The Globe and Anchor Men

The Globe and Anchor Men

U.S. Marines and American

Manhood in the Great War Era

Mark Ryland Folse

UNIVERSITY PRESS OF KANSAS

Published by the University Press of Kansas (Lawrence, Kansas 66045), which was
organized by the Kansas Board of Regents and is operated and funded by Emporia
State University, Fort Hays State University, Kansas State University, Pittsburg State
University, the University of Kansas, and Wichita State University.

Library of Congress Cataloging-in-Publication Data

Names: Folse, Mark R., author.
Title: The globe and anchor men : U.S. Marines and American manhood in the
    Great War era / Mark Ryland Folse.
Other titles: U.S. Marines and American manhood in the Great War era
Description: Lawrence, Kansas : University Press of Kansas, 2024. | Series:
    Modern war studies | Includes bibliographical references and index.
Identifiers: LCCN 2023037200 (print) | LCCN 2023037201 (ebook)
    ISBN 9780700636259 (cloth)
    ISBN 9780700636266 (ebook)
Subjects: LCSH: United States. Marine Corps—History—World War, 1914–1918.
    | World War, 1914–1918—Social aspects—United States. | Masculinity—United States—
    History—20th century. | Sociology, Military—United States—History—20th century.
Classification: LCC VE23 .F657 2024 (print) | LCC VE23 (ebook) | DDC
    940.4/1273—dc23/eng/20231102
LC record available at https://lccn.loc.gov/2023037200
LC ebook record available at https://lccn.loc.gov/2023037201.

British Library Cataloguing-in-Publication Data is available.

Printed in the United States of America

The paper used in this publication is acid free and meets the minimum requirements of
the American National Standard for Permanence of Paper for Printed Library Materials
Z39.48–1992.

To Sarah

Contents

Figures

Preface

The third thing they [the American people] believe about the Marines is that our Corps is downright good for the manhood of our country; that the Marines are masters of an unfailing alchemy which converts unoriented youths into proud self-reliant stable citizens—citizens into whose hands the nation's affairs may safely be entrusted.
— *Victor H. Krulak*, First to Fight

I cannot remember when I learned that my father was a Marine, nor do I recall when or how I learned he was a Vietnam veteran; in my mind those facts were just always so. As a young boy, that part of his past fascinated me, even though he never provided many details about his experiences to me or my two older brothers. There was an old picture of him and his recon unit in Vietnam that he hung on the wall. I stared at it often throughout my childhood. The men of his squad wear camouflaged utilities and have painted faces, everyone armed to the teeth. My father has a grenade launcher slung over his shoulder, the brim of his soft cover rolled up slightly at the front and back, a big white smile on his face. It was a powerful image, although I did not know how or why at the time. He also had a book from his boot-camp experience in San Diego full of pictures of his recruit training, with occasional images of him interspersed throughout, an "x" always marked above his head to make him easier to find. Growing up I felt lucky to have him as a father because he was a Marine as well as a combat veteran, which made him tougher, cooler, and more interesting than any of the other kids' dads. He was the personification of manliness in my eyes and to my brothers, too.

My father had to quit the oil business in the mid-1980s, shortly after I was born, and gained admission to law school. We moved to Clinton, Mississippi, so he could attend classes. He joined the Army National Guard to help make ends meet. So, he always had army boots and equipment in the house that my brothers and I loved to play with. Once, Dad dressed me up in his army-issue 782 gear and painted my face green for a Halloween party at my daycare. I remember walking into the classroom that day feeling on top of the world because I looked like my dad, the Marine. Even though he was in the National Guard at the time, I never considered him to be a soldier. To me, he was a Marine, and even at the age of four, I remember knowing there was a difference.

Through my father, the Marine Corps and the Vietnam War maintained a presence in my life, even if just in the background. He was usually a jolly, gregarious, and carefree fellow. Like many Vietnam combat veterans, however, he wrestled with demons. Those demons surfaced occasionally in terrifying ways during my childhood, and they became a part of his mystique and persona. My mother and relatives would blame drugs and post-traumatic stress disorder for his behavior, and that term became a part our of lives as well. That made me interested in his Marine experiences even more, though there was a tacit understanding in our house to just not ask about them. The demons had something to do ultimately with the end of his marriage to my mother in the early 1990s.

During my senior year of high school in Huntsville, Alabama, terrorists brought down the Twin Towers in New York City with hijacked passenger jets. The summer before the attacks, I vacillated between going to college and joining the military; September 11, 2001, pushed me toward the latter. My recruiter pitched the Marine Corps as a challenge, but it was the only option for me; I did not even consider any of the other branches. At eighteen I held the same convictions that I had at age four: Marines were tougher than everyone else. To make it through boot camp and come out the other side a Marine, to me, meant that you were a real man, one of a kind, one of the few and proud, like my father in the picture. I enlisted and went to boot camp in the summer of 2002.

Four years, two combat tours, and an honorable discharge later, I found myself in college interested in military history. Part of the attraction to the drum-and-bugle histories of war stemmed from the feeling that I had just participated in one. Serving on the front lines in two wars (Iraq and Afghanistan) as a Marine infantryman gave me a useful sense of perspective on my own studies. Many students find studying dull and tedious, which it certainly can be. But when I compared scholarly work with my past life as a grunt, I could not help but feel I was on the right path. I then went on to graduate school to continue studying military history. In searching for a dissertation topic in 2011, my old interest in the Marine Corps kept coming to mind. I realized then that through my father and even my own service, I had always been interested in the Corps.

But I was not interested in another purely operational military history of the Marines. I was interested in exploring the Corps's connections to society. I was fortunate that retired general Charles Krulak, former thirty-first Commandant of the Marine Corps and son of Victor "Brute" Krulak, became president of Birmingham Southern College, just twenty miles up the road from my house at the time. At the urging of some of my professors at the University of Alabama, I sent an email message to Krulak's office requesting an interview, and his secretary penned me in his schedule book.

I met General Krulak in his office on Birmingham Southern's campus on a beautiful, clear, cool November morning. With the overhead lights off, the morning light illuminated a room that was not quite moved into yet. We sat at a small pedestal table and spoke for a while. He asked me about my own time in service. I felt at home talking to him. He being a Marine, too, and a Vietnam veteran made something about the interaction feel familiar. We talked about military history, Marine Corps history, my father, his father, and his father's book, *First to Fight: An Inside Look at the United States Marine Corps* (1984). He saw that I had brought a copy with me and said, "Here, let me see my father's book." General Krulak then read the bulk of the preface out loud to me, the part explaining why his father believed the American people want a Marine Corps despite having a perfectly capable army, air force, and navy that collectively can do everything Marines can. It was a surreal moment.

The general then pointed to his framed shadow box given to him at retirement. In it, along with all his medals and other memorabilia from his career, was a round and rather inconspicuous cross-section of a tree. He pointed to that piece of wood and said that it was from a tree at Belleau Wood, then suggested that if I really want the answers to my questions about the Marine Corps and the American people, I needed "to start there." I knew immediately why he said that and like to think he knew that I knew.

Not one U.S. Marine currently living has not heard of Belleau Wood, and most would recognize it as the standard by which Marines are measured in the face of battle. Robert Coram's *Brute* (2010), a biography of Charles Krulak's father, Victor, had come out only a year before our meeting. Coram argues that "the Story of every Marine must begin at Belleau Wood."[1] In the 1990s Charles Krulak had drawn on that battle as an inspiration for instituting the Crucible, a capstone training event for Marines in boot camp that still exists to this day; I experienced it during my second to last week of boot camp in late October 2002.[2] He referred to the French forest as "one of the Marine Corps' most sacred battlefields . . . [that] forever cemented the Corps' reputation as the world's fighting elite."[3] He had argued that the Crucible would help imbue recruits with the character traits familiar to the Marines who had fought at Belleau Wood: confidence, courage, selflessness, resourcefulness, and esprit de corps.

The Battle of Belleau Wood in June 1918 not only influenced Krulak's effect on the Corps but also the Corps's effect on me. Before I left his office, the general signed the title page of his father's book: "Mark—Thank you for your selfless service to our Country & Corps. Semper Fidelis, CC Krulak, Gen., USMC, 31st CMC." When I returned to the car, I called my father. Afterward, I began exploring what exactly it was about Belleau Wood, and by extension the Great War—most often called the First World War—that was so significant to the Marine Corps.

What follows is an academic exploration and historical study of the Marine Corps during the Great War era, focusing on the Corps and its place in American society and history. It is not written as, nor is it intended to be, an extension and reflection of questions relating to my own experience as a Marine. Yet exploring how the Marine Corps appealed to Americans in World War I and how that war affected Marines' own image has illuminated how and why the Corps appealed to my father and myself. While reading about the promises the Marines made, the images of themselves they created, and how the Corps and the war changed those young men who joined in 1917, I could not help but think about the influence, both good and bad, of the Marines and Vietnam on my father and his family and of the Marines and the Global War on Terror on me and mine. While writing this book, I realized further that the Corps makes up a big part of my own and my father's character as men, just as it did for the Marines who appear in the following pages, for better or worse.

I would not have finished this project without the advice and encouragement from many people over the years. General Charles Krulak provided me with the initial push toward exploring the Great War–era Marines. My conversation with him at Birmingham Southern College solidified in my mind that I was going to write about the Marine

Corps. My advisor, Professor Andrew Huebner, has been a great mentor and teacher who has worked patiently with me on ideas, drafts, and my ignorance of proper comma usage. When scholars ask who my advisor was, I proudly say, "Andrew Huebner." Professor Dan Riches has been truly indispensable as a teacher as well and has nurtured my intellectual growth in every stage of my academic life. Professors John Beeler, Lawrence Kohl, Howard Jones, Lawrence Clayton, and Harold Selesky all shaped my interest in military and naval history and guided me into becoming a better practitioner of my craft. Professor Lisa Dorr was the first to steer me toward exploring masculinity in the Marine Corps. After resisting initially, I gave in because she was right.

I have the utmost gratitude toward the professionals at the Marine Corps History Division and Marine Corps Archives in Quantico, Virginia. Annette Amerman, who I interned under for two summers, has been an incredible source of knowledge, support, and friendship. Perhaps more than anyone, she showed me the ropes regarding Marine Corps historical research. Charles Neimeyer, Paul Weber, Chuck Melson, Breanne Robertson, and Paul Westermeyer all challenged me to think about and shape my project in ways I probably would not have come up with on my own.

Many archivists provided crucial help in tracking down obscure sources that were buried in the stacks. It is impossible to remember all their names, but two stand out. Alisa Whitley of the Marine Corps Archives (now at the U.S. Army Corps of Engineers Headquarters) consistently and cheerfully provided pdf scans and digital copies of records I needed whenever I could not make the trip to Virginia in person. She did this more times than I can count. Chris Killillay, of the National Archives and Record Administration in Washington, D.C., singlehandedly saved an entire research trip for me. A few days into my research, I and the archivists helping me could not locate the original orders and documents pertaining to the Corps's first enlistment of women, and I was running out of time. Apparently, Chris heard about this and, coming out of nowhere, began asking questions. After listening intently for just a few moments, he said, "no promises, but I think I may know where they are." He came back within an hour and dropped the files on the table in front of me. I was over the moon, thanked him profusely, and wrote down his name. Alisa and Chris exemplify all the best traits of archival professionals, and the quality of this project improved greatly because of them.

I am grateful for indispensable financial support over the years. The University of Alabama History Department's teaching assistantships and fellowships along with the UA Graduate School's Graduate Council Fellowship have helped sustain me and my family through this process. Many thanks are owed to the Marine Corps Heritage Foundation for seeing fit to award me their prestigious General Lemuel C. Shepherd Jr. Memorial Dissertation Fellowship in the summer of 2015. Their gift was more than financial—it was a crucial boost to morale that made me more determined than ever to see this project through. They saw the potential value of my study at a time when I still had many doubts.

I am eternally grateful to Bill Peerenboom and the class of 1957, who funded my postdoctoral position at the U.S. Naval Academy. Their support gave me the opportunity to teach U.S. Navy and Marine Corps history to midshipmen, which sharpened my understanding of both fields greatly. The postdoc also afforded me an ideal environment to research and write Marine Corps history. Most of the work done to transition my dissertation into my first book was done under the class of '57's support. It connected me to colleagues in the Naval Academy History Department who gave sage advice on life, publishing, and teaching. Professors Rick Ruth, Ernest Tucker, Mary DeCredico, Tom Brennan, Molly Lester, Jeff Hobbs, Miles Yu, John McManus, Kenneth Swope, and Marcus Jones as well as permanent military professors Mark Belson, Chris Rentfrow, John Freymann, and B. J. Armstrong, through conversations and feedback, were all very welcoming and encouraging of my endeavors. The Marine junior military professors, 1st Lieutenant Matt Mistretta and Captains Bill Fouse, Chris Hemler, Marko Stawnychzyj, and Major Kevin Boyce, made me feel right at home and provided attentive ears to my ramblings on Marine history and sometimes even about the "old unhappy far off things," pertaining to my own service years ago.

A special thanks to the inestimable Professor Kathy Broome Williams, who held the visiting Class of 1957 Distinguished Chair in Naval History while I was at the Naval Academy. Being the author of five books on naval history and a seasoned college professor, she provided a sterling example of the kind of teacher and historian one should aspire to be. Her office was a frequent stop for me in Sampson Hall, where we talked at length about history, teaching, publishing, our families, and sometimes nothing at all. It may have been a one-sided friendship, however. While I benefited from her wisdom and experience (she even babysat my child one evening), all she received in return were a few pointers on navigating Blackboard and email attachments. It was my great fortune to meet her, and I was sad when our time as colleagues ended.

Thank you to the editorial team at the University Press of Kansas, including Kelly Chrisman Jacques and Erica Nicholson. Copyeditor Kevin Brock displayed remarkable expertise, patience, and meticulous attention to detail during the editing process. Joyce Harrison, UPK's editor in chief, is a crucial reason why this book is before you now. She saw the potential in this project early on and has worked with me diligently over the past several years to get the project reviewed, then contracted, and finally published. She has a sterling reputation among military historians that is well deserved.

So much of a historian's life is made up of effort under criticism. Heather Venable, Janet Valentine, and Colin Colbourn all helped me tremendously in this regard. Their advice and encouragement along the way provided much needed morale boosts, which went a long way in helping me get through the review process. I must also thank my peer reviewers—the good, the bad, and the ugly, receiving all three types of feedback during multiple rounds of revisions for this book. The bad provided too little commentary to work from, while the ugly did not want this book published at all. Fortunately, the good ones won out because their constructive criticism and positive response gave me a path forward. Taken altogether, the project is much stronger because of all their efforts, and I have come to be very grateful for the process.

There are not enough words in the English language that could accurately convey the level of appreciation I feel toward my family for helping me see this project to fruition. Thank you to my parents, Lynn and Royce, for all the indispensable love and support over the years. Thank you to my father, Glenn, for the same and for starting my lifelong interest in the Marine Corps in the first place. A special thank you is owed to my mother-in-law, Barbara Meginniss, without whose help babysitting, the dissertation phase of this project would have ground to a halt at the birth of my daughter, Annette. I simply would not have been able to finish when I did without her.

And last, but certainly not least, my deepest gratitude and affections are reserved for my wonderful wife, Sarah. She has brought more joy and meaning to my life than I ever thought possible. The man I am today is because of her. No matter how miserable I made myself over the long course of this project, she was always there to remind me how great my life truly is and how thankful I should be.

Introduction

On April 27, 1914, a photographer captured an image of U.S. Marine first sergeant John H. Quick, Marine captain John H. Delano, and U.S. Navy ensign Edward O. McDonnell climbing a scaffold atop the Hotel Terminal in Vera Cruz to raise the U.S. flag. Marines and sailors had assaulted the city six days earlier in the face of stiff Mexican opposition. President Woodrow Wilson had sent Rear Admiral Henry T. Mayo with a small fleet of warships off Mexico's east coast as a force in readiness in case he deemed it necessary to intervene in the country's ongoing civil war. The arrest and release of nine American sailors in Tampico, followed by Mexico's refusal to offer a more grandiose apology than it already had provided, gave Wilson the excuse he wanted to put troops ashore to avenge American national honor. Marines suffered casualties of three killed and twelve wounded during the fighting, but the Corps gained significant positive publicity. Thirty-one years before the iconic Joe Forestall photo of Marines raising the U.S. flag atop Mount Suribachi on Iwo Jima in February 1945, this photograph communicated similar ideas—American military triumph and bravery.

Within a few years, the Marine Corps used this photo as inspiration for recruiting posters. It also used this image, along with its performance in the Vera Cruz affair, to persuade audiences that Marines represented the finest examples of American manhood. Civilian journalist Frederick J. Haskin wrote, "Wherever this country has need of faithful service and resolute hearts, there the marines have been on hand."[1] Another article declared that the "Gallant Soldiers of the Sea" had shown their quality during the amphibious attack.[2] The *New Orleans Times Picayune* published a report just after the Vera Cruz landings. There, the Marines advanced "steadily in the face of a hail of bullets from Mexican guns," the journalist wrote, "and showed what American manhood can do."[3]

This book explores two central questions and addresses several subsidiary ones. The first is concerned with how the Marine Corps's culture, public image, and esteem within U.S. society evolved during the

Fig. 1. "Raising the American Flag over Vera Cruz, Mexico, April 27, 1914." From *U.S. Marines, Soldiers of the Sea: Duties, Experiences, Opportunities, Pay*, 7th ed. (New York: U.S. Marine Corps Publicity Bureau, 1917), 13.

early twentieth century, the Great War era. Gender analysis provides the best lens to explore these issues because of how important and pervasive notions of manhood and manliness were to many Marines' identity, ethos, and world view. To answer the first question using a gender analysis, however, required exploring a second, very different question: how did the Corps define what it meant to be a Marine during the Great War era? While the former question is broad and requires examination of how the Great War influenced advertising, training, organization, and mission, the latter requires a deeper look into how Marines conceptualized themselves and what they believed they contributed to American society and its defense. Finding answers to these central questions led to others, including how Marines defined manliness and manhood and why they adhered to one cluster of interpretations over others. If Marines projected masculine imagery to promote their identity and to advertise their service, to what extent did that imagery evolve or change over time?

Gender influenced the Marine Corps's culture and identity during this period in several important ways. First, white manhood was a foundational element of the Corps's identity and institutional culture. While many white Americans began to embrace a "new masculinity" that emphasized consumerism and financial status, Marines held fast to older, more traditional Victorian, white middle-class notions of manhood that emphasized strength of character. While tending to share certain values such as self-control, honesty, bravery, and moral uprightness with the rest of white American society, they developed their own style of manliness. It is best described as a form of "martial manliness" that valued discipline, honor, and combat prowess. Despite these values being generally accepted as ideal character traits within the Corps, two forms of Marine manliness dominated the institutional culture: the rough-and-tough expeditionary Marine and the smartly dressed parade or staff Marine.

Second, Marines projected their culture of manliness outward with their recruiting, advertising, and public-image construction. Their efforts to build a rapport with society and convince Americans of their usefulness rested not only on claims to be great fighters but also through overtly gendered appeals. For example, Marines often claimed to be the finest examples of American manhood and promised to make men out of the recruits who joined their ranks. The Corps claimed to benefit the manhood of the country by developing men mentally, physically, and morally. It sought to imbue recruits' character with traditional manly virtues of honesty, selflessness, courage, integrity, and self-restraint and to subject them to a strenuous life that would make them mentally and physically stronger and capable soldiers and citizens. The Marines envisioned their institution as one that not only made the finest soldiers in the world but also made the finest men.

Additionally, the Corps created a masculine (that is, male) public image that it tailored to both war and peacetime depending on the context. Having a cluster of missions along with the characteristics of both soldiers and sailors has often convoluted the Marine identity throughout its history.[4] Marines created masculine images of themselves, in part, to clarify to the public who they believed they were. Whether working in a recruiting office, serving at sea, marching in an evening parade, patrolling the forests of Haiti, or fighting in France, U.S. Marines projected a white masculine public image to hold all of those duties together into a cohesive, recognizable form. But they altered this image over time. Before the Great War, Marines were men of action—America's quick-reaction force. During the war, they became chivalrous warriors on a quest to save civilization and destroy

America's enemies. After the war they briefly became fighters who could also sing and dance. As U.S. society wanted a return to normalcy and the military shrank in the face of demobilization and retrenchments, the Marines became not just soldiers of the sea but educators and shapers of men's minds and character as well.

Finally, gender was often the lens through which Marines and the public interpreted their experiences, service, and value. Gender played such a central role in the construction of the Corps's public face that discourses about Marine activities in peace and war often centered on notions of manliness and manhood. The public's esteem for the Corps tended to rise and fall, depending on how Marines represented American manhood at home and abroad. Their bravery, prowess, and sacrifice made Marines a positive testament to American manliness in France, which helps explain their sudden rise in popularity in 1918. Their treatment of Haitians and Dominicans in Hispaniola around the same time, however, made American manhood appear degenerate, callous, and murderous. Navy and Senate investigations of Marine behavior on Hispaniola reveal that despite their public proclamations to benefit the manhood of the young white men who joined their ranks, Marines frequently fell short of their own ideals. After losing some of the public's faith during these investigations, Marines attempted to win it back with public displays of manhood that included vaudeville shows, guarding the mail, public field maneuvers, and football games.

This book offers a critical look into an understudied yet important facet of Marine Corps history. It reveals the necessity of gender awareness when addressing the history of military institutional culture and identity. Marine historiography on culture during the Great War era is dominated by questions pertaining to mission development and to what extent the Corps was expeditionary, amphibious, naval, military, or even elite.[5] These questions, however, usually do not account for gender at all, nor do they help explain how Marines publicized a significant part of their culture to recruit and persuade Americans of their worth in relation to the army and the navy. Because they do not lead to answers that fully illuminate Marine culture, an incomplete understanding has remained of the effect of the Great War era on the Corps. This book illuminates how Marines have a long history of gender and race that informs much of their identity and purpose. Ultimately, however, it shows how the early twentieth century Marine Corps used gender to promote the benefits of war and military service over the associated costs, even when those costs were terrible to pay.

American Manhood

Historians of American culture have identified a shift in attitudes about what it meant to be a man in the late nineteenth and early twentieth centuries. Before industry and corporate capitalism changed the very fabric of life for the middle and working classes, a culture of individual production reigned in the United States throughout the nineteenth century.[6] Scholars have also identified two competing forms of male culture during that period, defined as *restrained* and *martial* manliness.[7] Restrained men were mostly of the urban middle class who valued domesticity, temperance, and forbearance. Martial men tended to be the hard drinkers and aggressive expansionists on the frontier who valued strength, courage, and the capacity for physical violence. Despite their differences, both sets held character—the inner qualities of honor, integrity, and moral courage—as central to their conceptions of manliness. Good character also meant working hard at a career or trade and practicing self-control. People frequently referenced these qualities in nineteenth- and early twentieth-century discourses about manhood, which historians have tended to associate with Victorian or "traditional" manhood.

But a new set of societal values grew out of the world of big steel, oil, manufacturing, banking, and international commerce. The ideal man of this burgeoning new culture was concerned less about production and more about consumption. His worth depended less on character and more on purchasing power. This "new" man cared very much about being liked and respected, as how one looked, dressed, and spent defined a respectable man. Subscribers to these ideas on male appearance used the term "masculinity" more than "manhood." Therefore, historians tend to identify these men and their use of the term "masculinity" to denote a shift away from Victorian manhood and manliness toward a newer twentieth-century male concept. There was no stark moment of arrival for this up-and-coming masculinity.[8] Technically, the Victorian age had passed by the coming of the Great War, but its cultural ideals still held sway throughout the first decades of the twentieth century. Victorian manhood, with its ties to the middle class and production and its emphasis on character and work, existed in tandem with the new masculinity, with its ties to the culture of consumption and its emphasis on appearances and leisure.

The U.S. Marine Corps, like the U.S. Navy and U.S. Army, was a conservative institution that held fast to older notions of manhood and manliness during this shift toward newer ideas about masculinity. Previous works have uncovered this conservative cultural tilt within the early twentieth-century U.S. military. For example, duty and sacrifice were important concepts in civilian masculine culture. One scholar has found that officers in the army adhered to these ideas even more strongly. But while middle-class Americans became more and more infatuated with monetary and materialistic wealth, in the military "the Victorian tension which linked sacrifice and duty to fulfillment remained strong."[9] The Marine Corps's own culture of manliness frequently followed the tenets of Victorian manhood.

Overlap between traditional manliness and the newer masculinity existed within the Corps, of course, especially when one examines its institutional magazines. On the very same pages slotted for stories that celebrated Victorian notions of manhood and character, one finds advertisements tailored to a male audience interested in commercial consumption. In this way the Corps's own publications mirrored popular civilian magazines of the time. Early twentieth-century creators of these periodicals pandered to men who identified with the newer masculinity and consumerism. According to Tom Pendergast, they "were themselves so indebted to the Victorian cult of character that they celebrated old styles of masculinity regardless."[10]

In the early twentieth-century United States, differences between Victorian (traditional) manhood and emerging notions of masculinity could be subtle, but they were important. Both had physical and mental aspects to differing degrees. According to American sociologists, physicians, politicians, and preachers, manhood was a many-sided thing. It was an achievement, a stage in one's life that came after boyhood and before old age. White middle-class Americans also understood it as a national resource, something grown and harvested. By the 1920s, the term "manliness" still tended to mean physical, mental, and moral manifestations of one's manhood, as people associated it with maturity, strength, self-control, courage, integrity, and mercy.[11] For many early twentieth-century Americans, therefore, manliness continued to mean a man's character, or how honest, moral, and hardworking he was. Manliness and manhood were things to be earned or achieved; childishness and childhood were their opposites.[12]

Manhood could be molded like clay and hardened like steel. Therein lay the foundation of the Marines' appeal: they shaped and molded men into their own image. The Corps claimed to recruit the finest specimens of American manhood and make them even better. The intended result through service was a strong, brave, and morally upright man, one with a wealth of travel and experience behind him. He would be a proud and worthy citizen who had earned respect through his years of service, training, and struggle in the Corps. Becoming a Marine benefited the man; the new Marine benefited the nation. As men became manlier, so the reasoning went, the country did, too.

Manhood could weaken or become sick, tainted, or corrupted. People took that risk seriously because many saw healthy manhood as essential for both the individual and the nation. Therefore, proponents of healthy American manhood, many of them progressives, advocated that men maintain their physical and mental health through exercise, religion, and "clean living." Clean living involved self-restraint. Too much alcohol, sex, or rowdy behavior could weaken or corrupt one's manhood, according to the prevailing middle-class wisdom of the time.[13]

Many Americans understood strength, assertiveness, bravery, and honesty as manly virtues.[14] Real manhood manifested itself, became stronger even, during times of trial, adversity, and struggle. According to Martyn Summerbell, a prolific writer of the time: "Spurious manhood encounters trials and succumbs before them. . . . [R]eal manhood meets the same obstacles, tramples them underfoot, and gains added courage and power by the very struggle and the joy of conquest."[15] The Marine Corps claimed to give young men the opportunity to live the strenuous life that President Theodore Roosevelt and other prominent citizens advocated.[16] Marines promised to provide the element of struggle and adversity deemed necessary for assertive, rugged manliness. Indeed, they seemed immune to the enervating effects of modern society that so worried educators, preachers, and doctors.

There is enough evidence to suggest, however, that competing forms of manliness existed among Marines. The gentleman/staff Marine and the field/expeditionary Marine were the most prominent styles, and they roughly mirrored the restrained and martial manliness dichotomy of the civilian world. The staff Marine worked in an office and valued the discipline, polish, and shine of military ceremony; the parades; and clean, crisp uniforms, while the field Marine preferred the dirty, rough-and-tumble life of being a field soldier on a campaign. The first often provided the public face of the Corps via serving on ships at sea, on recruiting duty, or on staff duty, while the second made up the operating forces that went ashore. Both types stemmed from the Corps's history of shipboard and guard duty on one hand and of amphibious expeditions on the other. The ideal Marine, officer or enlisted, was at home in either environment, although he most probably had his preference. It was a fine line to walk because one could easily slip too far into one side or the other to the detriment of one's status. A Marine who spent too long behind a desk and preferred the office or parade ground to field work could develop a reputation for growing soft and too refined. One who spent too long on campaign duty, however, risked becoming ill tempered and unrestrained.[17]

Both kinds of men pervaded the Marine Corps, and their names dot the pages of this book. On the field Marine side were officers such as Smedley D. Butler, Littleton Waller Tazewell Waller, and John Arthur Hughes as well as enlisted such as John H. Quick and Daniel J. Daly. Those who fell on the staff, recruiting, and more genteel side were officers such as George Barnett and Albert Sydney McLemore and enlisted men like Paul Woyshner and Thomas G. Sterrett, who would spend most of their time on recruiting and publicity duty. There were also Marines who walked the line between the two, including John A. Lejeune, John H. Russell, and George C. Thorpe. How often and to what extent these competing forms of manliness clashed is difficult to discern. But the most popular example of this is perhaps Butler's notorious dislike of some officers commissioned from the U.S. Naval Academy who he blamed for blocking his bid for Commandant of the Marine Corps in 1931.[18] That event is mostly beyond the temporal dimension of this book, but it does illuminate how competing forms of Marine manliness clashed occasionally.

Military Manliness

Of course, the kind of manliness the Marine Corps exhibited and offered recruits during this period was *military manliness*, a collection of values and behavioral norms that tends to exist within a society's armed forces. Like its corporate, working-class, saloon, or even middle-class counterparts, military manliness has its own distinct attributes particular to the historical context and the people who subscribed to it. I am deliberately using the term "military manliness" over "martial manliness" because the latter describes a much broader style of manhood that existed among civilians as well as the military. I also use it in preference to the more recent "martial masculinity" or "military masculinity," which can be defined as "a system of values that defines manliness through legalized violence against other groups," because it is more accurate within the context of the early twentieth century than these.[19] As the book makes clear, manliness and masculinity implied different things during the Great War era, although some scholars of the late twentieth and early twenty-first centuries have either used the terms synonymously or mixed their meanings.[20]

Within the context of the early twentieth century, military manliness is also defined by its peculiar ironies. It emphasized sacrifice, physical strength, and assertiveness while also demanding obedience and forbearance. The military required cleanliness and order but expected troops to serve in the filth and detritus of war. Officers expected toughness and stoicism out of their men but tolerated, if not encouraged, the emotional bonds that develop between troops on ship or in war, feelings that could be close and tender enough to be described as almost childlike.[21]

Medal of Honor citations provide perhaps the clearest examples of ideal military manliness. Today, the army, navy, and air force award them for "conspicuous gallantry and intrepidity of the risk of life, above and beyond the call of duty, in action involving actual conflict with an opposing armed force."[22] Congress and the armed forces have altered the award criteria over the years since its creation during the Civil War. For example, the army's original order for the medal excluded officers while the navy had a peacetime, noncombat-related award.[23] In the period covered here, the U.S. government awarded Medals of Honor to soldiers, sailors, and Marines mostly for conspicuous gallantry in battle. To receive one meant that the recipient displayed exceptional courage and skill in killing the enemy or in saving the lives of his comrades. It, therefore, was an award for the ultimate expression of wartime military manliness.

Medal of Honor recipients were some of the most respected men of early twentieth-century America. Leading up to and during the Great War, the army had won most of the Medals of Honor, but the Marine Corps had numerous awardees of its own. Dan Daly and Smedley Butler, both living legends in the Marine Corps during their time, had received two such decorations each. Daly's came from the 1900 China relief expedition and from Haiti in 1915, while Butler received his for actions at Vera Cruz in 1914 and in Haiti in 1915. The U.S. government awarded Butler both for "conspicuous" bravery in the face of the enemy.[24] Marine officer Hiram I. Bearss earned one in the Philippines for "extraordinary heroism and eminent and conspicuous conduct in battle."[25] Within the armed forces in general and in the Marine Corps in particular, men expressed the ideal form of manliness through acts of gallantry and violence. The emphasis on "violence" and "gallantry in battle" distinguishes military manliness from the more basic white middle-class version in civilian society.

Military manliness was not monolithic, however.[26] The U.S. Marine Corps, Army, and Navy had their own histories, cultures and subcultures, missions, purposes, and identities. Therefore, their general gender profiles differed. The navy, for example, tended to value the power of machines and technological expertise much more fervently than the army or the Marines, wanting men who would feel at home within the giant machinery of a warship at sea. The army and Marines, however, wanted men who found fulfillment on the parade grounds, in the wilderness, or on the firing line. The two services shared many basic "soldiering" characteristics, such as placing an emphasis on rifle marksmanship, bayonet drills, and training for and conducting overland expeditions and land warfare. But the similarities stopped there. The Marines' version of manliness (as will be illuminated further in chapters 1 and 2) stemmed in part from their history of being soldiers who fought on land *and* at sea. Although soldiering was a Marine's business, he was probably much more likely than a soldier to know where the fore and aft sections of a ship were and that a narrow beam meant that a ship would roll heavily in light seas.[27] This mix of "military" and "naval" characteristics has produced an institution that has emphasized men being just as comfortable fighting on ship as on land and being familiar with the inherent differences and necessities each domain requires.

Military manliness became all the rage during America's involvement in the Great War.[28] Scholars have identified the growth and spread of military jingoism and the heightened value Americans placed on military (also male) virtues of aggression, duty, obligations to the state, and courage since at least the Spanish-American War (1898).[29] There is merit to this interpretation, considering the correlating expansion of both the size and the responsibilities of the U.S. armed forces after Spain's capitulation. Americans avoided war in Europe initially due to strong residual isolationist sentiment, but clamorers for military readiness and intervention grew louder every month from 1914 to 1917. When President Wilson asked Congress to declare war on Germany in April 1917, a *rage militaire* swept the nation as discussions of duty, obligation, and citizen-soldiers concerning American manhood flooded public and private talks. At that moment American military manliness became the country's predominate wartime ideal for men.

Despite the challenges brought on by wartime expansion, the U.S. armed forces benefited from the fact that their esteem with the American people grew to great heights during the Great War. This was particularly true with the Marines, who perhaps gained the most in public opinion. Their claims to enhance the manhood of boys who joined them suddenly began to fall upon an audience now more receptive than ever to such rhetoric. Even after the war, when a strong argument could be made that military manliness no longer held the dominant position it once had, Marines continued to capitalize on the hard-won reputation they had earned in France. An indicator of how successful the Corps was in pitching its gendered image can be found with the U.S. Army, who's postwar manpower needs outweighed substantially those of the other services. By 1919, the army, having the greatest reach and resources, had learned from the naval services and began pitching itself explicitly as a "man-making" institution.

American Masculinity

Providing a concrete definition of "masculinity" ("femininity," too) is difficult. It can be just as hard to define clearly as "manhood" because its many different meanings make outlining its contours impossible. What is clear is that people use these meanings to describe and define the differences between men and women. On one hand the term applies to people who are biologically male. Defining it in this way alone is problematic, however, because people commonly associate masculinity and femininity with not only certain body parts but also behavioral patterns. Women, therefore, can *look* and *act* masculine and men can *look* and *act* feminine. Depending on the cultural context, both sexes behave and present themselves in ways that run the spectrum between *hypermasculine* on one end and *hyperfeminine* on the other, with more androgynous elements toward the center. For many gender historians, masculinity is a behavioral pattern associated with biological males to differentiate them from femininity and biological females.[30] Today, many historians see it as a social construct that conforms to cultural ideals particular to a certain time and place in history. It is also understood as a power dynamic that exists between peoples' interactions with each other via socialization, politics, sports, art, literature, and even war.[31]

This book uses "masculinity" and "manliness" to convey different things. In the late nineteenth and early twentieth centuries, many Americans understood "manhood" and "manliness" to mean a man's physical, mental, and moral strength, something men earned or achieved, while the term "masculine" meant simply male, a physical or anatomical state of being. Manliness *and* masculinity both denote physical characteristics most associated with adult males. Manhood and manliness, however, add moral and ethical dimensions. An adult male could appear and behave decidedly *masculine*, but his peers may not consider him *manly* or may question his *manhood* if he were a liar or a perceived coward.[32] Throughout this text, "masculinity" and "manliness" are *not* synonyms. I employ "masculinity" while discussing male physical characteristics and actions, Marine imagery and artwork, and early twentieth-century understandings of the term. I deliberately use "manliness" and "manhood" when sources imply both physical *and* moral characteristics of men. Applying the terms in this way accounts for the subtle yet significant differences between them. It also fits best within the time period, as their meanings conform most closely with how Americans and Marines of the early twentieth century would have likely understood the terms.

Hegemonic Masculinity

Most associated with the works of R. W. Connell, *hegemonic masculinity* is a term used by political scientists and historians of the late twentieth century to describe the predominate form of masculinity in any given context. It rests upon two assumptions. The first is that masculinity is a socially constructed "configuration of practice," or acceptable modes of behavior, that exists within the relationships between people. Masculine practices and behaviors differ to varying degrees between and within cultures. The second assumption is that masculinity is not monolithic. There are innumerable manifestations of masculinity, and there are power dynamics between them. "Hegemonic masculinity," then, is the dominant (more or less) form of masculinity within a particular culture that subordinates and marginalizes other manifestations of male behavior.

Hegemonic masculinity has limitations, however, particularly for the Great War era. Historians have argued that the armed forces generally conformed to early twentieth-century American hegemonic masculinity, especially in their recruiting advertisements.[33] This book does not employ the term often for several reasons. First, "hegemonic masculinity" is of limited value given the definitions of "manhood" and "manliness" versus "masculinity" noted above. Manhood and manliness reflected one's maturity, character, and morality. The "new masculinity," however, reflected one's social/political status, access to resources and women, and capacity for physical violence. This kind of masculinity can be understood, therefore, as a *power* that individuals possess within a culture or group. Men can wield it for altruistic or misanthropic purposes. Too much masculinity has been defined recently as "hyper-masculine" or, in twenty-first-century parlance, "toxic masculinity." Too little, and one is said to be overly feminine and thus subordinated among other, more masculine, men. Second, "hegemonic masculinity" obscures how, in the context of the early twentieth century U.S. military, manhood and masculinity were linked in an important way. One's manhood acted as a valve controlling the release of masculine behavior. Therefore, *hyper* and *toxic* masculinities are indications of sick or faulty manhood. A man with status, resources, and access to women behaves in a perfectly acceptable way if he is self-controlled, honest, faithful, and morally upright—in a word, manly.

Additionally, it is difficult to identify the dominant form of masculinity on a macro or even an institutional level given its many representations in the early twentieth-century United States. "Masculinity," as the term was most understood then, diverged along racial, class, and regional lines. Different manifestations like southern masculinity, working-class masculinity, Black masculinity, and urban or rural masculinity all existed simultaneously at the various local, regional, and even national levels. Because of their dominant positions in government, politics, and business, it appears that middle-class white men subordinated all others as the most popular and ideal form of masculinity in U.S. society. Were it used in this book, hegemonic masculinity would *look* like a heterosexual, healthy, assertive, confident, intelligent, and financially independent white man secure in his world of work in the public sphere and his circle of family in the private sphere.

Even if one asserts that white middle-class masculinity held the dominant position in relation to all others, that itself remains problematic to define within the Marine Corps. The early twentieth-century U.S. armed forces were largely homogenous in terms of race and gender. White men composed the enlisted and officer ranks, although they may have come from different economic, social, and regional backgrounds. Using "hegemonic masculinity" implies power relationships that research has not substantiated. This book makes no claims as to whether officers were "more masculine" than enlisted, whether staff Marines were "more masculine" than field Marines, whether the working class was "more masculine" than the middle to upper classes, whether white men were "more masculine" than men of color, or whether the Marines were "more masculine" than soldiers or sailors.

Crisis of Masculinity

Gender historians have asserted that masculinity in the United States underwent periods of upheaval, "crisis," and reconfiguration throughout the twentieth century. To what extent there was a "crisis of masculinity" in Great War–era America is not the point of this book. There was at the time, however, much concern over the character, education, employment, and development of manhood. It appears evident that white middle-class men perceived challenges to their dominant position during the early twentieth century.[34] As the woman's suffrage movement seemed to batter down the walls of the exclusive male public domain, men reacted by finding ways to recapture their lost sense of ruggedness and control. These male insecurities help explain the rise of physical culture, "muscular" Christianity, and outdoor adventurism among middle-class white men around this time.[35]

Many Americans during the Great War era, therefore, valued physical culture, strenuous exercise, and even early forms of bodybuilding to make up for the deficit of physical exertion in daily life.[36] Americans across class and racial lines enjoyed competitive sports during the early twentieth century. For the white middle class, however, athletics offered more than leisure, allowing people to reinject physical struggle and hardship into their lives. "Battle of Life" metaphors pervaded discourses on manliness and manhood. These metaphors harkened back to times when men proved themselves through literal battles with their enemies or figurative ones against their own vices.[37] The gymnasium, the boxing ring, the baseball diamond, the tennis court, or the football field served as sites where physical struggle could make one more masculine and thereby reinvigorate one's manliness.[38]

The Marine Corps offered this strenuous life to young men. Recruiters responded to concerns over weak manhood by offering a path to manly regeneration through their own ranks. While largely adhering to Victorian manhood, the Corps also used imagery that appealed to the newer notions of masculinity to attract recruits. Sharply dressed Marines pervaded their own imagery. So, too, did pictures of them exercising and playing sports both in the United States and abroad. Images that emphasized what life in the Marine Corps could do to the male body fit along with these appeals.[39] The Marines promised to enhance recruits' manhood by bolstering their character and giving them opportunities to serve their country. They also assured potential recruits that the Corps would reinject the element of struggle back into young men's lives, harden their bodies, and pay them all the while.

Fig. 2. A "Walking John" poster by Sidney
Reisenberg. Marine Corps Publicity Bureau, ca. 1915.

Identity and Iconology

Masculine imagery, both graphic and verbal, play an important role
throughout this study. Recruiting posters, paintings, sketches, and
cartoons constitute the bulk of the graphic images Marines produced
for each other and the public. These images are not abstract in the
sense that they appear divorced from any clear visual representation.
They are not about their own material elements per se; rather, they
are about who the Marines believed that they were and what they believed they contributed to society. Historicizing these images reveals
how they represented the Corps and how the artists designed them to
attract positive attention. This approach reveals that Marine imagery
communicated and touched on many pertinent themes at the time in
which the artists made them. Military and civilian artists portrayed the

Marines as white, male, sober, elite warriors; soldiers of the sea; physically well-built and conditioned; brave; and ready for anything. The extent to which Marine imagery communicated these things depends not just on the eye of the beholder but also on historical context.[40]

Images are powerful things because of what they mean to observers. Take, for example, the drawing of a Marine walking at right shoulder arms. Sidney Riesenberg drew this for the Marine Publicity Bureau just before the United States entered the Great War. Colloquially known as "The Walking John," on the surface its initial power is only descriptive. Here is a Marine in his element, on guard, walking his beat smartly. His uniform helps viewers distinguish Marines from soldiers in the army or sailors in the navy, although a U.S. warship is anchored behind him. Not only does the image convey what Marines look like but also where they serve: on land and sea. In this way the image is informative. Audiences can surmise all of this at a glance.

Looking closer, however, one may notice that the image possesses the power to illuminate who the Marines are, or at the very least, who the Corps wants the public to think that they are. They are soldiers, yes, but soldiers who serve from the sea and who are equally comfortable on land. They are a military service but are also naval. The sea element is what distinguishes Marines from regular soldiers, whose main element is land warfare, and their soldierly qualities set them apart from sailors, whose sole domain is war at sea. This Walking John looks more like a soldier than a sailor, which is deliberate. Marines are soldiers (albeit sea soldiers) who fight from the ocean, not sailors who fight on land. It is tempting to just describe the person in this image as a Marine and nothing further.

Yet there is still more to this image. There are class and race elements to this picture. This Marine looks white by early twentieth-century definitions, reflecting the policy that only white men could join the Corps. His uniform is clean and fitted; his shoes have a conspicuous shine. He appears to be a young man, and judging by his gait and posture, this fellow is no slouch. The Walking John's uniform makes it clear that he is not an industrial worker or a farmer, and the absence of any opulence or leisure in the image separates him from the wealthy elites. He is somewhere in the middle socially, yet it would be stretching the truth to say this man *is* middle class because of his military status. If he were an officer, it would be easier to connect him possibly to the higher echelons of society. But he is a noncommissioned officer as told by his sergeant's chevrons, and the single service stripe on his sleeve conveys that he reenlisted in the Corps after completing his first enlistment. Walking John looks disciplined, professional, vigilant, and sober, which makes him appear respectable and enhances the image's power to appeal to a broad cross-section of white America.

The Marine is also a *man*. This may seem obvious to most observers to the point of not being worth a mention. That the figure is unmistakably male, however, is not the extent of its significance. Everything about the figure that makes him appear sharp, disciplined, and confident also makes him look masculine. As Walking John is a visual representation of all Marines, he is a representation of the Corps's masculine image. He is a young but mature, healthy American man in uniform. His limbs are long and strong, his spine is straight, and his jawline is robust. The image derives much of its power by showcasing an idealized example of a man, one that exudes masculine physical display and prowess.

Yet the image's greatest attributes are not its descriptive and illuminative elements themselves; rather, its greatest power lies in its ability to persuade and inspire. It proclaims confidently that this is a Marine, this is what he looks like, and this is a sample of what he does. He is fit, he is disciplined, he wears attractive uniforms, and he is a "real man." The poster's most powerful message is that "you" can be a Marine, too. Walking John thus projects a template of who a young man will become if he joins the Marines, what he will look like, and how he will be seen by others. In this sense, it is a promise to potential recruits (and their families) that the Marine Corps will make a man out of them. That is the image's deepest power.

Marines also projected this self-image verbally in their poetry and prose. The "verbal imagery" that they conjured up supplemented and supported the Corps's pictorial imagery and identity, forming another primary, yet distinct, vehicle for the communication of its masculine image. While graphic imagery uses space, physical exaggeration, and the illusion of motion to communicate with viewers, verbal imagery relies on ideas, motion, and feelings.[41] In the written medium, authors during this period portrayed Marines every bit as elite and capable as graphic artists did. Their verbal imagery, however, most often communicated a type of manliness that was meant to come across as inherent to the Marines.

It is via graphic and verbal imagery that the Marine Corps most frequently appealed to white Americans' evolving notions of masculinity and manliness and promised to turn young males into real men. According to much of this imagery throughout this period, that is what it meant to be a Marine: a stronger, tougher, more efficient, and morally upright version of a man. When it came to recruiting, advertising, public relations, or any kind of controlled public expression of Marine identity, authors and artists made masculinity, the appearance and behaviors most associated with men, central to the message.

Structure

This book joins a small but growing body of scholarship exploring gender in Marine institutional culture.[42] While these histories often take masculinity and manhood into account to varying degrees, *The Globe and Anchor Men* places them front and center of the Marines' culture, identity, and image construction. The Corps's cultural notions of manhood and masculinity course through the chapters of this book, as do its claims to uplift and benefit the lives of those who join its ranks.

To better analyze the Marines' gendered appeals and culture, significant portions of the book are devoted to the social, cultural, political, and military context surrounding them. For example, there will be passages that veer away temporarily from explicit discussions of race and gender in the Marine Corps toward broader discussions of North American white middle-class manhood. There will be other portions of each chapter seemingly devoted to purely military, institutional, and strategic developments that appear not to address gender or culture at all. The reason for each of these instances is to provide the necessary historical context surrounding the formation and expression of Marine manliness and masculine imagery. Marine culture did not exist in a vacuum. Illuminating it, therefore, often requires discussing things of traditional military concern such as national security, strategy, training, recruiting, and occasionally tactics when they are necessary to explain the formation and expressions of Marine culture. The Marine Corps is a military institution after all, and to leave out those important pieces of their military history obscures the context from which its culture evolved.

Chapter 1 situates the early twentieth-century Marine Corps within the greater national-defense context. It explores how the Marines developed a culture of manliness from their very beginnings and how they fit within U.S. national strategy. It also illuminates the pervasive institutional insecurities that have plagued the Corps's existence from its founding. This analysis requires going back to the Gilded Age Marine Corps of the 1880s and 1890s and even earlier to give readers a broader sense of the institutional struggles and development the

Marines faced leading up to the Great War era. The Corps's force structure is also explained here to show how it has organized itself to meet the demands of its various missions.

This chapter also recounts how the Corps centralized its recruiting and publicity efforts after the war with Spain. Marines shaped and communicated their own public image with the establishment of the Marine Publicity Bureau, the *Recruiters' Bulletin*, and the *Marines Magazine*. The bureau and these publications promoted the Marine Corps as a man's institution that imbued young men with physical strength and the traditional manly virtues of honesty, selflessness, bravery, and integrity. Marine officers such as John A. Lejeune and John H. Russell brought up the increasing need for men of this caliber in the Corps's new professional journal, the *Marine Corps Gazette*, in 1916. Ultimately, this first chapter reveals how the Marine Corps's place within the defense establishment, and the debates surrounding its future missions and doctrine, intersected with its construction of a new masculine image.

The second chapter explores the culture of manliness that pervaded the Marines' rhetoric and imagery from 1914 through 1918. Marines often expressed themselves through gendered language to reinforce notions of their identity, justify their contributions to society, and bolster their public image. They tied ideas of Victorian manhood very closely to readiness, preparedness, and flexibility. These ideals stemmed in part from their history of service as an expeditionary force in readiness, which Marines used to forge an identity distinct from the other services. The preparedness movement that pervaded American politics after the eruption of the Great War in Europe informed their ideas on readiness. Marines linked manhood and race together, much like the society they served. The early twentieth-century Corps was the most racially exclusive of all the U.S. armed forces, and its racial homogeneity led to the construction of images and stories that promoted notions of white male superiority.

Chapter 3 examines the Marines' recruiting efforts from 1914 to 1918 and shows how they projected their notions of manhood outward in their public-relations and recruiting efforts. Marines aimed to recruit the "best" men while claiming that the Corps enhanced Americans' manhood. These claims became a major component to the largest recruiting drive the Corps had ever conducted in the spring and summer of 1917. Civilian journalists played an important part in this image construction. Marines followed advice from civilians who pushed them to advertise the Corps as a man-making institution. Journalists helped by publishing stories of manly Marines in newspapers. The Corps claimed to give young middle-class white men of sound body and mind a chance to become fit, develop good character, see the world, and become real men. In doing so Marines appealed to older notions of Victorian manhood through much of their rhetoric. They also, however, played to newer notions of American masculinity. Marines depicted on posters looked sharp, strong, and confident, which fit well with new ideas of masculinity keyed to the culture of consumption. Once the United States entered the Great War, the Corps produced more bellicose imagery to appeal to the growing popularity of military manliness. In doing so, it expanded from 12,400 to 30,000 men rapidly.

The Great War's effect on American politics, society, race relations, citizenship, woman's suffrage, and the size and scope of the federal government is hard to overstate.[43] Its influence on the Marine Corps was just as significant.[44] Chapter 4 explores how many Americans, both Marines and civilians, understood the Great War as a test and a sacrifice of their manhood. Military manliness became all the rage in the United States because German barbarity needed a manly response; America's national honor had to be defended. Therefore, Marines drew upon chivalric imagery and prose to portray themselves as righteous warriors and saviors of civilization. The Corps temporarily enlisted women for the first time in its history during this war. Placing them on recruiting and clerical duty allowed the Marines to incorporate women without upending popular gender norms. Far from weakening the Corps's masculine wartime image, the Marine Publicity Bureau presented female Marines in ways that seemed to enhance it.

Through their actions in the summer and fall of 1918, U.S. Marines demonstrated the strength and courage of American manhood. At Belleau Wood especially, they helped demonstrate that American manhood could pass the test of war. Journalists wrote of Marines as the pride of the country and portrayed them as proof that the United States still produced brave, strong, and morally upright men. Marines publicly and privately testified to the powers of war as a quickening agent for manliness and as a path to manhood.[45] They clung to this idea despite suffering the highest casualties in the Corps's entire history. The publicity bureau pitched these casualties as evidence of courage and the willingness of Marines to sacrifice themselves for the greater good. The true reckoning of the cost of the war would come later.

The Marines' deployments to the island of Hispaniola are as important as the Great War, as their actions there had serious implications for the Corps's identity and claims of being good for American manhood. Chapter 5 reveals that much like the U.S. occupation of the Philippines after the Spanish-American War, natives accused deployed Marines of illicit conduct. Histories of the 1915–33 occupation of Haiti and the 1916–24 occupation of the Dominican Republic are few to begin with, and fewer of them investigate Marine mistreatment of the native populations with any depth.[46]

Latin Americanist historians have produced a much more robust body of work on these occupations. Their histories often provide the perspective of people who lived under a foreign military occupation of their country.[47] *The Globe and Anchor Men* compliments Mary Renda's *Taking Haiti: Military Occupation & the Culture of U.S. Imperialism* (2001). Her exploration of how American notions of race and paternalism influenced Marines' interactions with Haitians has greatly informed this project. Here, however, Haiti and the Dominican Republic are examined together, which illuminates a broader pattern of Marine behavior across the entire island. Also, the discussion in chapter 5 centers around how the Corps's actions on Hispaniola created a profoundly negative masculine image of Marines, one that contrasted sharply with the reputation they had cultivated back in the States and won in France.

The implications of this are that American cultural conceptions about race and manhood influenced how Marines perceived and interacted with Haitians and Dominicans. Marines likened them to untrustworthy children, which was consistent with contemporary American discourses that denigrated the manhood of "colored" races. By 1917, Marines in Hispaniola had become embittered over having to miss the Great War to serve among people they deemed racially inferior. Some lashed out when insurgencies erupted in both countries in 1918. While fighting these undeclared wars, some Marines behaved antithetically to Victorian notions of white manhood. Their lurid actions seemed to indicate the breakdown and degeneracy of their manhood, something public discourses acknowledged happened to white men who lingered too long in the tropics. Ultimately, the Corps would survive subsequent investigations with its popular reputation intact because of the sympathy afforded them by the secretary of the navy, the naval and Senate investigation committees, and by some writers in the press. That good will was founded upon shared notions of the superiority of white manhood and the distrust of Haitian and Dominican testimony. Another reason the Marines survived this bad press was because of the activities of Corps headquarters back in the States.

Chapter 6 demonstrates how Major General John A. Lejeune focused

on manpower and recruiting during his first four years as Commandant of the Marine Corps (1920–24). Others have shown that Marines
during this time cared very much about public relations because of its
implications for recruiting.[48] But what is often missed is how important
the idea of manhood was to the Corps and its public-relations efforts.
The Marines appealed to the manhood of the nation, with claims of
how they could enhance and better young men's lives, which provide
valuable cultural and historical context.

As the Corps faced bad press from Hispaniola and postwar budget
cuts, it continued to promote itself as a man-making institution. Marines would stay on expeditionary duty in the Dominican Republic
until 1924 and in Haiti until 1933 during a long period of retrenchment
among the armed services. Postwar popular opinion shifted away from
military manliness as Americans wanted a return to peacetime endeavors. Marines responded in several ways. They softened their masculine
public image and created the "Roving Marines," who went around the
United States to demonstrate the kind of manhood that could not only
fight but also sing and dance. Marines wanted to increase the efficiency
of the men in their charge. American progressives of this time understood efficiency as an important component of traditional manhood.
Marines worked to demonstrate their efficiency by guarding the U.S.
Mail and conducting Civil War reenactments. Mission and doctrine
often preoccupied the minds and efforts of Marine leadership in the
early 1920s.[49] But they had to solve their recruiting problems first.

Chapter 7 explores the Corps's postwar educational and vocational
initiatives. The impetus behind these reforms came from lessons
learned in France during the Great War and from broader government
and civilian efforts to educate men. With the return of "peacetime
manliness" as the more popular form of manliness, all the services began advertising themselves as educational opportunities. The Marine
Corps established a vocational school in Quantico, Virginia, that they
claimed would enhance the intellectual and physical sides of manhood
via education and athletics. This chapter also explores how the army
learned how to advertise and gain favorable publicity for its own educational opportunities in part from the Marine Corps. The fact that
the army used the very same tactics and imagery as the Marines sheds
light on how persuasive gendered appeals were in the United States at
the time. It also demonstrates how influential the Marine Corps was
in the realm of military advertising and in appealing to the manhood
of the nation.

During the years covered in this book, Marines claimed to make men out of recruits, improve their health and character, and make them better citizens. No military institution could possibly live up to these promises for all its members, however. As chapter 8 shows, many Marine veterans like Thomas Boyd, Laurence Stallings, William Campbell, and even Smedley Butler rejected notions of the rejuvenating or beneficial effects of war. Those claims stemmed from the Marines' own culture of manliness, however, which endured after the Great War. The Corps's promises to uplift the young men who joined its ranks and make them manlier would resonate with succeeding generations. The Great War–era Marines, therefore, helped shape an important legacy. Through World War II, the Cold War, and beyond, Marines would contribute greatly to the idea that war and the military served as ultimate rites of passage into manhood. As veterans and their families would be able to attest, the enduring appeal of these claims often came with a terrible cost.

Marine Corps Identity

Elements of the U.S. Marine Corps

They are first in every skirmish,
   Either on the land or on the sea,
They're as fearless as the eagle,
   No matter what the cause may be,
They have been to Honolulu,
   Cuba and Philippines,
China and all other countries;
   Our Old Guard, U.S. Marines
— *"Our Marines," 1915*

A look back on Marine Corps history since its founding illuminates several important things. First, the Marines have a long history with the U.S. Navy marked by both discord and harmony, depending on the context. The Corps had been the junior partner in this close but rather complicated relationship, which challenged the institution to continuously be on guard against any perceived curtailments of its duties or threats to its existence. Institutional vigilance, therefore, is the second major historical issue for the Corps leading up to the Great War. From 1798 to 1914, the Marines fought efforts from the executive branch, the navy, and the army to abolish or diminish the service. Finally, what it meant to be a soldier, sailor, or Marine leading up to 1914 was greatly informed by society's definition of what it meant to be a man. Even a cursory exploration of the Corps's history reveals that manliness has always been a component of its institutional culture. These three themes are illuminated further by breaking the Marine Corps down to its essential elements of *missions, force structure*, and *public image*.[1]

The missions and force structure of the Marine Corps has stemmed from both tradition and the needs of the U.S. government and navy. The Marine Corps had a small but important role in the American defense establishment in the first quarter of the twentieth century. Marines made up the country's lightweight naval expeditionary force in readiness, whose missions stemmed from many Americans' expanding interventionist worldview. U.S. foreign policy shifted in the late nineteenth and early twentieth centuries from a traditional isolationism to overseas expansion. "Empire" no longer seemed to hold the same negative or despotic connotations that it once had for many Americans.[2] They now developed imperial ambitions because of what they believed an empire would mean for their nation's identity. As one recent historian has put it, "What committed Americans to imperial policies . . . was their dependence on empire for their prosperity, for their racial, social, and even moral identity as a people."[3] The army, navy, and Marine Corps secured that empire for the United States, particularly during the 1898 War with Spain, whether civilians believed it was an empire or not.

The navy, and thereby the Marines, became a highly active policing force to see to the nation's worldwide commitments of the early twentieth century. American corporations and the U.S. government had commercial and political interests all over the globe at this point: China, the Philippines, Central America, and the Caribbean, for example. Trouble for American lives and money could and did erupt at a moment's notice in any one of these places. Therefore, the armed forces' missions during this time involved policing actions that required rapid deployment. It was within this context of global, national, and military affairs that the Great War–era Marine Corps further developed an ethos that revolved around readiness and a cosmopolitan worldview that centered on a belief in the exceptional and "superior" nature of white American manhood.

Popular notions of manliness informed the Marine Corps's early twentieth-century public image as much as U.S. defense policy and its missions within the military establishment. Along with missions, force structure, and recruiting, the masculine public image of Marines, developed over the decades leading up to the Great War, was also one of the Corps's "essential" elements. A closer look at these reveals how the history of Marines and of American manhood are not exclusive of military and naval history. Writing on one while omitting the others would lead to impressions of a false dichotomy at best, an incomplete history at worst.

Missions and Institutional Vigilance

Like the U.S. Army and the U.S. Navy, the U.S. Marine Corps's reasons for existence since its founding have been involved with defense and the implementation of national policy. Its missions, therefore, have always been linked with the navy. The Marines trace their origin (or "birthday") to November 10, 1775, when the Continental Congress called for raising two battalions of marines to bolster a naval campaign against British-controlled Nova Scotia. In the age of sail, Marines of the United States, British, Dutch, and Spanish navies were as common a presence on naval vessels as guns and rigging.[4] They answered directly to the ship's captain, helped maintain shipboard discipline, provided insurance against mutinies, helped gun crews during ship-to-ship duels, and augmented sailors' boarding and landing parties. When the Continental Navy disbanded shortly after the 1783 Treaty of Paris, the marines disappeared with it. The United States needed a navy again in the mid-1790s to protect its commerce in the Atlantic and Mediterranean from French privateers and Barbary pirates. The construction of six frigates naturally meant the recruiting of sailors *and* marines to sail them. Congress established a Corps of Marines on July 11, 1798, which stands as the Marines' "second birthday" and the one that marks the beginning of its uninterrupted existence.[5]

Marines ingrained manliness in the service from the very beginning. In the late 1700s and early 1800s, American men began to derive their status less from their family's socioeconomic position and more from their own achievements. This change occurred against a backdrop of the birth of a new republican form of government and the proliferation of the market economy.[6] In this new nation the middle class began to grow. Men of this class began to define themselves by their work, or profession, and what they had accomplished through that work. The "self-made man" dominated society's idea of manhood during the early republic years.[7]

Being a gentleman and a man of honor greatly informed what it meant to be a military or naval officer during these early years. Reflecting greater society, navy and Marine officers knew that the status of being a man of honor derived from their individual achievements. These common beliefs pervaded life on ship and shore, where pride and anger often begot violence. In describing the developing American middle class, historian Anthony Rotundo writes, "Ambition, rivalry, and aggression drove the new system of individual interests, and a man defined his manhood not by his ability to moderate the passions but by his ability to channel them effectively." With this, Rotundo also provides an apt description of officer behavior around the turn of the eighteenth century.[8]

Early Marine officers, much like their navy and army counterparts, often "channeled" their aggression through dueling. Dueling involved defending one's personal reputation *and* the reputation of his respective service. Marine commandant William Ward Burrows set a precedent for all his successors by working to bolster and maintain the Marine Corps's public reputation. He would not suffer Marine officers whose honor had been besmirched by anyone. Navy and Marine officers often clashed with each other over professional duties and insults, real or perceived, which led to frequent duels.[9] "I believe Amongst officers, dueling is sometimes necessary," Burrows wrote, despite the fact that "great caution ought to be used, for my own part I think a Duelist a horrid character."[10] Writing to Secretary of the Navy Benjamin Stoddert in July 1800, he mentioned the mistreatment his Marines had received on the navy's frigates. "My officers are strictly charged to put up with no ill usage," he wrote. He then asked Stoddert to address the quarrelling between Marines and sailors, which might "prevent desertion and dueling."[11]

Burrows ended the letter with a prophetic sentiment that indicated how he was thinking about the future not only of his Corps but also of the U.S. naval services in general. "As our Navy is in its infancy, we had better begin early with these qualities that then form the base of our future conduct or disgrace must follow."[12] He wanted his Marines respected as men; if not afforded this respect, violence would surely follow. Humanity did not always prevail, and Marines would frequently defend their honor and their manhood with violence. Winning or losing a duel mattered less than being man enough to fight one. "I do not presume to judge who was in the right or wrong in the duel," Burrows declared to Lieutenant Phillip Edwards, who had just fought one, "you having behaved brave, satisfies me."[13]

Any Marine officer who had been assaulted by navy officers in port or at sea would have to receive satisfaction for the insult before being allowed to continue to serve. People during this era considered the opposite of manhood to be boyhood in many contexts. Thus, men who behaved foolishly, complained, or acted out without restraint needed correction. To be "corrected" as a Marine officer meant being treated as a boy, not as a man.[14] In the summer of 1800, a navy officer struck Marine lieutenant Henry Caldwell while on duty aboard the sloop of war *Trumbell*. Commandant Burrows informed Caldwell that "a blow ought never be forgiven, and without you wipe away this insult offered to the Marine Corps, you cannot expect to join our officers." He gave the lieutenant leave to handle the affair so "that you may be on an equal footing with the Captain or anyone who dare insult you, or the

Corps." But Burrows warned, "don't let me see you till you have wiped away this disgrace."[15]

The Commandant believed it his duty to support and defend his officers, but only when they had earned it. Burrows provided a past example. After a navy officer struck Lieutenant Anthony Gale (who would later serve as Commandant from 1819 to 1820) on a voyage, the latter waited until the ship returned to shore, challenged the former to a duel, and then shot him. "Afterwards, politeness was restored," Burrows observed.[16] In this way a Marine officer's manliness mattered a great deal because of how it reflected on the service's reputation. One historian recently found that between 1798 and 1826, four Marine officers died in duels while many more suffered serious wounds.[17]

The Marine Corps spent much of the nineteenth century serving with the various squadrons of the U.S. Navy around the world. After the War of 1812, the navy took a subordinate role in national defense policy during much of the 1800s as Americans' primary security focus was often the western frontier. At sea the navy defended the coasts and protected overseas trade. Marines fell under the navy's purview in implementing this policy. Their fortunes rose and fell with the navy during the Barbary Wars and the ship-to-ship duels during the early stages of the War of 1812. Marines participated in the frigate *Constitution*'s famous victories over HMS *Guerriere* and HMS *Java*. They also fought aboard the frigate *Chesapeake* against HMS *Shannon* in Boston harbor in June 1813 until the British forced the crew to surrender.

After the War of 1812, Marines served with the Navy combating smugglers, pirates, and showing the flag around the world. Marines served on the sloop of war *Vincennes*, which was the first U.S. warship to circumnavigate the globe in 1830. They also accompanied Lieutenant Charles Wilkes's 1838 exploration of the Pacific. Marines participated in the navy's shelling of Quallah Battoo in 1832, accompanied Commodore Matthew Calbraith Perry's expedition to Japan in 1853, and took part in the seizure of the Barrier Forts in China in 1856. Throughout the American Civil War, U.S. Marines served on blockade duty with the Union navy and made occasional landings against Confederate coastal fortifications, most notably Fort Fisher outside of Wilmington, North Carolina, in January 1865.

The Marines, however, also served detached from the navy on land campaigns from their very beginnings. Continental Marines under Colonel John Cadwalader accompanied George Washington's army on his famous raid on Trenton and Princeton in late 1776. In 1805 Marine lieutenant Presley O'Bannon and eight Marines accompanied a small

Arab army overland from Egypt to Tripoli. This expedition culminated in the Battle of Derna in April and May, after which O'Bannon was awarded a mameluke sword—such swords are still worn in ceremonies by Marine officers to this day. At Bladensburg, Maryland, in the summer of 1814, Marines fought alongside militia in defending against a British advance on Washington, D.C.

Archibald Henderson's rise to Commandant of the Marine Corps in 1820 was a significant event for the service. Anthony Gale, the fourth Commandant of the Marine Corps and Henderson's predecessor, had been summarily dismissed for drunkenness and "conduct unbecoming an officer and a gentlemen."[18] Henderson quickly sought to make a course correction from the Gale scandal. He made sure that a small force of Marine infantry was always on hand at the Marine Barracks in Washington for whatever use as the president may direct. This meant that Marines got opportunities to respond to riots, insurrections, and various small wars that had little to do with the navy. When Henderson offered Andrew Jackson a ready contingent of Marines to help fight the Seminoles in Florida in 1836, the president accepted. President James K. Polk accepted Henderson's offer of a regiment of Marines to bolster Major General Winfield Scott's army being organized for a landing at Vera Cruz. This expedition would lead to Marines assaulting the fortress of Chapultepec in Mexico City in September 1847.

Despite the consistently active service of Marines with the navy and army, threats to the Corps's existence plagued its history. Marines faced threats of being merged or defunded out of existence several times in the early nineteenth century. In 1821 Secretary of the Navy Smith Thompson wanted to abolish the Marine Corps as an official branch of the military to save money. President Jackson in 1829 reflected the thoughts of many outside the then-tiny Corps who found the Marines to be administratively troublesome and an expensive redundancy and favored merging it entirely with the Army.[19] Public and congressional support, however, with the help of naval officers who wanted to hang on to the Marines, led to the passage of an 1834 act called "For the Better Organization of the Marine Corps," which made the Corps a separate sea service within the U.S. Navy. Through eleven presidential administrations and eighteen secretaries of the navy, Henderson argued that the Marines served as the military arm of the navy, tasked with aiding its mission in protecting U.S. commerce around the world. The Marines' mission would not change until the navy's did. And that would not happen until a significant shift occurred in U.S. strategic thinking.

The Marines in the capital responded to numerous crises in the Washington area. They helped put down riots sparked by armed Baltimorean ruffians known as "Plug-Ugglies" in 1857. Henderson died in the spring of 1859 after thirty-eight years as Commandant, but the Marines he stationed in Washington would remain busy. In October 1859, when the abolitionist John Brown raided the federal arsenal at Harpers Ferry, Virginia, U.S. Army colonel Robert E. Lee brought Marines from the Washington Barracks with him to put a stop to it. Their place in Washington also ensured that Marines fought at the First Battle of Bull Run in July 1861.

By 1861, Americans had many competing definitions of manhood. Geography, race, and socioeconomic class influenced the kind of manliness one subscribed to during the Civil War era. Scholarship has shown that whether a man haled from the North or South; was from the middle, lower, or planter class; or was white and in the military, honor strongly informed his conception of manhood.[20] Historian Amy Greenberg has found that the westward expansions of the 1840s–50s, including the victory over Mexico, led many white Americans to embrace a martial and aggressive form a manliness. Forcing their civilization westward became an outlet for men to show their worth.[21] The Civil War provided another opportunity to test one's mettle. As a form of identity, masculinity operated on personal and macro levels. Wartime manly values such as bravery, toughness, steadfastness, and physical prowess could be associated with divisions and battalions as easily as with individuals.[22] For many Americans of this era, according to Bertram Wyatt-Brown, the war itself "was reduced to a simple test of manhood."[23]

This being the case, the Marine Corps's performance in the Civil War, although often conspicuous and gallant at the individual and small-unit level, never achieved the depth of respect the relatively gigantic armies of the North and South did. Marine ship detachments served with distinction in Flag Officer David Farragut's fleet at New Orleans in 1862 and then at Mobile Bay in 1864. Marines earned thirteen Medals of Honor during the Civil War, eight of those while serving as members of the ships' gun crews at Mobile Bay.[24] But the Corps was incredibly small (eighty-seven officers and around 3,700 enlisted men by 1865), and its effect on the outcome of the war was minimal. Marines clashed with the navy, again, over heavy losses they sustained during the January 1865 assault on Fort Fisher on the North Carolina coast.[25] Rear Admiral David Dixon Porter ordered 1,600 sailors and 400 Marines to divert the attention of the Confederate defenders by assaulting the fort's seaward side while the army attacked from the northwest. Union forces captured Fort Fisher, but the "Naval Brigade" suffered heavy casualties, losing 354 sailors and 61 Marines. Porter, among other navy officers, blamed the Marines for not providing enough suppressive fire on the Confederate breastworks during the assault.[26]

All of this would hurt the Corps's prestige and strain its relations with the navy. Marines could not serve with all the Union navy's vessels during the war, which led some naval officers to believe that Marines were unnecessary on ship. Historians have often referred to the years between 1865 and 1890 as the "doldrums" for the U.S. Navy and Marine Corps.[27] The post–Civil War years shifted U.S. security concerns back to the western frontier. No longer needing a navy of extravagant size and cost, Congress shrunk the naval services precipitously and returned them to the role of protecting U.S. trade and defending the coasts.[28] By 1870, the navy had only 52 actively serving vessels (down from 671 during the Civil War), and the Marine Corps had dwindled to fewer than one hundred officers and around two thousand enlisted men.

It was the lack of strategic purpose that really hurt both naval services. For the navy, this meant halting technological advancements in steam power, ship armor, and gunnery. Thus, its warships remained armed with old muzzle-loading guns and its auxiliary steamers relied on wind and sail to traverse the seas, only using their steam engines during emergencies. The Spanish navy's capture and execution of fifty people (many of whom were Americans) on board the *Virginius* in 1873 for transporting weapons to rebels in Cuba was a low point for the U.S. Navy. Diplomats avoided an all-out war that the service was not prepared to fight. Lack of interest in the navy meant that it fell behind the navies of Chile and Peru (which fought each other from 1879 to 1884) in both technology and size. For naval enthusiasts, all of this felt like stagnation at best and huge steps backward at worst.

For the Marine Corps, however, this retrenchment meant talk of disbandment. Between 1867 and 1868, Congress considered abolishing the Corps again for the sake of economy.[29] Commandants Jacob Zeilin (1864–76), Charles G. McCawley (1876–91), and Charles Heywood (1891–1903) all struggled to keep the Corps manned, equipped, funded, relevant, and even in existence. While the navy became more professionalized, the Marine Corps struggled to keep up. The founding of the torpedo school in 1869; the U.S. Naval Institute in 1873 along with its principal publication, *Proceedings*; the Office of Naval Intelligence in 1882; and the Naval War College in 1884 all provided educational and professional outlets for naval officers. The Commandants of the Marine Corps, however, had trouble sending their officers to the new navy schools *and* keeping up with the Corps's duties. Marines still served onboard warships as guards, aided in both gunnery and landing parties, and guarded naval yards and government property.[30] With only between eighty-five and seventy-five officers in any given year, the Commandants could not spare many men for professional advancement no matter how potentially beneficial.

The Marine officer corps needed this professional development for both efficiency and respect. Patronage appointments and political favors reigned supreme in officer selection; West Point and Naval Academy dropouts tended to fill the rest of the Corps's officer billets.[31] All of this damaged the Corps' public reputation. This situation led Marine lieutenant Henry Clay Cochrane to conclude, "there is a deep seated and wide antipathy toward the Marine Corps only the blind and imbecile can doubt." He declared that the Corps was "neither respected nor respectable."[32]

A significant step toward greater professionalization of the officer corps occurred in 1881 when the U.S. Naval Academy began commissioning officers for the Marines. In fact, from 1883 to 1898, the Marine Corps only accepted officers who had graduated from the Naval Academy.[33] During this period, they included many notable names in Marine Corps history. The class of 1881 included Charles A. Doyen, Henry C. Haines, and future Commandant George Barnett. John A. Lejeune placed sixth in his class of 1888, and Charles G. Long and Benjamin H. Fuller received Marine commissions a year later. Many of these graduates would become leaders of the early twentieth-century Marine Corps. George Barnett (class of '81), Lejeune (class of '88), Wendel C. Neville (class of '90), Fuller (class of '89), and John H. Russell (class of '92) all served as Commandant of the Marine Corps one right after the other. So, from 1914 to 1935, a full two decades of the Corps's history, Naval Academy graduates led the Marines.

Unlike their predecessors, these new officers received their education in a military environment meant to develop them physically, intellectually, and morally so they would become proficient and trustworthy officers. The Naval Academy of the 1880s and 1890s did not have a singular mission statement declaring this explicitly as it does today. In fact, it did not have one at all other than to produce officers for the navy. But what it meant to be an officer was informed by certain acceptable forms of behavior. Franklin Buchanan, the first superintendent of the Naval Academy, identified as early as 1845 the objectives of the school as "obedience, moral character, and temperance."[34] Captains Francis Ramsay and William T. Sampson (superintendents from 1881 to 1886 and from 1886 to 1890 respectively) still considered discipline and moral conduct to be important in midshipmen cadet development throughout the 1880s. Based on the list of behaviors that qualified as "scandalous conduct" according to the academy's own regulations during that period, officers and professors expected honesty, integrity, abstinence from alcohol, and self-control from all midshipmen cadets.[35] According to the rules, students had to conduct themselves as gentlemen at all times or risk accruing enough demerits to warrant dismissal. One of the faculty members during this period observed, "the Cadet is educated not only in professional branches of knowledge, but also in the principles and practice of morality, sobriety, industry, and the strict sense of honor."[36] In a sense, the academy aimed to produce not just officers, but upstanding young men as well.

Marine officers commissioned from the Naval Academy between the years 1881 and 1898, therefore, grew in soil rich with the manly virtues of discipline, honor, integrity, and self-restraint. This is an important correlation to point out because it was around the time these men become field- or general-grade officers (between 1914 and 1924) that the Marine Corps claimed to benefit young men mentally, physically, and morally. It was also during this time that the public image of Marines began to take on overtly masculine contours. Before then, however, these new Marine officers, imbued as they were with "gentlemanly" standards, went into a Corps rife with officers and men who valued expeditionary expertise and leadership as much as "gentlemanly restraint."

The navy modernized slowly in the 1880s. In 1883 Congress approved the construction of four new steel-hulled warships—*Atlanta*, *Boston*, *Chicago*, and *Dolphin*—in the first significant effort since the Civil War to modernize the fleet. Lawmakers approved two more vessels officially designated "battleships," *Maine* and *Texas*, in 1886. But this construction pace was rather conservative and reflected the prevalent thinking of using the navy to defend commerce and the coasts.

Issues surrounding the manliness of sailors relative to Marines came up during this modernization process. More ships usually meant more Marines, but missions were changing. Commodore James A. Greer headed the Board of Organization, Tactics, and Drill in 1889, which investigated the composition of landing parties and manpower on the new ships. Navy officers like Lieutenant William F. Fullam argued in *Proceedings* that the new ships needed more technically proficient crews, and Marines proved detrimental to ship discipline. "Nothing could be more harmful to the sailor than the presence of the marine guard afloat," he asserted.[37]

According to Fullam, the presence of Marines as ship's guards implied that the navy did not trust their own sailors to maintain discipline and professionalism. This further implied that Marines could be trusted as upstanding soldiers and men, but sailors could not. It was here that manliness became an important part of the discourse. According to Fullam, removing the Marines would attract better recruits from society because it would better enable the navy to "cultivate the manliness, utilize the intelligence, and win the hearty loyalty of 8000 men."[38] The lieutenant frequently referenced the sailors' "manliness" that needed to be cultivated, respected, and appealed to. He wanted Marines off warships, therefore, not solely because of limited room on board or because they no longer had a purpose but specifically because he thought their presence "repressed" sailors' manliness and thereby impeded their development. First Lieutenant Paul Murphy was one of the several Marine officers who argued against this reasoning. Based on his own service at sea, which spanned over eleven years, Murphy argued, "I have failed to see in the blue-jackets any evidence of repressed manliness due, in even a remote degree, to the presence of marines."[39] Men drilled in the military arts helped foster in sailors the very discipline Fullam advocated, according to Murphy.

Although Fullam represented a significant group of naval officers who believed that Marines had no place on modern warships, he was not interested in disbanding the Corps. He wanted the roles and missions of Marines changed to better reflect the needs of the navy. Specifically, he wanted the Corps restructured to form three permanent battalions that could be deployed when needed for expeditionary duty.[40] "The Corps would be invaluable as a highly trained, homogenous, and permanently organized body of infantry, ready at all times to embark and cooperate with the navy," he wrote.[41] By this time, however, Marines had developed a strong sense of institutional vigilance against actual and perceived threats to their existence. They did not want to relinquish any of their traditional duties because to do so, they believed, risked taking the first steps toward extinction.

This rhetoric linking manliness and manhood to sea duties came at a time when the navy needed to evolve to meet the new economic and maritime needs of the United States. By the 1880s, the telegraph and the railroad connected Americans and their businesses to an extent never experienced before. The proliferation of cheaper and more efficient transportation and communication, coupled with the growth of finance and domestic oil and manufacturing industries such as steel and textiles, precipitated an economic boom.[42] Protected partly by its own navy but mostly by British naval supremacy at sea, the United States expanded into global markets as well, which further enhanced its economic wealth. Not all Americans benefited from these changes. Jim Crow reigned supreme in the former Confederate states, labor problems grew, and occasional recessions occurred, the worst being the panics of 1873 and 1893. But the overall growth catapulted the nation into economic powerhouse status. The middle class grew both in size and wealth, and Americans began looking beyond the seas for expansion.

A couple of crucially important things occurred in 1890 that meant drastic changes for the U.S. strategic outlook, the navy's and Marine Corps's missions, and the Corps's public-opinion trajectory. First, the western frontier officially closed, marking the end of centuries of Euro-American expansion across the continent. With the frontier gone, national-security concerns now came from across the seas, where policymakers saw significant naval powers in Europe and Asia. Second, Alfred Thayer Mahan published his profoundly influential *The Influence of Sea Power upon History, 1660–1783* (1890), which argued that Great Britain had become the greatest global power in the world by seizing command of the sea with its fleet of capital ships. Mahan argued that *guerre de course*, or commerce raiding, which had been the United States' principal form of naval warfare, could never win command of the sea. Only *guerre d'escadre*, war of squadrons or battles between fleets of battleships, could do this. His book held strong implications that the United States could duplicate the success of Britain because the nation had all of the requisite national characteristics to become a first-rate naval power.[43] Global economic hegemony stemmed from sea power, according to Mahan, and many naval enthusiasts became taken with his arguments. Staying away from world affairs no longer seemed to serve U.S. interests. More and more Americans became less and less interested in continental insularity. An already evolving policy now had an intellectual rationale and justification.

Many Americans now *wanted* a stronger U.S. Navy replete with a fleet of capital ships capable of winning and maintaining command of the sea, if necessary. In 1890 Congress funded the construction of three state-of-the-art 10,000-ton battleships designed to traverse the oceans—*Indiana*, *Massachusetts*, and *Oregon*. Numbered BB-1, BB-2, and BB-3 respectively, indicating that there would be more, designers meant these warships to conduct oceanic battle, not commerce raiding.

The Marine Corps attempted to keep up as U.S. naval policy shifted. Commandant Heywood tried to expand the Corps in tandem with navy growth to help operate secondary batteries on the new battleships. Having already infused the Corps with Naval Academy graduates, Heywood created the School of Application for all new Marine officers to further reform and enhance the officer corps.[44] He consistently requested higher personnel ceilings throughout his tenure.

But friction with the navy over Marines on ships surfaced again in the mid-1890s. Captain Robley D. "Fighting Bob" Evans in 1895 requested the customary Marine detachment be left off the *Indiana*'s manifest. Secretary of the Navy Hilary Herbert denied the request and outlined Marine duties while on board.[45] Lieutenant Fullam published another article in *Proceedings* soon after in which he argued *again* for the removal of Marines from vessels. There was no task on ship or shore that Marines and their officers could do better or more efficiently than sailors and naval officers, he asserted. Manliness again became a central issue in this discussion. "Manhood must surely be recognized more fully in our navy than in any other navy in the world if we are to be properly prepared for war," Fullam asserted.[46] In the discussion that followed, Commander J. N. Hemphill went so far as to assert, "Regarding the marines, I think that they should be turned over bodily to the Army."[47]

Once again, however, Fullam did not want to disband the Marines. He recognized the necessity of landing parties and the need for an expeditionary landing force. He was well aware of the fact that the Marines had made over thirty landings with the navy around the world between 1865 and 1895.[48] Fullam now wanted six permanent Marine battalions, two on the West Coast and four on the East Coast, with transports that could bring them when and where needed.[49] The naval officers were not of one mind about the removal of the Marines from their ships, however. Admiral David D. Porter and Stephen Luce, for example, argued against it. Fullam and the officers who supported his views simply could not convince enough people in the navy or Congress, so Marines remained on board U.S. warships.[50]

The Spanish-American War of 1898 brought about the expansion of the navy and the Marine Corps's manpower and duties. The U.S. Navy defeated the Spanish fleets at Manila Bay in the Philippines and at Santiago harbor in Cuba. A Marine battalion under Lieutenant Colonel Robert Huntington won public acclaim in Cuba by defeating a small force of Spanish soldiers at the Battle of Cuzco Well (June 14, 1898). After the war Congress and President William McKinley allowed the Corps to expand to six thousand enlisted Marines, with two hundred officers along with the promotion of Commandant Heywood to brigadier general.[51] With the acquisition of island bases from Hawaii to Midway, Wake Island, Guam, and the Philippines, the United States had become a global power. A large, technologically advanced navy made more sense now than ever before. This navy would need to use advanced bases around the globe to refit and refuel its warships. In 1900 the navy's newly established General Board tasked the Marines with forming and training a battalion-sized force for advanced-base defense and seizure.[52]

During and immediately after the 1898 war, many young but prominent politicians argued that this new overseas empire was good for American manhood. Indeed, many progressive Republicans like Theodore Roosevelt, Albert Beveridge, and Henry Cabot Lodge interpreted U.S. overseas expansion as maturation of a young nation into full manhood.[53] These men also celebrated martial manliness and the apparent manhood of soldiers, sailors, and Marines for their victory over the Spanish. Roosevelt himself went so far as to resign his position as assistant secretary of the navy in the McKinley administration to fight in Cuba. Anti-imperialists, many of them much older than their opponents, countered that the United States did not need an empire to prove its manliness among nations. But the war with Spain made empire a fait accompli. As the imperialists saw it, the United States had grown into manhood.[54]

Roosevelt believed that a robust navy was necessary for a strong and manly nation. As president, he authorized the addition of thirteen new steel-hulled battleships to the fleet. Roosevelt's defense policy involved protecting and increasing the U.S. sphere of influence in the Western Hemisphere. His "Corollary" to the Monroe doctrine stated essentially that the United States would intervene in the affairs of Latin American and Caribbean countries to preclude European intervention. Part of the reason for this was to protect U.S. businesses and assets overseas, such as banking, fruit, sugar, and tobacco companies, from being destroyed during civil wars.[55] Another reason was because Roosevelt took Mahan's axiom, that concentrated fleets of battleships were the essence of sea power, to heart. European intervention in the Caribbean threatened the security of the Panama Canal, which remained under construction until 1914. A threat to the canal meant a threat to the America's future maritime economic growth and its ability to concentrate its fleets in either the Atlantic or the Pacific Ocean.

Therefore, Presidents Roosevelt, William Howard Taft, and Woodrow Wilson used the navy to secure the U.S. sphere of influence in the Western Hemisphere. This is where the Marines fit in with national policy during the World War I era. The navy would land Marines on foreign soil to protect American interests and forcibly pursue U.S. policy directives. Under these auspices sailors and Marines landed in Cuba in 1906, 1912, and 1917; the Dominican Republic in 1903, 1904, and 1916; Panama in 1903 and 1904; Nicaragua in 1912; and Haiti in 1914 and 1915.

During this period, however, there was one more push to get Marine detachments off battleships for good. In 1906 navy officers of the Bureau of Navigation persuaded both the president and some members of Congress that Marine services on ship were no longer necessary. Roosevelt and his friend Major General Leonard Wood (U.S. Army) took this a step further and agreed that the Marine Corps should be handed over entirely to the army. The navy did not want that. Both it and the Corps wanted some assurance that removal of the ship's detachments would not mean losing the Marines to the army, so they asked for a clearly written definition of Marine duties. The Commandant, Brigadier General George Frank Elliott, and his staff offered a draft of what would become Executive Order 969, which clearly spelled out Marine duties. Marines would guard navy yards and stations within the United States and abroad, provide the first line of defense of naval bases overseas, garrison the Panama Canal, and provide expeditionary forces as needed for overseas deployment.[56] Roosevelt signed the order in November 1908, and Marines began coming off the warships. But that order failed to remain in the finalized naval appropriations bill of 1909, as Congress wanted the Marines to remain on ship. The president let them have it their way.

There would be no more attempts to remove Marines from U.S. warships, and there would be no serious threats to the existence of the Corps until after World War II. This lull in overt attempts to shrink or do away with the Marines led historian Robert Heinl to call the period between 1909 and 1932 the "Quiet Interlude."[57] The Marines would finally establish a small but permanent advanced-base force in 1912 while holding on to its traditional duties. By 1914, however, despite no real threat to the Corps's existence, Marine senior leadership remembered well the various attempts by some army and navy officers to do away with the service or seriously curtail its duties. Although they would not find any during the World War I era, the Marines constantly scanned the horizon for new enemies within the armed forces and national politics.

Force Structure

The World War I–era Marine Corps was small compared to the army and navy, and its organization reflected how the government used it to implement national policy. In 1914 the Corps stood at roughly 341 officers and 9,988 enlisted men.[58] The navy, by contrast, had 1,872 officers and 52,293 enlisted men, while the army reported 4,936 officers and 102,450 enlisted.[59] The regular army divided itself among different branches—cavalry, field artillery, infantry, and Indian and Philippine Scouts. Tasked with defending national borders and possessions overseas, U.S. soldiers deployed to Alaska, China, Puerto Rico, Hawaii, and the Panama Canal, having taken over responsibility for its security from the Marines by 1914. Most soldiers served in the United States, but the Philippines held the largest forward-deployed element of the army, totaling just under 15,000 men.[60]

The Marine Corps' force structure was quite fluid because of its various missions. The navy and the government tasked the Corps with guarding warships and naval facilities. Marines also deployed rapidly for expeditionary and advance-base duties as needed. Up to 1912, no permanent regiments or battalions existed, only provisional ones that the Corps organized hastily when necessary and disbanded quickly afterward. The Marines operated this way during the Seminole Wars, the Mexican-American War, the Civil War, and the Spanish-American War. Corps headquarters formed provisional regiments (500–1,000 men) and battalions (100–200 men) by pulling Marines from various barracks and ship's detachments, assigning a command staff, and designating them a temporary unit number.[61] The Corps established the First Regiment of Marines for advanced-base duty in 1912, its very first permanent regiment.[62]

For the Vera Cruz expedition in the spring of 1914, the Corps sent the First Regiment and the provisional Second Regiment, together forming the Advanced Base Brigade, and threw together the provisionally organized Third, Fourth, and Fifth Regiments to meet the needs of the mission.[63] None of these regiments have lineage connections with the Second, Third, Fourth, and Fifth Marine Regiments that exist in the 2020s. This amorphous structure surely caused confusion among civilians and politicians unfamiliar with the Marine Corps's ways.[64] But this fluidity was a strength in that it allowed the Corps the flexibility required to respond to its various missions. For example, Marines formed quickly the First Provisional Brigade for the Haiti expedition in 1915 and the Second Provisional Brigade for the Dominican Republic in 1916. The former brigade included the First and Second Regiments, while the latter comprised the Third and Fourth.[65]

Manpower was a perennial problem for the Corps. A flexible force structure may have been appropriate given the ways in which the Marines deployed, but it frequently meant that they spread out rather thin. While provisional regiments deployed, the Marines still manned as many warships as they could and struggled to keep up with their other duties. Commandants William P. Biddle (1911–1914) and George Barnett (1914–1920) never requested a scaling back of duties, however, only more men and money.

Public Opinion

For the Marine Corps of 1914, it had never been enough to simply win battles and fulfill missions. To justify their own expense, Marines had to garner public support and influence public opinion about their usefulness to American society and security. The Corps had not always enjoyed a good public reputation. Its small size largely kept it out of the limelight through much of the nineteenth century. Partially in response to its often negative post–Civil War reputation, civilian journalist Almy M. Aldrich, with the assistance of Marine captain Richard S. Collum, wrote *History of the United States Marine Corps* (1875), the first published history of the Corps. Their goal was to "bring more prominently to the attention of the country a history of services whose importance has failed to meet with that general recognition which it merits."[66] The book is full of stories of disciplined Marines behaving gallantly in the face of danger. Despite this effort to influence public opinion, desertion plagued the enlisted ranks in the 1870s, 1880s, and 1890s, which hurt the Corps's already tenuous manpower levels as well as its public image.

The quality of enlisted recruits was a noted problem, and military officers wrote that the types of men recruiters culled from the urban centers constituted the source of the problem. An 1887 editorial in the *Army and Navy Journal* accused the Marine Corps of recruiting only from the large cities, which allegedly provided men "oftentimes from the scum of the earth. . . . They, in turn, desert from the Marine Corps, or curse it with drunkenness and malingering, and swell the annual loss to more than one-fourth of the authorized strength."[67] For the Corps, however, available funds did not permit opening recruiting stations across much of rural America. Its recruiting infrastructure reached only major cities such as Chicago, Philadelphia, and New York. Commandant McCawley admitted, "Men enlisted in the large cities have always been of an inferior class, and yet these must be taken or none [at all]."[68] He made it a point to say, however, that the navy and army had the same recruiting issues.

Letting undesirable men into the Corps could damage recruiting efforts and its public image. The enlisted force during Colonels McCawley's and Heywood's tenures as Commandant lost nearly a quarter of its men to desertion annually; 419 Marines deserted in 1888 alone.[69] The officer corps blamed the inferior quality of recruits for such manpower problems, but they themselves did not always set a good example. Naval officers frequently court-martialed Marine lieutenants and captains for intoxication on ship and conduct unbecoming an officer during these years. Marine enlisted men and officers gained reputations for drunkenness and unprofessionalism on shore and at sea leading up to the war of 1898.[70] Henry Clay Cochrane, now a Marine captain in the early 1890s, pointed out the solution when he wrote, "good men will beget good men."[71]

Marines of questionable character led commanders of war vessels to "request the withdrawal of the marine guards from their ships if they cannot be furnished with a better class of men."[72] The 1892 La Guaira incident did not help. The commanding officer of the *Chicago* deployed twenty-five Marines to the U.S. consulate in La Guaira, Venezuela, to protect it from revolutionary troops. Six enlisted men got drunk at the consulate and frightened the staff. After recalling the Marines back to his ship, the captain publicly proclaimed them "worse than useless."[73] How such Marines performed left significant impressions on the public mind. Publicity, both good and bad, could affect recruiting, funding, and mission accomplishment, all of which had implications for the very survival of the institution.

The public profile of the Marines during this period was not all bad, however. The popular phrase "The Marines have landed and have the situation well in hand" came into use between the American Civil War and the Spanish-American War. The U.S. government dispatched the navy with detachments of Marines to China, Japan, Formosa, Uruguay, Mexico, Korea, Panama, Hawaii, Egypt, Haiti, Samoa, Argentina, Chile, and Colombia from 1866 to 1898.[74] Marines under the command of Captain Cochrane acted as guards for the 1889 Paris Exposition. On top of the guard duties, the detachment put on parades for the public and the French government.

Starting in 1880, John Philip Sousa led the U.S. Marine Band. Sousa was a talented composer who proved adept not only at producing marches but also at recruiting equally talented musicians. He offered the band's services for private parties as well as public parades and ceremonies. He also drilled the band hard and expected military-style precision during their performances. The effect of this was to raise the public esteem of the Marine Corps in the Washington area.[75] Sousa would go on to become somewhat of a "international march king" and compose world-famous marches such as "The Washington Post," "Semper Fidelis," and "The Stars and Stripes Forever." All of these marches would become associated with the U.S. Marine Corps.

The Spanish-American War brought the Corps good publicity from their service on battleships and in Cuba. It began with the tragic destruction of the *Maine* in Havana harbor in early 1898. When a catastrophic explosion rocked the warship, legend has it that Captain Dwight Sigsbee rushed to the main deck of the ruined vessel and encountered a Marine orderly named William Anthony. Surrounded by smoke and flame, Anthony snapped to "present arms" and was rumored to have said, "Sir, I have to inform you that the ship has been blown up and is sinking." A newspaper later reported, "When asked about this instance of cool courage and superb presence of mind, this specimen of American manhood said: 'Oh, that's nothing, any yankee marine would do that.'"[76] Anthony then escorted his captain to safety. Twenty-eight Marines perished in the explosion along with 266 sailors; American newspapers made martyrs of them all, and public opinion soon blamed Spanish treachery for their deaths.[77] The United States declared war a few months later.

In the June 1898 fight at Cuzco Well, the Marines were accompanied by journalist and novelist Stephan Crane, who published stories of the heroics of Lieutenant Colonel Huntington, Captain George Elliot (a West Point dropout and future tenth Commandant of the Marine Corps), and Sergeant John Quick.[78] Similar stories of brave Marines in Cuba popped up in the *New York World*, *New York Tribune*, *New York Herald*, *Chicago Tribune*, and *Harpers Weekly*.[79] The *New York Times* praised the Marines on the secondary batteries of the *Oregon* for helping destroy Admiral Pascual Cervera's fleet at the Battle of Santiago Harbor (July 3, 1898). "In every respect, and at every point, the marines were shown to be a well-disciplined, alert, brave, lot of men," the article stated.[80] Journalists, politicians, and many other middle-class Americans injected masculine-charged rhetoric into discourses about the war.[81] Within this context, the Marines began to promote themselves as the more masculine of the two naval services because of their greater willingness to risk bodily harm on sea or on land.[82] The subsequent acquisition of island territories across the globe, the increase in size of the navy, and this good publicity led to an increase of the Corps to over six thousand men. It is hard to imagine such an increase in size and expansion of duties if the Marines had performed badly during the war.

The Corps's forays into East Asia brought a mixed bag of good and bad publicity. Marines under the command of Major Littleton Waller Tazewell Waller deployed to the Philippines in 1899 to assist the U.S. Army in fighting insurgents intent on overthrowing American rule. Marines also served as part of an international guard force that protected the Legation Quarter in Peking (now Beijing), China. This force fought in the Boxer Rebellion of 1899, when the Society of Righteous and Harmonious Fists attempted to expel all foreign powers from China. When the Chinese government sided with the Boxers, an international army of 20,000 men, accompanied by 500 Marines under Waller pulled from the Philippines, responded.

While the "Open Door" policy continued to be wedged open by armed force, the Marines returned to the Philippines, this time to the island of Samar, where an army infantry company had been ambushed and massacred in September 1901. In an expedition across the island, Waller lost ten Marines to disease and dehydration. Close to death from illness himself, the major ordered the summary execution of eleven Filipino scouts he suspected of treachery.[83] Waller's subsequent court-martial found him not guilty (his commanding officer, Brigadier General Jacob Smith of the U.S. Army, apparently approved of the acts). Ernest Howard Crosby, a noted and respected author of the day, read about the actions of Marines and soldiers in the Philippines with alarm. His resulting article, "The Military Idea of Manliness," provided a cutting rebuke of their behavior. "Forgery, deception, the violation of the laws of hospitality . . . the wanton slaughter of troops drawn up under false representations of peaceful intention, all these things, we are assured, are manly in the eyes of a soldier," he wrote.[84] Although Crosby and some authors in the *Nation* criticized the army and the Corps within its pages, many U.S. newspapers remained sympathetic to the Marines.[85]

If how Marines conducted themselves overseas was important for public relations, then the role of recruiters back in the States was equally vital. The first decade of the twentieth century saw important developments within the Marine Corps recruiting service. Those who worked larger cities such as Chicago, New York, and Philadelphia developed tactics geared toward drumming up good publicity for the Corps to gain recruits. They did this by befriending journalists and reporters from local newspapers. According to some Marine recruiters, journalists would socialize at the recruiting offices or would meet up with recruiters on corners or coffee shops and swap stories. They passed along stories about the Marines in action at home and abroad to these journalists, who would then publish articles for their principal newspapers.[86] Marines in these stories portrayed a style of manliness that valued courage, honor, toughness, and the willingness to fight. This arrangement was informal and mutually beneficial: journalists got something to write about while the Marines got favorable publicity. Thus was born a significant relationship between the Corps and the press that would pay dividends throughout the twentieth century.

These kinds of interactions led to the organization of more centralized recruiting and publicity efforts. Recruiters in Chicago established their own publicity bureau in 1907, which had a single typewriter and a mimeograph machine.[87] They typed up articles about the benefits of service in the Marine Corps and then sent them on to the local papers. No centralized Marine publicity bureau, responsible for all Corps publicity and recruiting material, existed at that time. The Marine Corps Recruiting Publicity Bureau (later shortened to the Publicity Bureau) filled this role upon its establishment in New York City in 1912, during Commandant Elliot's tenure. Commanded by Captain H. C. Snyder, and staffed with four fulltime recruiters, this office began working the Corps's public image.[88] The office grew to a staff of fifteen Marines three years later. The establishment of the Marine Publicity Bureau and the subsequent founding of the *Recruiters' Bulletin* in 1914 are perhaps the most significant developments in Marine Corps public relations since Sousa led the Marine Band in the 1880s and 1890s.[89]

Starting in November 1914, the bureau published monthly issues of the *Recruiters' Bulletin*, mostly in the interest of recruiters stationed across the country but also serving as general source of news and entertainment pertinent to many other Marines. Recruiters, both officers and enlisted, contributed articles, editorials, artwork, enlistment figures, and poetry to each issue throughout its existence. The editors wanted civilians to read the *Recruiters' Bulletin*, too, in part because it might aid recruiting by informing the public about who the Marines were and what they did.

By 1914, there existed, for the first time in the Corps's history, a centralized and productive force within its force structure geared entirely toward pulling resources from society and protecting and bolstering its name and identity.[90] The Publicity Bureau's mission was to produce material and write stories to attract the men and the public attention the Marine Corps needed to fulfill its obligations to the navy and to U.S. defense policy. Just before the outbreak of the Great War, the bureau occupied a two-story office in New York City and had as staff of twenty-seven enlisted Marines and one officer, Major Albert Sidney McLemore, Naval Academy class of 1891. McLemore answered directly to the Commandant and oversaw the Marine Corps's three recruiting divisions across the country: the Eastern, Western, and Central Recruiting Divisions. Marines subdivided these divisions into twenty districts, among them the Philadelphia, Chicago, and Los Angeles Recruiting Districts as well as the Southeastern and Mountain Districts, which covered less-populated areas of the country.[91] These districts oversaw 132 stations combined.[92] Thanks to the Publicity Bureau and the expansion of recruiting quotas, the Corps by 1914 had the reach into rural communities that Commandants in the past would have envied.

Now Marine recruiters went into areas of the country previously covered only by army recruiters. Still, the military's recruiting power dwarfed the Marines. The army had up to 312 recruiting stations across the country and received 168,955 applications between July 1, 1913, and June 30, 1914, alone.[93] Marine recruiters, armed with the Publicity Bureau's literature, pamphlets, and posters, manned offices across the country in big cities and small towns, competing for young men to join their ranks. Every one of them served as public-relations officers and living advertisements through their interactions with citizens.

The Marine Corps Image and Mission Construction

These World War –era recruiters promoted a certain image of the Marine Corps. Marines appeared to be elite warriors, neither soldiers nor sailors, but somehow better than both.[94] They promised to benefit the lives of the men who joined mentally, morally, and physically. The

Marines pitched themselves, both implicitly and explicitly, as a corps of soldiers who would make a man out of any youngster brave enough to join, taking and molding them in their own image. That image was not just a warrior image, it was a decidedly wholesome and manly one. Marines, recruiters claimed, were imbued with not only strength of arm and mind but also of character.

They promoted within their ranks and to the public not only traditional manly virtues such as honesty and selflessness but also military virtues such as fighting prowess. "Who am I? I am a two-fisted fighting rover. I am a United States Marine," reads *The Marine's Catechism*, a pamphlet recruiters had used since at least 1914.[95] An image harkening back to Sergeant John Quick's signaling of the gunboat *Dolphin* at the Battle of Cuzco Well is on its title page. One question near the end asks, "How does an enlistment in the Marine Corps benefit one?" The authors of the pamphlet answer that, in addition to travel and pay, "service in the Marine Corps will also build him up physically, improve his morals and his mind, and in every way make a better man of him." These traits would greatly prepare him to face the vicissitudes of life.[96]

Marines made these assertions in their own institutional publications, the *Recruiters' Bulletin*, the *Marines Magazine*, and the *Marine Corps Gazette*. While the *Recruiters' Bulletin* was an official, government-funded publication, the *Marines Magazine* was not. First published in December 1915 by the Horn-Shafer Publishing Company in Baltimore, Maryland, it was tailored to the enlisted audience. The founder, Sergeant Edward A. Callan, wrote, "the men of the Marine Corps are desirous of having a magazine devoted solely to their interests as men of the Corps." The original form of this enlisted magazine came as *The Cavite News*, started by Callan in 1908 in the Philippines. Like the *Bulletin*, the *Marines Magazine* served as form of entertainment and news for Marines stationed at home and abroad. Bereft of long and serious pieces on politics and social issues that were common to magazines geared toward more affluent classes of civilians, the magazine contained lighthearted fiction in the form of short stories and novella-length pieces published chapter by chapter across several issues. It also gave plenty of space to Marine artwork, cartoons, poetry, and humor as well as advertisements aimed specifically toward male audiences.[97]

The *Marine Corps Gazette*, a more academic publication geared toward officers and first published in 1916, was the brainchild of a group of officers who formed the Marine Corps Association in 1911 while stationed in Guantanamo Bay, Cuba. A couple of years later, in 1913, Colonel Lincoln Karmany, Lieutenant Colonel Lejeune, Captain Har-

WHO AM I?

WHO AM I?

I am a soldier.
I am a sailor.
Yet I am neither.
I am older than the soldier and the sailor, although I am smaller in size.

I go everywhere—by land or sea—and to the very frontiers of civilization if need be, in the protection of American interests.

I raised the first American flag on foreign soil, more than a century ago.

I carried Old Glory into action in Tripoli, Egypt, West Africa, the Fiji Islands, Sumatra, Hawaii, Mexico, China, Uruguay, Paraguay, Alaska, Panama, Formosa, Korea, Nicaragua, Cuba, Santo Domingo, and Hayti.

I am a two-fisted fighting rover.
I am the United States Marine.

Fig. 3. Cover of *The Marine's Catechism—Who Am I?* (New York: Marine Corps Publicity Bureau, 1917).

old C. Snyder (all three Naval Academy graduates), and Captain Davis B. Wills formed its executive committee. In the first quarterly issue, they claimed that the *Gazette* was "for the purpose of recording and publishing the history of the Marine Corps, publishing a periodical journal for the dissemination of information concerning the aims, purposes and deeds of the Corps, and the interchange of ideas for the betterment and improvement of its officers and men."[98] Marine officers published articles on a wide variety of topics pertaining to military service, including machine-gun drill, service in Guam, and garrison training. The *Gazette* kept Marines around the globe abreast of the latest regulations and orders and also served an educational function by publishing articles on history as well as book reviews.

The Corps was a bit late on the professional journal and magazine publishing scene. The *Gazette* bore similarities to the U.S. Naval Institute's much older *Proceedings*, but the *Marines Magazine* and *Recruiters' Bulletin* looked much more like other popular magazines of the era. Neither the army nor the navy had equivalents to the *Recruiters' Bulletin* yet. Since the 1890s, national publications such as *McClure's* and the *Saturday Evening Post* began allowing advertisers to pay for marketing space in their issues. This small change precipitated a revolution in the U.S. magazine market as publishers began making profits more and more through advertising instead of subscriptions.[99] Magazine prices for consumers dropped, and the number of sales rose substantially. The cover price for the *Marines Magazine* was only fifteen cents per issue or $1.50 for a year's subscription. These Marine publications came at a time, therefore, when magazines and journals reached a zenith in popularity.

The editors of the *Marines Magazine, Recruiters' Bulletin*, and *Marine Corps Gazette*, therefore, not only wanted to entertain and inform Marine audiences but also wanted the public to read them as well. This made these periodicals important mediums through which Marines communicated their own culture to outsiders. "Send a copy for one year to Mother, or Father, or to a big or little sister or brother or to your old school chum, back in the old home town," Callan encouraged readers of the *Marines Magazine*. "They'll enjoy it and read it for news of where you are."[100] Because their audience included families and parents, all three publications presented carefully crafted manly and wholesome images of Marines.

The sudden deployments to Hispaniola and the eruption of the Great War had a significant effect on Marines' worldview, their sense of mission, and their identity as a military institution. Discourse on these missions and events took place frequently in their three principal publications. Important discussions of doctrine and mission popped up as well. Prompted by the war in Europe, an enlightening debate took place between field-grade officers in the *Marine Corps Gazette*, revealing that readiness, flexibility, preparedness, and offensive action were key elements in the Corps's identity.

Notions of manhood also came up in these discussions in the sense that the authors cared very much about the Marine Corps obtaining greater prestige and glory. They debated the identity of an institution of fighting men and how Marines should be employed in the future to earn the respect of the other service branches and society at large. Marine manliness, therefore, was a central part of this discussion. Within the pages of the *Marines Magazine* and the *Recruiter's Bulletin*, Marines communicated these ideas through manly images and stories designed for in-house audiences and, later, as images presented to the public.

Colonel Lejeune's article "The Mobile Defense of Advance Bases by the Marine Corps" continued a discussion in the *Gazette* about the service's identity and possible future ongoing since the turn of the century. "The most important factor," he argued, "is the determination of the *true mission* of the Marine Corps in the event of war."[101] The Corps that Lejeune envisioned would have a vital role in a war that required naval warfare as a leverage for victory. He asserted that Marines had a chance to become the first to strike the enemies of the United States if they identified and prepared for a new general mission: advance naval-base defense and seizure.[102] This new orientation would have a positive psychological effect on Marines. If the Corps made itself into "an Advance Base organization, it would have the opportunity to share with the Navy the glory always resting on those who strike the first blows at the enemy," he claimed.[103] According to his vision, Marines would be the first ground troops to fight on hostile shores to capture and defend naval installations.

While peace reigned, Lejeune argued that the Corps's posture should be readiness with the navy. Marines needed to develop and train the force necessary for advance-base seizure and defense. "All, I believe, will agree that our training as an Advance Base organization, both as a mobile and as a fixed defense force, will best fit us for any or all of these roles," he claimed, "and that such training should, therefore, be adopted as our special peace mission."[104] Preparing Marines for war would be the commodity that the Corps produced for society. Lejeune affirmed this goal when he argued, "Surely, this is a mission worthwhile, and one which furnishes a spur to energetic effort and zealous labor in time of peace, so as to attain the true soldier's Elysian state, 'preparedness for war.'"[105] In terms of what Marines communicated among themselves, especially among the officer corps, preparedness was a primary concern in their culture. Lejeune and others argued that the Corps had much work to do, especially with the supposed "war to end all wars" raging across the Atlantic.

It was the Great War itself, not solely advance-base seizure or defense, that prompted Major John H. Russell to publish "A Plea for a Mission and Doctrine" in the June 1916 issue of the *Gazette*. Russell wrote that the forces then engaged in Europe equaled the "Standard of Efficiency" to which Marines should measure themselves.[106] He had measured the Corps and found it wanting because it had not paid enough attention to its own mission and doctrine. Russell's hopes for its future, like Lejeune's, involved combat in a war similar to the one in Europe. He wanted the Corps ready if, or when, the time came for the United States to join the war.

Russell and Lejeune cared about the Corps's reputation, which they believed would be enhanced through advanced-base warfare and offensive action. They desired glory, prestige, and institutional survival, not just efficiency. For Lejeune, being the first to fight would give Marines "the glory always resting on those who strike the first blows."[107] And for Russell, the adoption of an offensive doctrine "would greatly increase the . . . prestige of the Marine Corps."[108] With these assertions, the authors drifted away from the more tangible principles of efficiency and into the realm of cultural beliefs about what it meant to be a prestigious and elite institution. The Marine Corps needed the type of manhood that could achieve this level of prestige. "Men who lead a clean life will, I feel certain, give better service to their country when the great test comes, than the drunkard or the debauchee," Lejeune asserted.[109] Russell argued, "With poor personnel, no matter how well organized and equipped, an organization will, in short order, deteriorate."[110]

Prior to the Great War, the Marine Corps used masculine imagery to depict the very ideals of prestige and efficient personnel that Russell and Lejeune espoused. Images of Marines storming beaches with rifles at the ready saturated institutional publications. The Corps placed three recurring illustrations on recruiting posters and in the *Marines Magazine*. Entitled *U.S. Marines: "Soldiers of the Sea," First to Fight*, and *Join the U.S. Marine Corps: Soldiers of the Sea!*, they depict Marines attacking from the sea. All three convey aggressive men on the offensive, plunging forward toward their objective. These Marines appear athletic, strong, and ready for a fight, qualities people associated with military manliness in early twentieth-century America.[111] "The Marines of our service are the finest trained body of riflemen in the world," declared the *Recruiters' Bulletin*, because they were "the first men to land when the Navy has to land forces in turbulent districts; scattered in advanced posts over half the world, where the United States holds sway."[112]

Although it is not clear how the debates in the *Marine Corps Gazette* and the imagery found in *Marines Magazine* and the *Recruiters' Bulletin* directly informed one another, gendered themes and rhetoric appeared in all three. Probably, the debates and contemporary manly imagery came out, informed by each other, from the same intellectual and cultural milieu. They serve as examples of how Marines expressed these ideas about mission and doctrine, both vital parts of the institution's identity, with gendered terms and imagery.

This public-image construction was crucially important to the Marine Corps of this early twentieth century because it helped communicate their identity and attract the recruits it needed to fulfill its

Fig. 4. *Join the U.S. Marine Corps: Soldiers of the Sea!* World War I Posters, Library of Congress.

Fig. 5. *First to Fight,* by Sidney Reisenberg. From *Marines Magazine,* June 1917, 1.

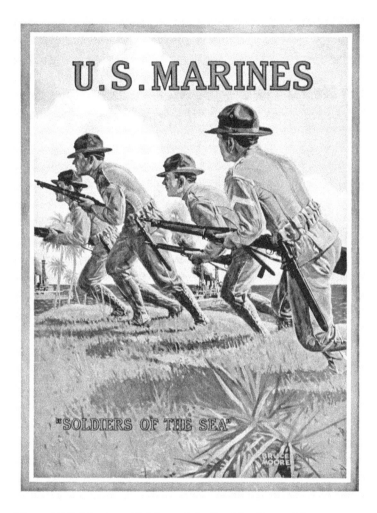

Fig. 6. *U.S. Marines: "Soldiers of the Sea,"* by Bruce Moore. World War I Posters, Library of Congress.

missions. With recent threats to its existence fresh in mind, the Marines remained vigilant and involved by continuing to push a narrative of turning young boys and slouches into men. The Publicity Bureau made sure the public saw this narrative play out as Marines deployed to Mexico, Haiti, the Dominican Republic, and eventually France. Manliness was a central element of the Marine Corps no less defining than its missions, force structure, and public image.

2

With Hard Two-Fisted Hands

They're first-class he-fighters, who uses their beans,
An'—only a fool would say "Damn the Marines!"
— *Berton Braley, "The Leathernecks," 1917*

Marines of the Great War era loved to tell stories about manhood. The *Marines Magazine* published one such fictional story in the spring of 1917. Jimmie Decker enlisted in the Corps but decided to desert after having trouble adjusting to military life. Jimmie claimed the recruiters lied to him. "Why had he enlisted, anyhow? To see the world, that was it," the author wrote. "And they had kept him drilling and hiking at a dull recruiting depot for a month, and then had shanghaied him to a dull station ship at an even duller northern navy yard where he would have to remain at least a year before he could even think of transferring."[1] Jimmie lacked discipline: he got in trouble for insubordination and for being late for duty several times. Unwilling to serve out his three-year enlistment in the Marine Corps, he opted to go absent without leave on a train to Montreal.

On the very train Jimmie boarded sat one Sergeant McNab, a long-in-the-tooth veteran and the personification of Marine manliness, who would attempt to talk the would-be deserter into changing his mind about the Corps and about himself as a man. The author described the scene:

Sergeant McNab, Irishman, five service stripes, and grizzled veteran of two wars, had seen and divined Jimmies' intention. He knew the signs only too well. Numerous young Marines had McNab seen in his twenty-two years of service who thought Uncle Sam too severe in the matter of discipline, and who, therefore, decided to separate themselves from the Corps via the dishonorable route. And numerous of these disgusted young men had the grizzled one caught in time to set on the path of an honorable career using as a means of persuasion coaxing, threats, coercion, and appeals to manhood, according to the temperament of the individual.[2]

McNab decided to sit next to Jimmie and have a chat with him. He aimed to change his mind by appealing to his manhood. Jimmie recognized the sergeant immediately and feared the old vet would turn him in. McNab informed the wayward youngster that he had nothing to fear from him, however, because he was not worth turning in.

The longtime veteran made Jimmie feel as though he was not man enough to serve in the Marine Corps. "Uncle Sam wants *men* only, not spineless scum," McNab said. "The best thing for such mollycoddles to do is just exactly what you're doing—run away." Good riddance, too, according to McNab, because "Old Glory is a jealous mistress, and will have none but strong men to serve her." By the time McNab finished casting aspersions on Jimmie's patriotism, loyalty, and courage, the young man had broken into tears. As the sergeant stood to leave, Jimmie reached for the older man's hand but got only this in reply: "No, I wouldn't shake hands with a man with no guts, that's not a part of my creed." McNab had accused him of cowardice and weakness, two of the worst transgressions a Marine could commit. He did not call Jimmie's physical abilities into question; he impugned his character. By doing so, McNab reflected not only Marine standards of decorum and behavior but also popular Victorian notions of manhood.[3]

From 1914 through America's entry into the Great War, U.S. Marines largely adhered to a style of manliness that stressed the inner qualities of courage, integrity, and toughness, all of which were in line with popular notions of Victorian manhood. These values existed in tandem with military virtues of readiness, preparedness, and flexibility. Taken together, these characteristics form the bulk of early twentieth-century Marine manliness. The outbreak of war in Europe, and the preparedness craze that swept the nation soon after, influenced much of the Marines' rhetoric regarding their public image and their usefulness to society. Marines saw themselves as men who could handle any situation. The color of their skin was also an essential ingredient of their manhood. Only white men without exception could become Marines during the Great War era, and their imagery and stories reflected beliefs of white superiority over other races.

Gendered notions of what it meant to be a Marine pervaded many of their public discourses. The Corps claimed to be a man-making institution that injected struggle and hardship into men's lives that toughened them and improved their character. Boot camp, for example, with its influence on both the mind and body, was supposed to enhance the manliness of recruits. Marines also valued the masculine qualities of being sharply dressed and physically imposing.[4] They tended to emphasize their manliness, with its mental and moral implications, and their masculine uniforms and physiques to boast that they were Uncle Sam's favorite body of fighting men.

Readiness Is Close to Manliness

Readiness, the ability to meet any one of the Corps's myriad missions quickly, coursed through Marine institutional publications. Ten thousand Marines served around the globe in 1914: twenty-six hundred in various barracks and naval stations in the United States; fifty-six hundred overseas in places like Peking China, Guam, Honolulu, Cuba and the Philippines; and the balance, over eighteen hundred men, on board the U.S. Navy's cruising vessels.[5] From 1914 to 1917, much of the Marines' discourses on readiness drew inspiration from their service at sea and in Latin America, the Philippines, and the far frontiers of American empire.

Marines aboard warships and in China had important military and ceremonial functions. These detachments had to be equally ready to operate the ship's secondary batteries, form a landing party, or don dress blue uniforms for onboard ceremonies and inspections. Most Marines coveted service in China. In Peking officers had three Chinese servants each, and enlisted men could hire locals to cook and clean for them. Although they had to be ready at a moment's notice to defend the lives of American and foreign diplomats living there, they also served as "one of the social adornments of the international community."[6] Marine dress parades, blue uniforms, and precision drills added a level of military pomp and prestige to the U.S. presence there. American diplomat Paul S. Reinsch, who served as minister to China from 1913 to 1919, was consistently impressed by their masculine appearance. He wrote of "fine looking companies of American marines, who among all troops in Peking are noted for their well-groomed, smart, and soldierly appearance."[7]

Most Marines stationed elsewhere around the world, however, had to be ready for labor well beyond military drills and security details. Major Henry C. Hines described a typical two days in the field for his battalion in Guam. "The men in Guam have done such a variety of work that to say they did this or that does not to any extent cover the ground," he wrote. His Marines built roads, bridges, dams, houses, and latrines. They charted maps, performed garrison duties, and served as local policemen. Despite the long days, wrote Hines, "a better trained, better spirited and willing body of men never lived."[8] What his men actually thought about all this labor on the island is left to the reader to surmise.

Charles A. Ketcham, editor of the *Marines Magazine*, offered another explanation as to why Marines cared so much about readiness. "The Marine Corps is prepared for active service," he argued, "because it is generally engaged in active service." Ketcham contended that the U.S. government's deployment of Marines on short notice to places such as Haiti, the Dominican Republic, and Vera Cruz demonstrated the importance of readiness. "A large percentage of our men in recent years have had real experience in the field— . . . actual service, demanding professional fitness and personal courage, and giving the men involved invaluable experience in the service of security and information and in actual field operations under fire." Being ready for any mission required a high level of flexibility, the ability to switch from one task to another seamlessly. Congress, he asserted, would be hesitant to fund and raise a large and expensive army for police actions in the Caribbean and Latin America. Yet U.S. interests in those regions meant one thing to Ketcham: "the Marine Corps is prepared and *must* be prepared." He concluded that for Marines to carry out their array of possible duties, they had to be "trained not only as infantry, but as artillery, heavy and light, as engineers, as sappers and pioneers, as signalmen, and even as cavalry when necessary."[9]

An image published in the June 1917 issue of the *Recruiters' Bulletin* graphically represented how Marines liked to portray their flexibility. *All in the Day's Work*, by Charles Gatchell, is a busy image. Marines are conducting landing parties, training for street riots, practicing saber and cavalry drills, and fighting sham battles. They are also marching, rowing, and wall climbing. This busyness is the point of the image, conveying a style of manliness that celebrates the physical and mental ability to do any task.

Marines thought of themselves as men of action, which, because their level of physical and intellectual activity, made them more useful to society. "When he ceases to be active he ceases to be useful and descends to the level of vegetable life," Corporal F. E. Turin wrote of his fellow Marines. "Certainly those pursuits which call into activity his intellectual powers must contribute to his felicity, his dignity, and his usefulness."[10] Another Marine warned, "If you are not ambitious; if

Fig. 7. *All in the Day's Work*, by Charles Gatchell. From *Recruiters' Bulletin*, June 1917.

you do not keep your brain active in figuring out what you would have done in some tight corner, in some special situation which required quick thinking, quick action, you are not a true Marine."[11] The Marines' ideal man was active and constantly adapting. A man with these attributes demonstrated an ideal character, one of the most important measuring sticks for Victorian notions of manhood.

Flexibility meant that Marines had to study various duties and undergo constant training for different tasks. "For the last sixteen years I have seen officers and men of the Marine Corps up late at night working on some detail," claimed First Sergeant Charles Dunbeck, "or trying to fathom some job or duties that had been assigned to the Corps . . . while their friends from the Army and Navy were lounging around the plaza listening to the evening concert." He claimed that a Marine had to be ready for anything: "tomorrow he must build a bridge, lay 50 miles of submarine cable, erect a wireless station, mine the harbor at Culebra, and next month mount 12-inch guns on Grande Island, and upon returning to the States he finds himself Captain of an infantry company, to drill against the crack outfits from the Army and Navy, at Madison Square." Dunbeck asserted that a Marine's education comes not from specialized study at schools or war colleges, but from doing the duty of a Marine around the world. "The Marine is not a soldier, sailor, nor a man from the engineer service corps, but nevertheless it takes all of these qualifications to make a good Marine," he wrote.[12]

When a Marine did not live up to these standards, his manhood came into question. A tactic recruiters used to fill manpower quotas was to entice former Marines to reenter the service. Ketcham printed a letter from Floyd M. Showalter to make a point about the manhood of the men who fell short of the Corps's ideal. Showalter wrote, "When there occurs a renaissance in military affairs . . . , when those in power cease to follow the English caste system . . . , when military and naval forces cease their ceremonies and circus parading . . . , when as in the French army, there is a better understanding and confidence existing between enlisted men and officer, then I shall return to the colors." Ketcham responded by casting aspersions on Showalter's manliness: "He was not big enough to impress his own worth and significance as a man and soldier upon his officers. A 'thin-skinned' man who does not possess a sense of proportion and of relative values conditioned upon time, place and circumstance, has a hard time in a military organization. Poor Floyd—good chap, no doubt, but he didn't 'catch on.'"[13] He claimed that Showalter was not man enough for the Marine Corps or any other military institution because he lacked a strong and assertive character. Being a "thin-skinned" man in Victorian cultural parlance meant being overly sensitive and thus unmanly.[14]

Marines did not pull these ideas from thin air. These discourses on readiness, identity, and manhood stemmed from the Corps's involvement in military actions in Mexico, Haiti, and Santo Domingo and from the influence of the Great War in Europe on American military thought. Leading up to the U.S. entry into the war, discourses on how well American forces would respond if drawn into a conflict with another major power had circulated around the country. Within these debates, preparedness often became a measuring stick for American men. Some people understood that it was the manhood of the nation who would have to chase the wolf from the door if necessary.[15] "If the scourge of war should visit this fair land, we would be found ready for it," Alfred Percival, a columnist for the *Syracuse Herald*, claimed. "The manhood of the country would rise en masse to drive the hated foe away from our borders."[16] Some people, however, questioned that premise.

The Preparedness Movement

Between 1914 and 1917, a military-preparedness campaign swept through the United States.[17] One historian argues, "by the fall of 1915, preparedness had become a popular fad and a craze, riding the progressive currents of national efficiency and individual duty."[18] Former U.S. Army chief of staff Major General Leonard Wood called for army reform and national military readiness perhaps louder than any general officer throughout the armed forces. The army he left for retirement in 1914 could not stand up to any military in Europe, he argued, because it was too small, too spread out, and too disorganized. It took the U.S. Army a long six weeks to assemble at the border of Mexico when the Mexican Revolution had erupted in 1911.[19] Wood claimed, "Our people have forgotten, in the rush and turmoil incident to the development of the national resources and the industries of our great country, the unnecessary cost both in blood and treasure of our past wars, and remember only that somehow or other we emerged from them successfully."[20] The U.S. Navy and Marine Corps became wrapped up in this campaign as well.

In response to the preparedness movement, Marines claimed that they were prepared to protect American interests at home and abroad. "Always prepared and ready for action" was how Sergeant Claud Johnson described them.[21] "While the entire country is crying 'preparedness,' the Marine Corps answers, 'we are prepared,'" wrote Captain L. M. Harding in a proposed recruiting pamphlet. As a recruiter, Harding wanted to use the preparedness movement to convince young men to join the Corps. He asked applicants to consider joining the only service that was always prepared to protect their country and each other. He supplemented this argument with a direct reference to Marine manhood: "Its ranks are filled with young men of the highest qualities and highest ambitions."[22] In doing so, Harding made the quality of manhood an ingredient of preparedness.

Recruiters were not the first to do this, as civilian writers had already begun to link preparedness to the strength of American manhood. If the former was weak, then so was the latter. The discussion evolved quickly into a contest between competing ideas of manliness that had been around since before the Civil War.[23] Preparedness advocates tended to espouse a martial form of manliness that valued aggression and valor. Their opponents, however, promoted restraint, patience, and civility. These ideas of contained manliness had been around for a few years by the time the Great War started. Homer Lea, a popular writer at the time, claimed that the United States was woefully unprepared for war and connected this with weak manhood in his 1909 book, *The Valor of Ignorance*. He argued that Americans suffered from several delusions: first, that they were safe from military invasion; second, that they need not concern themselves with military readiness; and third, that the United States could be a great nation without going to war. It took a certain level of valor to wallow purposefully in that kind of ignorance, Lea asserted, hence his book's title and central theme. "Whenever a nation becomes excessively opulent and arrogant," he argued, "at the same time being without military power to defend its opulence or support its arrogance, it is in a dangerous position."[24] He argued that both men and nations decay when they grow lazy and allow their strength to wane.[25] A weak nation defended by weak men meant that it was possible for German or Japanese armies to land on either coast of the United States without much resistance.[26] Lea's warnings tapped into a sentiment that also appeared in other works at the time.

According to numerous authors, the United States had much to lose if its manhood was weak. "The moment a nation loses its sense of manhood and strength," R. Swinburne Clymer wrote, "does it begin to decay and to decline."[27] A people without strong manhood risked decline and foreign subjugation at the hands of manlier nations. Therefore, the United States needed "manhood—virile, vigorous, strong, self-reliant, self-assertive manhood," to survive the age.[28] Officials in the federal government echoed the need for manliness but emphasized character over other attributes. "A nation stands or falls, succeeds or fails, just in proportion to the high-mindedness, cleanliness, and manliness of each succeeding generation of men," claimed a writer for the War Department.[29]

Frederick Louis Huidekoper's *The Military Unpreparedness of the United States* (1915) aimed to make Americans aware of the need to make ready in case of war. Major General Wood asserted that this book should be "carefully read by all Americans."[30] Huidekoper argued that the United States had been unprepared for every war it had fought and that defense policy as of 1915 was as inadequate as the policies of the past. He criticized army organization and size, recruitment policies, length of enlistments, dependence upon raw troops and their inefficiency in war, the combination of regulars with volunteers and militia, lax discipline, and the indifference of the government and the American people alike.[31] The *Marine Corps Gazette* published a review of it in June 1916 that said, "The work is invaluable as an authoritative reference and would be equally invaluable to the library of every student of the military art."[32]

Newspapers printed pieces that sharply criticized the manliness of antipreparedness types. John T. McCutcheon's cartoon that appeared in Missouri's *Joplin Globe* on August 7, 1915, presented nine different types of Americans he identified as "Dangerous Citizens" because of their unwillingness to support military preparedness. The first three examples appear guilty of gross ignorance concerning military affairs. "The man who thinks the United States can lick all creation," "the Man who thinks one American can lick any five foreigners," and "the peace at any price man who thinks that gentleness and persuasion can prevail against an envious and determined enemy" all knew little about the world and Americans' place within it.

The next three citizens in McCutcheon's lineup called for other people's sons to fight well-trained and dangerous troops but refused to let their own sons serve. "The man who wants the United States to adopt a firm stand against Germany, but who doesn't want his son to fight in case of war," "the man who would send untrained undisciplined troops against a trained and well organized enemy," and "the mother who didn't raise her son to be a soldier, but expects some other mother's son to protect her in time of national danger"—a direct reference to Alfred Bryan's popular antiwar song of 1915—all appear selfish and misguided. These parents who protect their children from military service do so at the cost of their sons' manhood. The man standing behind his mother holding a flower and dressed like a child illustrates this best.

The last three men McCutcheon presents are guilty of feigning both patriotism and support for military preparedness. "The man who doesn't know that an army without strong artillery would stand no more show in a modern war than a snowball in Mexico," "the yap statesmen who orates about the glory of the flag, but who voted against every attempt to provide adequate protection for it," and "the man who thinks that the richest most defenseless of all great nations can have a Monroe Doctrine and an Open Door in China policy without running the risk of getting into a war" are all just as damaging to the country as the others. Ignorant citizens and politicians, McCutcheon thus argues, shared the blame for America's unpreparedness.

These images of white middle-class American men (and one woman) drew their persuasive power from their various distortions of manhood. The man standing behind his mother, for example, has a jejune countenance and is wearing a child's sailor uniform. By hiding behind her, he is more like a child than a man. McCutcheon probably received inspiration from discourses on the perceived damage that overnurturing women inflicted on young boys in the United States. Renowned psychologist Dr. G. Stanley Hall influenced much of this thinking. "Feminization of the school spirit, discipline, and personnel is bad for boys," he argued, because women taught adolescent males genteel manners too soon, before "the brute and animal element have had opportunity to work themselves off in a healthful normal way."[33]

Leading up to World War I, many American intellectuals, public figures, politicians, and military officers argued that the manhood of their country had weakened. Between the Civil War and the Spanish-American War, they asserted, the closing of the frontier, the concentration of capital, and rapid industrialization had closed the traditional paths toward manhood. American males had lost their manly individualism and the ability to own their own land, control their own labor, and secure their own economic independence.[34] At the same time, Europe seemed in its death throes from the Great War, with men sacrificing their lives and putting their manhood to the ultimate test.

Military-preparedness supporters often targeted the "peace at any price man" as being particularly unmanly. McCutcheon depicts him with a naïve smirk on his face, preferring "gentleness and persuasion . . . against an envious and determined enemy" because he himself is too gentle in the face of danger, something not associated with martial manliness.[35] For example, Dr. William Lee Howard, author of *Sex Problems in Worry and Work* (1915), argued in a newspaper article that the "peace at any price" variety of man is the result of an embarrassing physiological condition. They suffer from being "hysterical, always voluble and argumentative, but never decided or physically pugnacious." Howard claimed this was the result of "early guiding of the boy through women's eyes, ideas and emotions."[36]

Not long after the appearance of the *Dangerous Citizens* cartoon,

Fig. 8. *Dangerous Citizens*, by John T. McCutcheon. From *Joplin Globe*, August 7, 1915.

some civilians used the Marine Corps as a willing prop to promote their preparedness agenda. A writer for the *New York Evening Post* wrote, "Let Congress look at the Marines" for preparedness. He pointed to the Corps as a service that Americans could be proud of because of "its admirable efficiency, the smartness, the neatness, the excellent set-up of the men[,] and the *esprit de corps* of its officers."[37] By addressing the Marines' physical appearances, this person homed in on their masculine features. His reference to "esprit de corps," however, with its connotations of honor, duty, and loyalty existing within groups, is an evaluation of the Marines' character. Making them appear both masculine *and* manly thus provides an even starker contrast with the more restrained parts of society, who's martial characteristics waned in comparison.

Of course, others promoted different narratives, even though many Americans probably paid little attention to these debates.[38] Still, isolationists, pacifists, and progressives who saw war as a potential hindrance to their social and economic reforms put ink to paper, proclaiming the futility of war and espousing the United States' need to stay out of world affairs.[39] While the proponents of military preparedness sided with Lea and Huidekoper in promoting a more militant and martial form of manliness, others agreed with Norman Angell's view that "military power is socially and economically futile" and that "war, even when victorious, can no longer achieve those aims for which people strive."[40] Angell argued that among industrialized nations, war would be too deadly and expensive to make any gains in territory worth the investment. William Jennings Bryan was a progressive "peace at any price" man who worked hard during his tenure as secretary of state (1914–15) to keep the United States out of conflict.[41] He wrote that military preparedness did not keep people safe but rather provoked war. "If preparedness would have stopped war there would be no war in Europe today," he argued. "Had we been prepared for war with a big navy and army then we would have been in it long before this time."[42]

Antipreparedness advocates evoked a different version of manhood when they claimed that real bravery did not constitute giving in to one's passions but rather restraining from violence. For the advocates of restrained manliness, self-control, the ability to subdue one's baser passions, was a common trait associated with manly character.[43] Reverend Arthur P. Schultz preached that battlefield courage was only one form of bravery, one "of very low grade" since animals have the same form of courage. The difference was that animals lack self-control. Moral courage to stay out of a fight is much more commendable because "the man who fights is only allowing the brute nature within himself to have full rein."[44] Authors like Shultz wanted people to divorce manhood and national honor from bellicosity, warmongering, and violence. They wanted American men to abhor war and did everything in their power to argue against it.

But Marines had their own thoughts on this of subject, of course. As if in a direct response to the song "I Didn't Raise My Boy to Be a Soldier," Sergeant W. W. Seibert published this poem in the *Recruiters' Bulletin*:

I didn't raise my boy to be a soldier
  But if this country calls him he must go

I'd rather see a musket on his shoulder
  Than see our nation beaten by a foe.
Our grandsires went bravely forth to battle
  And made the U.S. first in every way.
  If war should come today—
  I hope no mother'll say—
I didn't raise my boy to be a soldier.[45]

Between martial and restrained manliness, Marines leaned toward the former. They conveyed this preference in other poems that celebrated military glory and aggression. Jack O'Donovan's "Remember the U.S. Marine" starts out acknowledging the quality of the U.S. Army and U.S. Navy as military institutions. "But when going o'er the dispatches," he continues, "There's a name that is always seen / And when landing he's in the first batches / fore where work is, you find the / Marines."[46] Wherever the government orders them, Marines complete their mission with patriotic zeal, according to O'Donovan. "And no matter where you send him / To uphold the starry FLAG / He takes the job and goes in with a vim / And never a heart does lag."[47] One could not praise the U.S. military or the fighting spirit of its soldiers and sailors without including the Marines. "So, when singing the praises of Uncle Sam / And describing some desperate scene / twill be incomplete if you don't include / THE UNITED STATES MARINE."[48]

William J. Candee's poem "The Marine" emphasized the men's patriotism and fighting abilities. This poem is rife with Marine exceptionalism, a common trope in the stories and images Marines constructed for each other. "I am a soldier of the sea / With hard two-fisted hands / Old Glory's fought her way with me / Through many foreign lands / I place the way in mortal strife / Of fighters, I am dean / These words express my place in life: / UNITED STATES MARINE."[49] Like O'Donovan's poem, Candee links combat prowess and patriotism with a rugged manliness.

This rhetoric formed the context within which Marines promoted their manliness and masculinity. Collectively, it evoked images of the tough and exceptionally manly expeditionary Marine, the type of sea soldier who felt at home in distant places testing his mettle against peoples around the globe. Artists and authors used this image to define their identity and distinguish themselves in the early twentieth-century political and cultural environment. Their pictures and prose told stories about how a true Marine was a man ready, tough, and capable of any task put before him. They promoted readiness, preparedness, flexibility, and efficiency, in their discourses. By doing so they described the type of man Marines expected each other to be. Intended to be more than advertising slogans to fill the pages of recruiting pamphlets, they reveal that military manliness, one involving flexibility and readiness, was a foundational element of Marine identity and, at least in the Corps's view, set them apart from regular soldiers, sailors, and civilians.

White Manhood

Whiteness served as another crucial element of World War I–era Marine Corps identity. In the early 1970s, the director of the Marine Corps History and Museums Division wrote: "Today's generation of Marines serve in a fully integrated Corps. . . . Black officers, noncommissioned officers, and privates are omnipresent, their service so normal a part of Marine life that it escapes special notice."[50] The inverse was true six decades earlier: the complete absence of Black Americans from the ranks of the Marine Corps was so pronounced that it escaped any special notice at all.

Whiteness was a broadly accepted precondition to becoming a Marine. In fact, the Corps around this time was the only branch of service that had not enlisted men of color, a practice dating back to 1798. The army and navy had enlisted Black Americans to suit their needs in the War of 1812, the Mexican-American War, the Civil War, and the Spanish-American War. According to Ralph W. Donnelly and Henry I. Shaw, records exist of slaves serving with marines during the War for American Independence, but after the Corps came into permanent legislated existence in 1798, it did not enlist Black men until World War II. From 1798 until 1941, "the Navy restricted its black volunteers to steward duty," Shaw and Donnelly assert, "and the Marine Corps accepted no blacks at all."[51]

The U.S. military in general restricted Black Americans for several reasons that reflected the overt racism of the early twentieth century. First, the military did not want to mix the two races in close quarters, believing that violence would ensue. Second, officials feared that the presence of Black men might harm the recruiting of white men, the latter not wanting to serve with the former. Third, the military wanted to avoid at all costs placing a Black man in authority over any white man. The navy and army enlisted Black men, but they either served as cooks and messmen in the navy or in segregated units in the army.

Although the Marine Corps probably shared all these concerns about enlisting Black men into their ranks, there was another, deeper, reason to bar them. Put simply, the very definition of a Marine was a white man—no exceptions. In the Marine's mind Black men could be sailors, they could be soldiers, but they could not be Marines.

Perhaps because of this racial exclusion, Marine Corps institutional journals and magazines generally refrained from mentioning people of color at all. There are a few clues, however, that help shed light on how Marines perceived American Black men and women leading up to the Great War. The *Marines Magazine* and the *Recruiters' Bulletin* published anecdotes for enlisted audiences interspersed throughout each issue. The *Bulletin* recounted a story in 1915 in which two Marine sergeants, Perry K. Tompkins and James F. Taite, spotted someone wearing a Marine blouse on a street in St. Louis. This man was Rufus White, a Black man. Both sergeants first thought they were looking at a fellow Marine but were "greatly startled to see Rufus' dusky countenance."[52] Taite and Thompson would not stand for a Black man wearing a Marine uniform. He ran when the two servicemen approached, but they eventually cornered him. "Rufus said he found the blouse and that it was all he had to wear," the author related.[53] The two Marines took the blouse from him, returned to the recruiting office, and burned it.

A story in the *Marines Magazine* involved a joke about two army artillerymen, two Marines, and two Black men. The author referred to the last pair as "darkies" who could easily tell which two were Marines "cause on de caps I sees the picture of de rooster on de moon."[54] The "rooster on de moon" is a reference to the eagle, globe, and anchor emblem that Marines wear on their uniforms to distinguish themselves from the army and navy. As the passage implies, Marines promoted a popular racial stereotype at the time that Black Americans were intellectually inferior to whites. They also did not spare overseas people of African or Asian descent of racial categorizing and dehumanization. One author described service overseas for Marines as "chasing Southeast mongrels and niggers."[55]

Another story, which came out in the August 1917 issue of the *Marines Magazine*, illustrates how Marines perceived the valor of American Black men. Race riots in St. Louis reminded that author of his conversation with Corporal Louis Kroeck about a shootout between white and Black citizens that had occurred in a southern town a few years previous. He claimed that the white mob drove off the Black townspeople with ease. "I bet you ran like the wind," Kroeck said to one of the Black men who he had seen at the riot the day before. "Not 'exactly,' replied the negro, 'but I passed a whole bunch of othus who was runnin like the wind.'"[56] The author here associates Black men with cowardice under fire, the very opposite of a Marine's expected behavior in combat.

So, what did it mean exactly to be white in the United States during the Great War era and how did that concept inform or conflict with Marine interpretations of whiteness? Today, academics think of "whiteness" as a social construction, in no small part because skin color is not what made people white, according to middle-class popular thought in the early twentieth century. Whiteness, like manhood, had a great deal to do with intangibles such as character and morality, according to the racial dogma of the day. A man could have a white complexion, but if he were Irish or Serbian, for example, his whiteness and the quality of his character would be suspect. Levels of intelligence became a critical distinction between races as well. If a man who looked white was "feebleminded," then he was tainted and considered "off white," or less than white.[57] Such judgments were made by people who claimed to be, and who persuaded others that they were in fact, "white."

To look white was important for legal, social, and political purposes in early twentieth century America. But just as important to white Americans was racial heritage among themselves. In purely racial terms, this meant being Caucasian, which, according to late nineteenth-century understandings, was one of the three main subsets of human beings, the other two being "Negroid" and "Mongoloid," which included Japanese, Chinese, Native Americans, and Mexicans. In addition, people having Semitic ancestry meant they were Jewish.[58] Xanthrochroic—northern Europeans—and Melanchroic man—"darker" whites from northern Africa and the Middle East—constituted the two main groups of Caucasians. The Aryan race, ethnologists argued in the late nineteenth century, were an amalgamation of these two subsets. From there, whiteness broke down into even further subsets. Being Aryan meant being of Teutonic, Norse, Anglo-Saxon, or Celtic descent. Victorian-era anthropologists and ethnologists considered it scientific to class these groups as different and distinct races from each other despite all being "white."[59]

Because of this understanding of whiteness and despite racial exclusions, Marines of the time wrote as though the Corps was a melting pot of many races. Sergeant Luther H. La Barre used this idea to argue that American men were great soldiers and sailors because of immigration and "intermingling." "We have the Irish with their wit, the English stolidarity [*sic*], the Jewish thrift, the French valor and the Yankee progressiveness," he wrote, "intermingling in marriage and giving us children with a wider scope of knowledge and temperament, making them good citizens and better soldiers than an army composed of one nationality." It is doubtful that his omission of Latin, Asian, or African Americans would have received any special notice by white Americans during this time. But that simply illustrates further that, first and foremost, the Marines, "the branch with the greatest opportunities—sailor, soldier, and gentle-man," were of white complexion and/or of European descent without exception.[60]

While some Marines saw the Corps as a "white" melting pot, some also considered themselves superior to all other races. This came up in their poetry, especially the kind that drew upon the Marines' history of foreign intervention. The poem "Ask Them" mentions many of the different races that Marines had encountered to that time. "Mention to the swarthy greaser / 'Billy Blue U. S. Marine' / If you want to see a mortal / Turn in fright to shades of green," in all likelihood referring to Filipinos.[61] It then moves on to the island of Hispaniola. "Ask the coal black son of Haiti / What he knows of Billy Blue, / And he'll tell you he's a fighter, / For he has reason, too."[62] Finally, the poem reaches back to the expeditions of the nineteenth century:

Ask the haughty Spanish soldier,
   Ask the sons of Tripoli,
Ask the yellow skinned Coreans [*sic*]
   For the straight veracity.

And they'll tell you the same old story,
   That they'd rather tackle TWO
Howling demons linked together
   Than ONE sturdy Billy Blue.[63]

Marines used these campaigns against racially distinct foreigners as proof of their honor, prowess, and aggressive manliness. And by defeating these opponents in battle, they believed, the Corps had demonstrated the "superiority" of white American manhood.

Marines used this kind of racialized imagery to compare their manhood to that of other branches of the U.S. armed forces was well. One poem depicts a violent scene from the perspective of a sailor who does not care for Marines at all until one fateful day. It describes a landing party of sailors ("Blue Jackets" or "Jackies") on a tropical island being attacked by natives. "Was jumped on by niggers, a thousand or more, / An' there in the jungle we dropped to our knees / An' fought for our lives in the brush an' the trees."[64] The landing party feared the worst, but U.S. Marines came to the rescue, chased off the attackers, and saved the lives of all of the grateful sailors: "We seen their old khaki, an' say, in that muss / It looks like the garments of angels to us / The niggers they left that particular scene, / An' me—I was kissin' a U.S. Marine." The author depicts these Marines as the heroes of the story, men who proved their worth in a tight spot against tropical natives.

The author concludes the poem with a stanza praising the manhood of Marines. It includes elements they used to promote their own masculine image:

An'that's how I learned—as I should have known then—
That U.S. Marines is some Regular Men,
The first ones ashore, and' the last to come back,
When trouble is started with white men or black;
Yes, call 'em "ship's flatties," and "leathernecks," too, . . .
They're first-class he-fighters, who uses their beans,
An'—only a fool would say "Damn the Marines"[65]

Marines concocted stories like this that told of how they protected their fellow White men in foreign countries pervaded their institutional magazines. Quite a few of them communicated the idea that Marines, through their fighting prowess and penchant for action, were more manly than civilians, soldiers, sailors, and people of color.

Rudyard Kipling and U.S. Marine Identity

Some Marines took how artists portrayed their manliness and masculine identity in prose and imagery very seriously. An example of this was a discussion over how well Rudyard Kipling's poetry represented their lives. This had to do with popular conceptions of what a Marine was and what he could do as a man. One enlisted Marine described Kipling as having "won the admiration of thousands of service men all over the world by faithful portrayal of their life, his stirring narratives of their deeds of valor and his red-blooded tales of their noble sacrifices."[66] To be "red-blooded" in early twentieth-century parlance meant being a "man of action," or one who leads a strenuous life.[67]

Marines particularly identified with "Soldier an' Sailor Too," from Kipling's 1892 collection, *Barrack-Room Ballads*.[68] Great Britain's Royal Regiment of Marines inspired the poem, but U.S. Marines felt a common bond with this institution due to the similar nature of the service and history of each.[69]

By 1918, "Soldier an' Sailor Too" had been around for twenty-five years, and Marines adopted the poem as a literary representation of their institution. They seemed to like the following lines in particular:

> An', after, I met 'im all over the world, a-doin' all kinds of things,
> Like landin' 'isself with a Gatlin' gun to talk to them 'eathen kings;
> 'E sleeps in an 'ammick instead of a cot, an' 'e drills with the deck on a slew,
> For there isn't a job on the top o' the earth the beggar don't know, nor do—
> You can leave 'im at night on a bald man's 'ead to paddle 'is own canoe—'E's a sort of a bloomin' cosmopolouse-soldier and sailor too.[70]

Within these lines are characterizations of many things Marines liked to say about themselves leading up to the Great War. They served all over the world protecting U.S. interests. They served in the Philippines, Haiti, the Dominican Republic, Mexico, and Nicaragua to quell uprisings and guard American commercial property. Marines claimed they could do any job with which their government tasked them.

But not everyone appreciated Kipling's characterization of Marines in "Soldier an' Sailor Too." Sergeant Major Thomas R. Carney argued in the February 1917 issue of the *Marines Magazine* that the writer characterized Marines (and military men in general) as men culled from the dregs of society. "After toilsomely plodding through his pages," Carney asserted, "one cannot but conclude that the man in the ranks is an uncouth, blasphemous being, without principle or morals, devoid of human traits except thirst and appetite, and speaking a barbarous dialect unheard of until Kipling invented it."[71] He referred to the following lines as misrepresentations: "We're most of us liars, we're 'arf of us thieves / And the rest are as rank as can be. / But once in a while we can finish in style, / Wich I 'ope won't 'appen to me." Uncouth, blasphemous, immoral, and illiterate men of ill repute and bad character—these were not candidates for the rank and file of the Marine Corps, according to Carney.

Marines' fondness of Kipling irritated the sergeant major for a couple of reasons. First, Carney argued that language of the sort used in

U. S. MARINES

An' after I met im all over the world,
a-doing all kinds of things,
Like landing isself with a gatling gun,
to talk to them 'eathen kings.
'E sleeps in an 'ammick instead of a cot,
and 'e drills with the deck on a slew,
For there isn't a job on the top o' the earth
the beggar don't know nor do.
You can leave im at night on a bald man's 'ead
to paddle is own canoe."
                              —Kipling?

Fig. 9. "Kipling Poem." From *U.S. Marines: Duties, Experiences, Opportunities, Pay*, 9th ed. (New York: U.S. Marine Corps Publicity Bureau, 1918), 4.

the poem painted the speaker, who was taken as a representative of the enlisted man, as an "illiterate buffoon."[72] Second, he claimed that Kipling patronized Marines and even appeared contemptuous of them. For example:

I have never been able to discern, after all my ramblings through the overgrown fields of his verbiage, whether Kipling in his work is actuated by a patrician contempt for the man behind the gun, or whether he really holds him in some such patronizing regard as the pompous adult does the child whom he condescends to address in what he fancies is only language the object of his attentions is capable of comprehending. And still an innate viciousness displays itself ever and anon in the course of his maudlin vaporing that precludes an unreserved acceptance of the latter assumption.[73]

According to him, Kipling made Marines sound less like men and more like vulgar children in need of adult supervision.

For Carney, something important was at stake. The people who needed the most convincing of the Corps's value to U.S. manhood would be further convinced that the military was not for their sons if Marines kept using Kipling's work to promote their identity. They would pass their ill will on to succeeding generations, and antimilitary sentiment would grow. Worst of all for Carney was the fact that recruiters used quotes from this poem on recruiting pamphlets for Americans to read. "How far can we blame them," he reasoned, "when we have given place and publicity to the scurrility of this Cagliostro of Literature in our military papers, magazine, and—Heaven save the mark!—in our recruiting publications!"[74]

Marines responded to Carney's salvo against Kipling in subsequent issues of the *Marines Magazine*. Sergeant Paul F. Howard reported that a few members of his Iona Island, New York, detachment agreed with Carney to a certain extent. "First Sergeant Lewis thinks that the type of soldier described by Kipling is 'the liar, the thief, the reprobate,'" he wrote, but neither himself nor his first sergeant had ever met a man of that sort in the Marine Corps or in the British Royal Marines.[75] Howard asserted that those who condemned Kipling's characterization of Marines did so because they thought the poet used a negative stereotype, but very few Marines took issue with the poet's description of enlisted men in the military.

This discussion also hints at competing versions of manliness within the Marine Corps: the overly genteel intellectual versus the straight-talking expeditionary Marine. Corporal A. A. Kuhlen fell in with the latter when he defended Kipling and the servicemen who liked his work because the poet wrote in a manly style that Marines appreciated. Carney, who wrote in an erudite and verbose fashion, expressed too much genteel intellectualism, which reflected on his own manhood. Kuhlen argued that Marines preferred Kipling's style to Carney's because it was less pretentious. The sergeant major used phrases like "that *chef doeuvre* of vesicular vulgarity" and "the evil-smelling pen of this modern Thersites" that were much worse that Kipling's "'E sleeps in an 'ammick instead of a cot, an' 'e drills with the deck on a slew."[76]

Marines saw straight talk as a manly virtue and had little patience for ostentatious vocabulary, according to Kuhlen. "Why is Kipling the special bard of the service man?" the corporal asked rhetorically. "Because service men as a whole are red-blooded and vertebrate and prefer he-talk to meaningless twelve-cylindered words which express two cylindered ideas." He went on to explain in more gendered language why they identified with "Soldier an' Sailor Too" and why they liked the poet. Marines "like a man's man and have little use for the ninny or fossil," and they believe that Kipling "appeals to them as a man." While Carney complained that the poet made Marines look like reprobates, Kuhler argued that to characterize Marines as paragons of virtue was equally egregious. "We resent being styled angels, fully as we resent being called 'bums' and 'illiterates,'" he asserted, because neither represented the kind of men the corporal believed Marines to be.[77]

Kuhler also argued that Kipling made civilians more familiar with the manly superiority of the serviceman. "The average American fighting man is mentally and physically superior to the average American civilian," he claimed, "and Kipling has gone far towards acquainting the uninitiated with the life of the serviceman." For Kuhler and perhaps others like him, "Soldier an' Sailor Too" represented Marine manliness. Kipling had earned the admiration and respect of military men all over the world for faithfully portraying their lives and hardships. The Marines probably never settled this debate, however. When the United States entered the Great War, they appeared to drop this issue for more pressing concerns.[78]

Making Men

One of the most important services that Marines believed they contributed to society was making men out of its citizenry. They created images that suggested that young men underwent a physical and mental change during the process of becoming a Marine. Essentially, the Marines had improved their bodies and their character by joining the Corps, according to the imagery and stories they published for each other's amusement. Upon graduation from recruit training, new Marines had gone through an experience that brought them into manhood. Private William Honing reported from the recruit-training de-

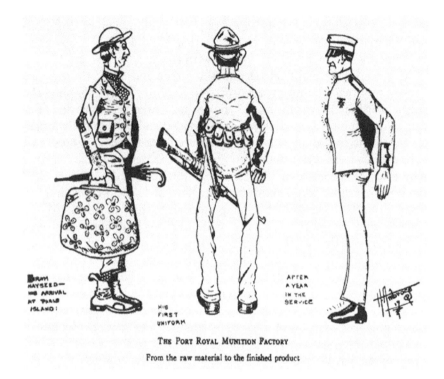

THE PORT ROYAL MUNITION FACTORY

From the raw material to the finished product

Fig. 10. *Port Royal Munitions Factory*. From *Marines Magazine*, April 1917, 13.

pot in Parris Island, South Carolina, that when a recruit graduates, he is not just a Marine, "he is a man—a real man through and through."[79]

Physically speaking, the men afterward stood more erect with protruding chests, their shoulders rolled back, and their heads held high. In *Port Royal Munitions Factory*, the artist presents three images of the same man. The first is *Hayseed on Arrival at Parris Island*, showing the raw recruit with a weak chin and shoddy clothing. The second image, *His First Uniform*, shows the same man in the process of transforming into a Marine. His posture remains slumped forward, and he appears uncomfortable. But the final image, *After a Year in the Service*, shows the finished product: a man with erect posture, a square jaw, a protruding chest, thicker legs, and an immaculate uniform.

This "finished product" was a man the United States could count on. The image entitled *Uncle Sam Knows* conveys the same notion. The Marines' ideal man, white, disciplined, and dressed as though fully prepared for an expedition, stands at attention next to Uncle Sam. He

UNCLE SAM KNOWS

Fig. 11. *Uncle Sam Knows.* From *Marines Magazine*, June 1917.

proudly points toward the Marine as though showing him off to an audience, pronouncing him "Always Ready."

The cover of the *Recruiters' Bulletin* issue for November 1917 plays on this same theme. Uncle Sam, his arm around a Marine with a square jaw and soldierly bearing, says, "My, how you've grown sonny!" Those who joined the Corps, so the reasoning went, became the pride of their nation. The physical stature of these men implied confidence, strength, and readiness. While these images show the advertised physical changes that men would undergo, Marines wrote stories demonstrating the improvement of their character as well.

Marine corporal C. Hundertmark published "The Three Sons" in the January 1917 issue of the *Marines Magazine*, a story that illuminates

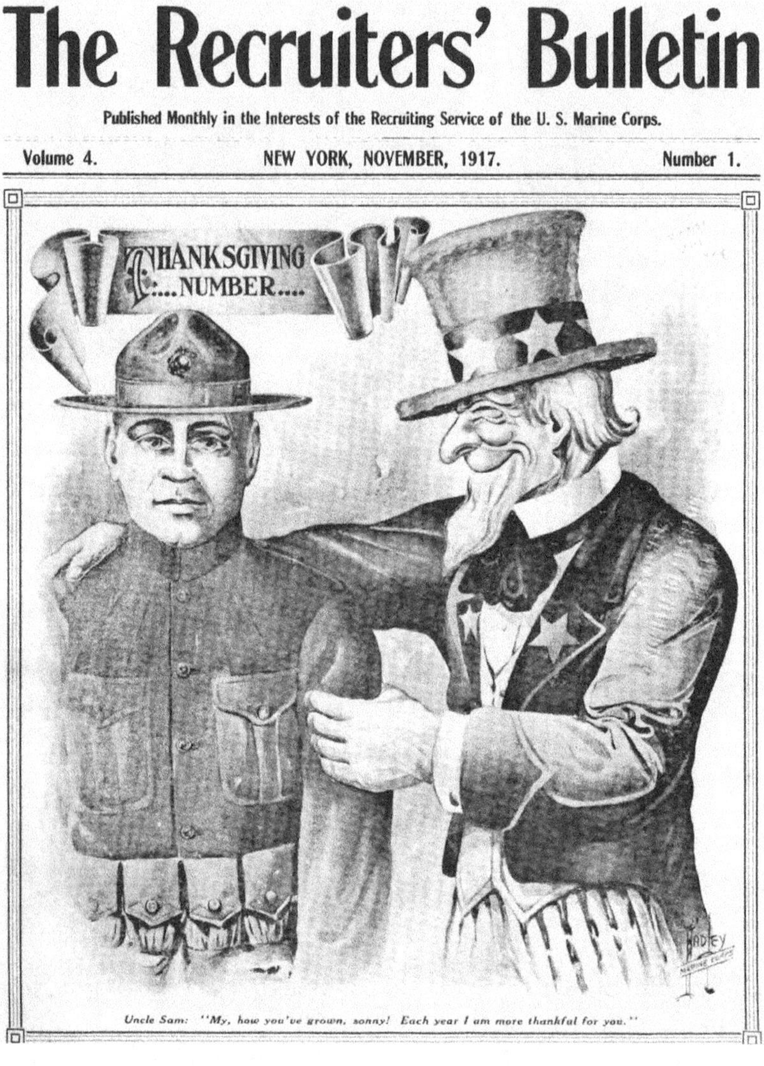
The Recruiters' Bulletin
Published Monthly in the Interests of the Recruiting Service of the U. S. Marine Corps.
Volume 4.
NEW YORK, NOVEMBER, 1917.
Number 1.
THANKSGIVING
....NUMBER....
Uncle Sam: "My, how you've grown, sonny! Each year I am more thankful for you."

Fig. 12. "Thanks Giving Number." From *Recruiters' Bulletin*, November 1917, 1.

how Marines thought life in the Corps benefited one's character. Jimmie Hopper owned a farm in South Carolina. He had three sons, only one of whom, Frank, joined the Marine Corps and, therefore, did not impose a burden on the family. Bob, the oldest, wasted his educational opportunity and his father's money in college by spending most of his time in a cabaret chasing women. John, the middle son, graduated high school and worked for a bank but took on debts through gambling. "His mother was heartbroken, and only for her I gave him what money we had on hand and what we had banked for a rainy day," his father confesses bitterly. "The last we heard of him was when he had to leave the country."[80]

Frank, "who never cared much about books," made a man of himself the way his brothers never did by joining the Marine Corps as soon as he was old enough. "I did not approve of it at first," Jimmie admits, "but finally I gave in, thinking the soldier life and the strict discipline might make a man out of him." With the money he earned in the Corps, Frank helped his parents get out of the financial trouble caused by his older brothers. Also, while at home on leave helping his aging father with farm work, Frank met a pretty, young local girl who, Jimmie relates, "is going to be Frank's partner for life in running things on this farm."[81] By saving his parents' farm and winning the affections of a respectable young lady, Frank has demonstrated that he is a man his family can depend on. According to this story, the Marine Corps enhanced Frank's discipline, virility, and devotion to family and duty. It imbued him with a style of manliness valued in Victorian culture.

Personal reminiscences of boot camp reveal how recruits experienced the change from civilian to Marine. These men underwent a brief period of quarantine, inoculation, and medical examinations upon arrival at Parris Island. Once recruits joined their training platoons, Marine drill instructors attempted to wipe away individuality and most semblances of their civilian identities. With their faces shaven, their hair trimmed short, and their bodies stripped of civilian attire, recruits donned uniforms and were "put through their paces."[82] Drill instructors trained them to salute, march, and obey commands quickly. Recruits had to exert themselves physically throughout each day of training. But boot camp was not solely about physical drills. It was a ritualized rite of passage one had to complete to become a Marine and a man, both literally and metaphorically.

The uniform dress, discipline, and collective suffering wore away the superficial distinctions between individual men from various backgrounds in the platoons. It mattered not if one were working class, middle class, a farmer, or a college athlete, everyone underwent a forced transformation into a different kind of man. Levi E. Hemrick, who enlisted in 1917 and went on to fight in the Great War, wrote in his memoirs that boot camp had a leveling effect on the men from disparate social and economic backgrounds. "The rich and the poor, the educated and the illiterates, the cultured and the rough necks, the religious and the infidels, the farmers and the city slickers, all are forced into intimate association," he noted.[83] Put in uniform and exposed to each other within the strict confines of boot camp, these men tended to lose their most extreme features: "The cultured grow less refined, the slovenly become tidy. The educated add slang to their vocabularies, the unschooled improve. The over-weights grow slim, the slender ones fill out. The stoop shouldered straighten up, and the stiff backs loosen up. Pot Bellies and big behinds are pulled in, and caved chests are thrown out."[84] This emphasis on physical and mental development is notable because of what the Marine Corps was trying to produce. "Male ruggedness and physical fitness is the goal of every boot camp," Hemrick asserted; "all men envy it and the fairest of women fall for it."[85]

Hemrick suffered a rude awakening in boot camp when he asked a drill instructor's pardon for committing a seemingly minor mistake in training. After the drill instructor berated him, Hemrick felt he had been properly introduced to his new life in the Corps. "This began my indoctrination in the Marine Corps' successful method of issuing a challenge to an individual and daring him to prove himself a man of strength," he observed. "The Corps makes men out of boys and sissies."[86] Hemrick's account of improved physical fitness creates a more *masculine* image than a *manly* one, perhaps because he wrote his autobiography in the 1960s, when Americans used "masculinity" to define male behavior instead of "manhood."[87]

Other Marines noted the significant change one underwent in boot camp. One recruit wrote home to his mother from Parris Island, "The first day I was at camp I was afraid I was going to die" but, after two weeks of training, "knew I'd never die because I'd become so hard that nothing could kill me."[88] In a letter from the recruit depot at Mare Island, California, Rubin Jaffe claimed that the change in him was so dramatic that his recruiting officers would not recognize him. No longer a civilian, Jaffe sounded proud because he was a tougher, manlier version of himself. "I'm afraid you wouldn't recognize me now, my Dear Major —gun totin', rip-roarin', son-of-a-gun of a hard-boiled Marine that I am," he enthused. "Why, I have grown so tough that the gobs scurry to their holes when they hear my hobnails a-poundin' the deck."[89]

Jaffe acquired this toughness from the physical training (PT) he and his fellow recruits suffered through. The Corps and the army during this time used a system of PT called "Swedish Exercises" that involved various forms of stretching and calisthenics.[90] Jaffe described the regimen as "a cross between contorting, steeplejacking, and tail spinning and is designed to make either a man or a lunatic out of you."[91] He claimed that while the PT made grown men cry on occasion, they were instilled with the notion that Marines did not quit.

Jaffe described how the training exposed recruits to a physically and mentally challenging lifestyle. "This is rather a strenuous life," he wrote. "It is—but at the same time a most fascinating one, and we all love it."[92] He loved it, in part, because of the effect the whole experience had on him and his fellow recruits. "They aim to make Men of us in the Marine Corps." For good measure he added, "Please be sure to spell that 'Men' always in capitals."[93] Jaffe was becoming a man, but not just any man. He was becoming a man who was ready for anything his country required of him: "I cannot express the feeling, the wonderful morale, that comes on us as the weeks progress—the satisfaction that we are ready to do our damnedest for Uncle [Sam]—and every man is FIT for anything that may come up."[94] Recruits like Hemrick and Jaffe took on new identities during recruit training. They did not just become Marines; they became men.

Once they became Marines, they entered an all-white male world in which they would be judged by military standards of manliness. All the training, labor, drill, guard duty, and sea and expeditionary duty required of them took a toll on Marines. Like the fictional Jimmy Decker, many of the actual enlisted men undoubtedly resented the discipline and threats of punishment required to keep thousands of them in line. The irony of any military institution that claims to "make men" is that it does not always treat those men like adults. Officers and enlisted men must obey stricter rules of dress and decorum than civilians and require leave or liberty granted by their superiors to enjoy free time or to see their families.

While the *Marines Magazine* and the *Recruiter's Bulletin* conveyed positive gendered images of the Marine Corps, court-martial records indicate that Marines certainly did not live up to their own standards. Corporal Conrad Hundertmark alluded to this when he wrote: "This place is a home for the man who comes clean, / And a happy home as well, / But if you don't come clean, you may understand, / The Marine Corps for you will be HELL."[95] In 1914 there were 271 Marines who received court-martial convictions, 211 in 1915, and 267 in 1916. Marines valued honor and courage, and yet the most common offenses among the enlisted men were absence without leave and desertion, both considered acts of dishonor. Of those Marines convicted, 80 were for desertion in 1915, 66 in 1916, and 122 in 1917, while those for being absent without leave counted 54, 46, and 54 respectively.[96]

Marine manliness called for aggression and prowess against their opponents on one hand, but restraint and discipline among themselves on the other. Other common charges reflected moral infractions, such as theft, falsehood, "conduct to the prejudice of good order and discipline," and "scandalous conduct tending to the destruction of good morals." Marines also charged each other for drunkenness and assault—either with intent to kill or for "striking a superior officer or threatening to assault and strike a superior officer." Fewer Marine officers stood for courts-martial than enlisted men, perhaps because of being fewer in number. The most common charges against officers were for drunkenness, "conduct prejudice to the good order and discipline, and "conduct unbecoming an officer and a gentleman."[97]

Court-martial records, much like the *Recruiters Bulletin* and the *Marines Magazine*, illuminate to an extent how gendered notions of identity and behavior shaped Marines lives. If gender is constructed through language and performance, then charges of "conduct unbecoming of a gentlemen" or "conduct tending to the destruction of good morals" implicated a Marine's manliness by casting doubt on his character. Exceptional offenses could lead to "dishonorable" and "bad conduct" discharges, punishments given throughout the armed forces. In 1916 the army reported 2,501 soldiers tried by court-martial, with 1,116 dishonorably discharged for desertion. That same year the navy dishonorably discharged 1,000 sailors and 187 Marines. It also separated 2,296 sailors and 487 Marines with bad-conduct discharges for a variety of offenses. For Marines and the armed services in general, to fall short of their own standard of military manliness was not only taboo but also a chargeable offense.[98]

Conclusion

Within the Marine Corps's intraservice publications, gender worked in several ways. Marines espoused a style of manliness that valued honor, readiness, fighting prowess, and flexibility through imagery and rhetoric to distinguish their institution from the army, navy, and civilians. Doctrinal debates informed their discourses and imagery by proclaiming the importance of readiness and offensive action. The national-preparedness movement that stemmed from the Great War also contributed to these discussions by linking the strength of American manhood with readiness for war. Gender also worked as a means of promoting particular behaviors within the ranks. Often the Corps understood desertion, training, courage, and its broader identity as an institution in terms of manliness. Marines questioned the manhood of those whose courage faltered, who used language that was too intellectual, or who criticized the Corps. They saw themselves as soldiers of the sea who stood ready to fight when their country needed them. But they also saw themselves as members of a man-making institution, a service that churned out better citizens. Both ideas constitute how Marines understood their value to society.

By May 1917, the Commandant of the Marine Corps, Major General George Barnett, convinced the secretaries of the army and navy to send a regiment of Marines with the first American troops to France.[99] What would become the Fifth Regiment of Marines set sail in June 1917. These men exuded confidence going into the Great War. Drawing upon masculine rhetoric and imagery, they told each other there was nothing Marines could not handle. "That the Marine Corps will conduct itself in a manner agreeable to the glorious traditions of its long history is a foregone conclusion," declared an author in the *Marines Magazine*. "Always prepared and always faithful, ready and able . . . to do what it is called upon to do, the Marine Corps will demonstrate upon occasion its keen fighting edge and the vigor of its stroke."[100] Marines also continued to steel each other for the trials ahead. Charles Ketcham told readers of the *Marines Magazine*, "Start in right and square yourself with the best traditions of manliness and of the Marine Corps."[101] Those who did not do so, like Jimmie Decker on the train to Montreal, were not real men and, therefore, not real Marines.

Sergeant McNab's strategy of appealing to Decker's manhood had the desired effect. His shaming made the young man "square" himself with the Corps's manliness. The story ends with Jimmie wiping his tear-dimmed eyes, getting off at the next stop, and heading back to his unit to serve out his enlistment. A few years afterward, "James Decker had re-enlisted and had been reappointed a first sergeant."[102] McNab, the old expeditionary Marine par excellence, had helped the wayward young Marine realize that he risked becoming a fugitive and being labeled a coward. He learned that desertion from one's duty was not manly behavior. Jimmie, who at first did not want to finish his enlistment, could not bear the thought of being a coward after his encounter with Sergeant McNab. He thus returned to his duty in the Corps, which is what Marines expected of each other.[103]

Marines used appeals to manhood and masculine imagery to communicate with outsiders as well. The Marine Publicity Bureau and

Marine recruiters would advertise the Corps's manliness to the public and claim their institution was not only "the first to fight" but also good for American manhood. With the passage of the 1916 Naval Appropriations Act and the April 1917 declaration of war on the Central Powers, the Marine Corps would expand greatly. Appeals to manhood would become a central part of its recruiting efforts just before and during the Great War.

The Great War

A "Sure-'Nough" Man

The man from the Navy threw up his hands,
    And said that it could not be done.
The man from the Army gave up in despair
    Before he had ever begun.
And still the job was finished on time,
    As neatly as ever was seen.
The man who did it against all odds
    Was a United States Marine.
— *C. Hundertmark, "The United States Marine," 1915*

In the spring of 1918, a journalist interviewed Sergeant James F. Taite, a Marine recruiter stationed in St. Louis, about the Corps. "No other branch has turned out as many physically and mentally perfect men as it has," Taite told the reporter. "It made a man out me," he claimed. "I am better physically, mentally, and morally. I have been in a place that is among men." The sergeant said nothing different from what the Corps had been promoting to the public for the past several years. "Not every man is a Marine, but every Marine is a man . . . a rip-roaring he-man," as stated in a 1918 edition of the Marine Corps Publicity Bureau's recruiting pamphlet. The bureau had put recruiters to work delivering this message to the American people. They looked for the nation's best young men to serve in what they argued was the nation's best military institution. Recruiters like Taite manned their offices, placed posters in store windows, conversed with men on street corners, spoke at high schools, and walked the streets of cities and small towns, handing out pamphlets for prospects to read. Appeals to manhood and the use of masculine rhetoric and imagery coursed through this literature. "Assert your manhood and go around to the recruiting station today," one pamphlet urges.[1]

Marines made manliness and masculinity central components to their recruiting efforts before and during the Great War. Pre-1917 recruiters claimed to turn away most applicants, citing high enlistment standards and manpower restrictions. They wanted men who were healthy and strong, both physically and mentally. While the country was still at peace, the Corps claimed it would mold and shape recruits into assertive, confident, morally upright, and selfless men. Marines would enhance their manhood by developing their character, a key element of Victorian manliness. They would also harden and toughen men's bodies through training and strenuous living, which would make them look like the sharply dressed and physically impressive Marines on recruiting posters. In doing so they appealed to the evolving notions of masculinity that valued appearance and celebrated physical strength. Marines received important help in recruiting and image construction from civilian journalists. They advised advertising the Corps as a man-making institution to win over not just potential recruits but also their families. These claims became integral parts of the Marine Corps's largest recruiting drive in its history in the spring and summer of 1917.

But when the United States declared war on Germany, the Marines matched their recruiting imagery and rhetoric with the rest of society's bellicosity. The declaration of war made military manliness the most popular form of manhood. While the U.S. government pitched the war as a means to uplift men's lives, Marine recruiters claimed to give American men the chance to be the "first to fight" the Germans. Recruiting posters shifted from good-looking Marines on duty to Marines actively fighting, an image better tailored to the needs of wartime. Popular magazines like the *Saturday Evening Post* published articles and advertisements that espoused and celebrated military manliness. By an act of Congress, and with journalists' help, the Marine Corps doubled its size in the second half of 1917. The central claim of the Marines still stood through all of this, however, that the Corps was good for American manhood.

Prewar Recruiting

Manpower was one of the Marine Corps's chief concerns leading up to U.S. entry into the Great War. Commandant George Barnett wanted to increase the size of the Corps to perform its various duties as efficiently as possible and to maintain a high state of readiness.[2] He argued that the service's varied duties and expeditions in recent years (for example, Vera Cruz in 1914 and Haiti in 1915) necessitated shifting personnel away from advanced-base seizure and defense, fleet detachments, and guarding naval yards. "Indisputably this is not only a poor makeshift," Major General Barnett argued, "but furthermore its continuance will interfere materially with the efficiency of the fleet and of advance base work, and will endanger the safety of the navy yards, naval magazines, etc."[3]

Barnett beseeched Congress for more Marines at the propitious time of preparedness fever, which was indicative of a growing popularity in military manliness in the United States. Marines used the preparedness camps that sprang up across the country as opportunities to advertise themselves. Aimed largely at white middle-class businessmen who worked in offices all day, these camps offered attendees the chance to get outdoors, perform physical training, learn military drill, and shoot targets. "Get out of your automobiles, you bankers and business men," Admiral Fullam proclaimed to businessmen gathered in San Francisco, "and win four weeks of physical, mental, and patriotic satisfaction. . . . Get into the open, let the wind blow through your whiskers; quit talking about preparedness and act."[4] The U.S. Army took the lead in running these camps, and men from throughout the region went to them in Plattsburg, New York, and in Philadelphia, Pennsylvania. Marines, however, made sure to be on hand to show themselves and assist.

A small group of Marine noncommissioned officers helped run the Philadelphia camp, organized and run by A. J. Drexel Biddle, along with two dozen army officers.[5] Commandant Barnett inspected the camp and claimed afterward that it was valuable in getting masses of civilians acquainted with military life and duties. He also noted that this camp gave the American people exposure to the Marine Corps. "I feel that the whole affair was of great benefit to the Marine Corps," he wrote, "for it gave knowledge of the Corps to many people who knew little or nothing of it before." All three branches of the military used this opportunity to gain publicity and to recruit.[6]

The National Defense Act of 1916 represented a victory for preparedness advocates. This legislation called for a general increase in the size of the military. The army would grow to 175,000 men, and a new reserve component would be formed, the Army National Guard.[7] The Naval Appropriation Act, like the National Defense Act of the same year, increased the navy and Marine Corps. Secretary of the Navy Josephus Daniels advised President Wilson that the country needed a fleet "second to none," which precipitated the construction of ten new battleships, six battlecruisers, and 146 additional smaller warships, including submarines and destroyers.[8] Congress allowed the Corps to increase by 40 percent, from 12,400 men to 17,400. Barnett and the Marines had gotten the increase they wanted; now they would have to recruit the men.

Marine recruiters wanted the best of American manhood to join their ranks. They targeted intelligent, efficient, and physically fit men for several reasons. Men of good character and sturdy constitution stood the best chance of serving out their full enlistment and maybe even reenlisting at the conclusion of their contract. They could bolster the Corps' claims of being the finest fighting institution when people saw that upstanding young men joined their ranks. Good men also made the Corps more appealing to the parents of potential recruits. They would allow recruiters to assert to families that "the U.S. Marine Corps is made up of men such as your son; young men who are in a perfect state of health and are of good character, so you may rest assured that he will have the very best of associates."[9] Recruiters wanted people to believe that the Marine Corps was a wholesome and beneficial experience for those who served.

Military recruiters before 1917 continued to fight against a decades-old reputation. Since at least the nineteenth century, the navy had suffered from public images of sailors being mostly foreign born, alcoholic "riffraff."[10] The army, despite being the largest and perhaps the most ubiquitous service, suffered from this as well. "Soldiers are considered professional assassins, idlers or vaguely blended in mind with British redcoats who harassed our country during the Revolutionary War," wrote an infantry officer.[11] Marines, too, claimed that a significant number of Americans had an unfavorable opinion of enlisted men. "The civilian seldom sees the good enlisted man as he is usually in civilian clothing," wrote one recruiter, "but he does see the undesirables of the service as these men are usually in uniform . . . intoxicated, foul mouthed, and insulting."[12] Recruiters wanted their fellow Marines to avoid scenes like one depicted in the illustration *The Kind of Enlisted Man with Whom the Civilian Is Acquainted*. A surly and disheveled-looking Marine in uniform is walking down a street arm in arm with a civilian, both clearly intoxicated. The text at the bottom of the image reads, "For better recruiting results prevent scenes like this one."

One day in Chicago Captain William Brackett walked near the state unemployment office. A long line of men waited outside the building. "A Gentlemen of large affairs" approached the officer and asked him, "Brackett, there is a fine crowd of bums looking for work; why don't

THE KIND OF ENLISTED MAN WITH
WHOM THE CIVILIAN IS
ACQUAINTED.

For better recruiting results prevent scenes like this one.

THE PUBLIC'S MISCONCEPTION OF
THE ENLISTED MAN.

Fig. 13. *The Kind of Enlisted Man with Whom the Civilian Is Acquainted.* From *Recruiters' Bulletin,* January 1915, 11.

you enlist them?"[13] The captain wrote that this man revealed how little people knew about the kind of men Marines were and the quality of men they sought. Brackett contended that Marines did not accept just anyone into their ranks. For the Corps, "the greatest need is for the fit, the intelligent, the efficient and there is always room for them." The captain claimed that Marines avoided certain types: "the ne'er do well, the loafer, the drunkard, the debauche, and the diseased have about as much chance of a welcome awaiting them as the proverbial snow bird in Hades."[14] Their recruiting literature promoted this standard as well. "Men accustomed to a life of dissipation and irregular habits will find the regular life of the service irksome and distasteful," claimed one booklet. "But for men of good character and regular habits the military life is a very near approach to the ideal."[15]

In 1914 Sergeant Birger F. Westergard warned that most applicants did not fit the character profile that Marines sought. Recruiters came across plenty of physically healthy men within the desired age range. He observed, however, that an applicant's motivations often betrayed their character. One applicant, a painter by trade, admitted that he faced unemployment over the winter months but that if he had any prospects, then he would not be interested in joining the Marine Corps; he wanted to join to escape starvation. "We only want men in the Corps who go into it to better themselves," Westergard replied to him. The sergeant told the painter, "You are one of the men that just as soon as Spring comes and work is plentiful, would be dissatisfied with the service . . . and get into such a state that you would rather be kicked out or desert, and be of no use to yourself, the Marine Corps or the rest of the world." Despite manpower needs, Marines remained selective.[16]

This pickiness caused recruiters to reject many applicants. Corporal Michael DeBoo reported from the Pittsburg recruiting district that "were it not for the fact of the standard being at its zenith, this district would, without any trouble, run considerably over its allotted quota each and every month, but with the standard being so high at the present time we are hampered to a great extent."[17] Captain William E. Parker reported from Buffalo, New York, that of the 1,953 applicants received in 1913, only 220 actually made it through the screening process to enlist.[18] *National Service Magazine* reported that from January to September 1916, the Corps only accepted 167 of 5,082 applicants within the recruiting district of New York.[19] The army, by comparison, enlisted 14,051 new soldiers between July 1 and November 30, 1916.[20] If an applicant had a crooked spine, was obese, or had other physical problems, he could be rejected. He could also fail examination for less tangible reasons such as illiteracy or inadequate intelligence. Sergeant Frank R. Busch's poem in the *Recruiters' Bulletin* addresses these problems with a hint of frustration:

The Marines they are the best of men
   That Uncle Sam can get,
And if you're not perfect in eye and limb
   You'll be rejected, you bet!

You apply to the Recruiting Sergeant
   Who is healthy and proud and straight,
But after looking you over,
   He says you'll have to wait.

"We want only perfect men,"
   He tells you is the rule.
You look amazed and think him crazed,
   Or he surely is a fool.

But way out in the hay field
   Where they think you are alright,
You think you would make a good Marine,
   Because you like to fight.

"But come in," says the sergeant,
   "We'll make a test or two,
And see in a few minutes
   If we can really pass you.

"We find by examination
   Your lungs are out of whack,
Your back it is too crooked,
   And your feet they do not track.

"We find you are some underweight,
If you do not carry lead,
But the worst objection that we have is that—
you are crippled in the head."[21]

Marines knew that they competed with colleges and universities for the best of American manhood. Gendered discourses on the physical, mental, and moral development of young men pervaded academia as well. In 1907 Theodore Roosevelt argued before the Harvard University Union that colleges should turn out "vigorous men" instead of "mollycoddles." Students became the former by playing "manly" sports like track, football, and baseball to develop their bodies and character and by using their education to actively engage with and improve their communities. Colleges risked producing "mollycoddles," however, by making students "too fastidious, too sensitive to take part in the rough hurly-burly of the actual work of the world."[22] Reverend Jasper S. Hogan delivered an address to alumni of Rutgers College asserting that universities should improve their students' manhood. College administrations and professors should encourage young men to become physically as well as intellectually fit "to aid them to possess the qualities and traits of a true man."[23]

Knowing that they could not offer similar academic opportunities, Marines claimed to create "real men" better than colleges through physical training and world travel. They argued that at the end of four years of college, the average student's body had suffered from countless hours of study. The result was "a poor physical wreck and nervous man." After four years in the Marine Corps, however, a man would be healthier, smarter, and wiser. For a Marine, "his methodical and systematical physical training in the service is keeping him in the best of health, and the travels that he necessarily must do during the term of his enlistment, serve to broaden his mind, and give him that knowledge and experience which so many college men never attain."[24] Promoting physical, mental, and moral development allowed the Corps to better compete with universities and reveals how Marines could tailor their advertisements toward a particular audience. The message, however, remained one that emphasized the quality of manhood entering their ranks as well as the quality of manhood they returned to society.

It is difficult to tell if these high recruiting standards had a direct positive influence on the efficiency of the Marine Corps. By the second decade of the twentieth century, however, the percentage of desertions and dishonorable discharges among the enlisted ranks had dropped significantly compared to the 1880s and 1890s. In 1888 the Marine Corps reported a desertion rate near 25 percent.[25] In 1914, from a total of 341 officers and around 9,500 enlisted men, the Corps lost 1,091 enlisted to desertion and 273 to dishonorable discharge, a rate of approximately 14 percent.[26] That rate dropped to 10 percent the next year.[27] Then the Corps reported 659 desertions and 116 dishonorable discharges in 1916, a loss of only 7 percent.[28] The following year Commandant Barnett reported 701 desertions and 219 dishonorable discharges out of 10,896 enlisted men. equating to around an 8-percent loss.[29] These figures were much lower than the percentage lost to desertions the Corps suffered in 1888 alone.

Marines sought professional help from the growing and relatively new field of advertising experts to attract the kinds of men they wanted. Clifford Bleyer, of the Taylor-Critchfield-Claque advertising firm of Chicago, wrote two pieces for the *Recruiters' Bulletin* in

November 1916 and January 1917. He wanted Marines to expand their target audience and focus less on the fighting side of the Corps. His message was tailored to a peacetime audience that had yet to be swept up by the passions of war. "The Marine Corps is more than a fighting machine," Bleyer wrote, "and its presentation to the public as such frustrates the real purpose of publicity, not only at a time when war is a topic to be thoroughly abhorred, but even when the world is at peace." Recruiters needed to appeal to young men *and* their parents. "As we view the proposition," he cautioned, "the Marine Corps must be sold to the people of the United States—and by that we mean both adults and possible recruits—on its merits."[30]

To Bleyer, parents and elders held sway over young men's lives. Mothers, especially, could just as easily talk their sons out of joining the Marines as a recruiter could talk them into it. He reasoned that parents could be turned off of the Corps if recruiters placed too much emphasis on fighting. "This is especially true of mothers," he advised. "The woman who 'did not raise her boy to be a soldier' is very numerous, because her idea of 'mothering' is to see that the son has shelter at night, every delicacy he desires at mealtime, and a lot of 'petting' in between." Bleyer pointed out that many American families cared little for the military, signaled by his reference to Alfred Bryan's 1915 antiwar anthem, "I Didn't Raise My Boy to Be a Soldier." "We realize the fact that in better homes, particularly, there is a strong prejudice against military life," he reasoned. Therefore, Marines needed to emphasize the benefits afforded young recruits to assuage prejudices parents might have toward the armed forces.[31]

Since the nation was at peace, even advertisements that toned down the bellicosity and focused more on preparedness could discourage young men and their families. "The pugnacious appeal is not the one that will fill the ranks," Bleyer advised. "'Preparedness', in the fighting sense, will not [either], it is a problem of individualism." Surrendering one's freedom in peacetime to serve in the military could be a hard sell. Therefore, Bleyer urged Marines to make appeals centered on self-improvement. "Touch him with the appeal of personal advantage," and the Corps could make service much more attractive to a potential recruit.[32]

Bleyer wanted Marines to sell their institution to the young and old alike by promoting their service as beneficial to the potential recruit's growth, "to awaken the interest of the young men and their elders—not their interests in the Marine Corps as a mere fighting machine, but as an instrument for the promotion of personal efficiency and the building of manhood." Joining the Corps would enhance recruits by broadening their experiences through discipline, travel, and service. The end goal was to convince young men and their parents that "the Marine Corps may so establish him in discipline and in ability to serve when service is required—that he will be better equipped if he adopts a life vocation—such a recruit will not only make a good soldier, but he is well prepared to make a good citizen and worker if he is again a civilian." Advertising this way would allow Marines to appeal to notions of Victorian manhood that valued productive and trustworthy men.[33]

This idea of targeting sons and parents alike took hold among recruiters. Based on articles in the *Recruiters' Bulletin*, Marines understood that women needed convincing that the service benefited the manhood of their sons. In concurrence with Bleyer's suggestions, Captain C. S. McReynolds wrote that educating families would overcome public ignorance of the Marine Corps by communicating its advantages and opportunities.[34] He offered a letter written by Mollie Shelton of Placerville, Idaho, in support of this contention. Mrs. Shelton worried about her son, John A. Shelton, who had enlisted in the Marines and reported to boot camp in December 1916. "It is with a sad heart I sign my name on this card," she wrote to Captain McReynolds. "It is such a shock to me that I do hope and pray my Dear Boy will succeed."[35] His response to her, published in the *Recruiters' Bulletin* for other Marines to see, is a strong example of how Marines communicated their worth to outsiders.

McReynolds sought to reassure Mrs. Shelton, "Our aim is to make every man a good soldier, and a good soldier is always a good citizen." He continued, "The Marine Corps standard is high; we are satisfied only with the best." McReynolds ended by arguing that her son had chosen the best path to future employment and manhood: "Young men who have completed honorably an enlistment in the Marine Corps are able, almost without exception, to secure much more remunerative and promising industrial employment than they were able to do prior to entering the service." McReynolds admitted that military life would be difficult and potentially dangerous but concluded, "I know of no better place for a man to develop the best type of manhood and citizenship."[36]

Bleyer also suggested using pamphlets and motion pictures that show how physically fit recruits would become. "We would present it as a life that promotes good health and builds sturdy manhood," he wrote. Doing so, however, would steer Marines toward making appeals based on rugged masculinity in addition to those focused on more traditional notions of restrained manhood. Advertisements that displayed the service's "physical culture, outdoor exercises, and the various forms of wholesome sports" bolstered the Corps's masculine appeal and helped emphasize "the care the government takes to have its men healthy and strong." Bleyer reasoned that having a strong, sound body could be used by recruits to their own personal advantage in whatever profession they chose later in life.[37]

Personal advantage not only meant an enhanced manhood that prepared young men for the struggles of life but also the ability to advance socially and economically. Bleyer provided an advertisement example entitled, "THE U.S. MARINE CORPS TRAINS YOU FOR THE BATTLE OF LIFE." It argued that successful men in business all had discipline and leadership skills that recruits would gain in the service. "Today young men are joining the United States Marine Corps that they may form this habit of leading," this sample proclaimed, "that they may learn to shoulder the responsibility of directing the activities of other men, of being Generals in the Battle of Life." Because being a Marine made leaders of young men, the Corps thus offered them the chance at a great long-term career. But Bleyer understood that for most young men, their service would be temporary and worked that into the copy. "If you intend to return later to civil life you will have gained the tremendous advantage of facing the Battle of Life, strong in body, confident in mind, steady, courageous, a *man* in the finest sense of the word."[38]

Bleyer continued with the "battle of life" metaphor in another proposed advertisement, which stated, "Success is a survival of the fittest." Great leaders became businessmen and statesmen who derived their strength from self-discipline. "Men who rule themselves *first*," it stated, "therefore are strong enough to rule others," appealing to Victorian notions of manly restraint. The Marine Corps should claim to train, discipline, and teach men self-control. Bleyer's sample advertisement copy affirmed:

Marine Corps training is one of the surest methods to win this command of self—to acquire the strength of mind, will and body to win the battle of life. Every young man needs to discipline himself. One who learns how to take orders knows how to give orders. He who can obey can command. *Now* is the opportunity to gain a training *that will make a better man of you*, whatever your ambitions may be. The Marine Corps trained man is fitted to be a leader. Marine Corps training in itself is a recommendation for a responsible position in every line of business. Parents, reflect upon the future of your son.[39]

Self-control was important because it had a direct bearing on one's morality and character. One contemporary author identified "lust, uncleanness, drink, gambling, swearing, lying, dishonesty, [and] irreligion" as habits that destroyed manhood.[40] By 1917, the armed forces had developed a reputation for all these things.[41] Sexual immorality was particularly troublesome because proponents of healthy manhood believed it was harmful to the mind and body through the spread of venereal diseases.[42]

Authors who utilized this rhetoric relied on the assumption that strength of mind and body, self-discipline, and leadership were all elements of successful men. Recruiters relied on this understanding about traditional manliness and its appeal to applicants and their parents when they employed Bleyer's suggested advertising tactics.

The "battle of life" metaphor existed in tandem with the common belief that healthy manhood developed through struggle. Life threw obstacles in men's paths and they needed strength, endurance, self-control, and judgment to overcome them. Some considered those traits as "the young man's equipment to fight the battles of life."[43] George Walter Fiske, a popular American author on theology, wrote, "attainment of manliness . . . is a struggle . . . a splendid victory won through struggle," referring to it as "the battle royal of life."[44] Marines used this metaphor to explain how the Corps benefited American men.

In the February 1917 issue of the *Recruiters' Bulletin*, Captain Ross E. Rowell informed readers to find examples of former Marines who had led successful and prosperous lives as civilians. Rowell planned to publish the personal stories and photographs of these men, who reflected "credit on their old Corps in civil life" to aid recruiting. He was especially interested in former Marines who attributed their success to "their training and service in the Marine Corps."[45] A regular piece entitled Ex-Marines Who Have Made Good became a consistent item in the *Bulletin*. An example of a story in this series was Rinaldo Livingstone, a Civil War–era Marine who enlisted in 1863. Back then he had been a struggling actor; by 1917, he was the commercial editor of the *San Francisco Examiner*. The Marine Corps had "taught me many useful lessons," Livingstone stated, "not only to endure patiently the ills that could not be avoided, but at the same time inspired me with manly courage to fight the battle of life."[46] Former Gunnery Sergeant Walter Vincent, who enlisted in the Marine Corps in 1889, was another subject in the series. He served twenty-two years in the Marine Corps and pursued a life of business upon retirement. Vincent attributed his later success with his life-insurance and real-estate businesses to the training he received in the Marine Corps.[47]

The conclusion of the 1917 edition of the recruiting pamphlet *U.S. Marines—Soldiers of the Sea* summed up one of the central claims recruiters made to outsiders to enhance their service's appeal. "Enlistment in the Marine Corps is a loyal, patriotic act," the editors asserted. "A man who has the right stuff in him will leave the service better qualified to succeed in the *battles of life*." They summed up, "The Marine Corps gives him every opportunity to become a strong, self-reliant man and a good citizen."[48]

There was a clear social and economic advancement aspect to Marine recruiting. By promising recruits that the Corps would prepare them for the "struggles of life," it implied raising one up into the middle classes. A young man could be born on a farm or into a working-class family and raise his station in life through service with the Marines. Some enlisted Marines even had opportunities to become officers. The 1916 Naval Appropriation Act increased the number of enlisted appointees to the Naval Academy from fifteen to twenty-five, and recruiters began advertising the possibility using the Marine Corps as a stepping stone to Annapolis, "where they will be educated and trained as officers, and have a certain and profitable future."[49] When the United States entered the Great War, applications for officer commissions in the Corps quickly outnumbered the actual vacancies. There were so many, in fact, that in June 1917 Commandant Barnett mandated the temporary discontinuance of civilian appointments.

Barnett opted instead to fill all second-lieutenant vacancies during the war with noncommissioned officers. Of the 761 new officer appointments into the Marine Corps between April and July 1917, 122 of them classified as "meritorious noncommissioned officers."[50] Corps Headquarters instructed officers to select brave and competent enlisted men who had excellent character for a commission. Those who had distinguished themselves in combat had a good chance at selection. "Family influence will have no weight," read an order from the Sixth Regiment of Marines in France, "each man must stand on his own bottom."[51] By the time the war ended, the Marine Corps had commissioned 602 permanent second lieutenants from the enlisted ranks. Barnett thought very highly of this system for several reasons. It allowed the Corps to draw officers from a pool of candidates who already had Marine training and experience. It encouraged "the better class of enlisted men" to perform to their best abilities knowing that they could be rewarded with a commission. Ultimately, this system, the Commandant claimed, "tends to attract a higher class of recruits to the Corps."[52]

The Marine Publicity Bureau used three main recruiting pamphlets and booklets that utilized many of Bleyer's ideas: *U.S. Marines— Soldiers of the Sea*; *U.S. Marines in Rhyme, Prose, and Cartoon*; and *Who Am I?* Collectively, these booklets represented the Corps's main efforts in communicating its identity to outsiders over the span of several years leading up to the war. Marines designed this literature to inform the public about their history, persuade readers of their value to society, and attract potential recruits.

The Corps used these booklets and posters to communicate several ideas to potential recruits and their parents. First, Marines were soldiers who served afloat with the navy, but they were neither completely sailor nor completely soldier. Rather, they were a mix of both and better than either one.[53] Second, the Marine Corps offered young men not so much vocational skills, which are what the army and navy promoted around this time, but rather habits of mind, such as personal efficiency, discipline (both associated with traditional manliness), and masculine bearing.[54] Third, all of these things benefited the potential recruit and were much more useful to a man no matter what vocation he chose upon returning to civilian life.

U.S. Marines—Soldiers of the Sea, a broadly used recruiting pamphlet, made these claims. While at sea, Marines would train, drill, and maintain combat readiness. "Great mobility and facilities for quick action are required of the Marines," the booklet claimed. "They must be kept in readiness to move at a moment's notice, and be prepared for service in any climate."[55] While stationed in the United States, Marines had many opportunities for self-improvement, such as gymnasia for physical exercise and libraries for studying. Four years of training and world travel meant a Marine returned home "a healthier, *more self reliant and better man*."[56]

Echoing Bleyer's suggestions, the Corps promised to make men stronger and healthier. "Special attention and encouragement are given to athletic sports of all kinds," the authors of the pamphlet claimed. "This is done to encourage the men to take an active interest in athletics and physical culture, with the realization and appreciation of the fact that in so doing the men improve themselves physically."[57] Marines would have opportunities to box and play baseball and football, all activities identified as "masculine games."[58]

The Corps made these claims during a time when people advocated sports as being good for the development of vigorous manhood. One writer wanted men to avoid becoming "narrow-chested, slope-shouldered, squeaky voiced . . . flabby muscled, namby-pamby molly-coddle(s)."[59] Proponents of traditional manhood saw athletics as a crucial part of educating men on college campuses "to produce the muscular element of manhood."[60] Marines understood this idea and put their own spin on it. Sergeant Charles D. Baylis argued that most Americans did not know that the Marines encouraged athletics at all its posts. Potential recruits with athletic experience in team sports would be great for the Corps, he thought. "A man who can get out on the diamond and strive and struggle along for no other gain than to see his outfit come out on top," Baylis claimed, "can also de depended on to strive an' struggle, and to be sticking around the immediate vicinity whenever there is anything doin' requiring the services of a man with sand, who can also handle a rifle."[61] Therefore, he argued for more emphasis on sports in recruiting literature to attract those kinds of recruits. Informed by pieces like these, the Publicity Bureau provided pictures of Marines engaged in exercise of various kinds, such as rowing, wall scaling, and calisthenics, to demonstrate how men could improve their physical health while in the Corps.

Posters served as graphic representations of how the Corps made men more manly and physically fit. The Marines in these images share attractive physical attributes and appear brave, disciplined, and patriotic. Essentially, they show what the Marine Corps could do for a man in peacetime: "four years of training which will graduate him into the world equipped with a perfectly healthy body, an erect carriage, a broadened view of life from his contact with people and places, a quick, responsive intellect, a disciplined, reliable individual—an asset to any employer."[62] Marines promised to make men "more desirable and capable soldiers, and better and healthier citizens."[63] Getting an honorable discharge from the Corps could open new opportunities for men looking for work. Marines enticed readers by claiming that an honorable discharge made a man a preferred job candidate for government and civil-services jobs because of what their military service revealed about their character. Young men could "have no better recommendation to show to his prospective employer, as assurance of fidelity and good character, than an honorable discharge from the service of the United States Government."[64] Recruiters claimed that useful citizens stood a better chance of finding work after leaving the service.

The other branches responded to the expansion of recruiting quotas in a similar fashion to the Marines. The army and navy sought to re-

Boat Drill.

Fig. 14. *Boat Drill*. From *U.S. Marines Soldiers of the Sea: Duties, Experiences, Opportunities, Pay*, 7th ed. (New York: U.S. Marine Corps Publicity Bureau, 1917), 27.

Wall Scaling

Fig. 15. *Wall Scaling*. From *U.S. Marines Soldiers of the Sea: Duties, Experiences, Opportunities, Pay*, 7th ed. (New York: U.S. Marine Corps Publicity Bureau, 1917), 33.

AN OUT-DOOR GYMNASIUM.

Fig. 16. *An Out-Door Gymnasium.* From *U.S. Marines Soldiers of the Sea: Duties, Experiences, Opportunities, Pay,* 7th ed. (New York: U.S. Marine Corps Publicity Bureau, 1917), 28.

cruit men of sound body and mind, which reflected several trends pervading the early twentieth-century U.S. armed forces. First, modern technology had advanced to a point where the services highly valued mental aptitude. The modern steam-and-steel navy, with its advanced engines and electrical torpedo and gunnery systems, required men with the capacity to master technical skills. Historically, most sailors came from the coasts and port towns of the United States. Navy recruiters had sought men there to fill the various ratings on war vessels in part because they believed that the best sailors were men who already had some experience at sea. The new navy, however, switched to inland recruiting, much in the same way as the Marine Corps did, to reach a greater supply and a theoretically "better brand" of recruits. Historian Fred Harrod has noted, "The twentieth-century navy boasted that its personnel represented respectable families from the heartland of America rather than what it considered disreputable elements from the waterfronts."[65] Like the Marine Corps, the navy sought recruits from the nation's interior based on the belief that people there were a more dependable, trustworthy, and respectable lot.[66]

Like the Marines, the navy also promised to uplift the lives of those young men who would become sailors. But in the years leading up to the Great War, its pitch focused less on the physical and more on the intellectual. Navy imagery often made masculine appeals both explicitly and implicitly. Hilton H. Bancroft's *Enlist in the Navy* and Howard C. Chandler's *Gee I Wish I Were a Man* are two notable examples of naval recruitment imagery. They make patriotic appeals and claim the navy to be the first line of defense, but in the fine print they offer a different kind of manliness than the Marines.

While the Corps offered a strenuous life of training and expeditionary duty that would harden young men's bodies and minds, the navy advertised the opportunity sailors had to receive academic instruction. "The American Navy is largely a boy institution," according to the Navy's 1916 annual report, citing the young average age of sailors, which was twenty-two years old.[67] Those "boys" needed academic instruction to become efficient sailors. "Practically every fighting unit in the United States Navy is a floating machine shop," read one 1917 advertisement.[68] The navy promised to teach sailors reading, writing, and arithmetic in addition to the technical instruction they received pertaining to their jobs on ship or on shore. Officials reasoned that the study of the science of electricity made for better radio operators and applied mathematics made for better gunners. "If the enlisted man does not remain long in the Navy," according to Josephus Daniels annual report in 1916, "his usefulness to his country as a citizen is nevertheless enhanced by what he has acquired in the Navy schools."[69]

The army faced the challenged of staying abreast of the latest implements of war that wreaked havoc on soldiers across the Atlantic. The early twentieth-century military needed men of good character because of their numerous constabulary missions in the Philippines, Cuba, and China. Army officials had learned in fighting long counter-guerrilla wars in the Reconstruction-era South, the western plains, and the Philippines that men with patience and restraint fared better than those without.[70] But now, in addition to being ethically disciplined, soldiers had to be cognizant of advanced weaponry such as machine guns, high-caliber artillery, high explosives, communication systems, airplanes, and poisonous gas. New weapons systems required more-complex training in terms of how to operate, maintain, and deploy them in battle. Army recruiters, therefore, sought as many recruits of good character and intelligence as possible.

While the navy and Marines frequently used explicit appeals to manhood, the army often chose recruiting imagery that was decidedly more implicit. They tended to focus more on patriotism, adventure, and opportunity without making the direct link to benefiting the soldier through education and physical exercise. In Michael Whelan's

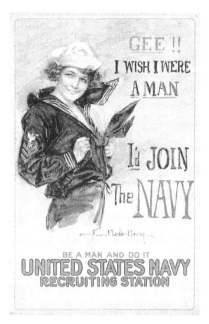

Fig. 17. First World War navy recruiting posters. *Enlist in the Navy*, by Milton H. Bancroft and *Gee I Wish I Were a Man*, by Howard C. Chandler. World War I Posters, Library of Congress.

Men Wanted for the Army and James M. Flagg's *Our Regular Divisions*, the men showcase an ideal military masculinity. In these posters they appear sturdy, upright, brave, and wrapped in patriotism. But their military's text advertisements were often more muted than those of the Marines or the navy. One read, "Men who *feel inclined* to join the Army are invited."[71] These appeals worked well, however, considering how much larger the army was compared to the other services leading up to U.S. entry in the Great War.

Wartime Military Manliness

Military manliness became more popular in the United States as the winter of 1917 turned into spring. With the declaration of war that April, it became the dominate and most appealing form of masculine culture. The military and naval recruiting services shifted gears in their advertisements. Their imagery now became more imperative and patriotic, and their masculine appeals became more explicit and

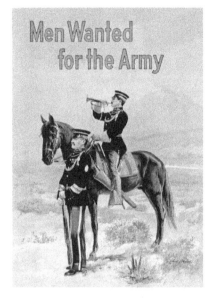

Fig. 18. Army recruiting posters. *Men Wanted for the Army*, by Michael Whelan; *Our Regular Divisions*, by James M. Flagg; and *Men Wanted for the Army*, by Isaac B. Hazleton. World War I Posters, Library of Congress.

emphatic. When the United States officially entered the Great War in April 1917, the Marine Corps, like the army and the navy, undertook a substantial public-relations campaign.

Commandant Barnett and the Marine Publicity Bureau designated June 10–16, 1917, as U.S. Marine Corps National Recruiting Week.[72]

The slogan for this recruiting drive was "Four Thousand Enlistments by Saturday Night." Barnett meant Marine Corps Week to break all previous recruiting records and take advantage of the *rage militaire* and surge of patriotism that swept the country in the spring of 1917. For Marine Corps Week, recruiters received packages containing fresh printings of literature and posters. Each package contained copies of *U.S. Marines—Soldiers of the Sea*; *U.S. Marines in Rhyme, Prose, and Cartoon*; and *Who Am I?*[73] But they would have help from civilians who were caught up in the fervor as well.[74]

Barnett and the Publicity Bureau made sure that recruiters had plenty of pamphlets and posters of to attract recruits, win the hearts of the American people, and portray the Corps as the premier military service. Newer editions of the pamphlets pushed more stories that reflected the fighting side of Marine Corps life to make it more attractive in wartime. They added James J. Montague's poem about Marines that further supported their claims about being fighting men. Regarding the dangers these men faced, the poem is forthright:

> Killed and wounded? Yes, a plenty, though their jobs are
>   Always small,
> That don't make a bit less deadly a careerin' rifle ball.
> In a war or in a scrimmage half an ounce of flying lead
> Is as dangerous to soldiers, and will kill 'em just as dead.
> They may not be splendid figures in historic battle scenes,
> But there are able-bodied fighters—those Marines.[75]

Here, Marines played to what they perceived were their strengths—courage, toughness, and aggressiveness—which people frequently associated with military manliness.[76]

The Corps made additional efforts to attract men who wanted to fight, especially those who were more athletically inclined. Now that the United States had finally entered the Great War, Sergeant Bert Van Moss advocated for the importance of intensified self-defense training among recruits. Close-quarters combat, he argued, was more likely now in this war than ever. Prior athletes would be more responsive to Marine physical and self-defense training. "Let us mobilize the boxers and wrestlers and other athletes of the country and put them in our training camps," Van Moss urged, "and we will turn out a corps of fighters that will win with the least loss, let the enemy choose any weapons." Doing this would enhance the physical strength and endurance of recruits and, thereby, raise the quality of the Marine fighting man. Van Moss was certain that a physically fit and properly trained Marine would "make the name American synonymous with supreme, in the art of war as well as the pursuits of peace—a competitor to be feared and as a neighbor admired."[77]

Recruiters received three posters in large quantities and meant for display across the United States to aid in attracting more men. "Stores of the institutional type—the Jordan Marshes, the Wanamakers, the Marshall-Fields, all over the country, stand ready to help the Marine Corps," Barnett assured recruiters.[78] Displaying posters would be mutually beneficial for these stores. "Marine Corps Recruiting Week," the Commandant claimed, "gives them the opportunity—and it is one of which they will be glad to take advantage; for it enables them to link up their store-news and their window displays with a current event of general popular interest."[79] Recruiters fanned out across the country with three different posters: *Active Service on Land and Sea*, *The Colors!*, and *Marine Corps Week*.

These illustrations display the kinds of men recruits would become. They portray Marines as soldiers of the sea, possessed of masculine and soldierly qualities. The men appear confident, courageous, disciplined, and controlled. *A Man's Game* was an updated "Walking John" and makes an explicit appeal to the manhood of the country. It asserts that the Marine Corps is an institution of men while also describing where they serve, now on land, over the sea, and in the sky instead of just on land and sea. Recruiters wanted these posters placed around police stations and firehouses. The Marine appears ready for anything, which may be why they specifically targeted those locations. Policemen and firemen, whose jobs require flexibility and readiness to answer an emergency at any time, might have identified with this image of a Marine.[80]

L. A. Shafer's *The Spirit of 1917—Join the U.S. Marines* shows four Marines of a landing party carrying the United States and Marine Corps flags ashore. These Marines are not calmly marching; rather, they are moving forward quickly, with rifles at the ready, as though toward the enemy. Behind them are U.S. Navy vessels in support. The message here is that Marines are not just security guards at naval stations or on a warship. They are soldiers of the sea, the vanguard of American forces, who carry their nation's flag onto foreign shores. The creators of this poster designed it for placement in store windows.[81] Its appeal comes from the adventurous spirit of the image. Many commentators leading up to World War I tended to believe that young men and boys who had been overexposed to women (mothers, schoolteachers, and

Fig. 19. *A Man's Game*, by Sidney Reisenberg. Paul Woyshner Papers, Marine Corps Archives, Quantico VA.

others) were becoming "sissies."[82] Emasculated American men could look at this homosocial image and see joining the Marines as a path to recapturing their manhood.

These posters contained images that the Publicity Bureau used frequently leading up to America's entry the war for additional posters. *The Spirit of 1917—Join the U.S. Marines*, for example, had at least two versions. The bureau entitled the original version of the image *U.S. Marines—Soldiers of the Sea*, in order to promote the Corps's identity to the public. They used a revised version to appeal more to young men's patriotism and to connect their institution with the country's history of fighting bravely when necessary. *The Spirit of 1917—Join the U.S. Marines*, appears inspired by Archibald Willard's *The Spirit of 1776*, which would have been a well-known image at the time. Both images communicate with audiences along emotional lines. Together, they represent not just bravery, determination, and patriotism but reveal a gendered representation of the nation and the Marine Corps's manly

Fig. 20. *The Spirit of 1776*, (above) by Archibald Willard; and *The Spirit of 1917—Join the U.S. Marines* (opposite page) by L. A. Shafer. From *Four Thousand Enlistments by Saturday Night: Plan of Action U.S. Marine Corps National Recruiting Week June 10 to 16, 1917* (Washington, DC: Headquarters U.S. Marine Corps, 1917), 12.

resolve as well. The spring and early summer of 1917 saw an uptick in spirited bellicosity across the nation, as many Americans began to embrace war.[83] By making the connection between these two images, Marines linked themselves with the country's earliest history of men answering the call to fight.

The Corps designed the poster *Marine Corps Week* to spread the word about its recruiting drive. This poster is a slightly different representation of the same theme: a Marine with a formation of troops

"SPIRIT OF 1917"

JOIN THE U. S. MARINES
AT
113 EAST BALTIMORE ST., BALTIMORE

standing at attention under the big guns of a battleship. While *A Man's Game* depicts a Marine on guard duty and *The Spirit of 1917—Join the U.S. Marines* a Marine landing party, this image shows a ship's detachment of Marines on a war vessel. This image as well as the others are masculine in the display of a sharply dressed, square-jawed Marines. Yet they are also manly in the sense that they present Marines as disciplined men of action. *Marine Corps Week* "is to be used universally," instructed the writer, "barber shops, pool rooms, cigar stores, neighborhood stores; everywhere and any place you can get it before the public."[84]

Major General Barnett and the Publicity Bureau's efforts to advertise through magazines during Marine Corps Week was part of a much larger phenomenon of the U.S. government and the American media networks cooperating on a grand scale. With the U.S. declara-

Fig. 21. *Marine Corps Week.* From *Four Thousand
Enlistments by Saturday Night: Plan of Action U.S.
Marine Corps National Recruiting Week June 10 to 16, 1917*
(Washington, DC: Headquarters U.S. Marine Corps,
1917), 12.

tion of war, the Wilson administration enlisted the help of scholars,
artists, editors, and journalists to convince the American people of the
righteousness of the cause against the Central Powers. George Creel
and the Committee on Public Information worked hard to whip up
patriotic fervor through posters, billboards, and other advertising media. Creel, according to one historian, "believed that America's vast
network of newspapers, libraries, schools, universities, and citizen associations could be used to promote the country's war aims and poli-

cies."[85] The army, navy, and Marines would benefit from this, as many newspapers and magazines jumped at the chance to advertise for the military and promote government propaganda.[86]

The Marine Corps received help from Donovan and Armstrong National Advertising of Philadelphia in tailoring its advertisements to the needs of wartime recruiting. The agency created recruiting posters for the Marines that appealed explicitly to the manhood of potential recruits. One image, *Man Wanted—To Fit This Hat*, shows a steel helmet with the Marine emblem on the front. The poster challenges its readers: "Can you fit the hat? It's no place for a man who must be cushioned against shock; who shuns risk or loathes adventure." In another image a Marine is about to throw a hand grenade. "Can you qualify?" the poster reads, "Clear-eyed, alert-minded, vigorous manhood comes first." A third poster echoes the others: "The U.S. Marine Corps is to be increased. A real red-blooded man's opportunity for enlistment. . . . Men of vigor in body and mind, ambitious for adventure and advancement are wanted." Like the Publicity Bureau's own recruiting literature, these images pitched the Corps as a challenge to potential recruits while lauding the manliness of Marines. By asserting that "the man who makes good at the Marine Corps Recruiting Station, will serve with men stalwart and square and valorous," Donovan and Armstrong reinforced the Corps's claims about comprising good men who could mold and shape young newcomers into their own image.[87]

Barnett and the Publicity Bureau also enlisted the help of the *Saturday Evening Post* to place numerous Marine advertisements in issues between May and June 1917. "This publication blankets the United States with remarkable thoroughness," the bureau observed, "upwards of eight millions of magazine displays pages and half pages, on the opportunities and allurement of patriotic service with the U.S. Marines."[88] Marines advertised in the *Saturday Evening Post* because it was one of the country's most widely read men's magazines. Tom Pendergast has argued that it "was the first American magazine to appeal directly to a male audience, and for the first four decades of the twentieth century was the champion of Victorian masculine ideals."[89] George Horace Lorimer, the chief editor at the time, made sure that the *Saturday Evening Post* published stories that appealed to white middle-class men. These were often about young men on the make or a "self-made man." The magazine, therefore, targeted young males who "started with little and, through the diligent application of habits and values, became something and someone much richer."[90] The Marines' advertisements claimed to fit this image of the "self-made men" by

Fig. 22. *Man Wanted—To Fit This Hat* (above),
Strike 3! (opposite above), and *Devil Dogs!*
(opposite below), by Donovan and Armstrong
National Advertising. Box 7, Entry 18, RG 127,
National Archives and Records Administration,
Washington, DC.

presenting the Corps as an organization that can put them on the path
toward personal and economic betterment.

Through the *Saturday Evening Post*, Marines got a chance to promote themselves on a scale unlike ever before. Through it, the Publicity Bureau planned to attract the "high type of men we all want to see
in the ranks of the Marine Corps" by building up "appreciation for
the Marine Corps service as the super-service."[91] Assertive military
manliness coursed through Marine stories and advertisements in the
Saturday Evening Post. Edward G. Lowry, a popular journalist, wrote
a piece on the Marines for the publication's June 9 issue. His story,
"The Marines Have Landed and Have the Situation Well in Hand,"
ran for three and a half pages and described who the Marines were
and what they did. In the beginning of the piece, Lowry tells a story

Strike three!
Right over the plate!
He's out! Ah, it's a great old game.

But it's ten thousand times a greater game when the stake is Human Liberty; when you put 'em across "No Man's Land" loaded with America's blasting answer to the challenge of the Hun.

There is once again a chance to enlist in the U. S. Marines. Can you qualify? Clear-eyed, alert-minded, vigorous manhood comes first; then the capacity for training for service on land and sea, or in the air; men with self-reliance and self-respect, and ambitious for advancement. Age limits, 18 to 36 years.

REGISTERED MEN: Ask Local Board to let you volunteer. Unregistered men, enlist in the U. S. Marines quickly, while you can.

Apply at the U. S. MARINE CORPS RECRUITING STATION
1409 Arch Street, Philadelphia

14 Public Square, Wilkes Barre   Federal Building, Camden.
37-39 West King Street, Lancaster.   Federal Building, Trenton.

U.S. MARINES

U.S. MARINES

"Devil-Dogs!
"Look out for the
American Devil-Dogs!"

The news dispatches report a wild-eyed bunch of the enemy racing back into their own lines on the Western Front. They'd been out looking for trouble—and had found it! Those who escaped brought back the story of their first clash with the U. S. Marines.

The U. S. Marine Corps is to be increased. A real red-blooded man's opportunity for enlistment in the Three-in-One Service—land, sky and sea.

Men of vigor in body and mind, ambitious for adventure and advancement are wanted. 1800 officers will be commissioned; and in the Marine Corps, officers come up from the ranks. Ages, 18 to 36.

REGISTERED MEN: Ask your Local Board to let you volunteer. Unregistered men, enlist in the U. S. Marines, while you can.

Apply at the U. S. MARINE CORPS RECRUITING STATION
1409 Arch Street, Philadelphia

14 Public Square, Wilkes Barre   Federal Building, Camden.
37-39 West King Street, Lancaster.   Federal Building, Trenton.

of how he had met a Marine sergeant named Jantzen. He sums him up by calling him "a sure-'nough man"—a brave expeditionary Marine competent for any task put before him. Lowry recounts how he and his party of Americans on assignment in Cuba ran afoul of a group of rebels near Trinidad. He telegraphed the U.S. consulate in Havana for help, and the ambassador dispatched twenty-five armed Marines to assist: "Jantzen and his party arrived. They were received like Caesar's conquering legions returning to Rome. I telegraphed the usual message to Mr. Taft, 'The Marines have landed and have the situation well in hand,' and sailed away to Batabano with my nose out of joint. That was a simple routine job such as the Marines are always doing."[92] Lowry made Jantzen and his Marines look aggressive, on one hand, but cool under pressure, on the other, ready to fight yet also restrained and disciplined. He made them out to be what Marines thought the United States needed at the time: men of action.

Lowry affirmed that Marines sought real men to join their ranks, those who wanted action and were not afraid of a fight. They wanted "men who take nobody's dust." "ROMANCE, action, adventure, active service, the lure of far-off horizons, strange lands, and the queer, hot, outlying places of the world where trouble is bred—these are the things that bring men into the Marine Corps and keep them there every year," he swaggered. Referencing the military-preparedness movement that had swept through the nation recently, Lowry claimed that these men were always ready: "Don't talk to the marines about preparedness. It makes them yawn. It is old stuff. They invented it. Whatever may be the state of readiness of the army or the navy, or the militia, or the citizens on foot who will make up the volunteer army, the marines are there, set, on their marks, and all their gear polished and scrubbed and ready for instant use." The Corps claimed to be prepared long before President Wilson asked Congress to declare war against Germany. Because Marines were ready, new recruits stood the best chance of being the first to fight the Germans if they joined the Corps. "This is where the first flight of keen fighting men will turn," Lowry boasted, men who "know the knack Marines have for getting into the thick of it first."[93]

The *Saturday Evening Post* published another piece associating manliness with the Marines: Mary Roberts Rinehart's "The Gray Mailed Fist." This article is mostly about the U.S. Navy and how it fought to keep up its readiness and stay abreast of the latest technological advancements in the face of public apathy leading up to the war. While Rinehart spent time with the Atlantic Fleet at sea, she came across the various Marine ship's detachments. She referenced people's general knowledge of Marines and added that "peace and order follow the marines like the pause and hush after a cyclone." Like Lowry, Rinehart mentions all of the things Marines wanted the public to know about them: they were manly, tough, ready, and flexible. "They are a highly mobile force, carrying with them practically all they need," she observes, "including the best brand of courage in the war market; each man has his packed kit ready." She makes them appear masculine by promoting their fighting prowess, claiming that Marines can handle "about twenty times their weight in German avoirdupois." She also advertises their manliness by mixing their mental and physical characteristics to make them seem "clear-eyed, businesslike, alert fighting men to their fingertips." Rinehart assures her readers, "They are as fine a body of men as our county can produce. And that is a large order."[94]

Barnett and the Marine Publicity Bureau also made sure that the *Saturday Evening Post* had advertisements promoting the Corps's military manliness on a weekly basis. "Enlist in the U.S. Marines!—the masters of any situation," claimed one of the larger ones, entitled "Where There's Action."[95] This advertisement referenced the Corps's history by claiming that Marines are "a tight little band—occupying a distinctive place among America's defenders."[96] It attempts to appeal to men who want to fight: "even more than a glorious past—to men of fighting blood—enlistment in the Marines means ACTION." To the left of its copy is an image of a Marine with the U.S. flag caught in a breeze. The headline reads "Where There's Action," and the armed Marine stepping on shore coolly and confidently seems to have found it.

The manliness conveyed in these images stem from the Marines' apparent confidence, discipline, and readiness to fight. Another advertisement proclaimed, "If you have the ambition and grit to render *first line* service to your country, and desire military experience in both naval warfare and land operations—abroad and at home—there is a place ready for you in this famous corps of fighting men."[97] An image of an armed Marine, with the same look of ambition and grit the text mentions, resides atop the advertisment. These are masculine images in that they highlight the Marines' physical appearance; all are once again armed and appear healthy, sturdy, and strong.

These images collectively attempt to convey how the many land and sea duties of Marines are exciting, fun, and beneficial to one's manhood. At sea Marines helped man the naval artillery; on land, they were the first to fight. An advertisement from June 30, 1917, explicitly conveys this idea.[98] A June 2 advertisement informs readers, "So, whether

Fig. 23. "Where There's Action." From *Four Thousand Enlistments by Saturday Night: Plan of Action U.S. Marine Corps National Recruiting Week June 10 to 16, 1917* (Washington, DC: Headquarters U.S. Marine Corps, 1917), 4.

U.S. Marines

THE SOLDIERS of the Nation's first line of defense!
"Ever Ready and Ever True!"

If you have the ambition and grit to render *first line* service to your country, and desire military experience in both naval warfare and land operations—abroad as well as at home—there is a place ready for you in this famous corps of fighting men.

The U. S. Marines are drilled as infantry, naval gunners, field artillery and machine-gun companies; and especially trained for instant duty as landing parties from the ships of the Navy.

About enlistment and opportunities for patriotic service, enquire at

Marine Corps Recruiting Stations

in all the principal cities

Separate from recruiting places of Army or Navy

Send the Corner Coupon or drop a Postal for free Book—Soldiers of the Sea—illustrating and describing the duties, adventures and experiences of U. S. Marines the world around.

U. S. Marine Corps Recruiting Publicity Bureau
117 East 24th St., New York

Fig. 24a. Recruiting advertisement. From *Saturday Evening Post*, May 19, 1917, 37.

The Soldiers
That Go to Sea

Young man!—Go to sea with the United States Marines; or ashore: wherever there's action!

The Marines are the "'Minute Men' of Today"—the first to fight.

On battleships they are naval gunners—manning the torpedo-defense batteries and anti-aircraft guns. On land they are infantry, field artillery, machine-gun companies.

U. S. Marines

So, whether the fighting is on sea or land or in the air, you will find the Marines in the thick of it.

The Marine Corps offers not only splendid all-'round military training, but plenty of opportunity for patriotic service—with the fleet and in duty ashore, at home and across the seas.

Fighting, travel, adventure, fun—it's all one to the U. S. Marine! Come on and join!

MARINE CORPS WEEK, June 10 to 16. "Four Thousand Enlistments by Saturday!"

About enlistment apply now, to—

Marine Corps Recruiting Stations
which are located in all the principal cities
Separate from recruiting places of Army or Navy

*Send the Corner Coupon or drop a Postal for free Book—
"Soldiers of the Sea"—illustrating and describing the duties
and experiences of U. S. Marines the world around.*

U. S. Marine Corps Recruiting Publicity Bureau
117 East 24th St., New York

Fig. 24b. Recruiting advertisement. From
Saturday Evening Post, June 30, 1917, 69.

Fig. 24c. Recruiting advertisement. From
Saturday Evening Post, June 2, 1917, 37.

the fighting is on sea or land or in the air, you will find the Marines in the thick of it . . . fighting, travel, adventure, fun—it's all one to the U.S. Marine!"[99]

But one must remember that these are recruiting advertisements, designed to cast the Marine Corps in as positive a light as possible to gain recruits. They offered young men a chance to see action, become fit, and travel the world. They claimed to make men more masculine by improving their bodies and more manly by enhancing their character. In doing so, however, they purposefully omitted anything about the Marine Corps that would be unappealing. The Publicity Bureau dispersed these advertisements during America's initial involvement in a terrible war that, by 1917, had claimed hundreds of thousands of lives. The U.S. government and all of its military branches, particularly the Marine Corps, took advantage of the hightened patriotism and the popularity of martial manliness that swept the country to get men into the armed forces. In doing so they focused on the benefits of service, making no mention of the potential dangers.

Marine recruiters only enlisted 1,700 men nationwide between June 10 and June 16, well below the 4,000 they wanted. "Many causes contributed to the small number enlisted," claimed Charles Ketcham, editor of the *Marines Magazine*, including other patriotic campaigns that "occupied part of the same week, and apparently diverted much of the public attention."[100] But the Corps grew quickly over the summer months. By August 1917, the Corps had expanded to 30,000 men.

Some Marines worried that the influx of so many new men would bring enlistment standards down. Colonel Albert S. McLemore tried put those worries to bed. "We have reached the thirty thousand mark and have not lowered the standard," he wrote. The colonel congratulated recruiters not only for getting the quantity but also the necessary quality of men. McLemore insisted, "Twenty thousand men—and real men too—in less than five months is a record of which you have every right to be proud."[101] In August, Major General Barnett ordered recruiters to start accepting only a very limited number of applicants while still "maintaining the highest standard."[102]

Although the Corps expanded, it was still quite small. While Marine recruiters took in 17,748 new men in 1917 (an increase of 360.7 percent), the U.S. Army enlisted 160,084 new soldiers, while the U.S. Navy brought in 84,229 new sailors.[103] The Selective Service Act of 1917 would push millions more men into the army. Marines claimed their fewer enlisted numbers and their lower draftee numbers indicated their high standards and "elite" status.

Marines were proud of the recruits they enlisted and even advertised some of them in the *Recruiters' Bulletin*. They were particularly proud of any college graduates who enlisted in the Corps. "Crack Yale Athletes Join Marines," proclaimed one piece in the *Bulletin*. One was Harry Le Gore, captain of Yale's baseball team and a football player, too. Among the others were Johnny Overton, a cross-country track champion, and Louis Ferguson, who led Yale's swimming team.[104] Another piece entitled "College Students 'Doing Their Bit'" boasted about how 119 University of Minnesota students joined the Corps compared to only 31 and 20 who joined the army and navy respectively.[105]

Perhaps the most famous enlistee the Marine Corps gained was former congressman and successful Detroit, Michigan, attorney Edwin Denby. Nearly fifty years old and weighing over 250 pounds, Denby was overage and did not meet the Corps's physical standards. Nevertheless, Major General Barnett could not pass up on the opportunity to enlist a somewhat prominent American citizen. The Corps sent Private Denby down to the newly established recruit-training depot at Parris Island. While there, he served as a motivational speaker for the other new enlistees. When asked by the press why he joined, Denby replied, "The country needs men."[106]

During the summer and fall of 1917, the U.S. Marine Corps became a source of manly pride for the nation. Newspapermen wrote of the Marines as the beau ideal of American manhood and did yeoman's work pitching the Corps as a source of confidence for a country already swept up in a passion for arms. This pride stemmed in part from the type of men editors believed the Marines to be. One claimed that its "ranks are filled with a class of men who rank second to none in the United States."[107] Pride also came from what they believed Marines could do. "The American Marine is the handiest man around the place," F. M. Knowles of the *New York Evening Mail* boasted. "He can do any sort of chore, go on any sort of errand, and he always brings home the bacon."[108] Yet at this time the Marines had not fought anyone in Europe. "Looking at their sturdy figures in the serviceable outfits of the Corps," wrote the editor of the *Buffalo Courier*, "there is no doubt in the minds of those who stay at home that the ever swelling Marine Corps will 'come through.'"[109]

Doubt in the ability or virility of Marines cannot be found anywhere in these journalists' writings. A Marine impressed William Richardson of Richmond, Virginia, for two reasons: "His manly bearing and his loyalty to the service of his choosing." "It takes a man to get into the Marine Corps," Richardson wrote, "and in the service it takes a

gentleman to live up to its standards . . . not a namby pamby fellow."
He advertised the Marines as the service for a "man that wants to fight
and fight hard."[110] For these newspapermen, the Marines indicated that
American manhood was strong and ready for war.

For those around the country who had just enlisted in the Corps,
the Marines were supposed to make real men out of them. Their personal manhood, like that of the nation, would be molded and tempered
by the Corps and the war. The Marines' nationwide advertising and
public-relations campaigns of 1917 helped win thousands of recruits
using such appeals. "My pal and I thought we ought to be two atoms
in the great struggle, so we enlisted," Thomas Boyd, future author
of *Through the Wheat*, wrote to his mother from Parris Island. Boyd
endured the struggle that the Marines had promised. Parris Island was
a new training station, and recruits had to construct their living quarters, dig latrines, and fell trees in addition to their military training.
"Believe me, it is no simple matter to become a Marine, it takes four
months of hard training in time of peace before one is a full-fledged
Marine so just imagine how hard we have to drill in order to get it in
within ten weeks." But his spirits remained high. "Unquestionably,"
Boyd wrote, "it is a gay life."[111]

Despite the recruiting drives and all of the advertising about being
ready to fight the Germans, nowhere was it written at the outbreak
of war that Marines would be guaranteed the opportunity fight in
France. There was no advanced-base mission in the war that the Marines could fill, and ship duty would be decidedly antithetical to their
"first to fight" advertising campaign. There was a great deal at stake
for the Corps if it missed out on the war entirely and stuck strictly
to the creed of being the military arm of the navy. That the American Expeditionary Force would be manned and led by the army was
perfectly natural and questioned by no one. Marine captain John W.
Thomason, who would go on to fight in France and became a noted
artist and storyteller of the Corps, remembered a decade afterward,
"Headquarters realized that the Marines must get into the German
War or become quite ridiculous."[112] Despite Barnett's claim that "the
Marine Corps should do its full part in this war, and for that reason I
feel it was absolutely necessary that the Marines should join the Army
on the western front," it is more likely that the American war effort
did not technically need any Marines in France.[113] But they went anyway—Commandant Barnett and Navy Secretary Daniels made sure of
that.

Barnett and Daniels had undoubtedly been in the ear of Secretary of War Newton Baker by May 1917. Baker wrote to President Wilson about early plans to send 12,000 men to France as soon as possible. This force would be soldiers of the regular army "with the possible exception of one regiment of marines, the Marine Corps being particularly anxious to participate in the first expedition, because of a tradition in the Marine Corps that it has always done so in our past history."[114] On May 27 Wilson accepted Secretary Daniels and Commandant Barnett's offer of one Marine regiment to cross the Atlantic with the initial wave of American troops.[115]

Much in the way President Jackson did in the Seminole Wars and President Polk did in the Mexican-American War, President Wilson supplemented his expeditionary force with Marines out of expediency. The allies in Europe wanted U.S. troops in theater as soon as possible to shore up morale. High-ranking Marines such as Barnett and Assistant Commandant Colonel John A. Lejeune believed that the Corps's concerns lie principally with the navy. The war, however, created an exceptional circumstance in which the Marines' "latent possibilities" for service could be utilized in a time of national emergency. When Wilson and his cabinet needed ready infantry to send to France, therefore, they included the Marines. A few years after the war, then Commandant Lejeune considered the Marines' presence in France to be the exercise of good economy of force "in accord with the patriotic principle that, in the event of war, everyman, especially those trained for war, should do his uttermost to aid in the winning of the war."[116]

This special circumstance, the expansion of personnel ceilings, and its growing appeal and advertising power gave the Marine Corps its opportunity to fight in the Great War. By July 3, the Fifth Regiment of Marines had landed in France. Barnett ordered this unit thrown together quickly from veteran Marine companies in early June 1917. The first Marines in France, therefore, were mostly seasoned veterans, many of whom had deployments to Vera Cruz, Haiti, Nicaragua, and Santo Domingo under their belts. As the Corps grew to its new wartime strength of 75,000 men, some 23,000 Marines would follow the Fifth Regiment to France. But most of the new men inducted into the Corps never saw France.[117] Only two regiments, the Fifth and Sixth, plus one machine-gun battalion would see major combat action against the Germans in the summer and fall of 1918. A year after the United States entered the war, these Marines would turn their worst combat action into their most glorious, one of the most horrendous sacrifices of American manhood into its supreme test. It was a test that both the Marines and the American public believed was passed with flying colors despite the high casualties. The battles of the summer and fall of 1918 would come to be understood as testaments to the strength and courage of Marine and American manhood.

The Cleanest and Strongest of Our Young Manhood

Pompous, and blatant and arrogant,
Bedecked in their new array;
So sure were the Huns in their thick-
    skulled pride
That nothing on earth could stem the tide,
Or block them on their way.
Eight thousand men were pitted then
    'gainst the Prussian Guard of fiends.
In the power of might for the cause of
    right
Went the Fifth and Sixth Marines.
— *Isabel Likens Gates, "The United States Marines," 1919*

Lewis A. Holmes wrote to his mother from France, where he served with the Fifth Regiment of Marines, that would get bloodied at Belleau Wood two weeks later. "The only thing I live for is to do my bit and then return to you a brave, strong man, both mentally and physically, and prove to you that I am," he told her. The *Marines Magazine* published a poem by Private Rueben E. Goldblatt that spoke to how many Marines thought about the war's meaning. "And they thrill with the adventure / for they know that it will be / A task to match the manhood / of the soldiers of the sea."[1] Many in the States understood the Great War as a new test for American manhood. The time had come for the men of the nation to do their duty, defend their country, and show the world that Americans could fight when pushed too far. Many wanted to stay out of the war, but German treachery forced the U.S. government's hand. President Wilson and others now saw the conflict as a matter of honor, and chivalric ideals manifested themselves in popular culture, government speeches, and Marine imagery. Harkening to traditional notions of manliness, the Marines presented themselves as heroes on a knightly quest to defend their nation's honor and rescue civilization.

Testing manhood in war meant sacrificing lives. Falling in battle proved manliness in some contemporary visions, and Marines experienced relatively high casualties from June 1918 until the end of the war in mid-November. The Corps and journalists claimed those sacrifices were necessary for victory. When word arrived of Marine battlefield successes in the early summer of 1918, the country was ebullient. Never in their history had the Marines enjoyed such public praise. Upon the return of the Marines in August 1919, the press heralded them as heroes and fine examples of American men in part because of their sacrifices for their country. Having witnessed the high casualties firsthand, Marine colonel Albertus Catlin wrote that young men could still become Marines, but only if they were "man enough."[2]

The Great War was significant for the Marine Corps for several reasons. The war gave many officers important lessons in tactics, logistics, artillery, and air support that would be used later in amphibious-doctrine development.[3] Some have argued that the Marines also "proved" that they were elite warriors.[4] The focus here, however, is how the war gave Marines the opportunity to prove their worth along traditional lines of wartime manliness.[5] The U.S. government expected its servicemen to fight honorably and courageously while adhering to strict moral standards. These expectations were a part of a broader trend in progressive thinking during the early twentieth century.[6] American wartime propaganda sanctified women and children and demonized Germans. Men, being the traditional protectors of the home, thus embarked on a crusade to protect their families and save civilization. Marines established a reputation of fighting bravely and honorably while supposedly maintaining the moral and physical-health standards advocated by progressives back home. They may have persuaded some that they were elite warriors, but deeper than that, the Great War helped Marines convince many observers that they were exceptional men.

The Test of Manhood

The test of manhood was how many justified conscripting hundreds of thousands of young men into the military and then sending them overseas to fight the Germans. A month after Congress declared war, it passed the Selective Service Act of 1917. The U.S. government would organize a national army for war with Germany made up of conscripts. Despite the animosity a significant portion of the country held toward the draft, those that were in power favored it.[7] Nearly three million men would end up being drafted into service during the war, and President Wilson wanted to make sure that they did not fall to the traditional military vices such as alcohol and prostitution. This army would be organized with the purpose of not only defeating Germany but also of uplifting the lives of men composing it. "I do not believe it an exaggeration to say that no army ever before assembled has had more conscientious and painstaking thought given to the protection and stimulation of its mental, moral, and physical manhood," the president wrote shortly after the declaration of war.[8] Many Americans accepted this line of thinking. A preacher who addressed Congress in the spring of 1917 called the draft "legislative action which will prepare and build up the young manhood of America" so it would be "fit to take its place and to defend American rights and liberties."[9]

Marines understood and used these ideas about manhood. The former congressman turned Marine, Sergeant Edwin Denby, made sure recruits at Parris Island understood what was at stake for their manhood. They had to conduct themselves honorably while in service and afterward return to their homes clean and upright. "Nowhere in the world does a man stand more squarely on his own feet, to make or mar his character, than in the military service," he said. "If you want to go back worthy to look your women in the face . . . it is up to you, men; it is up to you."[10] Life in the military could bring honor or shame to a man. Denby spoke of the deleterious consequences that alcohol abuse and sexual contact with women of ill repute had not just on men's honor but on their health as well. Often, when progressives spoke of "cleanliness," they meant clean bodies free from not just dirt and grime but also venereal diseases. American physicians and preachers associated "clean living" with strong and healthy manhood, while "lust, uncleanness, drink, gambling, swearing, lying, dishonesty, [and] irreligion" could "ruin our Christian manhood."[11] The U.S. government promoted this idea as well: "A nation stands or falls, succeeds or fails, just in proportion to the high-mindedness, cleanliness, and manliness of each succeeding generation of men."[12] Sergeant Denby drew on all of these ideas when he spoke with recruits about how the Marine Corps and the war would test them.

The war would also test their courage. "War puts manhood to a tremendous test, and be it said to a man's credit, that the coward is the exception, not the rule," a writer for the *Marines Magazine* claimed.[13] Cowards and shirkers harmed their personal reputation. "The man who fails in his duty to his country, or to his comrades or to himself, creates a ghost which will haunt himself forever," one Marine warned. "Never in his conscious moments can he drive away the specter of his failure to do his manly duty."[14] Manly, Marines did their duty in war, while those who did not were simply not real men. The consequences of failure were profound because an unmanly Marine failed not only himself but also his fellow Marines and his country.[15]

The test itself made men out of those with the courage to face it and pass. Those who rose to meet the challenges of their times with bravery would be richly rewarded. Courage was a common aspect of manliness in the World War I era. "Without courage a man is a poor specimen of a man, hardly worth calling a man," wrote one contemporary author.[16] "Never was [a] time in the history of the human race when real sturdy manhood, manly vigor and manly courage counted for as much as they do now," claimed another.[17] This rhetoric linking courage with manliness pervaded Marine writings as well. "If he plays a man's part," one wrote in the *Marines Magazine* in July 1917, "he is consciously the victor over danger, over hardship, over the temptation to avoid the difficult duty, over himself; he can look upon his destiny—yes, upon death itself—with clear eyes, unashamed and unafraid."[18] Essentially, this author encouraged readers to live up to the Victorian manly standards and imagery that the Corps promoted among its men. But these messages were conveyed in the early days of U.S. belligerency, a full eleven months before any Marines saw combat. The test for veteran Marines would not come until the summer of 1918.

Putting American manhood through the ultimate test of war meant sacrifice. Remarks by Secretary of the Navy Daniels reflected this line of thinking. In March 1918 he spoke before the Society of the Sons of St. Patrick in New York City. The central theme of his speech was this test for U.S. citizens. "There is no place in this country to-day," he explained, "for any man who is not ready to give all he is, all he has, and all he hopes to be to bring victory to American arms."[19] American men had to be ready to sacrifice themselves for their nation's cause in the Great War. Essentially, that was the test itself. In a time when people claimed "America for Americans!" demonstrating one's patriotism could come in the form of sacrifice. "The supreme test for an American," Daniels claimed, involved asking the following questions: "Does he love this country better than any other country under the sun? And will he gladly give his life to preserve the liberty which has blessed mankind?"[20] The war required sacrificing American manhood, if necessary, to the causes of democracy and liberty.

President Wilson attempted to persuade audiences of the need for this sacrifice by describing it in terms of honor and duty. His conscription proclamation of May 18, 1917, spoke of American manhood rising en masse to do its duty. Conscription, just like the preparedness movement, had been a contentious issue in U.S. politics during the Great War. Each had strong implications concerning the power of the federal government and citizens' individual rights and obligations to their country.[21] Many people saw the draft as a gross overstep of federal power. But Wilson wanted them to see its passage as "nothing less than the day upon which the manhood of the country shall step forward in one solid rank in defense of the ideals upon which this Nation is consecrated."[22] The war required men to serve in some form or fashion.[23] Obligations involved sacrifice. Wilson reasoned with his audiences further: "The stern sacrifice that is before us urges that it be carried in all our hearts as a great day of patriotic devotion and obligation, when the duty shall lie upon every man . . . to see to it that the name of every male person of the designated ages is written on these lists of honor."[24] For idealists like Wilson, conscription and war could be a good thing. It would teach men about honor, duty, obligation, and sacrifice, all popular notions of Victorian-era manhood.[25]

While on a brief furlough from his duties at Parris Island, Sergeant Denby witnessed in Detroit a parade of men who had been drafted into service. Having a sentimental and idealist nature, Denby felt inspired by the display of American manhood in the parade. "How American they were, these men who had welcomed the stern mandate of the government and were leaving their all to take up arms," he wrote. To him, these draftees embodied American loyalty, courage, and patriotism. Their government forced them into a war they did not volunteer for, true. But that only called for more praise because the ideal American preferred peace to war and only fought when absolutely necessary, like the men the sergeant saw in this parade. "There can be no question about the men, they are strong of heart and sound of limb," ready to perform their masculine role of protecting their homes.[26]

Denby highlighted the masculinity of the men in the parade by also commenting on the femininity of the women in the crowd. While the draftees marched, their wives, mothers, sisters, and children stood by in solemn support as though they offered their men up as "willing sacrifices" to the alter of liberty. While the men performed their masculine duty to march and fight, "there can be no doubt about the women, they will wait and hope that their men will come back to them as clean and honest gentlemen as they leave." And if their sons or brothers were to fall in battle, "then in the splendor of their spirit, our women will give thanks that their men have died so well."[27] Despite Denby's description, it is doubtful that all of the women in the crowd felt this way.

To criticize the war effort or the draft in 1917 was to invite public scorn and the threat of vigilante violence. Hundreds of thousands of Americans resisted or refused to answer to the draft.[28] The demographics that became associated with such opposition—German Americans, Irish Americans, socialists, and even populations of farmers—became the victims of this anti-antiwar movement. These groups suffered from intimidation, threats, and even lynching in their communities.[29] Women who publicly opposed the draft faced similar dangers. The "postmistress" of Bowman, North Dakota, allegedly proclaimed, "Women who do not oppose the draft are no better than brood-sows producing men for slaughter in defense of J. P. Morgan's billions."[30] Opponents accused her of being a "Kaiser Booster," a "copperhead," and a "traitor." Jeannette Rankin, the first woman to serve in Congress, also came out against the draft by calling the conflict a "commercial war."[31]

Denby's views of the draft, the war, men, and women represent dominant opinions in the United States and the Marine Corps at the time. These were not dominant in the sense that they were in the majority, rather that they were held by those in power. The government expected men, if drafted, to go into uniform willingly. It expected women to support and encourage men to do so, to keep the home fires burning, and to engage in volunteerism for organizations like the Red Cross.[32] According to the federal government and the armed forces, people who opposed the draft and the war effort failed in their prescribed roles not only as patriotic Americans but also as men and women.

Many Americans perceived the war as a matter of honor. Wilson described the situation as such to persuade the American public of what was at stake. "This flag under which we serve would have been dishonored had we withheld our hand," he declared.[33] This sentiment reflects how American writing around this time took on chivalrous tones. The Germans had insulted the United States with unrestricted submarine warfare that drowned American civilians. Minister Zimmerman's telegram to Mexico City had called on Mexicans to invade the United States. To restrain from violence would have meant shrinking in the face of an aggressor, which was a decidedly unmanly thing for a nation to do. On the floor of the House of Representatives, one orator proclaimed:

> I regret that we are to have war; but if we are to maintain our self-respect, *if we are to encourage the cultivation and development of those virile and patriotic virtues among our citizens*, without which our Government cannot and should not survive, if we are not to become the laughing stock of mankind, mocked at and reviled by every other nation of the world, if we are not to be derided and sneered at as a Nation of degenerates, of money changers, and of cowards, is anything left to do consistent with a decent self-respect than to acknowledge the unquestioned fact that the German Government has waged war against us, to accept the challenge that has been so recklessly repeated in continued acts of war and aggression against us, and *to meet it like and in the only manner befitting a great and a patriotic and manly nation?*[34]

Germany had thrown down the gauntlet, and American manhood would have to accept the challenge or live in disgrace.

Chivalry coursed through Americans' perceptions of their own manhood. Courage reappears in these discussions of manly behavior because that, too, was linked with chivalry. Popular Victorian conceptions of true manliness consisted of self-control and common sense on one hand, and possessing the courage to sacrifice for the greater good on the other.[35] Men needed courage to "to play the man in life, to put his life in for all it is worth—this sort of manliness rings true, and often sounds its clear note of chivalry, nobility and Christian knightliness," as George Walker Fiske puts it.[36] Even before the United States declared war on Germany, writers described American men as chivalrous. One author declared, "we can no longer accuse it of being immersed in materialism, but on the contrary, must recognize our American man as the knightly soul of the twentieth-century."[37] This comment speaks to the lingering concern that the expansion of material culture in the United States had diluted the country's manhood. Despite these doubts, men stepped up to the challenge. In the context of the Great War, Americans and Marines saw themselves as chivalrous crusaders coming to the rescue of Western Europe and democracy.

An image in the June 1917 issue of the *Marines Magazine* shows Marines connecting themselves directly to Christian crusaders and chivalry. In the foreground is one man charging through the fire-and-

THE CRUSADERS
The Old and the New

Fig. 25. *The Crusaders: The Old and the New,* by Paul
Woyshner. From *Marines Magazine,* June 1917, 2.

smoke-licked door of a church. Behind him is a crusader bedecked
in armor with his sword drawn. The artist saw the Marines as the
modern-day equivalent of crusaders of old—sent to fight for a high and
holy cause (democracy in this case) in a foreign land against infidels
(the Germans). The Marines, "neo-crusaders" sure of their cause and

Drawn by Pvt. CHARLES ELDER HAYS

Fig. 26. *U.S. Marine*, by Charles Elder Hays. From *Marines Magazine*, October 1917, 5.

confident in the outcome, would fight to save Western Europe like the chivalrous Americans they believed they were.

Two additional images convey this same theme of Marines coming to the rescue of Western civilization. The first depicts a small Marine with a rifle chasing a caricature of the European war fleeing in terror. Above him is a feminine-looking angel of peace. The second image again shows a Marine but this time confronting a savage-looking German to save civilization, which is personified here as a helpless woman on the ground. Behind them, Europe burns.

This imagery was founded upon the demonization of the German, the feminization of civilization, and the masculinization of Marines. Germans thus appear barbaric. Civilization in these images is either a woman supporting or being saved by the hero—the U.S. Marine. The savagery of the German is important because of the stark contrast it creates with the other two figures. In these images German barbarity reveals the manliness of the Marine and the femininity of the woman he protects or rescues.

This artwork reflects American writings and speeches that similarly dehumanized German soldiers. The wartime imagery and rhetoric of

THE RESCUER

Fig. 27. *The Rescuer*, by J. H. Ambrose. From *Marines Magazine*, August 1917, 2.

the army and navy aligned with that of the Marine Corps and the broader national message that the war was an opportunity for men to fight defend their homes. The army used the now world-famous image by Harry R. Hopps entitled *Destroy This Mad Brute* while the navy used William Allen Rogers's *Only the Navy Can Stop This*. In both images Germany's masculinity has been corrupted by militarism. The result is a form of hypermasculinity so severe to the point of being animalistic. Each shows Germany attacking the symbols of home for many white middle-class men: white women and children. Collectively, this imagery helped American men understand the overseas conflict in more visceral terms. Many indeed saw this as "the war to end all wars" and as a fight between the ideals of freedom and the oppression of authoritarianism and militarism. But intellectual, economic, and political reasons for going to war, as important and real as they were, were not enough to inflame the passions of people in the United States to fight an en-

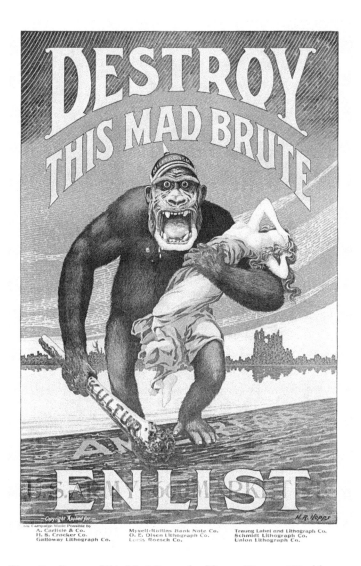

Fig. 28a. *Destroy This Mad Brute*, by Harry Hopps. World War I Poster, Library of Congress.

ONLY THE NAVY CAN STOP THIS

Fig. 28b. *Only the Navy Can Stop This*, by William Allen
Rogers. World War I Poster, Library of Congress.

emy an ocean away. The war had to be presented in terms of American
manhood defending not freedom of the seas or self-determination of
peoples, but their very own families against destruction and death.

President Wilson claimed that Germans "have regarded smaller
states, in particular, and the peoples who could be overwhelmed by
force, as their natural tools and instruments of domination."[38] Professor John Tatlock of Stanford University concurred, writing, "Our

sense of humanity, justice, and chivalry was horrified by the German invasion of Belgium, a weak and innocent nation."[39] American authors and artists portrayed the Germans as murderers of Belgian priests and children.[40] According to one, such vicious brutality caused the German soldier to lose his manhood. He was "bidden by his officers to shut his heart to every tender feeling," Ralph Flewelling claimed. "And the result has been that his manhood is lost somewhere in the meshes of military training, so that he has been guilty of barbarities and refinements of cruelty that savages would despise and be incapable of conceiving."[41] The Marines would have to stand up to the Germans and help put a stop to their barbarity.

Secretary of the Navy Daniels spoke of this quest as a great opportunity for the young men of the United States. Fate had given them the chance to be heroes and to make the world a better place. To the Naval Academy's 1918 graduating class, he said:

> Fortunate youth! Fortunate because it is given you to prove that the age of chivalry is not dead—that chivalry was never more alive than now. The holiest of crusades was motivated by no finer impulse than has brought us into this war. To prove that life means more than force; to prove that principle is still worth fighting for; to prove that freedom means more than dollars; that self-respect is better than compromise; to be ready to sacrifice all so that the world may be made the better—what nobler dedication of himself can a man make?[42]

The young men going off to war had the chance to demonstrate American valor and honor. An entire American army and two regiments of Marines in France were about to get this opportunity.

On the Western Front

The pitched battles that the Fourth Brigade of Marines fought against the Germans in the summer and fall of 1918 are very important to the Corps's history and have received a great deal of both professional and amateur historical attention. A brief recounting of these battles helps explain their significance to the Marines and American society. The Sixth and Fifth Regiments of Marines and the Sixth Machine Gun Battalion formed the Fourth Brigade of the U.S. Army's Second Division. The brigade itself formed in France in October 1917, with Brigadier

General Charles A. Doyen (USMC) in command. Brigadier General James G. Harbord (U.S. Army) replaced Doyen as Fourth Brigade's commanding officer in May 1918 and would serve in that capacity until July. In late July 1918, Major General John A. Lejeune (USMC) assumed command of the soldiers and Marines of the Second Division. Lejeune was the first Marine officer to command an army division in war.[43]

The Marines experienced their first major battle near Château-Thierry in May and June 1918. In late May the German First and Seventh Armies launched a massive attack at Chemin des Dames, driving the French Sixth Army before them. The Germans aimed to make the allies shift troops from Flanders to the Château-Thierry sector closer to Paris. General Erich von Ludendorff hoped this feint would allow his armies to knock the British Expeditionary Force in Flanders out of the war entirely.[44] The French high command hurried American divisions into the line to stem the German assault bearing down on their capital. They ordered the U.S. Second Division to move up to defensive positions near the Paris–Metz highway. This division, including the Fourth Brigade, helped stop what was left of the German offensive momentum in the final days of May.

The Germans in this sector then took up defensive positions in Belleau Wood, the town of Bouresches, and on Hill 142 to the northwest of the woods. From June 6 until June 26, Marines conducted frontal assaults on enemy positions in and around Belleau Wood. Hill 142 and Bouresches fell to them on the sixth. But it took three weeks of heavy and costly attacks and artillery barrages to force the Germans out of Belleau Wood.

For many Marines, including Private Elton E. Mackin of the Sixth Regiment, this was their first taste of combat. In his memoirs penned after the war, Mackin described his first engagement as a rite of passage, a turning point from boyhood to manhood. A young friend had just been killed by enemy machine-gun fire during a night movement to the front lines. Shortly afterward, Sergeant John C. McCabe found Mackin sobbing uncontrollably, what he later described as "his last boyish tears." The sergeant brought him back to his senses by challenging his manhood: "Hell, Bud, you'd think you were the only guy in this man's outfit to lose a pal. We've all lost 'em up here, an' we want *men* in their places—not babies! Now, dig in!"[45] McCabe would be killed in action four months later at the Battle of Mont Blanc, but he helped Mackin survive the battles to come. Mackin believed he had become a man at Belleau Wood, "boyhood lay forever behind, a page of life's story had turned."[46]

Marine historians place a great deal of significance on a hastily planned and poorly supported assault against a heavily defended German position at Belleau Wood. That costly attack across a wheat field holds a strong place in Marine legend, as the Fifth and Sixth Regiments suffered 1,087 casualties in a single day. Those who lived to write about it, like Colonel Catlin and Lieutenant Clifton B. Cates, were lucky. Catlin, who commanded the Sixth Marines that day, was evacuated after a German's bullet struck him in the right lung.[47] Two platoons of the Sixth Regiment assaulted across the wheat field toward Bouresches in four waves, the first and second armed with automatic rifles and grenades, while the third and fourth carrying 1903 Springfield rifles. Thomas Boyd, an enlisted man with First Battalion, Sixth Regiment, remembered: "They attacked, four short waves of sweating men in olive drab, stalking across that unfriendly wheat field. Men dropped without a sound and the four lines merged into three, two, one. When they reached the gray stone buildings of the town there were twenty soldiers on their feet."[48] Lieutenant Cates, a future Commandant of the Marine Corps, nearly died leading his company to take Bouresches. "We charged across an open field for eight hundred yards," he wrote to his family, "and there were eleven machine guns playing on us. . . . [Bullets] hitting the ground were as thick as rain drops—one hit me solid on the helmet—denting a dent in it the size of an egg—it knocked me cold for a minute."[49] One of his Marines revived him, and Cates carried on the attack.

Brigadier General Harbord ordered the initial attacks on Hill 142, Bouresches, and Belleau Wood without appropriate artillery support, leading to horrific casualties. General John Pershing, commander of the American Expeditionary Forces (AEF), along with Harbord and his subordinate Marine commanders were proponents of "open warfare," which emphasized massive infantry assaults on major objectives. Machine guns, artillery, and trench mortars had sent British, French, and German troops into trenches, which led to tactical stalemates along the western front. But the commanders of the AEF and its Second Division were determined to make progress with the rifle, the bayonet, and the infantryman, often without adequate artillery support.[50] Marines did not make serious progress into the woods until June 10, after friendly artillery had "blown the Bois de Belleau to mincemeat."[51]

During and immediately after Belleau Wood, a new moniker for Marines appeared: *Teufel Hunden*, German for "Devil Dog." It is not clear exactly when, where, or by whom this nickname appeared, but it seems connected with these Marine/AEF assault tactics on the western front. According to Marine private Francis A. Williams, German prisoners told him "how surprised they were to see us keep coming through their machine gun fire, while the French always retreated. They thought we were devils, and that is where we got this nickname of 'Devil Dogs.'"[52] There are no known German sources that corroborate these claims. By June 11, the Marines had taken nearly 400 prisoners, transferring them through the lines under guard.[53] With that many prisoners passing through the lines, it is possible that "Teufel Hunden" was heard somewhere by someone and then spread from there, but it is impossible to know for sure.[54]

Germans described Marines at Belleau Wood as good troops who were in fine spirits despite their casualties. "The Qualities of the men individually may be described as remarkable," one soldier admitted, "they are physically well set up, their attitude is good and they range in age from eighteen to twenty-eight years."[55] Marines were brave, which was respectable, but they "lack[ed] at present only training and experience to make formidable adversaries."[56] The Devil Dog nickname stuck, however; it continues to be used to this day as a reference to the frontal assaults the Marines made into Belleau Wood and its environs.

But "Devil Dog" also alluded to courage, which was inseparable from what it meant to be a man on the battlefield, according to Marines who fought in the Great War. The epitome of manliness for Boyd was John Quick, of Cuzco Well (1898) and Vera Cruz (1914) fame. In 1918 Quick was a sergeant major in the Sixth Regiment of Marines. Boyd recalled how, just after a depleted unit of Marines took the ruined town of Bouresches, they called for more ammunition. Boyd recalled Quick responding, "We'll take 'em a whole truckload." The sergeant major organized the loading of a creaky old wagon, pulled by a team of mules, with as much ammunition and ordnance as it could hold. Over gullies, rocks, and craters and through hellacious artillery and machine-gun fire, Quick drove the mules onward. The resupply effort could have easily failed. With all of the machine-gun fire and shelling in that area, it would not have taken much to incapacitate one or both mules—not to mention the cargo itself was highly combustible. But onward went Quick until he made it to Bouresches and resupplied the besieged Marines.

The young man witnessed Quick demonstrate all the hallmarks of Marine manliness: courage, confidence, selflessness, and self-control.

"Once more he had performed great service at great risk; once more he was decorated for bravery," wrote Boyd some years later. The sergeant major did not risk his life for medals or notoriety, but to help his fellow Marines. "And Quick? He said nothing about it; he had accomplished only his duty; *semper fidelis*, that was all."[57]

Marines had a long summer of sacrifice ahead of them as they and the AEF continued to use such tactics. The Second Division and its Marine brigade assaulted headlong into German positions at Soissons in mid-July. The Fifth Regiment of Marines took the town of Vierzy, followed by the Sixth Regiment's advance that pushed the allied lines forward almost a mile. Sergeant Arthur Ganoe wrote that he was terrified at the Battle of Soissons. During the division's assault under heavy German artillery fire, he came to an inflection point. He had just seen a shell decapitate a fellow Marine, so he paused briefly and vomited. At the same time, inside himself, "a battle between fear and duty was fought then and there—a brief, but painful fight." Knowing that he could die if he turned and ran just as easily as if he simply pressed forward, Ganoe decided that he "would rather be a dead hero than a dead coward."[58] He wrote that the young Marines at Soissons had developed "an old man's realization of the mournful beauty of all this sacrifice and devotion."[59] Ganoe would survive the battle, but his unit would be put out of commission temporarily. The frontal assaults at Soissons almost ground the Marines as well as the entire Second Division into dust. The Fourth Brigade suffered more casualties at Soissons (2,015 men) than at Belleau Wood.[60] "In June the Second Division had spent three weeks in the line in Belleau Wood," explains one recent historian. "At Soissons, it lasted two days before collapsing in exhaustion and having to be withdrawn."[61]

Until the armistice, Marines fought and died steadily alongside their army comrades as the allied armies kept up an intense and steady offensive along the western front. After a brief period of rest and refitting, along with taking on replacements, the Fourth Brigade participated in another frontal assault at Saint-Mihiel in September (903 casualties), then again at Mont Blanc in October (2,369 casualties). By early November, Marines on the front lines were aware of the peace talks, and no one wanted to be the last man killed. Corporal John E. Ausland of the Fifth Regiment wrote on November 9, "if, between this hour and the hour of the armistice we attack again, it will be just plain, damn, deliberate murder."[62]

Murder is what they got. Private Francis Williams recalled a sergeant who witnessed a Marine killed just before the war ended. A shell hit the young man below the waist and blew him in half. The sergeant was the first man to get to the poor Marine, who asked him to dress the wound. "Lad, you cannot live but a few minutes," the sergeant replied. With an astonishing smile on his face, the dying Marine looked up and spoke his last words, "Sergeant, this is a hell of place for a fellow to die isn't it?" For Williams, that unfortunate Marine's fate "goes to show the splendid courage of the men we sent 'Over There.'"[63]

Marines would eventually be awarded five Medals of Honor from the army and at least four from the navy. Sergeant Major Ernest A. Janson, Sergeant Matej Kocak, Corporal John H. Pruitt, and Private John J. Kelly received one each from the army or navy. Their citations all mention conspicuous gallantry, quick action, initiative, and the killing of German troops. Several hundred Marines won the army's Distinguished Service Cross, while the French government awarded 1,237 of them Croix de Guerre medals. The Croix de Guerre citations for the Fourth Marine Brigade referenced the overall character of the men in its composite units, not their physical or masculine traits. The Marines achieved success because of their "brilliant courage, vigor, dash, and tenacity."[64] By referencing the men's character under fire and in the face of danger, these medals reflected the value placed on manliness in war.

November 11, 1918, dawned on the Marines as they began their last hours of the Meuse-Argonne campaign (1,218 casualties).[65] Offensive tactics dominated European and American tactical thinking throughout the war.[66] Marines were quite susceptible to the allure of offensive doctrine as well, even before the United States declared war on Germany. In 1916 Major John H. Russell had asked, "Why should we not have a 'cult' of the Offensive?"[67] Russell got his wish on the fields of France, and the Marines paid for it. The AEF's offensive tactics resulted in the highest casualties the Marines had ever suffered in their entire existence up to that point: 11,968 officers and enlisted men.[68] Yet these casualty figures became a testament to Marine character and manhood more so than the number of awards they won.

Shortly after the armistice, three veteran Marines—Kemper F. Cowing, Courtney Ryley Cooper, and Morgan Dennis—published *"Dear Folks at Home—": The Glorious Story of the United States Marines in France as Told by Their Letters from the Battlefield.* Cowing compiled wartime letters penned by Marines, Dennis provided illustrations, and Cooper served as the editor. The book is full of gendered imagery presented in prose and graphic art. They selected letters suitable for public consumption, which transformed them from personal missives into public expressions of Marine manliness. Through these, the book also captures a carefully curated version of Marines' combat experience.

Cowing and Cooper used the selected letters to tell a glorious story of the brave, young American Marines who stopped the German drive on Paris in the summer of 1918. For much of the collection, they offer ripping yarns of combat, danger, and Marine prowess. There was no cynicism or irony in these letters, which would become common themes in post–Great War literature.[69] These accounts were full of bravado to show readers the stuff of which Marines were made. Private Walter Scott Hiller expressed this pride to his mother when he wrote home from the front, "Do you think any man would regret being a part of such an organization, that have proven to be real fighters, that can go up against the Kaiser's best-equipped and well-trained forces and give them the defeat we did? Not this man."[70]

These letters from Marines not only express notions of manhood and sacrifice but also occasionally describe combat as enjoyable, despite the danger. Lieutenant Merwin Silverthorne told his family that his men were happy to go over the top and fight the Germans: "The first time I went 'over the top' was on June 6th. Oh, what a happy bunch we were! I and the best friend I had were shaking hands with one another, happy and exultant in the fact that at last we were 'going over.'" When Silverthorne's buddy (Steve Sherman, a fellow Marine) died from machine-gun fire during their assault across a wheat field, "he had met his end, but he met it like a hero, an American, and a man."[71] The lieutenant's friend apparently died happy, at least according to the Marines who saw him fall: "they all are unanimous in saying he fell fighting with his face toward the enemy and a smile on his face."[72] Corporal John F. Pinson's letter also speaks of Marines enjoying the battle because it got them out of the trenches and into open warfare: "It was a real battle, and being in the open through wheat-fields and farm lands, was much to the Americans' liking."[73]

Apparently, Marines like Pinson felt comfortable charging across a field with bayonets fixed, closing with their enemy. "The boys all swung into action," he wrote, "laughing and kidding each other as they charged the German machine guns as if they were at a drill, dropping every twenty yards or so to rake the German lines with rifle and machine-gun fire."[74] The editors of the collection must have found this last quotation particularly inspiring. They used a drawing by Dennis to depict the very scene Pinson described. The Marines in this picture seem happy conducting the attack, exploding shells notwithstanding.

Cowing and Cooper used other images by Morgan to depict scenes

"THE BOYS ALL SWUNG INTO ACTION LAUGHING AND
KIDDING EACH OTHER"

Fig. 29. *The Boys All Swung into Action Laughing and
Kidding Each Other*, by Morgan Dennis. From Kemper F.
Cowing, comp., *"Dear Folks at Home—": The Glorious
Story of the United States Marines in France as Told by Their
Letters from the Battlefield*, ed. Courtney R. Cooper (New
York: Houghton Mifflin, 1919), 160.

of aggression and bravery that Marines described in their letters.
Private E. A. Wahl wrote: "The spirit of our men is wonderful. It is
beyond the wildest imagination. They walk right into the rifle and
machine-gun fire in the most matter-of-fact way. They have just taken
the Boches off their feet."[75] Captain George W. Hamilton wrote about
the first day of the Battle of Belleau Wood (June 6, 1918), when his
company assaulted across a wheat field under heavy German machine-
gun fire. The Forty-Ninth Company, Fifth Regiment of Marines

"IT WAS ONLY BECAUSE WE RUSHED THE POSITIONS THAT
WE WERE ABLE TO TAKE THEM"

Fig. 30. *It Was Only because We Rushed*, by Morgan
Dennis. From Kemper F. Cowing, comp., *"Dear
Folks at Home—": The Glorious Story of the United
States Marines in France as Told by Their Letters from
the Battlefield*, ed. Courtney R. Cooper (New York:
Houghton Mifflin, 1919), 127.

suffered heavy casualties that day. But his account, accompanied by
a drawing of a Marine charging a German machine-gun crew, gives
the impression that this was just another day of courage and prowess.
"It was only because we rushed the positions that we were able to take
them," Hamilton claimed, "as there were too many guns to take in any
other way."[76]

Another image depicts a story told by Major Henry N. Manney, the
quartermaster of the Sixth Regiment. The battle was deadly, but ac-

cording to Manney, "the Marines lived up to their reputation and even bettered it." "This is open warfare, just our style, and nothing could be finer than the way our men went to it."[77] The image that accompanies this letter depicts a Marine zealously protecting a wounded comrade. Together they lay next to a thicket, with artillery shells bursting midair in the background. The wounded Marine stares off into the distance, while dogged determination marks the face of his friend, protective but still fighting.

To Cowing, Cooper, and Dennis, tales of bravery and sacrifice meant Marines were exceptional men. Lieutenant Silverthorne wrote of losing some of his friends in combat. "A pang of deep sorrow will always pierce my heart when I think of some of my bosom friends," he reflected, "men young in years, but men from the ground up, who have made the supreme sacrifice."[78]

Their sacrifices on the battlefields of France revealed that Marines' identity went deeper than their warrior image. One of the book's creators wrote:

> And these letters, with their optimism, with their cheer and their smiles, show that the Marines who were battling against the Hun were something more than fighters. They were men—men in action and men in thought, men who were big enough men to be tender and gentle, and who, while those they left behind "keep the home fires burning," help to supply the spark that gives life to the flame of hope.[79]

The level of hope and emotion conveyed in their letters home meant the men's fighting spirit was restrained enough to hold on to their humanity. They had not given into the barbarism that American propaganda claimed had corrupted Germany's manhood.

Lieutenant Silverthorne claimed in a letter to his parents after the Battle of Belleau Wood that combat had made a man out of him. Facing death as a Marine was "an experience that has changed me overnight, from a youth seeking adventure to a man who has shaken dice with death."[80] Corporal Willard P. Nelligan wrote home after Belleau Wood that fighting the Germans had forced young men to mature quickly. "I know from that battle that they (the Germans) are whipped, because those kids (men now every one of them), in the face of that awful machine-gun fire, hollered at the top of their voices, ducked in, and came up hollering for more," he wrote. "The Germans can't stop that spirit."[81] The idea here, and the image pitched to the public, was that

"THIS IS OPEN WARFARE, JUST OUR STYLE"

Fig. 31. *This Is Open Warfare, Just Our Style*, by Morgan Dennis. From Kemper F. Cowing, comp., *"Dear Folks at Home—": The Glorious Story of the United States Marines in France as Told by Their Letters from the Battlefield*, ed. Courtney R. Cooper (New York: Houghton Mifflin, 1919), 137.

with courage, grit, and luck, these Marines had survived the rigors of training and combat and had come out the other end stronger. Taken at face value, the war and the Marine Corps gave them the opportunity to prove themselves men.

Although using letters from the front, *Dear Folks at Home* should not be taken as representative of the Fourth Marine Brigade's experience in combat. The creators of that book compiled and published only letters that portrayed the Corps in the best light, those that espoused the hallmarks of idealized wartime manliness. Its overall message is that the Marines who fought did so bravely, and those who died did

so honorably. By using only positive letters to paint the war as beneficial to the men who fought it, however, the book is best regarded as
propaganda. It was a part of an early wave of postwar American books
that, even though sacrifice was a significant part of the stories told,
nevertheless emphasized the benefits of war over the human costs. But
very different interpretations would come out later.

Passing the Test

Floyd Gibbons, a *Chicago Tribune* correspondent embedded with the
Marines at Belleau Wood, also provided significant accounts of combat
and sacrifice. He wrote that the Marines attacked German positions
with shoulders squared, heads down, and rifles and bayonets pointed
forward, and they paid the price for it: "In such fashion did the Marines go through the Bois de Belleau. Their losses were heavy, but they
did the work. The sacrifice was necessary. Paris was in danger. The
Marines constituted the thin line between the enemy and Paris. The
Marines not only held that line—they pushed it forward."[82] Inspired by
their courage, tenacity, and sacrifice, Gibbons would go on to portray
the Marines as prime examples of American fighting manhood.

Sacrificing their own lives, in part, won Marines great acclaim despite official policies regarding press censorship. General Pershing's
press policy followed U.S. government guidelines laid out in part by
the Committee on Public Information. The committee dictated that
no specific information regarding individual units could be reported
by American journalists.[83] Reporters, however, could label troops as
"Marines" or "soldiers" if they omitted designations of division, regiment, or battalion. Through this censorship loophole, the American
public in June 1918 received joyous news of U.S. Marines defeating the
Germans in battle. Floyd Gibbons had much to do with this public-
relations boon.[84] After Marines successfully assaulted Hill 142 in the
early morning hours of June 6, he sent a brief report of it to Paris,
which then went on to the United States. The front page of the *Chicago
Tribune* that day read, "U.S. Marines Smash Huns: Gain Glory in Brisk
Fight on the Marne."[85] That evening Gibbons accompanied the Fifth
Marine Regiments' assault into Belleau Wood. A German machine-
gunner shot the reporter three times—twice in the left arm and once
in the left eye. A few hours later Gibbons crawled to safety under the
cover of darkness.[86]

What happened once news reached the States of the Marines "victory" (the battle was not over yet) against the Germans was nothing short of a public-relations dream for the Corps. "The United States Marines were the toast of New York yesterday," the *New York Times* reported. "Everywhere one went in the cars, on the streets, in hotels or skyscrapers, the topic was on the marines, who are fighting with such glorious success in France."[87] Finally, the Marines were the first to prove what many Americans wanted to believe: that American manhood could pass the supreme test of combat. "The battle on the entire front has lifted the Americans into the spotlight and convinced everyone that if needed the Americans have the spirit, dash, and tenacity to fight as well as any living soldiers," proclaimed one column in the *New Orleans Times Picayune*.[88] The Marines "have proved that the American can fight, even if he wasn't brought up to be a soldier," affirmed another article.[89] Marine combat prowess became something to brag about, something that made Americans feel good about themselves. People asserted that U.S. Marines had turned the tide of the war. The *New York Tribune Review* reported, "The European battlefield has seen no omen carrying such portent to the German nation as the small but sweeping victory by American troops."[90]

World War I brought more positive attention to the Marine Corps than any other event in the service's history up to that point.[91] Marine manliness, performed and demonstrated on the battlefields of France, was central to that popularity.[92] "What sort of men are they?" asked Reginald W. Kauffman, a journalist for the *Living Age*. "'The best,' they will say—and, after living among them, I am not so sure that they are wrong."[93] Gibbons wrote that the Marines at Belleau Wood convinced the enemy that Americans were a superior class of men. "The German has met the American on the battlefield of France and knows that man for man, the American soldier is better," he boasted.[94]

Gibbons constructed one of the most significant and powerful images of the Great War–era Marine Corps. Unlike Vera Cruz (1914) and the battles that came a generation later in World War II, there were no heroic photographs taken of Marines in France. But Gibbons's description of a Marine gunnery sergeant's talk to his men right before they attacked across the machine-gun-swept wheat fields created an indelible image:

> The minute for the Marine advance was approaching. An old gunnery sergeant commanded the platoon in the absence of a lieutenant, who had been shot and was out of the fight. This old sergeant was a Marine veteran. His cheeks were bronzed with the wind and

sun of the seven seas. The service bar across his left breast showed that he had fought in the Philippines, in Santo Domingo, at the walls of Pekin[g], and in the streets of Vera Cruz. I make no apologies for his language. . . . To me his words were classic, if not sacred. As the minute for the advance arrived, he arose from the trees first and jumped out onto the exposed edge of that field that ran with lead, across which he and his men were to charge. Then he turned to give the charge order to the men of his platoon—his mates—the men he loved. He said: "Come on, you sons-o'-bitches! Do you want to live forever?"[95]

Gunnery Sergeant Daniel J. Daly is thought to be the Marine described by Gibbons.[96] By 1918, Daly had been in the Corps for nineteen years. He won his first Medal of Honor in China during the Boxer Rebellion in 1900 and his second in Haiti in 1915. Daly was the epitome of what a tough expeditionary Marine should be among his contemporaries.[97] Through this gunnery sergeant, Gibbons would help paint the soldiers of the sea as fearless and heroic men.

French accolades lent further credence to the notion that American manhood had passed the test of war. The government of France renamed Belleau Wood "Le Bois de la Brigade de Marine" in honor of the victory "where the American Marines vanquished the flower of the Kaiser's army."[98] Their success inspired their allies. "The Americans advanced in a solid phalanx, their strong determined faces and great physique an inspiration to their gallant French comrades," claimed the *Washington Post*.[99] The famous French painter Georges Scott created *La Brigade Marine Americaine au Bois de Belleau* to commemorate the U.S. victory there.[100] Full of the detritus and drab colors of modern war, the artwork presents a powerful scene of Marines driving the Germans before them. The Germans, so often depicted as monsters in other images, are shown reeling in defeat.

Lady Leathernecks

From 1917 to 1918, American society mobilized on a scale not seen since the Civil War to help defeat Germany. Men who left their jobs in the fields, factories, and offices to fight needed replacing somehow, as the war necessitated the increased production of food and matériel. An editorial for the *New Republic* had an answer to the labor shortage: "It is now incumbent upon us to see how far we can substitute the labor of

Fig. 32. *La Brigade Marine Americaine au Bois de Belleau*, by Georges Scott, 1919.

women for that of men."[101] As women began entering the work force in greater (though not dramatic) numbers they entered the armed forces as well.[102]

Secretary Daniels authorized the enlistment of women into the U.S. Navy in early 1917, and there were over two hundred female sailors by the time Congress declared war on Germany.[103] Marine Corps expansion and its wartime activities increased the volume of paperwork and made administrative duties substantially more complex. Added to the administrative mess were the many requests from Marine clerks for transfers to fight in France before the war ended. On August 2, 1918, Major General Barnett requested authorization from Daniels to begin enlisting women in the Marine Corps Reserve, "where their services might be utilized to replace men who may be qualified for active field service."[104] Recruiters had already used women, sometimes even wearing Marine uniforms, to motivate men to enlist since the United States entered the war. But now women could enlist and wear the uniform officially. On August 13, 1918, Opha Mae Johnson became the first woman to join the Marine Corps.[105]

Female Marines served on clerical and recruiting duty in the United States between August 1918 and August 1919. According to Cowing and Cooper, women enlisted in the Corps so that "a real 'he-man leatherneck,' as the Marines call themselves, might take up his gun and march away to war."[106] Once given authorization, recruiters began targeting women to enlist with slogans like "Free a Man to Fight."[107] They sought out only "women of excellent character, neat appearance, and with some business of office experience."[108] By November 1918, only 277 female Marines served on active duty; it is not known just how many male Marines they had replaced, if any, so the men could go to France.

The idea that female Marines would only work office jobs and recruiting duty conformed with the traditional gender roles of the time. As Heather Venable has argued, the addition of women in the Corps "symbolically created a division of labor based on gender, reinforcing the image of the male Marine as a fighter."[109] Women had never served in the Corps before (at least not officially), and there were fears that military service would cause an upheaval in American gender relations.[110] Service in the armed forces, long understood as an exclusively masculine domain, might cause women to pick up masculine vices or, even worse, lose their femininity. Their service might even help them accumulate civic credibility and lead to greater cries for woman's suffrage. The Corps, however, made sure that enlisted women maintained their feminine appearances and qualities. Female Marines would wear heels instead of hobnail boots, long skirts instead of trousers, and even though "a man's work will be required of all feminine Marines," they would be exempted from "heavy muscular work."[111]

The September 1918 cover of the *Recruiters' Bulletin* conveys this idea well. In her skirt and heels, a female Marine takes over the domain of office work while a male Marine, equipped with his rifle and campaign hat, is out the door to fulfill his traditional gender role of warfighting. *The Girl He Left Behind* is a Marine, but more importantly, she is still feminine and ready, as he is, to do her part in winning the war.

Although female Marines of the Great War era did not attend boot camp or train to shoot or construct field fortifications like their male comrades, they nonetheless participated actively in promoting the Corps's masculine image.[112] As members of the "gentler sex," they were considered ladies first, Marines second. "Since that fateful day last August when for the first time a lily white hand was raised at the Devil Dog recruiting station while a feminine voice sang out in dulcet tones 'I do,'" according to the *Recruiters' Bulletin*, male Marines had been curious to know more about these women. "What are they like, these lady leathernecks, these hundred percent feminine Hun hunters?"[113]

Corporal Martha Wilchinski helped shape the public's and the

Fig. 33. *The Girl He Left Behind.* From *Recruiters' Bulletin*, September 1918, cover page.

Corps's own perceptions of Great War–era female Marines. Wilchinski served as one of the editors of the *Recruiters' Bulletin* and the *Marines' Bulletin*—a short-term revamping of the *Recruiters' Bulletin* to a wider Marine audience beginning in November 1918—where she published short stories and letters to her fictional fiancé, "Bill." Using a comedic tone for her namesake literary alter ego "Martha," she writes of the trials and tribulations of a young female Marine getting used to the masculine world of the Corps. "I've got the greatest news,

Fig. 34. *Martha the Marine! The Uniform Is the Thing!* From *Marines' Bulletin*, November 1918, 31.

Bill," she states in one her first published letters. "Are you ready? Well, then—I'm a lady leatherneck; I'm the last word in hun-hunters; I'm a real, live, honest-to-goodness Marine!" Martha's prose is full of confidence. "Well, if a regiment of Marines can make the Germans stand on their bone heads and yell 'kamerad,'" she boasts, "can you imagine what a regiment of female Marines can do?" To a certain extent, the Corps has changed her. In an implicit jab at its reputation for sternness among its men, she concludes, "I can't sign myself as affectionately as I used to Bill, you understand, I'm a soldier now and you wouldn't want me to do anything that wasn't in the manual."[114]

But Wilchinski had not parted with her feminine ways completely. In a cartoon of her, entitled *Martha the Marine!*, she is presented as a woman who has joined the Corps not because of the traditional masculine reasons such as being the first to fight or to kill Germans, but because "they have the prettiest uniform!" She imagines that the uniform would look good on her and attract male admiration. The punchline of the cartoon, however, is that the uniform does not fit. In another letter to Bill, Martha writes, "When I put my uniform on I looked like a physical map of Colorado."[115] But this is highly disappointing for Martha: "You know I joined the Marine Corps so I could get my clothes for nothing."[116]

Martha is a woman in a masculine world, hence her comedic appeal. She writes of situations in which Marines struggled to get used to her presence. In one story Corporal Martha reports for sea duty on the USS *Arizona*. She approaches the officer of the deck: "'You're reporting for duty?' he asked incredulously. He was looking down at a blushing and stammering Marine; rank: corporal; sex: female."[117] This encounter leaves the officer tongue tied. He calls for one of the orderlies and says, "Turn this man—er—lady—er—Marine over to the first sergeant."[118] Martha then goes on about getting acquainted with ship life. She is introduced to hammocks, guard duty, and inspections. Morgan Dennis illustrated this story with several images that convey the surprise Marines probably had encountering their first woman in a men's institution.

In another letter to Bill, Martha writes of an awkward encounter she had with a Marine lieutenant in front of an elevator. As the doors opened, Martha and the officer dithered and just looked at each other, not sure what to do.

> Now, here's the question. If I am a lady and he's a gentleman, I go first. If he's an officer and I'm a corporal, he goes first. It all depends on how you look at it. I didn't know how he'd take it, so I thought I'd wait and see what he'd do. I guess he thought the same thing. So we both stood there eyeing each other up on the right oblique. Then he stepped forward and I stepped back. Then he stepped back and I stepped forward. Then we both stepped back. I was getting pretty dizzy by that time. I guess he was, too.[119]

In the end they both entered the elevator simultaneously. This incident illuminates two things: first, that regardless of rank, women were not seen as equals in the Corps. This situation would have been completely different, perhaps, if it involved only two male Marines. Second, Martha and the officer were faced with a conundrum. What takes precedent—traditional American gender relations or Marine Corps customs and courtesies? The officer was not sure whether to treat Martha like a lady or to treat her like a subordinate. The very fact that she was a woman forced him to vacillate on Marine protocol regarding officer and enlisted relations.

Nevertheless, the presence of these women enhanced the Marines' masculine wartime image. The November 1918 cover of the *Marines' Bulletin* presents an image of a female Marine walking arm-in-arm with

"It's a very simple thing—provided
you are a trapeze swinger."

"See that each man
has a hat, shoes
and a shave,"
said the
Major.

Fig. 35. *Martha on Ship*, by Morgan Dennis. From
Marines' Bulletin, January 1919, 7–8.

a male Marine as though she is guiding him into the future. The image provides a contrast between the two. She is smiling and dressed in the Corps's female uniform, while he is in dress blues, serious, straight faced, reserved, and saluting goodbye to the woman on his right. On the surface this image represents the Publicity Bureau's temporary switch from the *Recruiters' Bulletin* to the *Marines' Bulletin*. But it also illuminates how Marines perceived the service of their new female comrades. These women had a supporting role within the Corps and helped male Marines perform their duties. They also signified how the Great War had changed the Corps. Wartime necessitated the employment of more and more members of American society, women included. And so it was with the Marines. This was a new Corps, one with room for women who, instead of weakening the Marines' masculine image, threw it into greater relief.

Female Marines were not entirely shielded from the realities of war, however. Pearl Chandley Oagley was one of the first women who enlisted to help with recruiting. She worked directly for Colonel A. S. McLemore, who oversaw the Publicity Bureau. Oagley hung posters, talked to men on the street, and participated in parades. Part of her job and that of the other female Marines, however, involved writing letters to Marines in France. "A lot of spare time was spent writing to our service men," Oagley recalled, "for we realized that good letters did help a lot as we worked and waited for our boys to come home." As August turned to September, then October to November, these women became more aware of the human toll of the war. "We took this all very seriously, we had no inkling the war would not last long," she said. "Many did not get back." While Wilchinski, who made the Corps appear fun and comical published stories, Oagley handled casualty correspondence. She wrote letters of encouragement to wounded Marines in France and forwarded news of those killed in action to their families. "It was not a fun job," Oagley admitted, but she and her comrades "instinctively developed a flair for words in such cases, and shared them with the loved ones, their grief, and also the pride of sacrifice made for our country."[120]

The Pride of American Manhood

For many Marines in France, occupation duty kept them busy along the River Rhine until the summer of 1919. Most of them shipped home by August. When they arrived, combat had been over for nine months,

Fig. 36. Cover page of the *Marines' Bulletin*, November 1918.

and most of the other troops had already returned to the States. When the Second Division reached American shores, however, the press treated them like heroes.

On August 8, 1919, the Second Division, comprising both army infantry and Marines, marched in New York City in a grand parade. Leading the column was the division commander, Major General Lejeune, astride a bay charger. The parade drew huge crowds of people who cheered them on, waved American flags, and pelted the troops with roses. "This beats hand grenades," a Marine sergeant reportedly said after catching some flowers for himself. Lejeune greeted the crowds with broad smiles and waves as the Marine general led his division down the street and through the throngs of people to where the president, the secretary of the navy, the Commandant of the Marine Corps, and other high-ranking military officers waited to review the troops. Near the public library stood the reviewing stand and about five hundred wounded veterans of the war. The crowds cheered even louder when they saw Lejeune remove his hat and nod in tribute to them.[121]

Four days later the Marines marched in Washington, D.C. "Here come the Marines!" many cried as the Fourth Marine Brigade began to approach the reviewing stand, led this time by Brigadier General William C. Neville. "West Pointers never marched with more dash or vim than did these men," a reporter claimed. "Everyone agreed that a finer body of men was never seen in Fifth Avenue than the men commanded by Neville," his account read. As the column passed the reviewing stand, the wounded Marine veterans standing near the public library "simply went wild." Major General Barnett stood next to Assistant Secretary of the Navy Franklin D. Roosevelt. Roosevelt turned to Barnett and said, "I never saw a finer looking body of men and I never witnessed a more inspiring parade." The Commandant replied, "No wonder the Germans lost."[122]

The Marines became a source of national pride. They did not defeat the Germans on their own, of course. The army deserved more credit than it received from the press, despite attempts of some Marines and journalists to correct misinformation.[123] But people frequently connected the Corps to Germany's defeat. The *Washington Post* published poems that credited the European victory solely to the Marines. Isabel Likens Gates wrote one about the Marine fight at Belleau Wood:

> Awful and fierce the combat raged.
> As the huns came, wave on wave,
> Against our men, and steel to steel,
> Mid shot and shell, they'd break and reel
> And at last before us gave.
> Our loss was great, but it sealed the fate
>   Of the Huns—and the world esteems
> Like Spartans of old this tale will be told
>   Of Uncle Sam's marines.[124]

The battles in the summer of 1918 were fresh in Bessie B. Croffut's mind as she praised the returning Fourth Brigade. She called them "invincibles" who, with courage, blood, and righteousness, "stayed the Hun and there his lesson taught." Croffut celebrated the moral and mental strength of the Marine Corps, "where brave men battle for the right and true," and finished with, "there's not a thing on earth U.S. Marines can't do!"[125] Marines had worked hard to get the American public to associate manliness and combat readiness with the Corps. Published work like this suggests that the prestige they sought before the war had finally been obtained.

A crucial aspect of their newfound prestige was the kind of men Marines were. By the war's end, former sergeant, now major Thomas G. Sterrett served as the lead editor of the *Marines' Bulletin*. He and his team began soliciting journalists, politicians, and others from around the country to comment on the prowess of the Marines in the war, publishing the responses in the *Bulletin*. The December 1918 issue was a celebratory one that highlighted Marine victories in recruiting, in advertising, and in France. The editors even collected a dozen magazine covers that showcased the Corps's masculine image. Marines appeared on the covers of the *Independent, Cosmopolitan*, and the *National Magazine*, which indicated how far the Corps had come in terms of public recognition. It further reveals the extent to which Marines reached new heights of popularity at the same time as military manliness.

Good publicity was the goal, so Sterrett and his team collected and published positive responses that commented on the manliness of Marines. Kenneth C. Beaton of *Hearst's Magazine* called the U.S. Marine a "first-class fighting man" while Theodore Niver of the *New York Evening Post* compared them to the Spartans at the Battle of Thermopylae. Frederick Palmer, an American war correspondent, wrote that the Marines' victories, particularly at Belleau Wood, demonstrated the superiority of American men over Germans in combat. "They are known as fighters second to none among the troops of the Allies," W. S. Baker of the Salvation Army wrote. "They have shed honor and glory upon American Arms." The only Marines who complained in the field hospital where Elsie Janis worked during the war were the ones who lost limbs "and would not be able to go back and get even!"[126]

Another collection of praise came in the from advertising experts who linked the Corps's publicity and appeal to its manly reputation and masculine image. The power of its advertising, wrote William H. Rankin, the president of his own advertising agency, was that the Corps built it "around a central, well considered idea—the readiness and the ability of the U.S. Marines to fight."[127] The Marines were "picked men, an all-star team, world champion's among soldiers," according to one

Fig. 37. Marines on the covers of national magazines. From *Marines'
Bulletin*, December 1918, 71.

magazine writer. The Corps's slogan "First to Fight" attracted the very best potential soldiers, "the cream and flower of American manhood," who knew that becoming a Marine would test their mettle as men.[128] The service appealed to young men in the cities, towns, and farms of America. When the Marines wanted for volunteers, "red-blooded, 'he-men' responded to the call."[129] Another respondent wrote that putting on the Marine uniform meant "dressing up in the garb of clean, honest, unfaltering manhood" and that there was no greater honor a man could obtain than becoming a Marine.[130]

Many respondents saw Marine battlefield prowess as representative of American manliness. Horace Lorimer of the *Saturday Evening Post* wrote that the actions of the Marines in France, side by side with the U.S. Army, proved that the AEF was "a man's army" and that "nothing could sum it up better; nothing finer could be said about it."[131] The Marines quoted Melville E. Stone, the general manager of the Associated Press, with saying that "they saved Paris, they seriously injured the morale of the best German troops and they set the standard and fixed a reputation for American troops that none other dared tarnish."[132] Harkening back to the type of manhood in which worth was measured by production more so than by consumption, one advertiser wrote: "They have produced. They have been equal to the great cause. They are the personification of the American spirit."[133] Marines "revealed to the world . . . that this great non-militant nation could produce the finest fighting men on the globe, and must henceforth be regarded, not as an easy mark for militaristic aggression, but as a giant in capacity to do as well [as] in strength."[134] Major Sterrett and his team continued to collect as much praise as they could well into 1919.

When the editors of the *Recruiters' Bulletin* asked governors from around the country to record their thoughts on the Corps, especially its performance in the Great War, many of their responses were unequivocal. "In the Marine, the bloody Hun met his master," Frederick D. Gardner of Missouri proclaimed, "the dauntless courage, the intrepidity and the dash of the Marines . . . filled the German soldiery with fear, sent a thrill through the armies of democracy and struck the world with wonder and amazement."[135] If American manhood defeated Germany, then Marines were among its best examples.

Not only did the Marines win, but they also supposedly kept their bodies and honor clean while doing it. "Our boys are the bravest of the brave," Sergeant Ganoe wrote, "they fight hard and clean, in a crusading spirit that wins."[136] This is what Marines claimed in print anyway, which went right along with their promise to benefit the men who joined the Corps. The U.S. government also promised the nation that military life would be good for American men. The Commissions on Training Camp Activities aimed "to make the men fit for fighting, and after, to bring them back from war as fine and as clean as they went."[137] That meant keeping them away from sexual encounters with prostitutes. Contracting venereal diseases while in service would sully the reputation of American men coming home from war. As of 1919, Marines at least appeared to have resisted such temptations. The Corps had become an example of a healthy, clean, and strong body of men. "The splendid achievements of the Marines in the World War are well known," wrote Hugh M. Dorsey of Georgia. "They were the cleanest and strongest of our young manhood."[138] "The Marine Corps stands for all that is good in the ideals of manhood—for strength, for loyalty, for fidelity and for cleanliness in mind and body," Colorado governor Oliver H. Shoup asserted. "If you are a he-man, if you want action—enlist in the Marines!"[139] The Corps enjoyed high popularity after the war because it convinced many that it included some of the hardiest specimens of American manhood available, unsullied by the potentially deleterious effects of war.

Prominent officials seemed more convinced that wartime Marines had improved their character and their health. They had "demonstrated the incalculable value of military training as an aid to character building, and to the highest degree of physical fitness," claimed Governor Simon Bamberger of Utah, "therefore the benefits attending the training of the Marines are obvious in view of the fact that he is probably the most efficiently and variedly trained soldier in the world."[140] Some Americans wrote that the Marines benefited the nation's manhood because they transformed young boys into men in their own image. Therefore, they learned from the Corps how to live an honorable and successful life. "Any young man who enters the Marine Corps gains entrance into a selected company of manly, virile and helpful Americans," the governor of Maryland wrote. "He is finding a career full of honor and opportunity."[141]

A cartoon image entitled *Honest Pride* shows a diminutive Marine private who had just entered the Corps looking up to a sergeant who is taller and has a thicker chest, broader shoulders, and stronger jawline. The new Marine is impressed by the veteran's medals and exclaims, "Gosh, I'd never have room on my chest for all them medals." The old timer replies: "Don't worry; you'll have enough chest when you're with us a while. We guarantee to put a chest on an eel."[142] This contrast in body types conveys the physical attributes men supposedly

Fig. 38. *Honest Pride*. From *Recruiters' Bulletin*, December 1919, 21.

gained while in the Corps. In addition, the sergeant's service in the Great War adds to his masculinity and prestige. In the background is a picture of him wearing the uniform that Marines wore on the western front, with combat medals on his chest.

Of course, not all Marines could live up to this level of hyperbole. Court-martial records tell of alternative stories. In 1918 throughout the Corps (not just in France), 2,395 Marines faced courts-martial.

This meant that the number of triable offenses went up that year from 1,995 in 1917 and 1,856 in 1916.[143] According to the annual report of the secretary of the navy, 555 enlisted Marines received convictions for a variety of offenses. The most frequent convictions involved desertion, absence without leave, and sleeping on post: 66, 95, and 102 cases respectively. There were 10 cases of drunkenness and 21 cases of drunkenness on duty. The more serious infractions of manslaughter and assault with a deadly weapon were 3 and 5 cases respectively. There were 26 theft convictions. The U.S. Navy, a much larger institution, not only had more total convictions (4,213) but also more in every category. There were some offenses, such as forgery and sodomy, where the Marine Corps had no convictions compared to the navy's 8 and 19 respectively.[144] Four Marine officers faced court-martial convictions—mostly for drunkenness while on duty—compared to forty-nine navy officers.[145]

The report blamed this larger number of crimes on the increase in personnel. It also made note that the actual percentage of general court-martial trials was down in each service. The navy's ratio decreased from 1.75 percent in 1917 to 1.17 percent in 1918, while the Corps's dropped much more significantly, from 2.72 percent in 1917 to 1.2 percent the following year.[146] Obviously, not all Marines lived up to the public image promulgated by the Publicity Bureau and American newspaper propaganda. But none of these trials had yet to dent the Corps's public profile, meaning its reputation for upright manliness remained unchallenged in the press.

One of the only stories to make the papers of a Marine officer in France being tried before a court-martial was the case of Captain Edmund G. Chamberlain, one of the first Marine aviators. His alleged crimes were "scandalous conduct tending to the destruction of good morals" and "falsehood." Captain Chamberlain claimed to have shot down more German planes during the war than authorities thought credible, which led to his trial and eventual conviction.[147] A much more prominent story regarding courts-martial involved Oregon senator George E. Chamberlain (not related to the captain) who proposed a bill later in 1919 to give clemency and pardons to all convicted soldiers, sailors, and Marines for all minor charges less than a felony.[148] Even more prominent than that at the time were the stories of race riots in Washington, D.C., and elsewhere throughout the country.[149] No significantly controversial case about Marine behavior in France came out during or immediately after the war.

That does not mean that all Marines had acted honorably during the Great War. Some undoubtedly committed offenses in France worthy of a court-martial but went unreported. How many exactly is not known. It is likely that Marines executed German prisoners, but it is impossible to know to what extent or even where or when. After the war Thomas Boyd and William Campbell, two enlisted Marines who had fought at and survived the Battle of Belleau Wood, wove instances of Marines murdering German prisoners into their novels that were inspired by their own experiences in the war.[150]

Years after the Great War, Graves Erskine, by then a retired general, recalled a young Marine who had executed a German prisoner at Belleau Wood without cause. Erskine, a platoon leader in the Sixth Regiment at the time, had ordered the Marine to escort the prisoner at gunpoint to battalion headquarters. When he returned too soon to have completed the task, Erskine confronted him and accused him of shooting the prisoner. The Marine replied, "yes, but I haven't had a chance to kill one of the bastards all day, all they are doing is killing us, and I can't go back to Minnesota and tell them I didn't kill a German."[151] Brigadier General Harbord's memorandum of June 8, 1918, to his Marine officers further suggests that illicit killings took place. "The enemy have been told that Americans do not take prisoners, which makes their men fight to the death rather than surrender when they think they will be given no quarter," he wrote. He reminded his officers that if Marines execute surrendering Germans, it could cost the brigade many unnecessary deaths.[152]

Executing surrendering soldiers represented moral degradation and was completely antithetical to the notion of Marines as paragons of manly virtue. Instead of making men out of boys, the Corps risked looking like it made monsters out of them. These actions would further suggest that Americans were just as susceptible to acting out the brutality associated with German troops in allied propaganda. None of this made it into the newspapers back in the States, however. It would not be until the 1920s that the dichotomy between how the press and the Publicity Bureau portrayed Marine conduct in France and how the servicemen actually behaved would become apparent in the public sphere. Postwar cynicism and irony were on the horizon. As of 1918–20, however, it had yet to develop fully in American public opinion.

For the time being, the heroizing of U.S. soldiers and Marines would continue despite any evidence to the contrary. In his memoirs published within a year of the war's conclusion, Colonel Catlin remarked with pride on how Marines had conducted themselves in battle. They proved to him that the United States still made men of great quality, ones who could proudly stand with the manly generations that came before. "Can we read what our college boys did in Belleau Wood," he asked readers, "without thanking God that the soil trod by Washington and Lincoln, the Pilgrim Fathers and the builders of the great West, can still produce men of such stuff as that?"[153] The Marines' cause was a high and holy one. The United States "went into this war solely to save the ideals of Christianity from destruction," he believed. "It is my country that sent the flower of its manhood to fight and die for that cause."[154] Not long after the war, Reverend F. M. Johnson, a U.S. Navy chaplain, spoke to this sacrifice in verse:

> At the outposts of our Government,
>   Neath the snows or tropic skies,
> You will find the Globe and Anchor men
>   Where e're the Old Flag Flies;
> For these soldiers of the ocean
>   Lie in graves that few have seen,
> But they gave for God and Country,
>   Each one called—U.S. Marine.[155]

Conclusion

The Marine Corps came out of the Great War with a heightened masculine image and a public reputation for combat prowess and morally upright manhood. It had placed Marines in a large and terrible conflict in Europe that tested their mettle as an institution. The war also subjected their usefulness to the court of public opinion. Plenty of Americans saw the Marines who fought and died in France as heroes. The Marines also got the opportunity to construct images of themselves like never before. They did this in part by publishing letters home from the front and drawing pictures of Marines saving civilization or charging across wheat fields. Through their bravery and sacrifice, they had helped prove that American men could fight and win on the battlefield. The war could now be used as a new justification for older claims of manly resolve. Just like before, the American press helped the Corps with this image construction. It is hard to imagine Marines taking as much credit as they did during the Battle of Belleau Wood without the work of Floyd Gibbons. He staged a sweeping public-relations coup for the Corps that put the deeds of fighting Marines on the front page of many American newspapers.

In the public culture of 1918 and 1919, Marines came to embody all the very best of traditional American manhood. Their combat victories inspired citizens to write about them in heroic terms. The old insecurities concerning the weakening of American men that seemed to pervade pre–Great War cultural discourses on manhood fell silent for the time being. The army, the navy, the Marines, and the war helped change all of that for the moment. It is for these reasons that, when one looks at the public face of the Marine Corps in late 1918 and early 1919, one sees a military institution basking in the approbation of the country.

The Corps expanded to unprecedented numbers during the war. Starting with only 13,000 men in April 1917, by August 1918, it sat at an authorized strength of 3,017 officers and 75,500 men, while its actual strength was 67,000 total, including 7,000 reservists. From April 1917 to November 1918, Marine recruiting stations received an unprecedented 239,000 applications for enlistment, over 23,000 in the month of June 1918 alone, which corresponds with Marine combat action at Belleau Wood and all the resulting favorable press. The Marines only accepted just over 60,000 of all the applicants.[156] The secretary of war and the Department of the Navy ordered the Marines to accept draftees for the first time in the Corps's history late in the war, which could have potentially harmed its elite "all-volunteer" reputation. But Marines crafted a way around this by calling the resulting 7,000 draftees "voluntary inductees," meaning that although they had been drafted into the armed forces, they had to "volunteer" to serve in the Marine Corps. Although the War Department accorded the Corps "the privilege of individual induction," Marines retained the right to reject draftees if they did not pass their physical, mental, and moral standards. Only around 6,600 draftees actually became Marines.[157]

American attention soon turned away from war and toward other pressing issues, such as the League of Nations, the influenza pandemic, immigration, prohibition, race relations, and woman's suffrage. While these swirled around in American culture and politics, the Corps demobilized, discharged thousands of volunteers and draftees (including all of the female Marines), and made Major General Lejeune its new Commandant. The airplanes, chemical weapons, machine guns, and rolling barrages of the Great War demonstrated that the Marine Corps had to continue to emphasize the need for intellect *and* physical strength in its ranks. After the war the Corps, as well as the other services, would attempt to educate its enlisted men to make them better fighters and to enhance recruiting. It would claim to remain a fighting man's institution, but one that evolved to place greater emphasis on education and sports, in part to appeal to Americans who had returned to a peacetime mindset.

By 1919, the Marines had drifted out of the public eye. Unfortunately for the Corps, its men would not stay out of the newspapers for long. The Marines fought three small wars simultaneously in the summer and fall of 1918. While the Marines in France won acclaim for themselves and their country, those then in Haiti and the Dominican Republic did not fare so well. Only the war in Europe, however, received any special notice in the press. When public attention swung back its way in late 1919, the Marine Corps had a public-relations nightmare to handle. News of atrocities committed by Marines against Haitians and Dominicans would threaten to undo the reputation the Corps had worked hard to build. This information had serious implications for the Marines and their manly image. Americans would soon be reminded that the Marines—the first to fight, the heroes of Belleau Wood, the saviors of civilization—had a dark side.

Consequences of War and Counterinsurgency

5

Tropicalitis

So come along, you Leatherneck—tell us what you
  know,
Goin' down to Haiti, Bo, to make the niggers dance,
The way you used to strafe the Hun on the fields of
  France?
— *James Bardin, "Hi, There, You Leatherneck!," 1922*

Marines are much exposed to the strange degenerating magic of the
tropical sun. In the generation since the Spanish War our Corps has
never known a day of peace. Marines have grown grey in the banana
wars under the equator while the rest of the country has enjoyed unex-
ampled quiet and prosperity. The history of our Corps is an unwritten
saga of these unofficial wars. But service under the equator exacts its
penalties.
— *John H. Craige*, Black Bagdad

On June 11, 1917, Smithson Taylor of New York City sent a letter to the
Office of the Commandant of the Marine Corps in Washington, D.C.
The previous day Marine Corps Week, the Corps's largest recruiting
drive in its history, had kicked off around the country. Taylor used this
opportunity to tell Major General Barnett precisely how he felt about
the service. "Today's papers are full of praise of the Marine Corps,"
he pointed out. "Until a short time ago, I had considered the Marine
Corps the finest branch of the military service in the U.S.A." But Taylor had recently returned from Marine-occupied Santo Domingo. "I
wish I could give you a movie film of what I saw, to show you why I
have refused to allow my son to join the Marine Corps," he wrote.
There, Marines could always be found at the bar drunk, disorderly,
and unkempt. Occasionally, they bullied the locals. Taylor described
the behavior of one Major Davis as being particularly egregious: "Major Davis sits in that café, with coat open and under-shirt displayed,

then goes out and hits a coachman over the head with a bottle." He implored Barnett to act soon. "For the good name of your Corps, and the hope of someday creating good feeling towards Americans down there," he wrote, "DO SOMETHING." But nothing would be done for the time being.[1]

Taylor had witnessed what many other American observers would see in the coming years: Marines guilty of drunkenness, hair-trigger violence, and assault. The Marine Publicity Bureau had worked hard to persuade Americans that Marines were fine examples of manhood and that their sons would be, too, if they joined the Corps. Yet the behavior of Marines in Hispaniola produced a counternarrative that they were uncivilized and murderous. Marine manhood would no longer appear so wholesome and chivalrous, and white American manhood would be guilty by association.

Marines' notions of race and manhood guided their interactions with Haitians and Dominicans in the early twentieth century. Many of them operated under the assumption that people of color were inferior. Their racial attitudes are not surprising considering that contemporary discourses in the United States frequently asserted the superiority of white men over Black or brown. Paternalistic racism dictated that Black and Hispanic men were ignorant and lazy children in need of guidance—sometimes punishment—to set them straight. Shortly after the United States declared war on Germany, Marine and indigenous relations on Hispaniola worsened as disgruntled citizens of Haiti and the Dominican Republic launched insurgencies against occupation forces. In the undeclared wars that followed, Marines lost their sense of restraint and behaved contrary to Victorian notions of white manhood. Marine heavy-handedness would lead to investigations and courts-martial. On one hand, the Publicity Bureau used the deployments to Hispaniola to promote the Corps's manliness. But when things went bad, Marines attempted to excuse their behavior by referencing a common claim made by American travelers, psychologists, and medical professionals at the time: that the mental and physical health of white men degenerated in tropical zones.

The Marines Land

The Marine occupation of Haiti began under controversial conditions in the summer of 1915.[2] Fearing that President Vilbrun Guillaume Sam would surrender Haitian sovereignty to the United States, a group of revolutionaries attacked the presidential palace on July 27, 1915. Guillaume Sam fled to the French legation close by. When Haitians learned of the summary executions of political prisoners in Port-au-Prince, a mob entered the legation, dragged the president into the street, and literally ripped him to pieces.[3] Woodrow Wilson deemed this action a threat to American lives and interests on the island and ordered Rear Admiral William B. Caperton to land Marines from the USS *Washington* near Port-au-Prince. The First Marine Brigade transferred from Guantanamo, Cuba; established martial law; and restricted freedom of the press. Rear Admiral Caperton and the State Department then set about rebuilding Haiti's government.[4]

In May 1916 Marines took over the Dominican Republic's government under similar auspices. As per Theodore Roosevelt's 1907 customs treaty with that country, the State Department oversaw Dominican customs revenues and forbade its government from increasing the national debt. President Juan Isidro Jiménez had come to power with the support of the department. Jiménez promised to allow the United States to supervise Dominican finances and to create a national army to help keep the peace. The country's national assembly, however, opposed him because they understood financial independence was a necessary component of national sovereignty. When his own war minister, General Desiderio Arias, attempted a coup, Jiménez accepted an offer of intervention by U.S. naval forces waiting offshore. The USS *Prairie* landed 150 Marines in Santo Domingo, and they were followed quickly by hundreds more. Jiménez stepped down because he could not stomach regaining power with the aid of foreign troops.[5]

These were separate conflicts on Hispaniola, but Marines operating in both countries faced similar challenges. They fought insurgents and established tenuous military and political control over the fractious regions as best they could with the help of newly formed, local constabularies: Gendarmerie d'Haiti and La Guardia Dominicana. Low-ranking enlisted Marines often served as officers in the Gendarmerie and Guardia.[6] With the Marines, the State Department aimed to end the two revolutions on Hispaniola and to set up lasting, peaceful, and cooperative governments. While war raged in Europe, and over a year before the U.S. entry into that conflict, the Corps fought smaller wars of its own in Hispaniola, marked by counterguerrilla and counterinsurgency operations.

Racialized Manhood in Imagery

By 1917, Marines had a long history of fighting small-scale wars on foreign shores. Whether it was the Boxer Rebellion in China, the Spanish-American War, the 1914 landing at Vera Cruz, or the occupations of Haiti, the Dominican Republic, and Nicaragua, Marines used these events to bolster their public reputation. They frequently used the image of the rough-and-tough expeditionary Marine to do so. From these frequent deployments came the slogans "First to Fight" and "Always Ready" as well as the saying, "The Marines have landed and have the situation well in hand."

Such imagery graced the Corps's own recruiting literature. The *U.S. Marines in Rhyme, Prose, and Cartoon* used stories of Marines' abilities to quell uprisings among the country's southern neighbors. "He is America's 'handy man,' always ready to go anywhere and do anything, especially as a pacificator in struggling countries that run the risk of ruin through chronic revolution."[7] It also reprinted a piece from the *Literary Digest* that described Marines as "'Johnnies on the spot,' who are ready whenever there is a dangerous, difficult work to be done in a hurry." This item claimed that the popular phrase "Tell it to the Marines" stemmed from the fact that they frequently deployed to cope with emergencies in the Caribbean and Latin America, where revolutions threatened to tear countries apart. "Today 'Tell it to the Marines' means tell them to get busy on a man size job that calls for courage and strength and determination to see the thing through to the finish," it claimed.[8]

The deployments to Haiti and the Dominican Republic also inspired the construction of an array of graphic imagery driven by themes of race and gender. Cartoons portrayed the expeditionary Marine as manly and strong while casting Haitians and Dominicans as infantile and weak. Marine artists promoted a kind of racial paternalism that reinforced narratives of "superior" white manhood governing the "infantile" peoples of Hispaniola.

One image serves as a graphic representation of the phrase "Tell it to the Marines." It depicts a large Marine walking onto a beach occupied by a small Latino man. Labeled "Insurrecto" by the artist, the small man flees immediately at the sight of the large American and drops a sign that says "down with the government." "What did you say?" asks the Marine the way a father would address an unruly child. *Tell It to the Marines* offers a simple story: when there are revolutions or

"TELL IT TO THE MARINES"

Fig. 39. *Tell It to the Marines*. From *U.S. Marines in Rhyme, Prose, and Cartoon*, 3rd ed. (New York: U.S. Marine Corps Publicity Bureau, 1917), 12.

insurrections in Latin America, Marines will land, chase the insurgents away, and restore order.

Another image, entitled *Cheese It! De Cop!!*, tells the same story but expands the list of characters that Marines considered less manly than themselves. The artist shows small and terrified people fleeing a Ma-

"CHEESE IT! DE COP!!"

Fig. 40. *Cheese It! De Cop!!* From *U.S. Marines in Rhyme, Prose, and Cartoon,* 3rd ed. (New York: U.S. Marine Corps Publicity Bureau, 1917), 20.

rine marching confidently ashore while twirling a nightstick in his hand. Craven "revolutionaries," "disturbers" of the peace, "bandits," "rebels," and "insurrectos" all flee when the American arrives.

Marines also saw themselves as missionaries of sorts, sent to spread democracy and to teach Black people and Hispanics how to run a peace-

Fig. 41. *The Missionary*, by Paul Woyshner. From *Marines Magazine*, April 1917, 2.

ful government. Implicit behind these beliefs were racial assumptions about Haitian and Dominican inferiority. Historian Gail Bederman's assertion that white men linked "whiteness to male power" is evident here.[9] Paternalism, underscored by these assumptions, tended to tint the lenses through which Marines saw the population of each country.[10] These elements are present in an image from a 1917 issue of the *Marines Magazine* entitled *The Missionary*. A comically large Marine kneels on a tropical beach, holding an obstreperous but small and armed Latino man. "Listen Son!" the Marine says to the man as an adult would say to a child, "do unto your brothers as you'd hav'em do unto you! Savvy?"[11]

Another image likewise infantilizes the people of the Dominican Republic. Uncle Sam, wearing a Marine Corps uniform, has a wailing child across his knees with the words "Santo" on one leg and "Domingo" on the other.[12] Depicting Haitians and Dominicans as children only bolstered Marines' senses of their own manhood and perceived superiority. As historian Michael Kimmel has argued about American men at the turn of the twentieth century, "Manhood had been understood to define an inner quality, the capacity for autonomy and respon-

Fig. 42. *A Bad Child.* From *Marines Magazine*, January 1917, 37.

sibility, and had historically been seen as the opposite of childhood."[13] This kind of imagery repeated the infantilization of "Others" around the world and had been used to make military interventions seem benevolent since at least the Spanish-American War and the Philippine-American War (1899–1902).[14]

Marines also used artistic representations of their deployments to Latin America to demonstrate their superiority over other branches of the U.S. armed forces. Drawings that portray Marines as America's favorites show how they liked to see themselves compared to soldiers and sailors. For example, in A. H. Newman's *Uncle's Pet Nephew*, Uncle Sam is watching a group of children playing, each representing either the "Militia," "Army," "Navy," and "Marines." "Some boy!" he exclaims

Fig. 43. *Uncle's Pet Nephew*, by A. H. Newman. From *Marines Magazine*, April 1917, 5.

while watching with admiration the pluck and exuberance of the boy in a Marine uniform who yells, "Wee-e! I'm Fightin' Spicks!"[15] The dog (perhaps representing Dominican or Haitian rebels) is frightened and runs away. The Navy child is clearly overweight and clueless. The Militia boy sits while nursing a bottle as the timid-looking Soldier, with his glasses and his toy howitzer, looks at the Marine and says, "He's too rough to play with." Newman portrays Marines as more active, more experienced, and in possession of qualities Uncle Sam and the nation want most in a fighting man—the readiness and willingness to fight.

The Great War enhanced even further Marines' perceptions of their own racial and manly superiority over Haitians and Dominicans. One image that appeared in the July 1919 issue of the *Recruiters' Bulletin* depicts a Black man wearing nothing but a crown and a straw skirt.

The crown on his head implies that he is a chieftain of some sort, but he looks worried. His eyes are fixed on a German helmet attached to the belt of an armed Marine. "Your Crown is safe—as long as you're good!" the Marine exclaims with a smirk. The chieftain stands with his toes pointed inward and his stomach pointing forward, an insecure and childlike pose. The Marine, on the other hand, looks confident and assertive.

Marine perceptions of Haitians and Dominicans extended from American beliefs concerning race and manhood. While middle-class American doctors, journalists, and politicians understood race and manhood to be inextricably linked, some writers, both white and Black, associated specific types of manhood with each race. They often disagreed, however, over what kind of manhood *should* be associated with the two races. White authors would either imply or explicitly state that white manhood was stronger and more valiant and vigorous than Black manhood.[16] They argued that it had reached the furthest extent of human development, while Black manhood lagged. White civilization, they continued, was older and more mature than Black culture. According to them, comparing one to the other was to compare a fully grown adult to an adolescent. One author argued, "Infancy, childhood and youth precede manhood in the life of a nation as well as that of the individual," and Africans lacked "dignity, self-consciousness, perseverance, and steady application . . . , all characteristic of a race in its childhood."[17]

Some Black American authors and activists argued the opposite but used the same metaphor. "The growth of a boy into manhood is the point of evolution that our race has reached today," Roy Thomas Smith wrote.[18] Francis J. Grimke, an early twentieth-century pastor of the Fifteenth Street Presbyterian Church in Washington, D.C., as well as prominent member of the National Association for the Advancement of Colored People (NAACP), claimed explicitly that "the Negro is a man, and he will never be satisfied with anything less than a man's treatment."[19] He asserted this at a time when he and others believed that Black men had proven their manhood fighting for their country in France.[20] The war was supposed to change their lives for the better. But many white Americans, especially in the South, would have none of this. A disconcerting race problem, or the "Negro Problem" as white Americans tended to call it as if to shift the blame upon Black citizens, had befallen American society around the turn of the century. Tensions between white and Black people led to race riots across the country between 1910 and 1920. World War I exacerbated this racial

Fig. 44. *Your Crown Is Safe—as Long as You're Good!* From
Recruiters' Bulletin, July 1919, 24.

strife as Black veterans returned home from the war determined to
receive better treatment.[21]

Marine imagery, therefore, very much reflected the racial and gender norms of many white Americans. Most grew up in a nation where
people of color were seen as inferior by law and by custom. In the South,
where the great majority of Black Americans lived, state governments
denied them suffrage and spent a relative pittance on their segregated
schools, communities, and public spaces. This neglect ensured that
Black men, women, and children had little to no opportunities for intellectual, social, or economic advancement and no recourse to change
through elections. But most Marines grew up in a society that saw the
"childlike" characteristics of Black Americans as inherent qualities of
their race, not as direct and viciously cyclical results of white society's
own racial policies. As men of a self-proclaimed "superior race," many
of them believed they would naturally dominate "lesser peoples" in
order to help them, to protect them from themselves, and to punish
them when necessary, all for "their own good." The ease with which

Marines supposedly imposed order over "lesser races" enhanced their manly image and fit nicely within the world view they had accepted from home. For many Marines deployed to Hispaniola, however, these images would not accurately reflect the difficulties of counterguerrilla and counterinsurgency warfare.

Effects of the Great War

The Great War would have a significant influence on both occupations. Once the United States declared war on Germany, the government pulled companies of Marines off Hispaniola, much to the chagrin of the brigade and battalion commanders there. One officer in Haiti reported: "The reduction of the number of Marines in Haiti by two companies is, in my opinion, a serious mistake. . . . [I]t is necessary in my mind that we increase our influence in this Island and not weaken it. . . . [T]o withdraw troops just at this time . . . cannot but have a very unfortunate effect."[22] Stripped of much needed troops, matériel, and leadership, the Marine brigade in the Dominican Republic began to bend under a revival of insurgent activity in 1918.[23] "To face this situation what do we have?" remarked another officer. "Men of experience . . . have gone, other men . . . are on the limit of their two-year period and probably on the eve of their departure."[24]

Marines in Haiti and the Dominican Republic faced serious insurgencies in the spring and summer of 1918, but they would receive little press recognition. While the Fifth and Sixth Regiments of Marines in France won laurels fighting the Germans, elements of the First, Second, Third, and Fourth Regiments of Marines stayed in Hispaniola. Establishing and maintaining control over the countryside became more difficult. Marines often resorted to harsh measures to do so.

The race of the inhabitants made a significant difference in the attitudes of Marines in Haiti, the Dominican Republic, and even France. After landing in Europe, one Marine wrote enthusiastically, "here in France, among people of their own color and race, of paved streets and taxicabs . . . coming and going in a steady stream to and from the front, the Marine is learning new things every day."[25] Meanwhile, in Haiti, where the men were trying to teach people they considered "inferior" how to run their own country, Colonel L. W. T. Waller wrote to Colonel Smedley Butler to describe the Gendarmerie as "niggers in spite of the varnish of education and refinement. Down in their hearts they are just the same happy, idle irresponsible people we know of."[26]

Captain Adolf Miller, a Marine company commander who spent two years in Haiti, held similar beliefs. He kept an extensive journal of his time in country that illuminates Marine attitudes toward Haitian natives. He believed all of them were "child-like" and "highly excitable." He thought the men were stupid and cowardly, while the women were all of "easy virtue."[27] Miller read H. Hesketh Prichard's *Where Black Rules White* after being in country for eight months. The book argues that as a race, Black people are incapable of ruling themselves peacefully by Western that is, white) standards. In his journal Miller calls the book "very interesting."[28] By February 1916, he had been in country for over eighteen months and claimed explicitly that he had developed no respect for Haitian people at all.[29]

Many Marine officers in Hispaniola felt left out as the United States went to war in Europe, and some desperately tried to get orders to France. Captain Alexander A. Vandegrift (future hero of Guadalcanal and Commandant of the Marine Corps) served in Haiti throughout the U.S. involvement in the Great War. He had spent much of his adult life preparing to fight in just such a war as in Europe only to be "shunted aside despite the most ingenious attempts and pathetic appeals directly to the Commandant to send us over there."[30] Vandegrift described missing this chance as "a personal calamity of tremendous proportions" and recalled taking on an increasingly bitter and negative attitude toward his duties in Haiti because of it.[31]

Colonel Butler, a giant figure in Marine Corps history, was another officer who wanted out of Haiti as soon as possible.[32] The consummate expeditionary Marine who preferred life in the field to the barracks, he was an experienced officer who had served in the Spanish-American War, the Philippines, China, and Mexico. By 1917, he had won two Medals of Honor, one at Vera Cruz in 1914 and the other for actions at Fort Riviere, Haiti, in 1915. One would expect Butler to be content, serving as the well-respected commander of Marine and Gendarmerie forces in Haiti and having proved his manhood over and again. But everything changed once the United States entered the Great War. "This work here would be more interesting and worthwhile," he wrote his parents in October 1917, "but under the circumstances it is unbearable. . . . This thing of being left out of the show is really more than I can stand and I tell you both very truthfully that I shall never show my face in West Chester again if I am not allowed to go to France."[33]

In his letters to his family, whenever the subject of the war came up, Butler sounded profoundly depressed, even to the point that he questioned his own manliness and his life decisions. "Had I remained in civil life," he lamented, "I could have gone to France at least as a Lieutenant, and saved my face, while now . . . I must sit here under a foreign flag, while my country goes to war."[34] Butler was willing to do anything to go to Europe, including being reduced in rank: "It isn't as if I asked to be sent as a General or even a Colonel or *even* a Lt. Colonel, I would welcome any position from private on down."[35] Even the thought of his in-laws going to serve in France caused him mental anguish:

> Bunny [Ethel Peters Butler, his wife] has 14 near male relations in the Army, from Privates up to lieutenants and all my able bodied kinfolk have gone—all males on both sides but *me* the one professional soldier. . . . [T]hey can readily see why I could never associate with anyone after the war. Someday my grandchildren will be subjected to the remark "where was your grandfather during the big war?" And they will have to lurch their heads in shame and either lie or say "he was a policeman in the service of a foreign and black Republic."[36]

Butler's sense of his own white manhood was at stake here. Missing the fight to police a "black Republic" would lessen his worth as a white man despite his many years of service in the Corps. In part because of his political connections through his father, Butler shipped out to France in March 1918 and was replaced by Colonel Alexander S. Williams. Butler would never reach the front lines, however, instead spending his time in France as the commander of Camp Pontanezen in Brest, where he oversaw the debarkation and embarkation of troops to and from the front lines. Many officers stayed behind in Hispaniola, however.

Those remaining in the Dominican Republic expressed similar sentiments. Lieutenant Colonel John H. Russell requested a transfer from Santo Domingo to France only to receive the reply, "The work with which you are engaged in, whilst it may not bring as much notoriety as will the work in France, is equally important as makes for the good of the Marine Corps."[37] Brigadier General Joseph Pendleton, who commanded Marines in the Dominican Republic, wanted to go, too, but was told by the Commandant, "as a matter of policy the War Department is opposed to sending general officers to France who are beyond a certain age, which unfortunately leaves you and me out."[38]

The Great War made the image of aggressive and powerful expeditionary Marines easily defeating Haitians and Dominicans decidedly less fulfilling and less manly. Now, Marines claimed that too much service in the tropics was bad for their manhood. Corporal H. W. Houck wrote a poem for the *Marines Magazine* in September 1917 that illustrates perhaps how many enlisted men felt about having to serve in Latin America rather than France. Houck wanted to fight the Germans in Europe, where he and his fellow Marines stood the best chance of demonstrating their manhood.

> Now, we are not complaining, but here is our
>   Appeal,—
> Return us to the USA, you know how
>   We feel.
> *Our minds are only wandering now, but later*
>   *Will go wrong*
> *And then you'll all be sorry, for you'll miss*
>   *us when we're gone.*
> One hundred and eight men are all we have,
>   And brave lads every one;
> So give us a chance to go to France, for
>   We're rip-roaring sons of guns.[39]

Instead, Houck was doomed to wither away in the tropics. In Corps literature, withering is what happened when Marines served too long in the Caribbean or Latin America: their minds degenerated, their morals loosened, and their health waned.

Racial Degeneracy

These manly "rip-roaring sons of guns" suffered from "Tropicalitis," a Marine colloquialism that historian Mary Renda describes as "the mental and emotional degeneration that often afflicted or threatened to afflict White men on duty for any length of time near the equator."[40] John Houston Craige, a Marine officer who served in Haiti, described the condition in his 1933 book, *Black Bagdad*. For many white men who stayed in the tropics too long, "the stolid slow up, the nervous blow up."[41] Marines believed that one could waste away mentally and physically in the constant heat or heavy rains of tropical climates. Insanity or death could be the result.

The environment took a toll on Marines. Colonel Russell wrote that Marines in Haiti were constantly "subjected to tropical rains and sun."[42] Captain Miller reported throughout his time in Haiti how sickness among his Marines was a constant concern. In May 1916 his entire company reported ill in some form or fashion to the point that "the surgeon strongly recommends that the 15th Co. be transferred to some northern port to recuperate."[43] Contemporary authors frequently wrote about the insalubriousness of the Caribbean, where white men were susceptible to all manner of diseases. Too much sun was bad for the skin, but it could also cause much more serious damage. "Excessive exposure to the sun . . . almost invariably produces headache, slight fever, and ultimately a high degree of nervous irritability ending not infrequently in a nervous breakdown," declared one author at the time.[44] On Hispaniola, Russell would have agreed: "Malarial fever in Haiti is endemic and practically all officers and men who did patrol duty sooner or later acquired it."[45] Lieutenant Colonel Frederic M. Wise, who had served in France, the Dominican Republic, and Haiti, concurred. Much of the Marines troubles in Hispaniola "that could not be justified could at least be explained by the effect of long periods of isolated service in the tropics on northern men." He asserted, "Too many White men had had to sit alone for months in a shack in the jungle, looking at a couple of palm trees until they began to look at a rum bottle."[46]

Craige wrote of the deleterious effect of the sun. "There is a strange magic in the rays of the sun," he observed. "A short exposure, bareheaded, brings sunstroke to the newly arrived white man."[47] Craige told the story of one unfortunate Marine lieutenant named South who was full of romantic notions of adventure before arriving in Haiti. After a couple years, however, he began to lose his mind. For this young officer, the tropical sun had leached his strength, turning him from a man of vigor to a nervous wreck. South's comrades noticed him mumbling to himself increasingly, withdrawing from the company of others, and sometimes passing into fits of hysteria. "The Tropics have got him," his fellow Marines would say.[48] To early twentieth-century American academics and Marines, the degeneration of white men in the tropics was real.[49] These fears and misconceptions reveal how the weakening of manhood pervaded Marines' understanding of service in Hispaniola.

"Tropicalitis" was not caused solely by the climate, however. By around 1915, academics had long asserted that too much exposure to "inferior races" caused white men to degenerate in the tropics. Ellsworth Huntington, a professor of geography at Yale University, argued, "Experience in all parts of the world shows that the presence of an inferior race in large numbers tends constantly to lower the standards of the dominant race."[50] Such scholars asserted that people native to the tropics were indolent, lewd, crude, and licentious, all character traits that white middle-class men and women tried to keep suppressed.

Through overexposure to native peoples of color, white men supposedly lost their sexual morality and work ethic. "All of these things may be looked upon as disadvantages of the lower race rather than of the higher," Huntington claimed, "but I believe that the higher race reaps by far the greater injury."[51] Colonel Butler seemed to agree with this assessment. A year after his own departure from Haiti, he wrote to a friend still stationed there, "trusting that the service among the blacks is not getting too much on your nerves, and that you will not stay there until you lose all your teeth as I did."[52] It is not clear if Butler believed that time with "the blacks" caused tooth decay, but he certainly believed that there was something inherently difficult about working with Haitians.

Illicit violence by Marines increased substantially in Haiti and the Dominican Republic in 1918. In Haiti the Americans reinstituted the notorious corvée labor system, which forced locals to construct roads without pay. One of the occupation's missions there was to build roads connecting the northern and southern provinces of the country. Marines meant this road to aid in the commercial development of Haiti and to increase their own efficiency. To acquire workers, they compelled Haitians who could not pay the road tax to pay with their own labor. Since the system had been used there before, the Marines assumed that it would work again. But many Haitians now viewed it as slave labor and resisted.[53] The Marines treated those who resisted as criminals, which led to imprisonments, executions, and more resistance.

Court-martial records from Haiti between the years 1915 and 1919 indicate a shift in the number and type of crimes Marines committed. From the beginning of the occupation until 1917, the most common offenses were being absent without leave, drunkenness, and scandalous conduct. By middle to late 1917 (after the U.S. entry in World War I), violent crimes became more common: "Murder; assault with a deadly weapon wounding another person"; "assaulting superior officer with intent to kill"; and "murder (of a native)."[54] Among the officers tried by general courts-martial, three stood trial in 1917, eleven in 1918 (which was the last year of the Great War and the period that saw a spike in insurgent activity), and twenty-six in 1919.[55]

Part of the reason for this behavior probably had to do with the Great War itself. Once the United States intervened in Europe, Marines quickly saw their missions in Hispaniola as part of the war against Germany. Americans had considered Germany their greatest economic and strategic rival in the Caribbean since the turn of the century.[56] Following America's entry into the war, numerous rumors began to fly among the local populace about U.S. and German intentions in Haiti. Colonel Eli K. Cole reported that some Haitian politicians "appeared to be laboring under the impression that our government was in danger of being overthrown by the Germans living in the United States, . . . having been told there were five hundred thousand armed Germans ready to start a revolution in the United States." Some even believed rumors such as "the United States Government will force every male Haitian between the ages of 15 and 55 to join a military force to fight against Germany."[57] Cole assured as many Haitians as he could that those claims were false.

Marines fell back on notions of paternalism, with their implications for racial manhood, to make sense of this situation. They often attributed Haitians' willingness to believe these kinds of rumors to their childishness. "The Haitians," Russell wrote to Commandant Barnett, "are a very hysterical people. Hundreds of rumors are circulated among them daily, that are simply ridiculous, but, like children, they believe them and completely lose their heads."[58] And Captain J. L. Perkins described the locals as "little more than children mentally."[59]

Because they seemed so infantile, it was simply impossible for some Marines to believe that the Hispaniola peoples conducted an insurgency on their own. From the Dominican Republic, Lieutenant Colonel Thorpe wrote to his superior that "the general opinion here is that whoever is running this revolution . . . is getting a lot out of the niggers." He and others blamed Germans for directing insurgent activity. Thorpe claimed that a recent spike in violence in the Dominican Republic "shows the handiwork of the German as certain as can be, there is no doubt in my mind that a German is commanding the enemy's campaign."[60] A Marine officer in Santo Domingo reported: "The pro German element is at work stirring up the minds of the people. . . . I believe that if the Germans had some big win in Europe we would have here a general insurrection."[61] General Pendleton wrote that Marines in the summer of 1918 "were campaigning against Germany, German influence, German money, and German inspired revolt."[62]

German-orchestrated attacks made more sense to the Marines than insurgencies led by "childlike" Black people and Hispanics. These beliefs, founded upon hierarchies of manhood and race, led to a misunderstanding of the situation in both countries. According to Bruce Calder's research, what the Marines saw as a German-led revolt conducted by insurgent leaders was actually a grassroots resistance by Dominicans, led by trusted local political and military leaders, fighting against foreign intrusion and economic exploitation. The spike in insurgent activity in 1918 stemmed in part from a misunderstanding of or disrespect for local politics in the eastern provinces of the country. *Cuadillos*, local men who had charisma, military skills, economic resources, and important family ties, controlled much of the eastern Dominican Republic. Marines "either failed to understand it or completely misjudged the strength of the *cuadillo* system," argues Calder.[63] World War I also seriously hindered the country's export trade, which negatively affected Dominicans' economic prospects.

Marine paranoia of German subterfuge probably extended from the very same anxiety Americans felt in the States, particularly in the South. Southerners in North Carolina, for example, feared that German agents would sow disloyalty and discord among African American communities. The *New York Tribune* claimed a few days before Congress declared war that Black southerners had shown "ill tempers," the telltale sign of an impending rebellion. Racism and systematic oppression of Black Americans had nothing to do with it, apparently. The paper instead blamed German agents, who had been "insidiously working to bring about a rising of negroes against the whites." According to the conspiracy, Germany would incite Black people to rebel in the South, followed by the spread of the insurrection throughout the United States. The rebels would then take over Texas and turn it into a Black republic. The assumptions here were not very different than those the Marines operated under in Hispaniola, namely that Germans had to behind the unrest. "Inferior races," according to this line of thinking, were usually content under the control of white men, and would only become discontented and rebel when influenced by perfidious outsiders.[64]

By 1918, newspapers in the United States frequently published columns that described a worldwide system of German espionage and subterfuge. Americans, and likely Marines, too, read about Germans hatching plots all over Europe.[65] They read about enemy "agents spreading pacifist propaganda all over the United States."[66] Journalists also published stories of Germans bribing Pancho Villa to attack Americans along the Mexico–U.S. border.[67] Given the frequent appearance of stories like these, Marines on Hispaniola certainly would not have thought it too farfetched to believe that Germans were on the island causing problems.

The Marines' War in Hispaniola, 1918-1919

Lieutenant Colonel Thorpe's war in the Dominican Republic offers a lurid example of Marine misconduct. Officers under his command began killing Dominicans in early 1918 in retaliation for the murder and mutilation of William Knox, a Marine captain liked, respected, and known as "a champion of civic improvement in his district."[68] By all accounts, Knox was very kind and patient with residents and worked hard to earn their trust. When he was killed, many Marines wanted revenge. The officer who replaced him allegedly executed eleven suspected "bandits" associated with his murder.[69] Knox's friend, Captain Thad Taylor, turned sinister as well. After the captain's death, Taylor believed "that all circumstances called for a campaign of frightfulness," so he "arrested indiscriminately upon suspicion; then people rotted in jail pending investigation or search for evidence."[70] According to Thorpe, Taylor's retaliatory methods sowed discord and anarchy in El Seibo Province.[71]

Encountering stiff resistance from insurgent bands, Thorpe and his men resorted to drastic measures. On April 14, 1918, Taylor and a group of Marines captured a Syrian national living in Hayto Mayor, known locally as Agapito José, who they believed was involved in Knox's murder.[72] After Marines shot and killed Agapito in the street, Taylor allegedly "took a dagger and driving it in his [Agapito's] throat slashed down to the abdomen."[73] Taylor's accomplices in this act were Captain Russell W. Duck and newly arrived Captain Charles F. Merkel. In August Thorpe instituted a campaign, known by the locals as *reconcentraciones*, aimed at gathering Dominicans from the countryside into camps located in the larger urban centers.[74] Thorpe probably learned this tactic from the Spanish during the Spanish-American War. In addition, the U.S. Army and Marines reconcentrated entire communities of people during the war in the Philippines immediately following Spain's defeat.[75]

Thorpe believed that placing populations of Dominicans under surveillance and control would allow his Marines to separate the good from the bad. But Dr. Alejandro Coradin of Hayto Mayor, who witnessed these efforts firsthand, later described them as the "concentration of the wretched inhabitants of the commune of Hayto Mayor who had been locked up like pigs in stockades under the pretext of investigating whether or not they were bad persons, a procedure which we can call puerile."[76]

Captain Merkel, commander of the Fifty-Second Company of Marines, proceeded to commit a string of notorious crimes during this campaign. He soon became known as the "Tiger of Seibo" after the eastern province of El Seibo that he terrorized under the supposed orders of his battalion commander, Lieutenant Colonel Thorpe. Throughout the month of September 1918, Merkel treated every Dominican he encountered outside of the concentrated zones as an insurgent. He captured, tortured, and allegedly murdered dozens of people.[77] Thorpe had Merkel arrested on October 1. While in his cell, the captain wrote a letter accusing Thorpe of ordering the killings. Merkel knew that the misery, death, and destruction he had wrought in El Seibo Province would damage the Marine Corps's reputation. "I am doing this in order to save disgracing the M. Corps and myself," he claimed, "but I sincerely hope that god will punish Thorpe someday for he is not fit to have command of anything and his sole object is to get people into trouble."[78] Alone in a prison cell, Merkel shot himself in the head with a smuggled .38-caliber revolver.

Thorpe denied involvement in Merkel's crimes, but in a letter to his own superior dated August 21, the lieutenant colonel implicated himself. To Brigadier General Pendleton, Thorpe indicated how he thought he stood to benefit from the deaths of many Dominicans. "If I do a good job of clearing these two provinces of insurgents *and kill a lot*," he claimed, "maybe I go to a more active field of endeavor too. . . . I ought to show that I'd be a good German killer."[79]

Merkel accused Thorpe of ordering the killings, but other Marines accused the lieutenant colonel of being too lenient on the Dominicans. According to Special Agent Carlos J. Rohde's report on conditions in the Dominican Republic, many Marines hated Thorpe for being a "nigger lover."[80] Shortly after Merkel's death, Thorpe released seventy prisoners, who Marines had captured in supposed "bandit" camps, upon their promises to live peacefully. Perhaps in response to Merkel's rampage, he had instituted an order forbidding all Marines from firing on anyone unless fired upon first. This order left the men feeling defenseless while patrolling the hills. Marines feared being captured by insurgents most of all, especially considering how Knox's body was mutilated. Some claimed they would commit suicide before being captured, believing that their enemy would torture them, dissect them, and then hack them to death with machetes. Rumors spread of captors cutting off the genitals of captured Americans.[81] So, Thorpe's leniency infuriated the Marines who would rather he prosecute "these bands as rigidly as might be expected under the circumstances."[82]

Thorpe reacted to Rohde's accusations the same way he reacted to Merkel's—denial. Calling Thorpe a "nigger lover" implicated his manhood and loyalty to his own men and race. He asserted adamantly, "I am not a nigger lover in any sense of the word."[83] Rohde further reported that Marines wanted to kill Thorpe. "I have had any number of Marines tell me that they feared that one of these days, when Colonel Thorpe might join them in one of their scouting expeditions, one of their own men would 'accidentally' shoot Colonel Thorpe," he wrote.[84] Painting a rather dark picture of the Marines' war there, Rohde's investigation has never been mentioned in any Marine Corps histories that address the Dominican Republic occupation of 1916–24. It and other disturbing reports from Hispaniola would remain out of the public eye for the time being.

Much of the resistance Marines experienced in Haiti stemmed from the corvée work system. Realizing the resentment coerced labor had caused among residents, Colonel Williams abolished it in October 1918.[85] But one of his subordinates, Major Clarke H. Wells, kept the corvée in the Hinche District through the early months of 1919—apparently without the permission or knowledge of his superiors. Wells claimed that volunteers worked the roads, which was news to workers themselves, who knew their labor was forced.[86] Lieutenant Colonel Wise described the corvée system as legal but overly used by the Marines. The result, he claimed, was that "the Haitians had started another revolution ten times worse than the one we had just suppressed."[87]

The corvée fanned the flames of an insurgency being conducted by Charlemagne Peralte. A charismatic leader who had been previously arrested for armed robbery and forced into hard labor, Peralte escaped from prison in the summer of 1918.[88] After he fled into the countryside, he gathered supporters who were angry over the corvée. Making clear allusions to Germany's oppressive occupation during the Great War, Peralte proclaimed to the people of Port-au-Prince, "Haitians, let us be firm; let us follow the example of Belgium," meaning resist the invaders at all costs the way the Belgians had fought the Germans.[89]

During this insurgency, Marines often had a hard time distinguishing innocent Haitians from dangerous ones, which led to indiscriminate counterguerrilla measures. Colonel R. S. Hooker became profoundly frustrated with those who would not help him find Peralte. Hooker undoubtedly encouraged many Haitians to resist his Marines by proclaiming through a public notice:

> I have told you several times to return to your homes and remain quiet. I have told you that I would accord protection to all those

who are honest citizens, but what have you done for me? Nothing! . . . In view of your negligence in failing to denounce these people, I have found it necessary to take very stern measures. What are these measures? It is becoming necessary to burn huts in order that the bandits are unable to find protection from the rain; it is becoming necessary to kill cattle so that bandits will not be able to find meat to eat; it is becoming necessary to destroy life-sustaining supplies of every kind so that the bandits will not have beans, sugarcane, bananas, etc., to eat. These measures hit the bandits, the innocent, and the good citizens equally.[90]

Marines then began to execute locals. They allegedly killed prisoners in January 1919. One Marine accused Major Clarke H. Wells of ordering that "prisoners, if any were undesirable, [or] useless . . . [be] bumped off, by this expression of course [he] meant to kill them."[91] Acting under these orders, Ernest Lavoie (an officer in the gendarmerie and also a Marine Corps private) ordered the execution of nineteen prisoners.[92]

Partly because of such killings, Peralte successfully painted the Marines as evil foreign occupiers bent on enslaving the population. He led organized attacks against the occupation government at Hinche, Grand Riviere, and Le Trou. Marines finally caught up with him in October 1919, when Second Lieutenant Herman H. Hanneken and a select team of Marines disguised themselves as Haitian insurgents (replete with blackface) and infiltrated Peralte's headquarters. While in disguise and with the Haitians' guard down, Hanneken and his men assassinated Peralte on the spot, later putting his body on public display.[93] The lieutenant and one of his Marines were later awarded the Medal of Honor for the "extraordinary heroism and conspicuous gallantry and intrepidity" displayed in killing Peralte.[94]

Although it undoubtedly took courage to infiltrate their enemy's camp, the irony behind this action was that sneaking around in disguise and assassinating an enemy was usually not considered manly and honorable behavior. The U.S. Army had been criticized for these tactics over a decade before in the Philippines.[95] The war in Haiti, however, was not the war in France. Soldiers and Marines believed that counterguerrilla operations required different tactics than a conventional war, and by 1919, special operations like Hanneken's were not uncommon in Marine or army occupation duty.

Benoit Batraville picked up the torch of rebellion and carried it another year. Around the time of Peralte's assassination, Colonel Russell assumed command of Marine and Gendarmerie forces in Haiti.

He immediately abolished all semblances of the corvée and increased the intensity of Marine patrols throughout the Haitian countryside. Eventually, these efforts led to the finding and killing of Benoit in April 1920, which precipitated a lull in organized resistance.[96] It was just after this campaign that negative images of Marines and their activities in Hispaniola began appearing in American newspapers. They now seemed less the saviors of Western civilization than white men succumbing to brutality.

Investigations

In September 1919 Commandant Barnett ordered an investigation of Marines in Haiti after he heard of the courts-martial of two Marines for killing a prisoner. The cases led Barnett to believe that "practically indiscriminate killing of the natives has gone on now for some time."[97] The incidents he referred to involved two Marine privates, identified in the records only as McQuilkin and Johnson, who executed two prisoners near their own graves, which they were forced to dig. An acting lieutenant named Brokaw (no first name provided), who was later committed to an insane asylum, ordered these men to shoot the prisoners.[98] Lieutenant Colonel Wise claimed, however, that Johnson and McQuilkin shot the men "just for excitement."[99] Barnett was one of the principle proponents of the Marines' positive popular image in the United States. He was "shocked beyond all expression to hear of such things and to know that it was at all possible that duty could be so badly performed by marines of any class."[100] Investigations in Haiti would lead to subsequent inquiries into Marine behavior in the Dominican Republic as well.

Newspapers in the United States acquired and published Barnett's remarks, which brought down a firestorm of bad press on the Marine Corps. Their coverage was sensationalist in tone. Long the darlings of the American press and the self-proclaimed finest examples of American manhood, Marines now were cast in a much more negative light. "The military record in Haiti is a blot on the administration and a stain on the honor of the American people," declared one columnist for the *New York Evening Post*. News of Marines killing Haitians indiscriminately was "a shock to those who have cherished the conviction that American military rule did not imitate the coercive methods of some experienced and more callous governments," he affirmed. The *Philadelphia Public Ledger* claimed, "While we were 'making the world safe for democracy' in France . . . , we were ruthlessly practicing machine gun imperialism."[101] And the *Baltimore American* used the most pointed rhetoric against the Corps: "If our marines in Haiti have been indiscriminately killing natives, the criminals should be brought to justice in a way to remove such a hideous stain from the reputation of a branch of service of which the nation is justly proud, especially since the splendid record the marines made in France."[102]

Two investigations took place in late 1919 and 1920, both conducted by high-ranking navy and Marine Corps officers. Brigadier General Albertus W. Catlin, recently recovered from his chest wound received at the Battle of Belleau Wood, conducted the first inquiry. He uncovered killings committed by Privates Lavoie, McQuilken, and Johnson but could not marshal evidence regarding other crimes. He relieved Major Wells and ordered a stop to all summary executions no matter what the circumstances. Secretary of the Navy Daniels ordered the new Commandant, Major General John A. Lejeune, to conduct another investigation in Haiti in September 1920.[103] While there, Lejeune, accompanied by Brigadier General Butler, ordered that any Marines who suffered from physical or mental breakdowns be sent home promptly.[104]

Journalists who traveled to Hispaniola to see the occupation for themselves came back with the impression that racism, often attributed to southern men, ruled the day. A frequent visitor to the West Indies named Harry A. Franck found "many earnest young Southern officers who . . . took a harsh view of their duty and placed too small a value on the lives of Black people."[105] He saw the predominance of Marines from the American South as part of the problem in Haiti. "These men were mainly men who did not get into the Great War," Franck asserted, "and were anxious to have military feats to their credit."[106] Gulian Lansing Morrill leveled explicit judgment on the occupation. He blamed "the 'nigger-hating' politicians in the U.S. who sent 'nigger-hating' marines here, recruited from the South."[107]

A writer for the *Nation*, Herbert J. Seligmann, visited Marines in Haiti in the spring of 1920 and came back with this accusation:

The five years of American occupation, from 1915 to 1920, have served as a commentary upon the white civilization which still burns Black men and women at the stake. For Haitian men, women, and children, to a number estimated at 3,000, innocent for the most part of any offense, have been shot down by American machine gun and rifle bullets; Black men and women have been put to torture to make them give information; theft, arson, and murder have been committed almost with impunity upon the persons and property of Haitians by White men wearing the uniform of the United States.[108]

While Marines from the Great War were portrayed as heroic, proud American fighting men, this kind of imagery made those stationed in Hispaniola appear cruel and murderous.

Internally, the Marines accused these journalists of exaggeration and distortion of the truth. Before Lejeune left for Hispaniola in 1920 to investigate the situation personally, he received a letter from Second Brigade commanding officer Logan Feland from Santo Domingo. Feland warned the new Commandant, "there are many wheels within wheels here, and always someone can be found to magnify and distort out of all proportion whatever may be found to the discredit of anyone connected with the military government."[109] Earl "Pete" Ellis concurred. As chief intelligence officer of the Second Brigade, he had tried to get to the bottom of rumors of Marine officers drinking and behaving poorly. He failed to find the source. "However, I have learned," Ellis informed Lejeune, "beyond doubt that some person or persons have started a concerted campaign to discredit the Brigade and the military government in general."[110]

Marines began a campaign that year to defend themselves against the perceived "sensationalism" of the press and protect their image. Lejeune wrote to the *Nation* in direct response to Seligmann's article, emphasizing the difficulties Marines faced in Haiti. They had made mistakes and courts-martial convictions had been doled out, but "it has been and is the duty and aim of the Marine Corps authorities here and in Haiti to work solely for the interests and advancement of Haiti and the Haitian people."[111] The *New York Times* interviewed retired major Philip T. Case, who tried to persuade readers that what they had read about Marines in Hispaniola was wrong. He claimed, "time and time again when I was with my men down there . . . , we would be fired upon by natives without returning fire because we did not want to injure women and children." Case proclaimed that despite the tough nature of the Hispaniola deployments, for the most part, Marines showed remarkable restraint and professionalism in keeping with their manly image.[112]

But others admitted that there were killings. One former Marine from the South, instead of denying that any illicit killings happened, defended and even attempted to justify them. "I am not trying to give the impression that there were no natives killed in Santo Domingo nor Haiti," he admitted, "for there were, in both places, and probably there were a few 'indiscriminate' killings, but no more than in any place in our own Southland, where there are more negroes than White men." This veteran spoke to the prevailing idea that white men would naturally abuse "inferior" races when outnumbered. "Why are they continually harping on the killings of natives," he asked, "and never a word said about the killings of lone marines and small parties, with never a chance of quarter, even if a marine would lower themselves to ask quarter of a negro."[113]

This former Marine's comments again brought up another perceived path toward racial and masculine degeneration—exposure. According to this idea, white men tended to behave savagely in the presence of too many people of an inferior race.[114] Richard Henry Edwards, an ordained minister and college professor, asserted that lynching was the ultimate form of white viciousness and atavism that "brutalizes whites and blacks alike."[115] It manifests from "the vague, rather intangible, but wholly real feeling of 'pressure' which comes to the white man almost instinctively in the presence of a mass of people of a different race."[116]

According to early twentieth-century racial theory, white people remained civilized only in areas where they made up a strong majority of the population. When outnumbered, however, these racial pressures would push men to violence. "A few of one race may be tolerated among the many of another race on condition of inferiority," wrote one author. "No instance in history is recalled where two distinct races lived together on equal terms—one must be dominant, the other subordinate."[117] To some observers and defenders of the Marine Corps, when the "subordinate race" seeks social and political equality, the "dominate race" resorts to brutality. This kind of reasoning is perhaps why many Americans did not see anything unnatural or necessarily wrong with white men killing people of color in Hispaniola.

Throughout the summer and fall of 1920, the press hounded Secretary of the Navy Daniels about the investigations into Marine behavior on the island. He repeatedly defended the Marines and claimed, "you cannot send a man to that country where they are shot in the back and expect them not to kill bandits."[118] He also greatly resented the portrayal of American servicemen as murders and reprobates in publications like the *Nation*. Daniels allowed for the fact that some Marines had acted harshly toward the Haitians but implied that the victims were the Marines themselves, not the Haitians. "There will always be a few people cracked by the climate, or shot in the back who do things they ought not to do," he told the press, "but the attack on the Marines as a whole is an attack on American civilization which they embody."[119] Occasionally, reporters would get snarky with Daniels. On December 27, 1920, one blurted out, "I don't suppose the Marines celebrated the day [Christmas] by killing a few Haitians?" Daniels, refusing to match the cynicism of the reporter, only responded with, "No . . . I think the Marines celebrated Christmas by the consciousness of having done a hard job and done it well."[120]

Daniels was no doubt relieved when the official navy investigation of Marine conduct in Hispaniola came back with a verdict of not guilty. After returning from his inspection tour in late September 1920, Lejeune submitted his official report of the situation in Haiti as he saw it. He claimed to see Marines in good health and high morale working with a thankful Haitian people. Lejeune felt proud of the men's service there and believed the American people should be proud of them as well.[121] The navy investigation regarded "the charges which have been published as ill considered, regrettable and thoroughly unwarranted reflections on a portion of the U.S. Marine Corps which has performed difficult, dangerous and delicate duty in Haiti in a manner which, instead of calling for adverse criticism, is entitled to the highest commendations."[122] With this finding, Marines tried to lay the issue to rest with the press and reestablish their positive image in the papers. With the headline "Marines Quieted Haiti," one newspaper quoted Lejeune as saying, "there exists throughout Haiti a strong sentiment of gratitude to the marines for their work for the welfare of the people."[123] The Commandant never abandoned the notion that Marines behaved well on the island.

Even papers that communicated a strong disdain for the interventionist policies of the U.S. government began to withdraw their criticism of the Corps. The *Washington Post* reported that "the opinion [of the American people] will probably be held that the Marine Corps was a victim of the orders from Washington, rather than a willful offender on its own account."[124]

In 1920 Lieutenant Colonel Giles Bishop Jr. published *The Marines Have Landed*, a book of anecdotes and lessons of manhood for an audience of adolescent boys.[125] Characters in the book included a Gunnery Sergeant Miller, who "strove at all times to teach his young charges the manly virtues of honesty, courage, self-control, obedience, industry and clean living."[126] There was also a First Sergeant Douglass, who would chastise junior Marines for being unmanly. "It's a sneaking, unmanly trick, and marines are supposed to be men, not sneaks," Douglass would say.[127] Because of the investigations, and perhaps also because of behavior like Hanneken's, Bishop's book was not received well by everyone.

A writer for the *Nation*, a liberal publication that was critical of the Wilson administration, accused Bishop of over-romanticizing the Marines. "His Marines are fine, manly youths who go ashore to help the Dominicans in the simple American way which consists of regarding the natives of Caribbean islands as 'niggers,' . . . shooting all who show signs of being stubborn in behalf of their rights. . . . In the book this is easy to justify, since these Dominicans are merely dirty bandits whom it is made almost an act of sanitation to exterminate." Bishop was also charged with attempting to make a wholly disreputable conflict into an honorable one. "It is bad enough to make out that wars are pretty picnics," the *Nation* continued, "it is worse to make out that they are all honorable conflicts between one's snow white countrymen and the sin-black foe."[128] For this publication at least, the Marines were not as manly, wholesome, and upright as Bishop claimed.

Marines continued to defend themselves into early 1921. In response to the allegations of illicit killings and Marine misconduct, Earl "Pete" Ellis published in the March 1921 issue of the *Marine Corps Gazette* an article entitled "Bush Brigades." He argued that the motives of the United States and the Marines in countries like Haiti and the Dominican Republic were purely altruistic. He understood the Marines' job as "creating order out of chaos," which was a very difficult task made harder by the American press. Ellis painted a negative picture of any journalist who "yells in print: Marines are down in Jungleland!—and killed a man in a war!—and we didn't know anything about it!" The result for Marines was bad press, which led to unnecessary investigations and being labeled "Hired Hessians."[129] Ellis believed that the best judges of the situation in Hispaniola were the Marines themselves, implying that journalists did not know enough about Haiti or the Dominican Republic to comment publicly. He concluded by reminding the public: "Yes, the Marines are down in jungleland, and they did kill a man in war, and a great many people did not know anything about it. This is most unfortunate, but—the Marines are only doing their job as ordered by the people of the United States."[130]

The Rape of Hispaniola

The negative press would continue through the 1920 presidential election. More information would come to light after the new U.S. presi-

dent, Warren G. Harding, and his new secretary of the navy, former
Marine Edwin Denby, took office. On May 9, 1921, delegates of the
Union Patriotique d'Haiti handed the U.S. State Department and the
Senate Foreign Relations Committee the most damning accusation of
the Haitian occupation: "Memoir on the Political, Economic, and Financial Conditions Existing in the Republic of Haiti under the American Occupation." Frequently referred to as the "Haitian Memoir," it
leveled charges of murder, torture, pillaging, rape, and the burning of
entire villages against the Marines. The *Nation* published a copy of the
"Haitian Memoir" in its May 25 issue.

According to this document, Marines killed men, women, and children while patrolling the hills of Haiti's various districts in search of
"bandits." Some specific charges included burning suspects with red-
hot irons, hanging and burning victims, and shooting down pregnant
women. For example, one group of Marines and Gendarmes reportedly assassinated and mutilated the body of an old man named Joseph
Duclerc. This same group then went on a spree of violence that included shooting a female teacher through the mouth, burning more
houses, and decapitating a blind man along with a child who was with
him.[131] The report described two dozen more cases of lurid Marine
conduct against Haitians. While on these patrols, Marines and Gendarmes arrested many people and sent them without trial to various
prisons around the country.

It was the prisons and detainment camps where the Marine occupation proved the deadliest. Between 1918 and 1920, over 4,000 prisoners
perished while detained throughout Cap-Haitien and 5,475 at Chabert.
Unknown numbers of prisoners died in other camps, according to the
"Memoir," which further claimed, "The ghastly mortality in the prisons together with confirmation by survivors reveals a record of atrocities, of brutality, and [of] cruelty which defies description."[132]

The "Haitian Memoir" also asserted that the naval court of inquiry
that led the investigation of Marine conduct on the island was a sham.
Admiral Henry T. Mayo, Rear Admiral James H. Oliver, Major General Wendell C. Neville (USMC), and Major Jesse F. Dyer (USMC
judge advocate) made up the court and initially inspired confidence in
the proceedings because of their credentials as professional military
officers. But the panel never established an effective system of hearing claims, collecting evidence, calling witnesses, and trying cases.[133]
Martial law throughout their country made it very hard for Haitians to
move around. So, even if those with grievances knew where the court
was being held, their journey could easily be precluded by military

authorities. The report also charged that many of the Haitians "who had anything to say regarding the numerous cases of murder, brutality, robbery, rape, [and] arson . . . were systematically excluded."[134] Therefore, the court found very little evidence in support of Marine misconduct.

Two months later the Anti-Election League of Santo Domingo published its own accusations against the occupation. Marines controlled the Dominican Republic, the report said, by "virtue of machine guns and bayonets." According to the Anti-Election League, the Marines were downright villainous: "They commit murder, burn, and concentrate the poor peasants of entire regions."[135] The league blamed them for nearly everything that happened during Thorpe's campaign and Merkel's rampage. These accusations began to raise the ire of notable former Marines, but not because they were disappointed with the actions of the Corps.

Former enlisted Marine Denby, now secretary of the navy, had visited Haiti during the investigation and characterized the charges within the "Haitian Memoir" as complete "rot." But the *Nation* challenged his credibility to comment accurately on the situation. "Mr. Denby is a former marine," an editorial pointed out. "Apparently, he considers that the honor of the Marine Corps must be vindicated by an absolute denial that any marines are in anyway guilty of wrongdoing. This is a poor conception of his office."[136] Denby responded that by spreading these stories, the *Nation* had dishonored the Marines who had worked hard to bring peace to Haiti and the Dominican Republic. The magazine's editors shot back, "The men who commit atrocities are the ones who 'besmirch the uniform'—not those who try for the sake of the good name of the entire organization and of the country to bring the offenders to book."[137] Its reporting cited Haitian newspapers and claimed that Denby's visit to the country lasted only twenty-four hours and simply was not thorough enough for him to know the truth, much less comment on it.[138]

The "Haitian Memoir" and the Anti-Election League ripped open unhealed public-relations wounds for the Marine Corps and the federal government. Using clear allusions to rape, the *Cleveland Gazette*, a notable Black American newspaper, printed an article titled "Southern American Democrats Despoil Little Black Republic."[139] Some writers argued that the country should be ashamed of the behavior of its Marines. The claims made by the "Memoir," it declared, "constitute an everlasting stain on American honor."[140] Regarding the Dominican Republic, the *Gazette* titled its report "Outrage after Outrage Perpetrated in the Little Mulatto Republic, as in Haiti, So [too] in Santo Domingo."[141] The author of this piece accused Marines in the Dominican Republic of using "Belgium Congo, or Prussian-Belgian methods of eliciting information," such as burning and torturing residents.[142] Only three years before, the Marines' image was one of virtuous manhood standing up to German savagery. Now it was the Marines, and American manhood by implication, that appeared savage.

Then more challenges to Marine notions of manliness and racial superiority appeared, especially in Black newspapers.[143] The *Washington Bee* published the account of a journalist on assignment in Santo Domingo who saw a drunk Marine officer verbally and physically abuse the staff at a bar. "Here was a fair sample of the superior American, just arrived, with superiority undimmed," the writer claimed. This Marine was not a man but an "overgrown boy."[144] Secretary of the NAACP James Weldon Johnson publicly accused such Marines of being low specimens of manhood. "Prejudice and small-calibre Americans had been sent down to Haiti," he claimed, "creating friction with the natives by reason of the color prejudice they brought with them."[145]

The Senate investigation hearings gave some Haitian and Dominican victims their day in court, and their testimony undermined popular perceptions of both Marine and American manhood. The committee took several days to hear testimony from witnesses and survivors of Merkel's rampage, for example, in which more specific details of murder and torture surfaced.[146] This final investigation called many Marine officers to testify, which made Lieutenant Douglas McDougal nervous, "as one false move at this time by any of our officers could place us in a very embarrassing position."[147]

Haitians brought charges against Dorcas Williams, Private Lavoie, and Captain William F. Becker, to name a few. Becker stood accused of particularly heinous crimes. Madame Celicourt Rozier testified that during a 1919 attack on her village, Marines under Becker's command shot to death and then burned all of her children.[148] Heraux Belloni claimed the officer had killed his parents; his father was tied to a tree first before being executed.[149] When Captain Becker testified during the investigation, he claimed that incidents like these were "battles" with insurgents. He did not remember any specific women being killed but did acknowledge that it was possible that some died in the fight: "we were fighting right in the main bandit camp and there were women all around."[150] According to author Martyn Summerbell, American men were "practical, and good humored, and courageous, and chivalrous, and generous, with warm heart that swells with compassion for any world-wide sorrow."[151] Accusations of the murder of women and children, no matter what the pretext, seriously contradicted that claim.

When word of these accusations got out, some writers accepted this news as fact—"The Rape of Haiti!" ran the headline of the *Cleveland Gazette*. One author claimed that "the Marines committed horrible rapes on Haitian women," further stating that "our own marines in Haiti are guilty of crimes that would have pleased Caligula."[152] Many Great War–era Americans considered rape one of the ultimate forms of savagery, white male degeneracy at its worst.[153] Western and allied propaganda painted Germans as savages attempting to defile a feminized representation of civilization during the Great War. Now, during the Senate hearings, U.S. occupation forces stood accused of the metaphorical rape of Haiti's and the Dominican Republic's sovereignty while numerous Marines were accused of literal rape against individual women.[154] This sexual crime revealed a breakdown in morality and a rise in atavism in the perpetrators. D. P. Rhodes argued in his 1919 book, *Our Immortality*, that "of all human acts, rape is perhaps the one most clearly indicating a crude social experience in the ancestral lineage of the agent"; in addition, "any but the most backward in general development may deliberately plan a rape."[155] Many also understood that rape could pose significant threats to the rapist's body; men who so succumbed to their baser passions risked catching and spreading venereal disease.[156]

But the rape of Haitians and Dominicans also meant miscegenation, one of the most insidious paths toward racial decline and masculine degeneracy according to white supremacists. Mixing white genes with "lesser" genes could reduce the purity of the white race. A white supremacist using the pseudonym "Junius Aryan" waxed fanatical about keeping the races separate. He defined racial interbreeding as "an unnatural and vulgar heterogenous union" that threatened to "overthrow Aryan civilization in the country, which if effected would also destroy the Aryan European civilization . . . thus retarding the world's civilization, which is entirely dependent upon the Aryan race in its purity."[157] Dr. Lothrop Stoddard warned, "If white civilization goes down, the white race is irretrievably ruined." He added, "It will be swamped by the triumphant colored races, who will obliterate the white man by elimination or absorption."[158] The rape of women in the tropics could lead to the end of white manhood and civilization itself. So, instead of reinvigorating white American manhood, Marines were now charged with potentially ruining it.

Conclusion

The insurgencies in Hispaniola proved that Haitians and Dominicans were not as easily conquered as Marines claimed. These were not the type of wars many Marines wanted to fight; that one was in France. The killings, torturing, rapes, bad publicity, and investigations demonstrated that Marines were not always paragons of manly virtue. It appeared that they, like any white men overly exposed to "lesser races" in the tropics, according to common beliefs of the time, had the propensity to slip into savagery. But the Corps did not implode, and the Marines did not lose the popularity they had won in the years leading up to and during the Great War. Why not? Why did so few people condemn the Corps or determine that the Marines would turn their sons into murderers? The answer revolves around how many Americans at the time understood race and manhood.

The Corps's defenders argued that a few bad Marines did not warrant condemning the whole institution. They tended to reference the more popular images of these servicemen over the negative images painted by the *Nation*, the Union Patriotique d'Haiti, and the Anti-Election League of Santo Domingo. They often referenced the restrained manhood that most Marines exhibited in dealing with people who they believed were backward and infuriating. Brigadier General Pendleton claimed that if journalists went down to the Dominican Republic with open minds, then "they will return . . . with entirely different ideas, and instead of decrying will give credit to the patient, tireless, human work and efforts of our officers and men who uplift and help the Dominican people."[159] In the fall of 1921, Major General Lejeune seemed confident that senators would find little fault with Marine conduct in Hispaniola because "the splendid work done by the Marines in Haiti has been placed before the Committee in a very favorable light by the Marine Corps officers who testified."[160] He was right to be optimistic. The Senate investigation committee itself was more inclined to praise than to condemn the Marines. "The very small number of such individual crimes reflects credit on the discipline of the Marine Corps," Senator Tasker Oddie determined.[161]

Throughout all the negative press, there were numerous instances where Marines won sympathy. Samuel Guy Inman, a noted writer and traveler, wrote that "the men who were actively campaigning in the bandit infested interior of Santo Domingo deserve our deepest sympathy."[162] He believed this because of their inglorious work and because they spent long periods of time away from modern amenities and recreation.[163] Former captain Craige echoed this sentiment ten years later. A Marine in Haiti "had no movies, no radio, none of the features of civilized life to which he was accustomed. He saw white faces rarely and white women hardly at all."[164] Even Seligmann, the journalist Marines accused of publishing false accusations against them, tried to paint Marines in a sympathetic light by claiming that they resented their missions in Haiti: "Officers and men have criticized the entire Haitian adventure as a travesty upon humanity and civilization and as a lasting disgrace to the United States Marine Corps."[165]

Some observers argued that the federal government, not the Marines on the ground, should take responsibility for any crimes committed in Hispaniola. "It is the machine, not the man, that is to blame," Inman wrote as he tried to defend the Marines on the island.[166] During the 1920 presidential election campaign, Republican candidate Harding claimed that the Democratic Party misused the Marines to bully weaker peoples. "I will not empower an assistant secretary of the navy to draft a constitution for helpless neighbors in the West Indies," he declared, "and jam it down their throats at the point of bayonets borne by the United States Marines."[167] The *Washington Post* blamed Navy Secretary Daniels for "the misuse of American forces," while the *New York Tribune* stated plainly that "the Marines were not primarily to blame."[168] According to this reasoning, any degeneration of Marine or American manhood that occurred on Hispaniola was not the Marines' fault, but that of men behind desks in Washington.

Additionally, many white observers cast the whole lot of Dominicans and Haitians as untrustworthy. Following popular white racial attitudes, Marines often described the people of both countries as habitual liars.[169] They criticized the manhood of Haitian politicians, who they considered the "lowest of all . . . who spread the improbable tales against our men and officers, which are there after repeated in the press of the United States by writers who are easily deceived."[170] The Senate committee itself sided with the Marines when it claimed that nearly all Haitians at one point or another resisted the occupation forces in some form. Members summarized the credibility of Haitian witnesses against Marines: "The testimony of most native witnesses is highly unreliable and must be closely scrutinized. . . . [M]any unfounded accusations have been made."[171]

The Marines may also have gained enough popularity in the summer of 1918 to see them through these dark postwar years for the U.S. armed forces. Lejeune and the rest of the senior Corps leadership would continue to assert that most Marines served honorably in

Hispaniola as they had in France.[172] In their minds the few isolated incidents of illicit behavior had been handled quickly and fairly by the military courts. They even argued that, in many ways, the Marines in Haiti and the Dominican Republic fought a harder war than the one in France and deserved more credit than they got from the press.

Perhaps just as important, military and civilian members of the investigating committees refused to believe that white American men could behave so savagely. "Ours is a Christian country," concluded one Haiti investigation board, and "we make war as a Christian country should."[173] Ignoring evidence to the contrary, the Senate inquirers asserted that "Americans are not given to mutilating their dead enemies" and stated their conviction "that these cruel or inhuman acts were probably never committed by Americans."[174] To these observers, it probably made more sense that American men never actually murdered, tortured, mutilated, or raped. Marines were supposed to be some of the country's best examples of manhood, not monsters. In a significant sense they simply believed what they wanted to believe.

Ultimately, Marines and many white middle-class American men subscribed to the notion that men and women of color were inferior. Marines wrote about Haitians and Dominicans as though they were wretched peoples. American college professors, preachers, politicians, and authors were of the same mind as them on the superiority of white manhood. Many white Americans would also find nothing untoward about white men using violence to keep people they believed to be from "lesser races" under control in another country.

The brutality of white manhood dotted American newspapers throughout the Great War era. White journalists reported the gruesomeness of African American lynchings in the same tone one would report the weather. Many of these public displays of violence had to do with perceived assaults on white women. As Stephen Kantrowitz has pointed out, "White women's sexuality constituted a crucial defensive perimeter for white supremacy."[175] A Black man's assault on a white woman was perceived as an attack on white supremacy itself, and white men would go to extraordinary lengths to impose vigilante justice. After almost killing the mayor of Omaha, Nebraska, a white mob lynched a Black man accused of assaulting a white woman.[176] In Texas a county judge physically assaulted a white representative of the NAACP for being a "Negro Advocate."[177]

Violence spilled forth against Black and white people who attempted to upset the social order. One of the deadliest race riots in

American history broke out in East St. Louis, Illinois, in the summer of 1917. Industries there replaced white laborers who went on strike with Black workers. Enraged and urged on by the police, white mobs killed over 100 Black people and left over 6,000 more homeless after burning their neighborhoods.[178] "The Black man must submit to the white or the white will destroy," William P. Beard claimed in 1917 soon after a wealthy Black businessman was lynched near Abbeville, South Carolina.[179] The savagery of white Americans could not be ignored by some observers. "It is not uncommon to read accounts telling that the victim was tortured with hot irons, that his eyes were burned out, and that other monstrous cruelties were inflicted upon him," Dr. A. A. Brill wrote. "Such bestiality can be recognized only as a form of perversion. . . . Any one taking part or witnessing a lynching cannot remain a civilized person."[180]

This brutality appeared in Haiti and the Dominican Republic as well. Historian Allan Millett's brief analysis is nonetheless true: Marines were "no more immune to racial prejudice than their fellow Americans."[181] Having sacrificed so much of the cream of American manhood to "save" Western civilization in the Great War, some Americans undoubtedly were shocked to hear of U.S. Marines behaving in a way reminiscent of German barbarity. Simply put, Marines made American manhood appear strong and chivalrous in World War I; they made it look cruel and degenerate in Hispaniola. But most white Americans probably did not see things this way. Nor would they have caught the irony in a poem by Percy Webb, a popular Marine writer of the day. He probably spoke for many Marines of his generation when he urged his fellow Americans:

> Drop your proud and haughty bearing
>   And your egotistic pride;
> Get acquainted with the soldier
>   And the heart and soul,—inside.
> Test and try to analyze him,
>   Criticize him thru and thru,
>   And you'll, very likely, find him
> *Just as good a man as you.*[182]

Even though only one Marine's interpretation, Webb's poem is an interesting indictment of all American men. The Publicity Bureau had published many of his other poems that celebrated Marine manhood.

Contrary to much of the bureau's images of Marines being paragons of military manliness, Webb describes them here as ordinary and imperfect. Written in private, never published, and bereft of the usual hyperbole, in this poem they, like those mentioned in the *Nation* and other newspapers that criticized the Corps, do not come across like supermen, just American men.

6

An Invitation to Brave Men

The trail leads through Cuba and
    Haiti,
  Or wherever our flag is unfurled,
    There's a chance for a rollick,
    A fight or a frolic,
  In any old place in the world.
Come, follow these globe-trotting
    Fighters
And learn about faraway scenes.
    Be a two-fisted rover
    And travel all over
  The trail of the Roving Marines!
— *"The Trail of the Roving Marines," 1920*

On a chilly Saturday evening in Washington, D.C., Marines from the Eastern Recruiting Division lined up on the stage of the National Museum auditorium to perform something the Marine Corps had never done before: a vaudeville show for the public. The men made a clean appearance, with their finest dress blue uniforms replete with brass buttons, golden-colored chevrons, black shoes shined to a mirror polish, and crimson red stripes along the seams of their trousers. A Marine jazz band opened, with trumpets, saxophones, trombones, drums, and clarinets accompanied by a chorus of a dozen enlisted men. In front of the singers and musicians, a spritely corporal swayed his arms and swiveled his feet to the rhythm of the music. Another noncommissioned officer, this time dressed in a khaki field uniform, followed up the song and dance with a lariat exhibition. The audience then witnessed a Marine burlesque his way through a hula dance. Soloists, comedians, and a ukulele quartet composed the rest of the show that ended with two short films about Marines in Haiti and Cuba. This initial performance was only a dress rehearsal performed to an audience of fellow Marines, both officers and enlisted men, and their guests. The next day these newly dubbed "Roving Marines" went on a tour across the United States to show "the fine standard of men who make up the parties, both in the point of physique and intelligence."[1]

These shows were about displaying Marine manhood to boost recruiting. Rovers from the Eastern, Western, and Central Recruiting Divisions rented out music halls, theaters, and high-school auditoriums around the country. They performed skits meant to show audiences a flashy version of the life that Marines lived, one that included adventure, comradery, travel, and excitement. But at its fundamental level, "the idea was to show the country the sort of men that the Marine Corps makes out of the youngsters who enlist, as well as to advertise the service for the purpose of getting recruits."[2] The "sort of men" the Corps had in mind can be found in the following advertisement for the troupe:

> Are you looking for fun and excite—ment—
> Do you find civil life pretty tame?
>   Haven't you got a hunch
>   To be one of the bunch
> Who are ready and willing and game?
> Would you follow the Road of Adventure
> With fellows who know what life
>   means?
>   It's a pathway that's thrilling
>   For lads who are willing—
> The Trail of the Roving Marines![3]

The Marine Publicity Bureau wanted the rovers to be both physically and mentally impressive. With their emphasis on being adventurers, fighters, and world travelers who could also sing and dance, the rovers constituted one of the Corps's flashiest postwar exhibitions of Marine manliness.

The Roving Marines, were just one of the numerous attempts by the Corps to use gender to promote itself and to recruit in the immediate postwar years. The Marines continued to advertise traditional manliness that emphasized character, discipline, and self-improvement, but they employed much more creative methods.[4] They softened their wartime image with the rovers during the final months of Barnett's commandancy. When John A. Lejeune became Commandant, he emphasized efficiency more than his predecessor. Lejeune attempted to reform promotion policies and had Marines guard the mail, reenact Civil War battles, and conduct amphibious landings at Culebra, which created a public profile of the Corps being efficient and ready at a time when many people believed American manhood to be weakening once again. As prewar fears of emasculation and overcivilization returned in the early 1920s, Marines continued to pitch enlistment as a transformative and wholesome experience that would graduate recruits from boyhood to manhood. Collectively, all these efforts by the Corps to survive both postwar retrenchments and negative press associated with Hispaniola centered around persuading the public that the Marines remained an efficient organization that benefited America's manhood.

Wholesome Manhood

The U.S. armed forces shrank after the Great War as soldiers, sailors, and Marines left the services in droves from expired enlistments. This exodus became a serious concern for the Marine Corps, a small organization that needed enough men to carry out its missions across the globe and in the States. In 1920 it shrank to 15,249 men, which was 10,000 less than Congress had allotted in naval appropriations for 1919.[5]

The Publicity Bureau picked a select group of Marines to compose three roving bands. They chose as many veterans of Hispaniola, France, China, and the Philippines as they could to attract audiences and to project an image of Marines as tough and experienced soldiers. But they particularly wanted those who could sing, dance, or play musical instruments "to show the recreation which a man serving in the Marine Corps could enjoy, the manhood that the service develops, and the high intellectual qualities of the personnel of the corps."[6] The bureau especially sought veterans of the Great War to go on these tours.

Perhaps the most famous Marine among the rovers was First Sergeant Dan Daly, a living legend within the Corps itself. A salty expeditionary Marine, winner of two Medals of Honor (for service in China and Haiti), and veteran of the Battle of Belleau Wood, Daly had martial credentials that many in and out the Corps admired. To Marines, he was the "most picturesque of the old-school soldiers."[7] Brigadier General Smedley Butler, a Marine just as well known as the sergeant, said of him, "Daly is a real red-blooded Marine and it was an object lesson to have served with him."[8]

Marines knew Daly as a fighting man, but one wrapped in a certain mystique. Despite his hero status among Marines, he was exceptionally modest and private. Daly frequently refused to have his picture taken, and during interviews, he would never talk about himself for long. "Trying to gather biographical data about Daly from Daly is like quizzing the Sphinx," one Marine wrote, "both are non-committal."[9] "You'll have to be satisfied with whatever the corps officers tell you," Daly told one journalist later in his life, "I don't care for all this publicity, all I ask is to be left alone."[10] When a reporter from the *New York World* got a hold of Daly long enough to conduct an interview, the old Marine deflected every question thrown at him and talked about one of his favorite pastimes instead: "My own story of how I won those medals? Say we heard by wireless on the way home that New York has Sunday baseball now. Gee, that's the best news I've ever heard in a long while. That affair in China? That's a long time ago. That was about the time that Buck Ewing was good, wasn't it? That boy was some catcher."[11] Daly's modesty was a true part of his character, and it endeared him to his fellow Marines as much as his fighting reputation. He appeared to serve only out of love for them and of his own sense of duty, not because he wanted attention from the press.

Despite his qualms with publicity, the Publicity Bureau made Daly one of the main attractions of the Roving Marines. He headed an exhibit that displayed war trophies, such as German helmets, mortars, and machine guns captured by the Marines in France.[12] Rovers advertised Daly as the "only enlisted man in the United States who is the holder of two congressional medals of honor."[13] Other distinguished Marines, like Gunnery Sergeant Charles Hoffman, "another fighting man who has won the highest decorations of three nations for valor on the battlefield," joined the rovers as well.[14] Together, with their combat credentials and reputations for honor and service, Hoffman and Daly represented those Marines who had been through the ultimate male rite of passage—combat. They were the Corps's strongest examples of manhood to put on display to "show the young men of the country the type of men who make up the peace time corps."[15]

The rovers attracted just the kind of publicity the Marines wanted. Newspapers around the country reported favorably on how the shows appealed to male audiences. Reporters liked the Marines' comedic performances because "some of the jokes are regular he-man jokes that were never penned by any kimono-clad play wright in a pale-blue boudoir," wrote the *Richmond News-Leader*.[16] They also put on boxing exhibitions in which a Marine would "square up" with a member of the audience. "The boxing bouts were exceptionally clever, the opponents being types of manhood that are always looked up to by their fellow men for their prowess and manly art of self-defense," observed one spectator.[17]

The Marines' reputation for physical prowess could, in some instances, make potential recruits think twice about joining. The Publicity Bureau wanted the Roving Marines to change their minds. This is where image-softening came into play. "They tell me only about one in 20 can pass the doctor, and you have to be a regular bruiser," claimed one potential applicant. "Get that out of your mind," Sergeant James Higgins told him, "it isn't always size and brawn, (rather its only) proper, 'physical machinery' in him that we require."[18] Boxing, war trophies, and close-order drill made the Roving Marines look strong and exclusive, but the singing, dancing, and comedic acts made them also appear fun and more inviting. Now that the Great War was over, this reflects an important shift in emphasis to appeal to a peacetime society.

These shows demonstrated how malleable the Corps's manly image could be. Marines performed all the traditionally male duties of fighting overseas, but they also sang, danced, and played music and sports. Marines could do it all, so the reasoning went, for it was not just the Corps that was on display. Healthy, clean, and good-looking men on stage was an attempt to persuade audiences that the service was good for America's manhood. Newspaper responses to these performances often praised the men along these lines. "The Roving Marines are made up of as fine a looking set of men to be found anywhere, being a credit, not only to themselves, but to their country," the *Imperial Valley Press* in Southern California remarked.[19]

The Roving Marines did not target male audiences only. Reporters who witnessed their performances commented on the effect the uniformed men had on female members of the audiences. "Did you notice how the eyes of the Quincy girls roved yesterday every time a bevy of those roving Marines roved up and down the street?" one reporter teased. "They were just ordinary, healthy and husky young men . . . , but they had on dress uniforms—all neat and blue, with glaring read stripes you know!"[20] When the Roving Marines visited Montgomery, Alabama, a large number of the attendants were young women, "who gazed on the full-dress uniforms of Uncle Sam's choicest picked fighters with unaffected appreciation."[21] Apparently, this attention from women irritated some of the men at the show with them. "Some of the male members of the audience were heard to wonder why it is that so

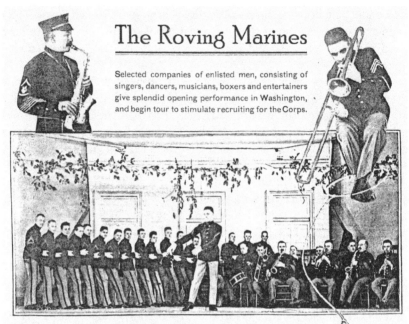

The Roving Marines

Selected companies of enlisted men, consisting of singers, dancers, musicians, boxers and entertainers give splendid opening performance in Washington, and begin tour to stimulate recruiting for the Corps.

THE ROVING MARINES got off to a flying start before a representative audience of officers, men and their invited guests in the auditorium of the National Museum in Washington on Saturday evening, January 31. It is significant that such an audience, comprising those of long service, others who were brought into the Corps by the recent war, and still others who watched the show with the interest of civilians, were a unanimous unit in pronouncing the program as an unqualified success. The Roving Marines are now roving in earnest, and when this article goes to press one detachment will be showing in Charleston, W. Va., another in Terre Haute, Ind., while the Rovers of the Pacific Slope will be delighting Los Angeles, Cal.

The initial show in Washington was in reality the final dress rehearsal of the combined forces of the Eastern and Central Divisions. There were some lively jazzing by two of the "jazziest" bands that ever made a Marine's feet beat time to syncopated melody; a roper who whirled a lariat *a la* Will Rogers and never missed a whirl; some ukulele players who can "uke" with the best Hawaiian impresarios in the business, singers, dancers ,comedians and—they were all Marines!

The program that follows shows the scope of the show, but only those who saw it could appreciate the verve, the pep, and the almost professional finish that the Rovers gave to their entertainment. Without making any invidious comparisons the greatest hits were scored by the Jazz Orchestra, all veterans of the Marine Band; Corporal Madden, well-billed as the Demi-Tasse Will Rogers, who gave an exhibition with the lariat that would make a sensation on the professional stage; Quartermaster Sergeant Levin in his burlesque Hula Dance; and the ukulele quartette that gave an unusually tuneful act, while Green and Healey, formerly popular

Fig. 45. "The Roving Marines." From *Recruiters' Bulletin*, February 1920, 3.

many girls get uniform struck," noted the *Montgomery Advertiser*.[22] The Publicity Bureau hoped that attracting women with the quality of the manhood on stage would stick in the minds of the young men in the audience, perhaps inducing some to enlist.

The tangible effect the Roving Marines had on recruiting is difficult to measure precisely, but recruiters often reported positive results following a performance. On a practical level, the rovers' variety of skits and exhibitions obscured what life was really like for most in the Corps. In celebrating Marine manliness, they omitted the boredom, danger, and risk involved with being stationed in Hispaniola or fighting in France. These shows were all about the supposed benefits of being a Marine and none of the costs. But, they increased the Corps's public exposure, provided information about the Corps, and gave local recruiters a chance to mingle with attendees and hand out literature. "This feature proves to be one of the best advertisements that can be obtained as the recruiters come in personal contact with the people on the street," one report enthused.[23] Recruiters often received more inquiries from potential applicants after the Roving Marines left town. That, in part, had to do with newspaper advertisements more so than actual personal attendance at the performance. After a show in Pittsburg, Pennsylvania, one recruiter reported: "Inquiries have increased very noticeably, especially by mail from the nearby towns which the Pittsburg papers have reached. This proving that the paid adverting is doing good work."[24] As spring turned to summer, however, the trail of the Roving Marines soon came to an end.

John A. Lejeune and Marine Manliness

In late June 1920 Major General Barnett waited in his office to be relieved of his post as Commandant of the Marine Corps. A few days prior he had received a request for his resignation from Secretary of the Navy Daniels. Furious and quite hurt, Barnett uncovered the secretary's plan to have him replaced by Major General Lejeune. By now, several separate issues had come to a head to precipitate his removal. First was Daniel's original policy of allowing service heads to serve only one four-year term. But the ongoing world war necessitated Daniels keeping them all in place until its conclusion. Out of the service chiefs, Barnett was the only one who did not tender his resignation at the conclusion of the war in November 1918, believing that he served at the discretion of the president, not the secretary of the navy.[25]

Barnett had also gone around Daniels's authority in May 1918 by seeking a promotion to lieutenant general through his own Republican friends in Congress. This attempt to gain a third star came to nothing when it ran afoul Thomas Butler, father of Brigadier General Smedley Butler and a leading member of the House Committee on Naval Affairs. The elder Butler strongly opposed the promotion bill and declared Barnett a "rocking chair warrior." That insult probably came from the representative listening to his own son's complaints about the Commandant, for General Smedley disliked General Barnett strongly. To refer to a Marine as a "rocking chair warrior" was to call into question his expeditionary and combat experience, two important elements of Marine manliness. While Barnett had a long and distinguished career as an officer, it appeared to his critics inside and out of the Corps that six years among the social circles in Washington, D.C., had made him soft.[26]

Secretary Daniels picked Lejeune for the post because his record as a leader on expeditionary duty and as a combat commander was second to none. An 1888 graduate of the Naval Academy, Lejeune was part of the first generation of Marine officers ever to be commissioned from the school. He led Marines on the cruiser *Cincinnati* during the Spanish-American War, commanded a battalion in Panama in 1904, and led a regiment at Vera Cruz in 1914, with recruiting duty and various staff and fleet assignments in between.[27] His stint at the Army War College in Carlisle, Pennsylvania, from 1909 to 1910 proved a crucial turning point in his career. While there, Lejeune developed professionally and intellectually and made himself a known and respected quantity among army officers. This eventually led to his most prestigious assignment, commanding officer of the Second Division, U.S. Army, during the Great War.[28] Lejeune led the division, comprising both soldiers and Marines, through the major offensives of 1918, including Saint-Mihiel, Mont Blanc, and the Meuse-Argonne offensive.

Lejeune, therefore, had the manly field qualifications that Barnett lacked. There were Marine officers who had more medals or who had more expeditionary experience. But Lejeune's command of the Second Division in France put him above the rest in combat leadership and command prestige. These two elements impressed Representative Butler, who wrote to Lejeune: "We are going to have a Marine Corps and it is to be commanded by a real soldier. . . . I am pleased with your appointment."[29] This reference to a "real soldier" was the opposite of "rocking chair warrior." It not only implied the value of Lejeune's combat experience over his predecessor but also his manhood. Within the Marine Corps, it was a fine line between being a gentleman staff officer and a rough-and-ready line officer.[30] Lejeune seemed to walk that margin better than any Marine at the time, which made him an ideal fit for the post. Secretary Daniels believed him to be "one of the ablest military men in the world" while also having the "confidence and the admiration of the great body of fighters in the Marine Corps, in the Navy and the Army."[31] Barnett simply no longer commanded that level of respect.

Barnett would not step down without voicing his grievances, however. According to one witness, when Lejeune arrived to assume command, Barnett refused to let him sit down. "John, stand up there just a minute, we've been good friends all our lives—close friends. Why didn't you let me know what was going on?" Barnett said that if the situation were reversed, "I would have come to you and told you exactly what was happening." "George," Lejeune replied, "my hands were tied." Barnett could do nothing now but accept the situation as a fait accompli. "All right. I stand relieved, you're the Commandant," he said before quitting the post he had held since 1914. Thus, on June 30, 1920, Major General Lejeune became the thirteenth Commandant of the Marine Corps.[32]

Many letters of congratulations arrived from officers around the Marine Corps. Feland, Waller, Ellis, and others all sent encouraging words and best wishes. Lejeune responded to as many as he could, which was no mean feat considering the situation he had just inherited. First of all, Secretary Daniels forcing General Barnett to resign from the post gave Lejeune's appointment a controversial feel.[33] In addition, and while still getting acquainted with the significant duties of his new job, rumors of Marine misconduct in Haiti and the Dominican Republic had spread and drawn the attention of the press, the secretary of the navy, and Congress. That fire would be put out in due time, but Lejeune's main concern was elsewhere.

To achieve his long-term goals for the Marine Corps, the new Commandant had to fix its immediate postwar problems: troop numbers and recruiting. To his former Second Division staff officer Ellis, Lejeune wrote, "The most pressing matter at the present time is that of recruiting, as I am anxious to see the Corps brought up to its full permanent strength as early a date as possible."[34] In his first month in office, the general sent letters to recruiting officers around the country letting them know the imperativeness of getting the Corps fully up to strength as soon as possible. "Please impress on all recruiters the fact that they are the missionaries of the finest Corps in the world and that its destiny is largely in their hands," he wrote. "The eyes of the whole Corps are turned towards him, and I take the deepest personal interest in the success of his individual efforts."[35]

Lejeune assumed the helm of that Corps as it faced drastic postwar retrenchments. Americans wanted a "return to normalcy," which meant, among other things, shrinking all of the armed services. The cuts in men, money, and matériel drove Lejeune to make efficiency and economy top institutional priorities. With this in mind, he laid out a plan on how the Corps would proceed:

> In a military organization quality of production is represented by the physical condition, discipline, morale, and degree of military training and instruction of the officers and men. It depends upon the physique and character of the men appointed or enlisted and on the manner in which they are handled during their military service. How to bring the quality of the troops to a high degree of perfection is the greatest of the problems confronting us.[36]

By emphasizing "physical condition," discipline, morale, and character, Lejeune focused on how the Marine Corps would continue to promote manliness and manhood within its ranks.

Commandant Lejeune worked to keep Marines in the public eye as much as possible. With the help of Brigadier General Butler, he would craft a peacetime image of the Marine Corps that promoted efficient manhood, its development, and improvement.[37] This effort would help accomplish two things. First, this evolving masculine image would run counter to the ongoing negative reports coming out of Hispaniola. It would also employ and promote the Marines' ideas of manliness toward the more practical concern of filling the ranks. Lejeune reported to Congress, "Discharges and separations from the service exceeded enlistments to such an extent that by the end of the calendar year 1919 the strength of the corps was over 11,000 short of that authorized by law, making it impossible for the corps to properly carry out its mission."[38] He convinced lawmakers of the need for adequate appropriations, but that did not stop the Corps from shrinking to 15,000 men during his first year as Commandant.

The Roving Marines ended when Lejeune took the helm. Although they worked mostly under his predecessor's watch, Lejeune was proud of what the rovers accomplished. He reported to Congress that in some towns after the Roving Marines left, public inquiries about enlisting increased as high as 1,000 percent.[39] Nevertheless, further budget cuts slotted for 1921 ended the trail of the Roving Marines. The recruiting service also took a big hit in manpower. In the summer of 1920, 845 Marines were on recruiting duty; that number dwindled to 375 by February 1921.[40] Despite this reduction of recruiters throughout the country, "at the beginning of the fiscal year 1921 recruiting was deemed the most important problem before the Marine Corps," the officer in charge of enlistments wrote to Lejeune.[41] Now the Marines had to pay greater attention to economy and efficiency.

Postwar Manhood and Masculinity

By 1920, the distinctions between *masculinity* and *manliness* in the United States began to blur more so than they had ten years earlier. "Masculinity," long used as a neutral term to describe all things "male," blended with "manliness" as it began to carry moral and mental implications.[42] The "new masculinity," which celebrated physical appearance and material success, grew in prevalence. Masculinity, therefore, began to take on new meanings. For a growing number of white-middle class men, to be masculine meant not just being male but also being successful in their profession or career. After the war American men had to perform their "masculine" duties as breadwinners for their families. If there was a hegemonic masculinity during the 1920s, it took of the form of white civilian men achieving in the public sphere, whether it be in the office, on the factory floor, or on the baseball diamond or football field. Millions of men who had just been discharged from the military were expected to find occupations, raise families, and be efficient, upstanding, and patriotic citizens.

"Masculinity" came into more popular usage as the prewar notions of "overcivilization" came back with the return of peacetime occupations. Men risked being "emasculated" by the entrance of women into the public sphere and the owners of companies and corporations who dominated their lives through wage labor.[43] Except for race riots, the early 1920s was a time of relative peace, Prohibition, and woman's suffrage. As women "encroached" upon traditional male spheres of influence, men found the activities that defined their gender compromised. With no war to fight, the armed forces became unappealing. Military manliness, which had been celebrated intensely during the war years, receded as the most popular form of male culture. Additional outlets such as bars closed due to Prohibition while others like politics opened to women. The spheres of the home (feminine) and the public realm (masculine) began to blend. Now that the Great War was over, white masculinity had to be played out in books, on the vaudeville stage, on the baseball diamond, and on the silver screen instead of on the battlefield. The men who were the most convincingly masculine in these arenas included Babe Ruth, F. Scott Fitzgerald, Buster Keaton, and Charlie Chaplin because of how successful, wealthy, popular, and influential they were. Traditional notions of ideal male behavior persisted in certain crowds, however.

While all of this was going on, the U.S. armed services, particularly the Marines, held fast to a traditional manliness that emphasized character and the production of reliable, active, and efficient men. Sensing that most Americans and Congress had lost the taste for extravagant military expenditures, Commandant Lejeune asserted that the Corps would shrink even further if people thought the Marines were idle and unproductive. "This belief we must combat by engaging in useful work," Lejeune wrote.[44] Reports of Marines indiscriminately killing Haitians and Dominicans increased between 1921 and 1922. Counterimages of Marines doing good work and producing dependable citizens were now more crucial than ever. By Lejeune's reckoning, Marines proved their worth in peacetime by guarding government property and by serving in Haiti and the Dominican Republic. "That work is worth-while," he claimed, "as is all work done for the benefit of other people."[45] He maintained, as he had done during the naval and Senate investigations of the occupation forces on Hispaniola, that the Marines were behaving chivalrously on the island.

One of the key services that the Corps provided, Lejeune claimed, was the development of manhood among Americans who enlisted in the Marines. "At Parris Island and Mare Island we are training young Americans to be better men physically, mentally and morally," he argued, "and this process is continued here, on board ship, and wherever they may go during their enlistments." Lejeune wrote that the Corps inculcated several manly virtues among its young recruits that included "self-control—industry, energy, fidelity, unselfishness, honor, courage, and self-sacrifice."[46]

Lieutenant Colonel E. B. Manwaring collected copies of letters written by a select group of recruits in boot camp that supported Lejeune's claims. Although the men were asked specifically to write letters describing life at boot camp, many of the responses were so positive that Manwaring wanted to publish them for publicity purposes.[47] These recruits claimed that life in the Marine Corps was making men out of them. One described boot camp to his friend, claiming that the hiking, drilling, and food had salubrious effects. "When you get out you will be a man," he asserted.[48] Others expressed the same sentiments when writing home. "Altogether, recruit training is pretyy [sic] hard work but if you go into it with the right spirit, it will certainly make a man of you," he declared.[49] But recruits had to be endowed with of the right "material," which the Corps would then mold into its own manly, Marine image. "To sum it up," wrote a recruit from Indiana, "the Marine Corps is just what I thought it was—a place where a man has to soldier to make anything out of himself."[50]

Recruits also wrote about the character of the Marines they met. Before the Great War, recruiters often harped on the idea that young men would be surrounded not by drunkards and reprobates, but by men of good character. "I found that the Marine Corps as a whole is composed of a very fine lot of men," assured one recruit.[51] "Our sergeant and corporals are very fine fellows," wrote another.[52] Recruits seemed to appreciate the cleanliness, discipline, and soldierly bearing of the Marines at Parris Island. "I can say that the sergeant in charge of us was one swell fellow," a recruit from Massachusetts claimed. "Of course he was strict with us in the line of discipline. . . . I don't believe he swore more than twice and believe me he was well liked by all the fellows."[53] Training could be harsh, but the Marines took care of them and treated them fairly, these newcomers claimed.

They often associated this good character with their drill instructors, who to this very day are often the most iconic Marines. The recruits were raw material, Parris Island was the anvil, and drill instructors were the hammers used to pound and shape that material. They turned recruits into Marines, and young boys into men, according to these letters. Recruits respected their drill instructors, not only because of their rank, authority, knowledge, and experience in the Corps but also because of what all of that added up to: they were real men in their eyes. "I was assigned to the 610th company with a real man over us," one recruit wrote. "My first impression of him was the he was the hardest and crankiest old fogy on the Island but I soon changed my mind; he sure was a prince."[54] They frequently described their drill instructors not only as "princes" but also as "swell fellows," meaning they were trustworthy and respectable. Letters painted these Marines as efficient, clean looking, tough, and "well-bred," all of which the recruits understood as indications of red-blooded manhood. A Kentuckian's drill instructor was quite simply "one of the finest men I ever knew."[55] The manliness and character of these Marines was a large part of the reason why some recruits saw the Corps as "the best man making outfit."[56]

But the recruits who wrote these letters were not typical trainees. They were chosen to "undergo a special course of instruction and training which would prepare them for the efficient performance of duty as Drill Instructors."[57] Upon completion of the course, they would have received advanced training on how to be instructors and rifle-range coaches. These men were likely the most highly motivated lot in training, which lessened the chances that any of them would complain about their experience. Additionally, they probably knew the letters would be read by their superiors. It is impossible, therefore, to gage the sincerity of these writings.

Recruits' parents also contributed to the idea that the Corps helped their sons transition from boyhood to manhood. One mother from Missouri wrote that she had tried her best to "teach him [her son] to be a man."[58] Before he went to boot camp, she had spent a fortune in tuition to send him to a military school hoping to facilitate that process, "and during the 2½ years he was there he never learned as much as he has learned in three months where he is now."[59] An ill father requested that his son be granted leave from boot camp to come home and be at his side. After his son's visit, he wrote, "When he left me just a kid in his second pair of long pants I was afraid I was doing wrong to let him go but when I lay there fighting the old grim reaper and looked up and saw a hard boiled *man* standing by my bed and realized that it was my little boy grown up I was glad I let you have him and commenced getting well right off."[60] During the postwar years, the return of peacetime manliness and the investigations of Marines in Hispaniola notwithstanding, some Americans still trusted the Corps to turn their young boys into men.

According to these letters, the moral, mental, and physical dimensions of manhood remained key components of the Marine Corps's postwar service culture. The fact that the Marines collected them for publicity purposes reflects their common practice of advertising their manliness to attract recruits. They did this purposefully to make the Corps look like it was still good for the manhood of the nation. This intentionality is further supported by the fact that negative descriptions of boot camp or of life in the service are completely absent from the stack of letters. It is highly unlikely that everyone enjoyed recruit training and liked their drill instructors. The Marines who picked these letters clearly wanted to highlight the benefits of recruit training over any burdens or costs. In doing so, they could pitch their service as a man-making institution, one that corresponded to Lejeune's vision.

Lejeune expected upright manliness from the officer ranks as well. He oversaw the completion of the 1921 *Marine Corps Manual*, in which he placed the responsibility for the betterment of enlisted Marines squarely on the officers' shoulders. The Commandant advocated that the relationship between officer and enlisted should be as between father and son. Officers should be looking out for their Marines' welfare, both physically and mentally. He wrote that this was "vital to the well-being of the Marine Corps" because young enlisted men "are in the formative period of their lives, and officers owe it to them, to their parents, and to the nation, that when discharged from the services they should be far better men physically, mentally and morally than they were when they enlisted."[61] Officers should encourage athletics and lead them in academic instruction whenever possible. Above all, Lejeune wanted his officers displaying the very same marks of manliness expected from enlisted men. The Commandant stressed "industry, energy, initiative, determination, enthusiasm, firmness, kindness, justness, self-control, unselfishness, honor, and courage." Every Marine, especially every officer, "should endeavor by all means in his power to make himself the possessor of these qualities and thereby to fit himself to be a real leader of men."[62]

While Lejeune characterized the relationship between Marine officers and enlisted men in paternalistic terms, a navy officer, Rear Admiral William L. Rodgers, defined it differently. During an address to the graduating class of newly commissioned Marine officers at Quantico in June 1923, he claimed that two classes made up the naval services: the working classes, which he equated to enlisted men, and the managerial classes, which meant the officers. Those graduates assembled, he said, would be a part of this managerial class and therefore needed strength of character to lead. To lead men, then, they must be "gentlemen" with "high character," which meant possessing courage, virtue, honor, and loyalty. This last trait, he emphasized, "is incompatible with self-seeking and the desire to get one's self in the limelight for selfish purposes."[63]

Rodgers's speech highlights both the similarities and the differences between how navy and Marine leadership defined the relationship between commissioned and enlisted ranks. Both services valued strong character and claimed to uplift men's lives. "The Marine Corps, and the service it, through you, is able to render to the country, will owe much to your development of professional knowledge here, but it will owe more to your character," the rear admiral advised.[64] Since before the Great War, however, Marines often presented themselves as a more "democratic" service, one in which class distinctions between officers and enlisted men had blurred.[65] Rodgers's ruminations on class reveal that some in the navy likened officers and enlisted men to managers and laborers, while Lejeune and others in the Marines preferred father and son or teacher and scholar.

Additionally, Rodgers promoted the virtues among officers that Lejeune expected of all Marines. In the Corps there was more continuity regarding expectations of character that went up and down the ranks. These "military virtues" aligned with traditional manliness that would have appealed to peacetime Americans, and Lejeune endeavored to get his Marines to display them publicly and often.

Efficient Manhood

Commandant Lejeune wanted the Marine Corps as efficient as possible in matters of recruiting, training, and expeditionary duty. In postwar America efficiency became even more necessary, as budget cuts and demobilization racked the armed services. "Demobilization is a bad thing for a service like the Marine Corps because it could affect efficiency," Lejeune wrote, "[and] lack of efficiency could be fatal for an institution that does nothing the army cannot do."[66] He held no delusions regarding the fiscal situation in Washington, D.C., and its potential to damage the Corps. "Officers and men are now filled with the determination to work unceasingly to maintain the efficiency of the corps. . . . It will be the mission of all to do all in their power to jealously guard its great reputation," he reported.[67] To clarify what Lejeune meant by "efficiency" and how it related to manliness requires some context.

In the 1920s efficiency equated to preventing or reducing the wastage of time, money, or resources.[68] Government bureaucrats, business managers, and industrial capitalists made it their watchword. "Efficiency" appears repeatedly in the army's and navy's annual reports, in which each branch divulged its expenditures to the public. Efficiency could manifest itself in many ways. Businesses, organizations, and individuals could be efficient by using their available resources to produce optimum results. Alternatively, they could work specifically to increase the efficiency of their own or another organization. To be efficient or to increase efficiency required many of the traits that Lejeune and the Marine Corps promoted, namely intelligence, selflessness, honesty, and discipline. To claim that a man or an organization was efficient implied that he or it had all of those characteristics.[69] Discourses on "efficiency" in the military, therefore, were about more than just economics—they were very much about an organization's or individual's character and manliness.

Officer Promotion and Retention

Lejeune endeavored to increase efficiency in the Marine Corps, in part, by ridding the service of physically, mentally, and morally unfit officers through reform of the promotion and retention processes. Marine officers promoted by seniority, meaning that those with the longest time in a particular rank advanced over officers with less time in the same rank when a vacancy opened. It did not matter how many medals, how much combat experience, or how reputable an officer's character was, only time in rank. Lejeune and many others wanted to promote by merit selection, whereby officers came before a selection board that weighed their performance, experience, abilities, and character. The ones with the highest marks in those areas would promote or be retained, while the rest, no matter how long they had been in a rank or the service, would not. This system, its proponents argued, would rid the Corps of "dead weight" and allow younger, more vigorous officers to achieve authority and responsibility faster and more efficiently.[70]

Commandant Lejeune had to tread carefully because his predecessor's attempt to institute promotion and retention reform had created tensions within the officer corps. Barnett had appointed Colonel John H. Russell in 1919 to chair a retention board for officers desiring to remain in the service after the armistice. Known infamously as the "Russell Board," it sought to create parity between officers who deployed to France and those who did not. The effect, however, was that those with major combat experience in Europe felt slighted. Additionally, rumors circulated that the Russell Board preferred officers "who will break bread with you and marry your daughters." True or not, the whole affair smacked of capriciousness and painted Barnett out to be a Marine who valued "headquarters types" over expeditionary and combat-tested officers.[71]

Soon after becoming Commandant, Lejeune appointed a fellow veteran of the Great War, Major General Wendell C. Neville, to chair a new board to fill vacancies in billets created by officers leaving the Corps after the war and reward those who had fought in France and Hispaniola and wanted to remain in uniform.[72] The "Neville Board" included Marines like Brigadier General Butler and Brigadier General Harry Lee, both of whom favored the retention and promotion of officers with combat and expeditionary experience. Their list of favored officers included many prior enlisted men who, although lacking political connections and formal education, had received commissions during the war and fought bravely. Based on appearances, the Neville Board differed from the Russell Board in that it gave the impression that Marines who had demonstrated their manhood in combat deserved preference in promotion and retention over those who had not. Based in part on this unofficial criterion, the board recommended 692 officers to be retained out of 1,118 applicants. Prior enlisted men numbered 489 of those who received permanent commissions.[73]

The Russell and Neville Boards revealed a divide between Marines who wanted younger, more energetic officers promoted by selection and those who preferred the traditional ways of seniority that rewarded time in service. The *Marine Corps Gazette* published a copy of the 1922 "Promotion Bill," which was set to go before Congress and proposed the establishment of permanent promotion boards throughout the armed services to determine the eligibility of officers seeking advancement. If an officer failed his first board, he could try a second time. If he failed again, then he would retire upon reaching a certain age. The *Gazette* also published Commandant Lejeune's explanations behind the proposed changes, declaring that for an officer "to oppose it [the promotion bill] is tantamount to admitting that he expects to be found disqualified by the board, or that he expects not to be placed on the eligible list prepared by the board."[74] Since these boards would be evaluating officers' mental, moral, and physical fitness, suggesting that one would not pass the examination was equivalent to challenging his manhood. In response, Marine officers *anonymously* came out against the proposed bill in the very next issue. Promotion by selection immediately after the Great War, they feared, would be unfair to the great majority of officers who did not get the opportunity to fight in France through no fault of their own. Several cited that promotion by seniority was fairest to all parties involved and that selection boards ran the risk of pressure exerted by outside political influence.[75]

Notions of manliness shaped this discussion surrounding Marine officer-promotion reform in several ways. By making the qualifications for promotion about mental, moral, and physical fitness, Lejeune attempted to make selection about efficiency but inadvertently made it about essential qualities of manhood instead. Those who did not measure up to the promotion boards' standards would have to retire. For officers who opposed the legislation, this was not about efficiency, it was about their fitness as men being judged unfairly. The proponents and opponents in this debate corresponded roughly to the two predominate forms of Marine manliness: expeditionary Marines, with combat credentials who valued battlefield prowess, against headquarters Marines, with less overseas experience who valued tradition. Congress in the end agreed with the latter group. Much to Lejeune and Butler's chagrin, the bill failed to pass. Promotion by selection would not be achieved in the Marine Corps until 1935.

Guarding the Mail

Guarding the U.S. Mail from November 1921 to March 1922 gave the Marine Corps an opportunity domestically to demonstrate its own efficiency. Due to frequent mail robberies around the country starting in 1921, the U.S. Postal Service requested help from President Harding. He delegated the task to Secretary of the Navy Edwin Denby, a former Marine, who notified Lejeune that the Corps had been selected to guard the mail. "I am proud that my old Corps has been chosen for duty so honorable and so hard as that of protecting the United States Mail," he stated in his notification.[76] Lejeune appointed Brigadier General Logan Feland to implement a plan whereby armed Marines protected post offices, mail trucks, and trains from robbery.[77]

This new mission required Marines to work with the Postal Service and the public, which caused concern due to the potential danger involved. Across the country, Americans saw sharply dressed Marines armed with pistols and shotguns at post offices and transportation sites.[78] New York City perhaps saw the highest concentration of these guards. Hundreds of men, pulled from Quantico, Virginia, and the Brooklyn Navy Yard, worked eight-hour shifts guarding post offices, railroad terminals, and mail trucks.[79]

Denby issued explicit orders to the Marines on guard throughout the country. Under no circumstances were they to surrender their weapons if suddenly held up by armed criminals; better a dead Marine than stolen mail, according to Denby. "Never forget that the honor of the Corps is in your keeping," he wrote, as though the Corps's manhood was at stake, "you must be constantly alert and you must, when on guard duty, keep your weapons in hand and, if attacked, shoot, and shoot to kill."[80]

And shoot they did. In Green Bay, Wisconsin, a twenty-two-year-old Marine named Marcus Hanson spotted two men hiding between two boxcars. Thinking they were criminals, he opened fire with his shotgun, hitting one of the men, Otto Lambrecht. Lambrecht's wounds

Fig. 46. Marines guarding the U.S. Mail, ca. 1921. History Division, Marine Corps Archives.

were not fatal, but he claimed to be an innocent bystander trying to hitch a ride on another train when Hanson shot him without warning. The governor of Wisconsin, John J. Blaine, ordered an investigation, which led to a warrant for Hanson's arrest. Thinking their mission a federal one that transcended local and state authorities, neither the Marine Corps nor the Navy Department agreed to hand over Hanson for arrest without investigating the incident on their own.

Governor Blaine then began to criticize publicly the policy of Marines guarding the mail on two levels. First, he accused the federal government of overreacting and putting innocent peoples' lives in danger. He saw it as an unlawful establishment of a "military regime" over society. Second, he called into question the security expertise of the Marine guards in Green Bay that day. "Innocent men will be shot down like so many rats," warned Blaine, "according to the whim, caprice, inefficiency, inexperience, mis-judgement, or even willfulness of the guard."[81] Ultimately, the governor likened the Marines to children requiring greater supervision rather than to grown men by saying, "youths should not have authority to shoot at their discretion."[82] The opportunity to provide efficient service to the nation appeared to be backfiring on the Corps. By January 1922, however, Secretary Denby had approved the findings of the naval investigation of the shooting, which exonerated Hanson completely.[83]

Incidents like this resulted, perhaps, from the conflicting nature of Denby's original message to the Marines, which many probably took as an order. On one hand, he gave Marines carte blanche to shoot but only "if attacked." He also said, on the other, that "the mail must be delivered or there must be a Marine dead at the post of duty."[84] Add Denby's claims of the Marine Corps's honor and reputation being at stake, and what the young sentry finds himself in is a situation where he and many of his comrades are looking for an opportunity to shoot. With potentially his, and the Corps's, manhood at stake, it should be no surprise that shootings occurred despite the absence of reports of Marines being held up or shot at by armed robbers.

Other examples of Marines shooting people popped up all over the country. A Marine named Carl W. Mays wounded two college students in Denmark, South Carolina, for refusing to leave the train he was guarding. The Postal Service defended Mays in this case and commended him for doing his duty.[85] Another Marine guard shot a civilian named George Reynolds in the leg as he attempted to board a mail car near Elkhart, Indiana.[86] In Texas a private killed Wiley Clarke after the latter, who had been previously removed from a train by the same Marine, approached menacingly and said, "I am not afraid of you and all your guns."[87] Near Savannah, Georgia, Sergeant N. S. Bethers expended five shotgun shells at three men whom he caught in the process of removing packages from an express boxcar, wounding two of them.[88] The exact figures of how many Marine shootings took place in the country are not available, nor is it known how many people were wounded or killed in such incidents.

The Marines on guard duty even clashed with local police. Captain Victor F. Bleasdale, the officer in charge of a 150–200 Marine guard unit in St. Louis, Missouri, informed his men that the only authorized persons allowed near the mail were properly credentialed U.S. Mail employees. He ordered them to stop and turn away everyone else, including the city police. The Marines believed they exercised federal authority and assumed that anyone, including potential thieves, could don a local police uniform and try to fool the guard on post. "This was sort of a shock to the police force," Bleasdale later recalled, because they were not used to anyone in their jurisdictions being beyond their authority.[89] He described one incident in which a young policeman approached a Marine on a loading platform in a railroad tunnel, even after being ordered to halt. The Marine shot a pillar right next to the policeman's head, which sprayed his face with concrete bits and precipitated his retreat. "I never had a damn bit of trouble with police after that," Bleasdale said.[90] Marine guards clearly did not wait to be attacked or fired upon before shooting.

The Marine Corps and the Postal Service put their own official spin on the whole operation, despite the many controversial shootings. After several months of working closely with the Postal Service, Lejeune reported to Congress that, while Marines were on post, armed robberies had ceased.[91] Acting Postmaster General Hubert Work wrote to him that the Marines "performed their arduous and difficult duty in a most excellent manner and they have my most earnest praise and appreciation for their invaluable service to the public."[92] Through that, Marines attempted to show themselves ready to serve at a moment's notice and that they could be trusted to do a dangerous mission among civilians efficiently and safely. Whether they did it safely is debatable at best. "When we are needed, we are needed in a hurry," a Marine wrote. "In the past we have never failed to respond, no matter what the call. The public expects us to be ready, able, and willing. We ourselves confidently expect in every year 'to lend a hand at every job'—to be Marines."[93] As far as Lejeune was concerned, the Marines who guarded the mail aided his efforts to "make the Marine Corps as useful as possible to the Government and the People of the United States in peace as well as in war."[94]

For the navy and the Marine Corps, guarding the mail went well. The Department of the Navy issued a press release that proclaimed, "It is an impressive commentary on the esteem in which Marines are held by the Nation's criminals as well as its law-abiding citizens that holdups almost ceased from the day the Marine Guards were placed in charge of mail shipments."[95] Colonel Rufus Lane suggested in a group conference with the Commandant that the Marines take over the job permanently. Lejeune agreed that guarding the mail afforded "a splendid example of the use to which our reserve may be put in time of emergency." It gave the Corps another chance to demonstrate its readiness, efficiency, and manliness. But he contended that Marines should only be used for operations like this in times of emergency. "The spirit of the country is against the use of the military forces as a permanent thing in domestic affairs," he told his staff officers at headquarters, "they are glad to have our men guard the mails now, but would not care to have them continuously on that duty."[96] Lejeune was also concerned that the allocation of Marines to such a permanent detail would take manpower away from potential expeditionary duty—the Marines' bread and butter. The federal government called upon the Corps to guard the mail temporarily again in 1926.

Marine publications spun the whole affair as a credit to the Corps's manhood. "The order assigning Marines to do this duty contains a phrase which should thrill every Marine who reads it," read an article in the *Leatherneck*, a relatively new Marine-operated newspaper out of Quantico. "The mails must be delivered or a Marine must be dead at his post. A threat to cowards, but an invitation to brave men! Such an order could be issued only to an organization known to contain *men*."[97] Like the Roving Marines, guarding the mail placed the Corps's manliness on display, although in a much different context. Percy Webb, the de facto poet laureate of the Great War–era Marine Corps, waxed heroic in the December 1921 issue of the *Leatherneck*:

> The Banker wasn't worried
> When he had bonds to send,
> For he had read the tidings
> That his troubles were to end.
> "Put those bonds in the mail," he said;
> "No one will dare to rob,
> For everything is lovely when
> Marines are on the job!"
>
> "Mother," said the daughter,
> "I might enjoy this trip,
> But I'm afraid that bandits
> Will steal my purse and grip."
> "Hush, daughter! Do not worry."
> The mother softly said;
> "U.S. Marines are riding
> In the baggage coach ahead."
> . . .
>
> The robber band was waiting;
> The train came around the bend,
> But when they saw the Leathernecks
> Their plans came to an end.
> "Lets beat it!" said the bandits,
> As they turned around to scoot;

"We're off of robbin' trains when the
    Marines commence to shoot!"[98]

Marines guarding the U.S. Mail may have halted robberies, but they
also endangered people's lives and upset local and state authorities.
That they spun these shootings into yarns about their manhood anyway is a testament to the influence of manliness on the Marines' public
image and its pervasiveness within their ranks.

Maneuvers

In addition to the Roving Marines and guarding the U.S. Mail, Marines turned their training exercises into public events to showcase
their readiness and, of course, their manliness. The new Marine Corps
base at Quantico was home to the service's recently established East
Coast Expeditionary Force. This unit would be the Corps's quick-
reaction force of the early 1920s and had to maintain a high level of
readiness. Always with an eye toward efficiency *and* publicity, Lejeune
and Butler concocted a ploy to gain more attention while sharpening
the Quantico Marines' expeditionary edge: reenactments of Civil War
battles. The four battlefield maneuvers that the East Coast Expeditionary Force conducted from 1921 to 1924 brought even more public
attention to the Corps.

On one hand, these maneuvers were about training Marines for
war. Butler argued that marching Marines around northern Virginia
to conduct in-depth training exercises for a fortnight would facilitate
combat readiness more efficiently than six months of in-class instruction. He wanted to demonstrate that "we are able to mobilize our
scattered forces and have a small, well-trained army [operational] in
a few days; any army of sufficient size to make some impression in
case it is needed for international police work."[99] Butler and his aides
assigned the Fifth and Sixth Marine Regiments opposing roles during
this maneuver, supported in the field by modern artillery and aviation
units from Quantico.[100] They conducted a reenactment of the Battle
of the Wilderness in September 1921, during which the Marines hiked
through northern Virginia to reach the site. Once there, and in public
view, the men built camps, conducted air raids, fired blank antiaircraft
rounds, supported infantry maneuvers with artillery, and showed the
public how the Civil War–era battle would be fought using modern
weapons and tactics.

Lejeune and Butler hoped that this and other reenactments would demonstrate that the Marine Corps could operate independently and employ modern weapons effectively and efficiently during a time when ideas about military power were changing. Seven months earlier, in February 1921, U.S. Army brigadier general William "Billy" Mitchell demonstrated the potential effectiveness of aerial bombing against warships in the Chesapeake Bay. Using 1,000-pound bombs, Mitchell's pilots sunk the *Ostfriesland*, a captured German battleship. Afterward Mitchell publicly announced that airpower, not seapower, was America's best defense.[101] That bold claim raised the ire of navy and Marine Corps leaders. Near the Chancellorsville battlefield in Virginia, Butler had his Marines place antiaircraft weaponry and searchlights in an array similar to that used on a battleship. The firing of these antiaircraft guns awed spectators and demonstrated "that the battleship, with proper overhead protection, is not an obsolete weapon as General Mitchell would have the country believe."[102] By doing this, the Marines helped the navy cast doubt upon any premature claims regarding airpower's dominance.

The Wilderness maneuvers also allowed the East Coast Expeditionary Force to practice the Corps's own developing advance-base seizure and defense doctrine. By 1921, Marine officers like Lejeune, Russell, and Ellis had been at the forefront of turning the Corps into an efficient body of amphibious warriors specialized in conducting landing operations necessary to a naval campaign.[103] "Wilderness Run was considered the shore line, and all terrain to the westward was considered to be the sea," read an official report, "the problem was entirely a naval one, and the colums [sic] that advanced from the imaginary transports and battle ships."[104] The Marines attacked positions as though they were "islands" and "landed" on the "beachhead" using trucks as though they were boats.

This training proved valuable in a limited sense by giving the men and officers experience in the field, whether they were marching, flying planes, or driving trucks. But it would not be until the 1930s that Marine amphibious doctrine would mature significantly and not until the next world war that the Corps would put this kind of training to actual use. Even the Publicity Bureau admitted, "While such pageants afforded entertainment for large numbers of spectators and brought the attention of the public to the Marine Corps, they were of little real value in training the personnel of the force in modern warfare."[105]

If this exercise was solely about military training, then Butler and Lejeune would not have turned it into a public spectacle. The immediate significance of the Wilderness maneuvers for the Marine Corps, therefore, had to do with public relations. The Marines had lost some public faith during the 1919 and 1920 investigations of their Haiti and Dominican Republic occupations. Things got worse in the spring of 1921, from a public-relations standpoint, when the *Nation* published the "Haitian Memoir" and its damning accusations of Marine misconduct. But the political environment had improved by the fall of 1921, when President Harding, cabinet members, senators, representatives, their families, and many other spectators from the Washington, D.C., area traveled to watch the Marines' reenactment of the Battle of the Wilderness.[106]

No doubt, the Corps's political connections in Washington helped convince powerful government officials to attend. Representative Butler and Secretary of the Navy Denby both had a hand in drumming up support in the capital for the Marines' reenactments. Harding, who had criticized the Wilson administration and the Marines during his 1920 presidential campaign, now sang the Corps's praises. "I shall not exaggerate a single word," he reportedly said to the Marines. "No commander-in-chief in the world could have a greater pride in, or a greater affection for, an arm of national defense, than I have come to have for you in this more intimate contact."[107]

The Wilderness reenactment was not just about training to be a modern fighting force. In an important sense, it was about showcasing Marine manhood and its efficiency, discipline, and capabilities to maintain public confidence in the Corps. The *New York Times* commented on the "the spirit and vigor" of the Marines that "made the mimic war seem most real."[108] Lejeune claimed, "Every person who was there came away with *renewed* confidence in the Marine Corps and with great admiration for its efficiency."[109] In response to the negative press the service had received that year from the Senate investigation hearings, one observer of the reenactment wrote to General Butler, "With such a reinforced brigade, the efficiency of which has probably never been equaled in any of our peace time forces, the Navy Department may well be proud and at ease regarding affairs in Latin America and throughout the Spanish Main."[110]

The Wilderness maneuvers proved successful enough to allow for another major exercise the following year. In June 1922 the East Coast Expeditionary Force took a barge from Quantico to Washington, D.C., then marched north through the verdant hills of Maryland and southern Pennsylvania to Gettysburg. It was to be "one of the greatest and most comprehensive of troops maneuvers in the History of the United

Fig. 47. General Smedley Butler leading the Marines through Gettysburg, 1922. Herman Priebe Papers, Personal Papers Collections, History Division, Marine Corps Archives.

States in time of peace."[111] Once again, high government and military officials attended the show, which lasted from June 19 to July 12. One of the most spectacular performances of the month-long exercise was the Marine aviators who flew scouting and bombing missions, aerial "gymnastics," and stunts. The flyers even shot down an old observation balloon to the glee of spectators. Tragically, however, two Marine pilots died on June 26 when their plane crashed—no cause was ever determined—while conducting maneuvers.[112]

Marine and naval airpower made a for a big show, but what the Corps wanted to display were the Marines themselves. Like at the Wilderness, it hoped the Gettysburg maneuvers would demonstrate how its service culture was beneficial to American manhood. One Marine wrote that audiences witnessed "the fitness of the Marine for any undertaking that might come his way and will show the benefit of intensive training that is given the Marine at Parris Island, S.C., Training Station and the Marine Barracks, Quantico, Va."[113] In late September 1923 the Quantico force reenacted the Battle of New Market in front of an estimated 150,000 spectators with the help of cadets from the Virginia Military Institute in nearby Lexington, Virginia. Following the reenactment of Antietam in 1924, the Marines' fall maneuvers would be discontinued for a decade partially because of further cuts in the military budget.

The East Coast Expeditionary Force conducted advanced-base seizure and defense training in tandem with the U.S. fleet from December 1923 to February 1924 at Culebra, Puerto Rico. The Marines had conducted a smaller-scale exercise there in the spring of 1922 and would conduct a larger joint-training expedition with the navy three years later. For many of the thousands of Marines and sailors involved at the winter 1923–24 landings, this marked their first large-scale landing based on the nascent precepts of advanced-base seizure and defense. Marine and naval officers realized that they had much to learn after this exercise, as it revealed glaring weaknesses in logistics, naval-gunfire support, landing coordination, and communication.[114]

But that proved to be only the view of experts. For one reporter, it was a different experience entirely as the exercises "revealed that the marine corps is being intensively trained with all the latest devices of warfare, and that the corps is remarkably efficient."[115] The Navy Department issued a press release that promoted the landings as "a crowning demonstration of the efficiency of the Marine Corps Expeditionary Force" and a great show of the Marines' "ability to land in a few hours' time a powerful force of fighting men such as only forces of the first magnitude could hope to cope with."[116] America's young men who served in the Corps were training hard and becoming efficient sea soldiers. At the very least, that is the impression they were trying to achieve. After 1925 the Corps's amphibious-landing exercises ceased until the 1930s.

Conclusion

Roving Marines, guarding the U.S. Mail, and Civil War reenactments as maneuvers provided a positive public image that centered around Marine manliness and manhood at a time when the Corps really needed it. Those activities demonstrated where the bulk of its attention was focused during Lejeune's first term as Commandant: efficiency, recruiting, and public relations. Military retrenchments necessitated this emphasis because Lejeune had to make sure he had enough Marines to carry out the Corps's missions at home and abroad. Throughout the early 1920s, however, recruiters turned away most applicants for enlistment just as they had done before the Great War. In 1920 the Corps only accepted 12,588 enlistees out of 51,359 total applicants. Two years later it was 9,499 out of 52,986, then 8,964 out of 48,597 for the fiscal year ending in June 1923.[117] Much of this selectivity had to do with the Corps's funding allotment from Congress, which provided only very tight budgets during this period. The service simply did not have the money or the room for as many recruits as Lejeune wanted.

The immediate postwar years were not all positive, however. The Senate investigation hearings and bad press remained a dark cloud hanging over the Marines during this time. Lejeune's efforts at officer-promotion reform failed in no small part because of how the proposed changes would implicate the manhood of those who failed to advance. Additionally, some Marines guarding the mail endangered people's lives and undermined local authorities. Promoting their own manliness and promising to enhance the manhood of the men who enlisted, however, remained central messages of Marine public-image construction in the early 1920s.

A significant difference between the Corps's postwar and prewar publicity, however, was the core public image it projected. Before the Great War, Marines pitched themselves as quick-reacting soldiers of the sea ready to fight anywhere. During the war, they doubled down on warrior imagery. With the return of peacetime in the early twenties, however, Marines began to present themselves as fighters who could sing and dance and as models of efficient manhood.

Another development was the extent to which Marines went to demonstrate their manliness. The Corps had never done anything like the Roving Marines in an official capacity in its entire history up to that point. Nor had it ever performed major training operations in the public eye like it did at the Wilderness, Gettysburg, Antietam, and New Market. Manliness proved so pervasive that officials even spun the shooting of civilians by Marine mail guards into a credit to their manhood. But during this same time, the Marine Corps's culture of manliness would also manifest in its education initiatives and sports teams. In addition to being models of military efficiency, Marines would become champions of the gridiron and educators of men's minds.

7

To Build Up a Class of Men

From the Barracks down at Quantico
  To the field at Baltimore.
We are here to let the doughboys know
  How the Devil Dogs can score.
We will let the whole Third Army see
  Just exactly what it means
To buck a line that's guarded by
  The United States Marines.
— *H.K., "Bits o' Mud from Quantico," 1921*

On December 3, 1921, the Quantico Marines football team shut out the U.S. Army's Third Corps team in Baltimore, Maryland. Tickets for the game had sold out, and prominent government officials such as Josephus Daniels, Edwin Denby, and Commandant Lejeune watched from the stands. Like all football games, this one tested the teams' grit, physicality, discipline, and toughness. It pitted U.S. soldiers, described as "bulky"—one army player weighed just shy of 300 pounds—and with a defensive line "like a stone wall," against a physically smaller but "speedier" Marine team. The Third Corps head coach, Major Dwight D. Eisenhower, had hoped his players' larger size would help dominate the Quantico team. The Marines, coached by Lieutenant John W. Beckett, used speed and their well-practiced playbook to beat the army team 20–0 that day. Their offense "uncorked a repertoire of plays so varied and so well timed that the army lads were left in a state of semiconsciousness." Marine fullback Lieutenant Frank Goettge, "described as foremost among the young gentlemen," repeatedly "tore huge gorges through the Third Corps line."[1]

American football in the 1920s was a masculine contest, and the Marines won this matchup using their speed and intellect.[2] Because the game is a controlled display of male physical, mental, and moral strength, it is also a test of manliness. If the Roving Marines, guarding the U.S. Mail, and the East Coast Expeditionary Force's maneuvers at Civil War battlefields were demonstrations of manhood, the Quantico Marines football team was about putting that manhood to the test on the gridiron. Throughout the early 1920s, the Quantico team played against numerous collegiate and armed-forces squads along the East Coast and achieved several winning seasons.

Marines formed the Quantico football program alongside their early efforts to create a Marine university. The idea behind this service school was paternalistic in that Commandant Lejeune and Brigadier General Butler believed Marines needed educational opportunities for their own good. They wanted not only to improve their physical and moral welfare but also to keep them out of trouble. The assumption that Marines "needed" schooling for moral uplift did not conform to prewar and wartime claims about their character and manhood. According to the Corps's recruiting and internal literature, they were already supposed to be men of good character. Technological advances, strategic changes, and postwar public discussions about the need for better-educated men in society, however, influenced all three armed services to make room for learning.

The Marines attempted to mix military life at Quantico with a more collegiate one, replete with schools for officers and enlisted men and sports teams, including football and baseball. Officials argued that these reforms would keep Marines of the East Coast Expeditionary Force actively engaged in educational pursuits in between training and other duties, leaving them little time for idleness. It was also a way for the Corps to compete with colleges and universities for the cream of American manhood. Marine advertising shifted from promoting discipline, drill, and fighting "bandits" overseas to the educational value of military service. While being a Marine was about being an efficient man ready for active service, the Corps's education initiatives also made it about preparing men for civilian life.

But the Marine Corps would not be the largest promoter of latent educational possibilities in the services. The War and Navy Departments promulgated this idea during the early 1920s as they sought to maintain smaller peacetime forces. With a little guidance from the Marines, the U.S. Army underwent a renaissance in advertising and publicity soon after the war. The sheer size and reach of the army's new advertising and recruiting apparatus would flood the United States with booklets, articles, and posters that promoted the military as a pathway to manhood and as a way for young men to get a useful education. Thus, it was the army that appeared to shape much of early postwar discourse surrounding the value of military training and education. But in the methods and messages it used, the Marine Corps's influence is evident. Although certainly not the loudest or most prevalent voice, the Corps nonetheless succeeded in being a significant contributor to the idea that military service made men through training and education.

Ultimately, these education efforts were part of a broader campaign by the armed forces to improve the well-being of servicemembers for recruiting and disciplinary purposes. The services evolved their war-time image of being warriors to one of being men actively engaged in vocational and educational opportunities. Through the Roving Marines, guarding the mail, and public training maneuvers, the Corps had already begun to shift its wartime imagery and appeals further toward a more popular postwar manliness, one that emphasized mental, physical, and moral growth. All of this reflected a postwar institutional culture that held fast to traditional manliness, albeit one that could now be improved in the classroom and demonstrated on the football field.

Postwar Strategic and Military Context

After the conclusion of the Great War, U.S. strategic interests shifted from Wilson's Fourteen Points. Protecting the continental United States and its overseas possessions, enforcement of the Monroe Doctrine in the Western Hemisphere, and defending the open door in China became the top three policy goals in the immediate post–Great War era.[3] Two major pieces of legislation would organize and structure the U.S. armed forces during this period: the National Defense Act of 1920 and the Washington Naval Limitations Treaty of 1922. Both had significant implications for all three services in terms of size, force structure, readiness, recruiting, and public relations.

The 1920 National Defense Act codified the nation's historical habit of maintaining a small peacetime regular army that would be responsible for leading and training an influx of citizen-soldiers in case of a major war. Congress capped the regular army at around 300,000 men (officers and enlisted) and the potential size of the National Guard at 435,000. The U.S. Army would be spread out across the country in nine corps areas. Each area would be home to one regular, two National Guard, and three reserve divisions, each in charge of its own recruiting. Army leadership made readiness to protect U.S. borders and territories overseas and to mobilize in case of a national emergency the rule of the day.[4] They also made education of officers and enlisted men a key tenant of their readiness posture. They believed that it would prepare the army for the growing complexity of twentieth-century warfare and entice young men to enlist during peacetime. In this process the army would become a self-styled "builder of men."

Navies became diplomatic bargaining chips soon after the Great War. At the Washington Conference of 1921–22, delegates of the United States accepted the Four, Five, and Nine Power Treaties. Participants under the Five Power Treaty—Great Britain, the United States, Japan, France, and Italy—agreed to halt new battleship construction that exceeded the tonnage ratio of 5 (Britain):5 (United States):3 (Japan):1.75 (France):1.75 (Italy). In the other two treaties, participating powers agreed to respect each other's Asia-Pacific holdings and honor China's geopolitical integrity. For the U.S. Navy, this meant shifting emphasis away from battleships, the traditional measure of seapower, toward other types of vessels, namely aircraft carriers and submarines.[5] Peace and arms limitation dominated U.S. popular opinion leading up to this conference, however, and the navy had already begun advertising itself as the service where one could be a man and gain an education. Manning this new "Treaty Navy" in peacetime would necessitate advertising service at sea as beneficial to the lives of the men who became sailors.

The Marines would continue to help the navy in its missions at home and abroad. They remained stationed in China and continued their presence in the Dominican Republic until 1924, Haiti until 1933, and Nicaragua from 1926 to 1933. Commandant Lejeune worked to structure and train a large segment of the Corps for advance-base operations with the navy, a task that had been a part of the Marines' cluster of missions since 1900 but had never received much attention due to other obligations and a sparsity of funding and manpower. The shift in emphasis to advance-base operations during Lejeune's tenure meant that Marines would be embarking on missions that would be more complex and require more knowledge of logistics, machinery, and combined sea, air, and ground campaigns. Marines needed to go back to school. The Marine Corps education campaign, therefore, derived in part from the very practical need to enhance its own readiness.

Educated Manhood

Some Americans had changed their minds about the quality of American manhood since the Great War. The war brought hundreds of thousands of American men to draft boards that examined them for physical and mental defects. These screenings resulted in startling conclusions. Based on this data, Brigadier General Charles E. Sawyer, a physician and surgeon for the U.S. Army, claimed: "Americans' physical manhood is materially deficient. Its mental capacity is of mediocre type." Less than 5 percent of drafted men scored above-average marks for intelligence, and only about 67.5 percent of them met the draft board's physical standards. Sawyer called for a systematized plan of education to develop America's manhood both physically and mentally. This plan, he hoped, would "change us from a body of men shot through with physical weakness to a physical perfection that will make us not only strong as individuals but will make us strong as a nation."[6] Studies like these broadened the postwar discourses on the quality of American manhood and how to improve it.[7]

Increasing efficiency through education was one way to do just that. Americans frequently linked efficiency with healthy and virile manhood during this time. For example, government pamphlets considered physical, mental, and moral efficiency as prerequisites of a healthy and productive male citizen.[8] "A man's value to society is determined by the amount of work which he can perform, mental or physical," the Young Men's Christian Association claimed.[9] James Samuel Knox, author of *Personal Efficiency* (1920), argued that the Great War had exposed America's need for more efficient men. "But scientific training of mind and body transformed many of these weaklings into strong, upstanding young men, full of ambition and initiative, who are now able to get things done."[10] Physical training and intellectual development through education benefited one's manhood by making him more efficient, and an efficient man could be successful in any walk of life. Like other authors of his time interested in efficiency and manhood, Commandant Lejeune would place heavy emphasis on education for Marines to achieve both. In addition to being a military institution, the Corps became an educating one, which was consistent with outside discourses on developing efficient manhood.

The nexus of Marine education would be the relatively new base at Quantico, Virginia. Located just thirty-seven miles south of Washington, D.C., the Corps broke ground at Quantico in the spring of 1917, immediately after Congress declared war on Germany. The site served initially as an advanced infantry-training facility where Marines, both officers and enlisted, prepared specifically for deployment to France.[11] After the war Lejeune became the base commander, and he envisioned Quantico, as early as 1919, as becoming the center of Marine Corps learning. Soon after becoming Commandant in June 1920, he moved the Marine field-grade and company officers' schools there. This would end up being significant because it not only turned Quantico into the intellectual hub Lejeune envisioned but also led eventually to the creation of the *Tentative Manual for Landing Operations* and the *Small Wars Manual* in the mid-1930s. The Commandant placed Brigadier General Butler in command of Quantico, now the home of Marine officer and enlisted education.[12]

According to Lejeune, the idea for the Corps to try its hand at educating Marines came from the Great War. While in France, he realized that the best way to improve and maintain the morale of troops in rear areas was to provide opportunities for voluntary schooling. In testimony before Congress, he pointed out that military men of experience know that "in times of peace you cannot drill men all day long; they become stale and tired." So the commands had to come up with other activities to fill out the rest of the day. Without these offerings, Marines would become idle in the afternoons and evenings, and "the devil finds a great deal of mischief for idle hands." Educating Marines, Lejeune believed, would solve morale and discipline problems. But the point of education went beyond these practical concerns.

Lejeune believed that education and vocational training were good for Marines' manhood. While drills and training were good for war and helped develop men physically, education better situated them for civilian life after the Corps. By having developed a Marine and given him access to a modicum of vocational education, "when he left the service, he would be a better man physically, morally, and mentally then when he came in, better fitted to grapple with the problems of life, a better citizen, a better son, husband, and father."[13]

Secretary of the Navy Daniels fully supported the plan. This is no surprise given the U.S. Navy's own efforts to emphasize educational opportunities for sailors while at sea. "Education is the basis of efficiency," read the navy's 1920 annual report, "to build up and maintain the intelligent and highly trained personnel required for the operation of modern warships."[14] In addition to the Naval Academy and the Naval War College, the navy sought to provide correspondence courses for enlisted sailors. Its leaders used the same reasoning as the Marine Corps in that the education the men received in the service would benefit them later in life. With the help of contracted civilian educators, the navy developed fifty-six courses "adapted to naval usage." These fell under different divisions such as navigation, steam, electrical, yeomanry, and primary courses. The USS *Rochester* (CA 2) was one of the first vessels to try out the correspondence courses. Over half of the ship's crew of 450 men enrolled in courses, among them spelling, geometry, algebra, and history as well as chemistry, physics, and magnetism and electricity.[15] The program soon spread throughout the Navy to many other ships, including the USS *Tennessee* (BB 43) and USS *Oklahoma* (BB 37).

Like the Marine Corps, the Navy did this partly to boost recruiting. The commanding officer of the USS *Rochester* concurred in this, noting, "The Navy will certainly be able to get a better class of recruits when the public at large can be definitely told that systematic instruction will be given throughout the Navy." Its leaders had been paying attention to popular opinion and knew recruiting in peacetime would require a different approach. "Military service which does not send men back into civilian life better trained, better educated, and better fitted," Secretary Daniels wrote, "is a failure and will not attract the finest young men in America." Navy leadership embraced the idea that "valuable experience, training, and education will in itself do more to aid recruiting than anything else we can offer."[16]

Daniels held fast to progressive ideas that linked patriotism and service to mental, moral, and social uplift. Scarcely able to conceal his own paternalism, he proclaimed that no military institution was worth its salt if it did not "seek to uplift, strengthen and make more efficient" the men in its ranks. This idea rested upon the assumption that new servicemembers were more like children in need of raising rather than adults in need of training. When asked by a journalist during a press conference about "projects under development" at the Naval Academy, Daniels replied, "Oh, making men."[17] In April 1921 the *Saturday Evening Post* published his article "Training Men for the Navy and the Nation," which promoted the navy as a teaching and educational institution. He also highlighted the kinds of skills necessary to the fleet. Manning a modern naval warship required electricians, gunners, cooks, plumbers, engineers, and mechanics, all very technical jobs. Consequently, sailors learned trade skills they could use in civilian life once their enlistments ended. According to Daniels, "The entire educational system of the Navy is designed to train men not only for the duties they are to perform but also to fit them so far as practicable for the trade profession they may select."[18] He not only aimed to bolster publicity for the navy but for the Marine Corps as well.

Daniels wove together a narrative for readers of the *Saturday Evening Post* that made the Marines look economical, efficient, and sensitive to the value of education. According to the secretary, Lejeune and Butler saved the postwar Marine Corps from low morale and injected life and purpose back into their branch. The war had taught them that providing troops stationed in France with educational opportunities after the armistice had "strengthened esprit among men and officers and had prevented deterioration of morale and physique." Therefore, "when these officers began the after-war task of recreating a strong Marine Corps, they came to the conclusion that the best way to build up and maintain the morale of the Marines was to give them a chance at an education."[19]

Therefore, Secretary Daniels supported the Marines' ideas on educating their force because it fit right in with what the navy was already doing. "Write me that letter with reference to the vocational school . . . make it as full as you can," he requested of Butler. "I think it would carry with all the papers and would delight the people of America and would help recruiting very much for the class of young men that we are anxious to get in the Marine Corps."[20] As Daniels explicitly stated, and as Lejeune and Butler thoroughly understood, there was a publicity side to this plan. The navy and the Marine Corps would enhance their claims of being beneficial to America's manhood by advertising themselves as educating institutions.

Butler felt that manpower reductions and the continuous bad news coming out of Hispaniola equated to a brief depression of spirit for the Corps. "The Marine Corps, like all other armed services, is pretty well down and out through lack of men," the general wrote from Quantico, "but we are slowly pulling ourselves together and will again be a 'Corps' I hope."[21] With Lejeune's support, he drafted a plan that called for the creation of "nothing more nor less than a huge military university" that would produce vocational and academic training for Marines. The school would enhance their efficiency while in the service and help their prospects of finding employment after discharge.

The general argued that the education Marines received would not interfere with "the military instruction necessary to produce the finest type of soldier." He continued, "Anyone familiar with the training of Marines will admit that as a steady diet, more than two hours of purely military training a day will make an enlisted man muscle bound and cause him to grow stale, except in time of war." He thought that military instruction alone was appropriate in times of war. But now that he was trying to build a university, Butler claimed that drill and combat training did not help young men learn useful trade skills that would help them in civilian life. He and Lejeune, therefore, oversaw the establishment of three schools: automotive mechanics, music, and typewriting and shorthand.[22]

Butler wanted the Marine Corps to enhance the ways it benefited the young men who joined and help them advance in life:

> Heretofore an enlistment in the regular service of the United States has been considered a waste of time unless a man intended to make it his life work, and as far as preparing him for any duty in civilian life aside from that of a policeman or a defender of his Nation in time of war, it certainly was. Men who had professions or trades when they entered the Corps necessarily ceased to advance during the period of their enlistment, and a man who does not continually advance goes backward; no man can stand still.[23]

Yet he contradicted Marine recruiters' claims regarding the value of military training. Since before the Great War, recruiters had argued that becoming a Marine enhanced recruits' manhood, which bettered their lives and prepared them for successful careers as civilians. Butler now suggested otherwise: the Corps, as of 1920, opened very few doors for those who returned to civilian life. While he would not have disagreed with the notion that the Marine Corps *should* enhance one's manhood, he only wanted it to better fulfill that promise with vocational and academic education.

Butler had an ambitious plan. The men attending a school would undergo military instruction in the mornings and vocational training of their choice in the afternoons. He wanted to invite employers from around the country to come and speak to the students about opportunities in their respective industries. Butler reasoned that this tactic would expose young Marines to possible avenues of career advancement and familiarize prominent businesses with veterans. His plan would thus help "secure positions for our men who complete their military training and . . . provide employment for them."[24] The Corps also would arrange for students to visit companies related to their vocational training to increase their chances of securing employment after their service. If these Marines decided to stay in, however, their training and education via the Corps schools would make them candidates for future commissions in the officer ranks.[25] In this way, what would eventually become the Marine Corps Institute (MCI) would grow to rival other military educational institutions such as the U.S. Naval

Academy in Annapolis, the U.S. Military Academy at West Point, and the Citadel. That was the plan at least.

Butler wrote to Secretary Daniels claiming that Marine schools at Quantico would benefit the Corps along several lines. First, they aimed to make the service more attractive to the American people and potential recruits in peacetime. Butler wanted the Marine Publicity Bureau to create a catalog of courses the way traditional civilian universities did. "Let the people who are paying the bills for this establishment see what we are doing with their children and their money," he suggested. The general reasoned that a vocational school at Quantico would help persuade the public that their sons were not just training to defend their country. When these Marines completed their enlistment, they would be "returned to civil life a good all-around American citizen."[26] Essentially, they would be better men.

Second, the instructors would be officers who would get valuable hands-on leadership experience. Those who led Marines in training could also lead them in the classroom. Butler argued that "the closer contact an officer can maintain with his men, provided he is a proper man to hold a commission, the greater will be his influence over these same men, and it follows, naturally, the better leader he will be." To illustrate this point even further, he recounted an incident at Quantico in which an officer discovered one of his junior Marines was illiterate. Another officer, First Lieutenant J. B. Neill, promptly offered to teach the young man how to read and write. Neill's classroom soon grew to seventeen students needing instruction in basic grammar. Butler used this story to make a point: "Mr. Secretary, the devotion of that young man to Mr. Neill is pathetic, and when you speak of leadership, that man will go through hell at the wink of Neill's eye. Neill has more control over that man than he could have gotten in ten years of 'right and left face' on a parade ground."[27] Officers educating young Marines would increase the bond between them. Those who did not want to teach their Marines would become suspect regarding their leadership qualities.

Ultimately, the schools would keep Marines on base busy and engaged in "wholesome" work, which reflected Butler's paternalistic notions surrounding troop morale and welfare. The year 1919 saw a general increase in courts-martial across the naval services. The Judge Advocate General reported 515 court-martial cases against Marines in 1919, 125 of which resulted in bad-conduct discharges.[28] Butler and Lejeune believed that boredom and idleness had to do with much of this trouble. If Marines were not honing their military skills, then they should engage in academic or vocational studies. "This, Mr. Secretary, will nearly close up our prisons; in fact, since we have started this teaching some six weeks ago, our punishments have dropped to practically nothing," Butler wrote.[29] Whatever claims he had about moral and physical uplift notwithstanding, the general envisioned education as a preventive measure to keep Marines in line and out of trouble.

These efforts at educating enlisted sailors and Marines occurred at a time when professors and government officials worried about the education of American manhood. Edward Garstin Smith, a conservative author who frequently criticized progressive movements and the Wilson administration, argued that American manhood was degenerating in part because of a lack of quality education. "America suffers from an over production of rich men," he asserted, and "an underproduction of educated men."[30] Threats from home and abroad, including tyranny and socialism, riddled the postwar world. Educated manhood, the idea went, was the best way to combat those threats. Thames Ross Williamson argued that educated men were an essential component of a fully functioning and safe nation.[31] Dr. Basil A. Yeaxlee, secretary of the Universities Committee of the YMCA, declared, "adult education is a permanent national necessity, an inseparable aspect of citizenship, and therefore should be universal and life-long."[32] Each of these authors spoke against the common idea that school was important only for childhood, not manhood.

Dr. Henry Louis Smith deemed education a crucial step toward manhood among boys. "Before the boy can become a real man," he must learn "independence, initiative, will-power, self-control, and self-direction," all of which he could gain through a proper education.[33] According to Louis Smith, education was more than just a rite of passage that young boys should endure to reach manhood, it was the surest way to improve one's economic and social standing. The Great War, he argued, made it clear that "never has the call for educated leadership been so insistent as now . . . and never has a thorough college education, backed by character and energy, promised such large and certain dividends of wealth, fame, and opportunity."[34] Some Americans like Garstin Smith, Williamson, and even Lejeune and Butler viewed education as a powerful force in their society, one that could make a man.

This power could be used for good or for evil, however; a man's character made all the difference. Education without moral direction and the development of character could be dangerous. The Christian Education Movement put advertisements in numerous newspapers around the country claiming that schools could save or destroy the world. They pointed to "Prussian Militarism" as being a product of an education program based on military might and physical prowess that had wrecked Europe.[35] "The more you 'educate' a man who is defective in the intellectual and moral fundamentals, the more dangerous a man you make him," Garstin Smith argued.[36]

Louis Smith identified bad campus atmospheres that enabled "childish, frivolous self-indulgence" as the threat to a good education's foundation in character. For him, character meant manhood. He offered this advice to young men about to attend college: "It then depends on your character and will power whether you will play with the shavings on the floor like a baby, look out the windows at the passers-by like a child, or use your tools like a man and make yourself a master workman. After you are once inside the college door, an ounce of manhood is worth of ton of units and ream of certificates."[37] Character and manhood, therefore, were foundational elements of a man's education.

With an education that bolstered his morality, a man then only needed the courage to follow his own moral compass. A "red-blooded man," according to Reverend Julius A. Schaad, a prominent preacher and author at the time, was one with strength through self-control and self-direction. He had "strong enough convictions on moral questions to lead him to make sacrifices of himself or his interests for a great cause."[38] These educated and morally upright men were the kind of good American citizens that the Marine Corps sought to produce through vocational training.

Marines were sensitive to the manhood-morality-education nexus. To persuade officers around the Corps of the value of the MCI, Captain Earl H. Jenkins published "Character—Building the Basis for High Morale" in the March 1920 issue of the *Marine Corps Gazette*. In a rare moment when a Marine of this time wrote on class, Jenkins argued that most men who joined the Corps came from the working classes. That group could be divided in two, "those whose social influences have inculcated a devotion to duty, a respect for established authority, a Christian sense of right and wrong and a brotherhood of man; and the *uneducated* man who has been surrounded by ignorance and prejudice from birth, who is suspicious of everybody and everything, who thinks every man's hand is against him and whose hand is against everyman."[39] The former, he argued, needed more prominence in the Marine Corps to maintain morale because "he is the material out of which a real guardian of American liberties can be made." Jenkins argued that the MCI served as a great tool for Marines to mold that material. "It is not so much in what is gained in knowledge as what is gained in character that makes school life a success or failure," he asserted.[40]

The Corps's efforts toward educating its enlisted Marines were a reaction to what was going on in the civilian world and the other services. Officers who helped Butler and Lejeune create the MCI heard the cries for more education coming from American society. "The subject of educating the nation's young men has become a problem and a duty more urgent than ever before, and the people and the nation's law-makers are thoroughly awakened and ready to support any movement looking toward that end," First Lieutenant John H. Craige wrote in 1920.[41] They also knew that, given the postwar economic situation, selling the Corps to potential recruits would be a challenge.

Advertising government pay would not attract the recruits Marines sought. "There is evidence also of a growing disposition on the part of young men to regard time spent in the military service as time wasted; years in which little is learned and no advance made in knowledge, capability and earning power," Craige pointed out.[42] The MCI, he hoped, would attract ambitious young men who appreciated the value of education in furthering their careers in postwar America. Turning the base into a college campus, albeit one where the students were Marines with military duties and training, would "make life at Quantico so attractive and profitable that the worst punishment which can be inflicted upon an offender against camp order and discipline will be dismissal from the service."[43]

The Marine Publicity Bureau soon took to the newspapers across the country to advertise vocational training at Quantico. The image of the Corps softened even further. Before the Great War, Marines were America's quick reaction force, rough men ready for anything. During the war, Marines had been chivalrous warriors, bent on the destruction of America's foes. After the war, Marines became warriors who could sing, dance, and play music. With this new publicity campaign, Marines now became educators, shapers of men's minds and characters. And the kinds of men the Corps produced became more nuanced. They would not just be warriors fit only for the battlefields of France or the forests of Hispaniola but also for the modern world of commerce, business, and industry. This image is a clear shift away from the wartime manliness that pervaded U.S. society between 1917 and 1919 toward the look of the new peacetime manliness to which the Marines now claimed to have no qualms conforming.

With information provided by the Publicity Bureau, newspapers around the country advertised the MCI as a place for only the most promising of American manhood. Like prewar recruiting efforts, writers presented life in the Corps as a privilege. It could mold and shape young men, but they had to have the right moral and physical material in the first place. "Recruits accepted in this class must be of the highest type and have the best qualifications of physique and character," reads one advertisement.[44] "For this branch of service attracts the sort of a man who has the makings of a 'good fellow,'" another advertisement states. "And no school, unless it is a military institution of the first rank, can approach the Marine Corps in giving a man the self-reliance, alertness and qualities of leadership which military training affords."[45]

Frederick J. Haskin, a notable author around 1920, wrote an advertisement for the Marines that centered around the MCI. He targeted an audience of young men "who have ambition, but not money, willing to work their way through a good education."[46] Haskin acknowledged that Marines designed vocational and academic training at Quantico to get men to serve. But he pitched the idea this way: "it is an effort to put the whole business of military service on a higher plane, and to attract to it a higher type of men."[47] The quality of manhood among potential applicants still mattered very much in Marine recruiting and publicity. The MCI helped them appeal to that audience in postwar America.

The institute enabled the Corps to further enhance the abilities of the young men in its charge. If they had the right physical and moral qualifications to enlist, the MCI would help mold them into a man, a Marine. Making men more efficient was essential. The idea, according to one advertisement, "is not to build up a class of men merely for work while in the Marine Corps, but to really educate them so that when their terms of enlistment have expired they can go back to civil life benefited by the broad education they have received while in the service."[48] One writer described the schooling for Marines as "a practical application . . . of the principle that 'the more a man knows the better soldier he makes.'"[49] Secretary Daniels echoed this very sentiment by arguing that educating Marines at Quantico made them better, more efficient warriors.[50]

Marines on recruiting duty claimed that the MCI worked well in gaining new, high-quality recruits. It "has, without a doubt, been the most attractive inducement offered by any branch of the service to the young men of America and it is making its influence felt very noticeably with this district," Major Feland wrote.[51] By 1923, recruiters still sang the MCI's praises. For example, advertising the educational benefits of the Marine Corps allowed them entry into events such as the Chicago Vocational and Trade Schools Exposition. Setting up recruiting booths at educational fairs like these gave recruiters more opportunities to appeal to their target audience. "Here is a chance to get off of South State Street where the recruiters pick up men who are more or less down and out and reach a class of determined young men who have gone into this exposition for the purpose of ascertaining how they can improve their condition in life."[52]

The Marine Corps's education efforts did not occur in a vacuum. Ultimately, they competed with civilian schools, the private sector, and the other services for young men. The Corps's small size was a double-edged sword. While it was hard to keep and recruit enough men to fulfill all its missions, this allowed the Marines to be pickier than the other services regarding who they let in and who they rejected; they could claim to be "elite" because of the math if not anything else. But it was the U.S. Army that was the most prolific in terms of claiming to educate men and make them manly in the post–Great War United States.

The U.S. Army Builds Men

In December 1918, three and a half weeks after the armistice, Secretary of the Army Newton D. Baker and Chief of Staff General Peyton C. March decided to push for a 500,000-man peacetime U.S. Army, a number twice as large as Congress had authorized in 1917. To get this many men to join, however, required rehabilitating the army's image from being a "ne'er-do-well's refuge" to something more respectable.[53] The task of figuring out how to do this fell to its Morale Branch, an office within the War Department's general and special staffs. Captain J. E. Cutler of the Morale Branch advised, "Service in the Army needs to be made more satisfactory and popular than it now is" because if not, "to promote enlistment in the Army would probably turn out to be a boomerang."[54] Lieutenant R. F. Fuller argued that the army could obtain and keep 500,000 men if the Morale Branch focused on how the service could benefit young men's lives. He wanted to emphasize its growing educational opportunities and vocational training. "Have it become generally known that the matter of education is as important in this new army as is the military training," he argued.[55]

The army experienced the same recruiting issues as the navy and Marine Corps. Morale officers believed that postwar Americans reverted to the notion that the peacetime army was as an institution for men who could not find employment in civilian life. Many saw it as an austere and unrewarding experience that offered no long-term benefit other than immediate employment. A man must be in dire straits to consider becoming a solider, the reasoning went, and if he does, then he will be a part of an organization of men only serving to makes ends meet. It did not help that the army had millions of men set to leave its ranks, many of them having endured hardships during the war and would likely advise others to not enlist.

Although the army had more resources and a more extensive re-cruiting apparatus than the navy and Marine Corps, their tactics and advertising had to evolve to acquire and maintain such a large force. Leadership figured out that prewar inducements of travel and pay were no longer appropriate for men who could find better-paying jobs in civilian industries. The wartime draft and calls to duty, patriotism, and honor appealed less to Americans after participating in the largest war the world had yet seen. But "if the parents of the country can be made to feel that the army is the best place for the sons to obtain a reasonable preparation for life, it is believed that recruiting can be greatly stimu-lated." The Education and Recreation Branch advised promoting the army as an institution that safeguarded young men and provided them with educational and "moral training." Morale officers had plenty of ideas, many of them revolving around improving men's lives, but they needed to research how this could be done and advertised effectively.[56]

Captain C. R. Dickinson conducted research on behalf of the U.S. Army's Morale Branch to come up with suggestions on how best to proceed with recruiting and advertising. He investigated the U.S. Navy, the Merchant Marine, and even the British Army's methods. Dickinson learned several things. First, these institutions considered morale and recruiting intricately linked. From this he suggested that army morale and recruiting officers work together closely, the former to improve life in the service via overseeing recreational activities and infrastructure, the latter to advertise such things for recruiting pur-poses. Second, he gleaned from the Navy Publicity Bureau that the army should place medical officers at each recruiting station to pre-clude instances of a man being accepted at the local office but rejected four hundred miles away at the medical examination. He also learned that each recruiting office around the country needed to be supplied with recruiting material from the main office "so that each station thus becomes a local agent under the jurisdiction of the home office."[57]

As useful as all of this information was, Dickinson wrote that he was most impressed with the Marine Publicity Office. He interviewed none other than Major Thomas G. Sterrett, who had been on the front lines of the Marine Corps's publicity and advertising efforts since around 1915. Dickinson described Sterrett as "an extremely able and alert newspaper and publicity man who has been promoted from Private to . . . Major on account of his extremely valuable service to the Marine Corps in the lines of publicity and salesmanship." Every day the major set about his mission of "selling a trade-mark soldier, the United States Marine, to the American public." He also worked to ensure every Marine know the Corps's traditions and history and to make each man proud of himself and his institution. Dickinson reported that Sterrett's work resulted in great publicity and good morale for the Corps, which had "worked out the most intensive and efficient method of accomplishing the above results that have so far been developed."[58]

During the interview, Dickinson learned how thorough Sterrett was and how seriously he took his job. With a small staff and a modest budget, the major could follow any Marine's career; when someone did something notable, he turned it into a human-interest story for publication in either the *Recruiters' Bulletin*, or syndicate newspapers, or sometimes both. Sterrett convinced the captain that New York City was the ideal location for publicity and advertising. "A thing done locally in New York City has national importance," he told Dickinson, "because New York City is the center of news, publicity, advertising, the motion picture industry, the actors, and every form of work which touches the imagination of the American public." Sterrett advised him that there existed no reason why the army could not have the same success as the Marines. They needed to place a publicity bureau of some sort in New York City and start advertising the engineer corps and the infantry first "because they already have hold upon the imagination of the American people."[59]

Although Dickinson saw the Marines as ahead of the army in advertising and publicity, it was not just because they were savvier. The Corps, according to the army captain's outsider point of view, had better morale and cohesion, which made it easier for them to advertise the benefits of their service. One reason for this was that "the Corps does not have any restriction as to social inequality between men and officers" and that "practically all promotions are made from the ranks." He also credited the *Marines' Bulletin* (the *Recruiters' Bulletin* temporary name in 1919 and 1920) for unifying the Corps and helping with both morale and advertising. Dickinson enclosed a copy of the *Marines' Bulletin* with his report. "A careful examination of this complete and valuable magazine," he concluded, "will give an idea of how carefully and well developed is the plan which the Marine Corps has adopted, and the results of their care in publicity, have undoubtedly been remarkable both in building up morale in the Marine Corps and in gaining the good will of the American public for the marine."[60]

The army took Sterrett's advice and, by the summer of 1919, established a publicity bureau in New York City. This office served as the command office of its two recruiting authorities: the General Recruiting Service and the more decentralized recruiting offices that ran out of the various army camps spread across the country.[61] Colonel Julius T. Conrad headed the bureau and assigned officers to head publicity and advertising efforts. By July 30, Conrad managed fourteen officers and twenty-one enlisted personnel. With the acquisition of job presses, linotype, and multigraph machines, the army's bureau began printing pamphlets and recruiting literature. The service also took Sterrett's advice to immediately make acquaintances with local newspaper editors, something the Marines had been doing for over two decades at this point. Army publicity personnel prepared "special matter" for the newspapers to publish on their behalf. With these, the army wanted to "acquaint the public with the educational and vocational value of the Army" and "to destroy popular misconception of the Army as a peace institution and to all irritation against the army resulting from the complaints of discharged soldiers." Once the newspapers distributed these messages, the bureau then sent the material out to army recruiters across the country.[62]

This bureau also took the Marines' advice by publishing its own equivalent to the *Recruiters' Bulletin*, the *U.S. Army Recruiting News*. Although just starting out, "the ambition of the Bureau was to develop the bulletin into an attractive magazine, or 'House Organ' for the recruiting service." The magazine provided news, ideas, and advertisements. It also helped unify the army recruiting and advertising efforts behind a common goal: presenting the service as one that made men.[63]

After this report came out, more soldiers began advocating for the army to promote itself as an institution that makes good men better. As early as February 1919, officers began pushing for changes in the army's public profile. Major William T. Morgan wrote to the chief of the Morale Branch, "The large number of desertions in the Regular Army, and the type of enlisted man often seen on the streets, with the great number refusing a second enlistment is the best evidence that something is radically wrong." He called for a nationwide advertising campaign that promoted the institution as one that wanted the very best men in every locale. The campaign should also communicate that "army training is a primary duty of good citizenship, and that the man who comes back from the army by the same token is a better citizen, a leader in local affairs."[64]

Army leadership concurred and began making top-down changes. In September 1919 the War Department issued a general order stating that the War Plans Division of the General Staff would direct the military's new education and recreation activities. The chief of this division would have civilian educators advising him on educational policies and would work to make all educational opportunities uniform and practicable. This initiative had two purposes. The first had to do with efficiency and coping with the army's increasing reliance upon complex machinery to function. Its goal was "to train technicians and mechanics to meet the Army's needs, and to raise the soldier's general intelligence in order to increase his military efficiency." The second purpose was "to fit the soldier for a definite occupation upon his return to civil life." For officers and cadets at West Point, this change was mostly bureaucratic. Officers would continue to attend the army's various general staff colleges and service schools, while cadets' lives would center around learning how to become officers and leaders. The most significant change was the development of post schools where enlisted men could receive basic general educational and vocational skills. With this change, the army could claim that it offered educational opportunities for all of its soldiers up and down the ranks.[65]

The army decided to rehabilitate its own image around a single slogan that would drive their recruiting and public-relations efforts: "The U.S. Army Builds Men." The service would achieve this personal growth along the same lines the Marine Corps claimed—mentally, physically, and morally. The mental development would come via basic training, vocational education, and professional schools. Physical exercise and sports activities would develop men's bodies. Soldiers with healthy bodies and educated minds would not suffer from poor morale and disciplinary problems, thus achieving development in that area, so the reasoning went. The army put this message on its recruiting posters, various pamphlets, and the covers of the *U.S. Army Recruiting News*. And not only was this used as an official slogan for recruiting, but it also staked the army's claim to a particular form of peacetime military manhood.

Having learned what to do and how to do it from the naval services, particularly the Marines, the Army Publicity Bureau began claiming to

Fig. 48. *The U.S. Army Builds Men*, by Herbert Andrew
Paus. World War I Posters, Library of Congress.

make men out of the recruits who joined the military. During the summer of 1919, the army undertook an ambitious recruiting drive to gain
50,000 men. Recruiters made education, travel, and self-betterment
the key incentives of the campaign. In support of this drive, newspapers printed O. S. Williams's drawing *He Won't Go Wrong*. It shows
Uncle Sam enticing a young boy to consider joining the armed forces.

Joining the army or navy, the image implies, means climbing higher in life. On their ascent young men would become accustomed to the "best food on the market." They would have a "chance to learn a trade" and "see the world." They would gain access to "free schools" and "lots of sports." Ultimately, they would achieve the pinnacle of what any institution could offer: "respected manhood."

The Morale Branch reported that the immediate effects of the 1919 recruiting drive were quite positive. Between February and July, the army enlisted 87,577 troops, 60,826 of which came from the camps across the country and 26,715 from the General Recruiting Service. The reason for this success had to do in part with better publicity. The Morale Branch claimed that army advertisements published in *Leslie's Weekly*, the *New York Times*, the *New York Herald*, and the *New York World* were picked up by other newspapers around the country. This greater publicity led to "changed public sentiment toward the Army due to a better conception of its functions and value in peace, as well as to knowledge of the great value of the training it offers." In the New England states particularly, the army's publicity "successfully neutralized hostile sentiment toward the Army as an institution, and thereby aided recruiting efforts materially."[66]

It appears that its message, not just its tactics, helped obtain these results. The army conducted a survey of men who enlisted in 1919 and found that most of the responders joined for self-improvement. Out of 327 men who completed the form, 182 of them enlisted because they liked army life, 123 checked vocational education, 212 included travel, and 104 also joined for adventure. These reasons were all different ways that the army "built men." The campaign slogan appeared to be working.[67]

Despite the positive outcomes of the recruiting drive, the post–Great War army suffered the woes of demobilization perhaps more acutely than the other branches. For example, between 1919 and 1922, the navy shrank from 191,000 to 112,000 sailors, and the Marine Corps likewise contracted from 75,000 men (on paper) to around 16,000. The army, however, discharged over *3 million* men within the *first year* after the armistice.[68] Although military leadership called for a peacetime force of unprecedented size, the period between 1920 and the 1930s for the army was one of deep cuts and retrenchment.[69] By the end of 1919, the regular army stood at 225,000 troops, although it would dip to around 130,000 in the coming decade.

But the army had committed itself to the ideas behind "The U.S. Army Builds Men" and continued to appeal to the manhood of the

Fig. 49. *He Won't Go Wrong*, by O. S. Williams. From *New York Herald*, June 16, 1919.

nation with promises of physical, mental, and morale development. To counter lingering opposition to military recruiting, officers began seeing their service as a "vital and natural part of the social organism of the Nation." Serving in the army was no longer just about duty or patriotism. Secretary of War Baker wrote that for soldiers in the new army, it was about "acquiring training in a useful trade, receiving the elements of an education and having their characters developed."[70] Like the Marines had done before the war, part of the reason the army changed emphasis was to continue building favorable impressions with the parents of young men. "All parents should be interested in the work the Army has undertaken," reads a recruiting pamphlet from Camp Gordon, Georgia, "and young men who feel the need of an education, cannot afford to overlook the opportunity that is now offered them for development into better trained, more capable and efficient Americans citizens."[71]

Now that all three services promised to make men out of the recruits who joined their ranks, members of Congress attempted to take these initiatives even further. Senator Kenneth McKellar from Tennessee proposed a bill that would require the armed forces to educate their men by law. "Compulsory education," he argued, would make "the service the alma mater of soldiers; it extends education to those who cannot otherwise afford it; it makes parents willing to enlist their sons; it makes peace service in the Army a useful and necessary period in a man's life, of great economic value, and gains for the respect of the people." He reasoned that the military benefited by increasing the intelligence and efficiency of its force and by solving its recruiting problems. Soldiers benefited by gaining self-respect, becoming well-rounded citizens, and becoming equipped "with weapons for the battles in civil life." Finally, the nation benefited from making education more readily available to citizens who cannot afford it on their own. McKellar believed that educated minds served as the best defense against bolshevism and militarism. It was also the surest way to endow men with an appreciation for education and for American institutions that they would then pass along to their children.[72]

The *U.S. Army Recruiting News* continued to publish the slogan "The U.S. Army Builds Men" throughout the early 1920s. The staff frequently placed it at the top of the editorial page, with "men" underlined for emphasis. Major A. G. Rudd thought the slogan and the promise it made to be the army's best method of attracting troops in peacetime. It communicated "that the soldier actually profits in many respects from his service in the Army."[73] In one advertisement the army claimed to develop health, loyalty, courage, character, leadership, responsibility, and self-control, all of which were attributes of idealized peacetime military masculinity.[74] Another showcased a letter written to "the mothers of America": "Bring on your boys from the cities! / Send us your lads from the plains!" No matter their nationality, or their features, it claimed (falsely) that the army would take them and, like the Marines had been claiming for years, mold and shape them into men. They would become "Deep chested, square shouldered and active / Erect, and with twinkling glance / Straightforward and true, we return them to you / . . . Just lend us your boy, we'll dissolve the alloy / in Our Army, the Builder of Men!"[75]

Another advantage the army had over the other services was the fact that they ran the various Citizens Military Training Camps (CMTCs) across the country at the time. The 1920 Defense Act authorized these camps as continuations of the prewar Plattsburg training camps. The army held CMTCs around the country every summer throughout the 1920s for men to attend and receive military training without any service obligation attached. The idea behind this was threefold: to train as many men as possible in case of another national emergency, to develop positive relations with society, and to aid recruiting efforts.[76] The War Department pitched the official purpose of the CMTCs as a way to unify the people of the country and "to show the public by actual example that camp instruction of the kind contemplated will be to the liking of their sons; that it will develop them physically, mentally, and morally; and will teach Americanism in the true sense."[77]

The army worked diligently to publicize these camps, beginning in 1921, as places where men could reinvigorate themselves. R. E. Greenwood's drawing *At a Citizen's Military Training Camp* sums up well how the army portrayed them to the public: men having fun, socializing, exercising, and getting a taste of what Army life was supposedly like. Another one of his works, the *Evolution of a Youth*, tells the story of what happens to a young man after spending a month at the camp. He socializes with plenty of "manly boys" through boxing and camp life. When he returns home, he is "an entirely different chap."[78]

Military leadership reasoned that the camps had other benefits to the country as well. They brought in white men from up and down the socioeconomic ladder to mingle, work, and learn together. The benefit of this would be unifying the country through training and learning about citizens' obligations to serve. "We want to make every person in the United States feel that there is a place for every man's son," said Major Archibald G. Thacher before Congress. Thacher helped set up the camp at Plum Island, New York, before the war and was instrumental in configuring the new camps.[79] By "every man's" son, however, he meant every white man's son. It appears that the inclusion of Black men in these camps did cross their minds as a possibility.

The CMTCs reflected a national movement, particularly in the early days of the program. All three armed services chipped in to help spread the word and run the camps, although the army clearly took the lead. Commandant Lejeune ordered all officers and enlisted Marines on recruiting duty to cooperate with the army generals in whatever corps area they operated. The navy's recruiting service helped spread the word as well, so long as it did not hinder their own recruiting efforts.[80]

Occasionally, the army would publicize efforts from people around the country who tried to convince young men to attend these camps.

Fig. 50. "To the Mothers of America" and "Notice to Recruiters" (opposite). From *U.S. Army Recruiting News*, May 1, June 15, 1924.

One of these was Adele Daniel's essay about a young boy named "Bud" who she thought should attend a CMTC. She described Bud as having a few "physical defects," a "dormant talent for leadership," and naught but a "common school education." The outdoor exercise would endow him with strength, endurance, and agility. He would learn the moral

ARMY TRAINING

DEVELOPS

SYSTEM
HEALTH
LOYALTY
COURAGE
INITIATIVE
EDUCATION
CHARACTER
LEADERSHIP
SELF CONTROL
RESPONSIBILITY

THE ESSENTIALS OF

SUCCESS IN LIFE

20,000 of these folders have gone out to each Corps Area. Have you received your share?

qualities of courage, discipline, and self-control. Finally, he would be able to take instruction in courses that "will interest and benefit him." Once Bud completed the camp training, "*America* will possess another *man*, another *citizen*, another *potential soldier*."[81] The army also published selected responses from employees of the Radio Corporation who had attended one of the CMTCs in the summer of 1924. These attendees were unanimous in their praise of the camps for the exercise, training, and instilling of self-confidence.[82] The CMTCs toed the mark regarding the military's advertising and claiming to make men more manly.

Fig. 51. *At a Citizen's Military Training Camp* (above) and *Evolution of a Youth* (opposite), by R. E. Greenwood. From *U.S. Army Recruiting News*, May 1, 21, 1921.

EVOLUTION *of* a YOUTH:

Speeding The Departure of The Son to The
C. M. T. C. Was Quite A Task.——AND

—When He Arrived He Wasn't Overjoyed
At The Reception Given Him——BUT—

After Spending Thirty Days In
Camp Among Manly Boys——

—We Find Him Back Home An
Entirely Different Chap.—

The army made no plans to include Black men in the summer camps. Neither the *U.S. Army Recruiting News* nor the War Department's annual reports mention their inclusion or their explicit exclusion at all. Racial segregation and discrimination guided much of government policy at the local, state, and federal levels throughout the country. As far as the War Department was concerned, allowing Black men to attend the summer CMCTs meant establishing and allocating resources for additional camps solely for their training. Officials would not abide racial intermingling, but if enough Black men applied, then they would consider developing "colored" camps. Throughout the 1920s, the army rejected many applications for attendance from Black men on these grounds, which ensured they would never need to build separate camps in the first place.[83] This unofficial policy resulted in all the CMTCs being for white people only; whatever benefits to manhood there were, they would be denied to Black men.

The NAACP sharply criticized the army for this blatant discrimination. In the *Crisis*, the organization's own periodical, W. E. B. Du Bois accused the War Department of "Jim Crowing the Negro." He saw the CMTCs as valuable opportunities for physical training and comradery that the government had denied Black citizens. Even though this was "but another phase of 'Jim Crow,'" Du Bois encouraged Black men around the country to apply in hopes that the army would keep its word and create more camps in order to accommodate them. The policy was shameful, but "unless we American Negroes go to these camps and get this training, when war comes our boys are going to be the dumb driven cattle of white officers."[84] The first camps for Black Americans did not appear until 1936.

Militarism and Criticism

Criticism of the camps and the education initiatives ran along two primary lines. The first was that they were an indicator of growing militarism in the country, while the second argued that the educational and vocational programs took too much time away from traditional military training. The fears of militarism stemmed from all the talk of recruiting, efficiency, training camps, and maintaining an army and navy that was hundreds of thousands strong. The Germany that invaded Belgium in 1914 remained the standard of militarism in the United States. Part of the reason the United States mobilized for war in

1917 was to defeat German militarism, after all. Therefore, many people across the U.S. political spectrum found the government's growing postwar preoccupation with military training, technology, and readiness quite alarming.[85]

These fears stemmed in part from the U.S. Army's own ambitious plan to maintain a 500,000-man force immediately after the armistice. The fact that the navy and Marine Corps continued to recruit as many men as possible did not help, but the army, being the largest service, took the lion's share of the criticism. Secretary of War Baker and Chief of Staff March both came under criticism within and without the military. "I cannot quite fathom why at this particular time, when we are facing an era of universal peace, we would have an Army many times larger than we have had in our history," one senator from California wrote.[86]

Proponents of the training camps and postwar military readiness, however, used the services' educational efforts as shields to defend their endeavors. The armed forces needed men to fill their ranks in order to fulfill their respective peacetime missions. With the army joining in after the Great War, all three services now worked in concert to convince Americans that young men benefited from their time in the ranks through educational opportunities. "When the soldiers of America become the scholars of the Nation, the safety of our institutions will be guaranteed by the irresistible force of intelligence actuated by patriotism," Senator McKellar proclaimed.[87] One critic of the CMCTs wrote a letter to Dr. Frank Crane asserting that the camps were inculcating militaristic values in young men that could only lead to "Prussian style" militarism. Crane responded that this was simply impossible in the U.S. military in part because of its relative inclusiveness and educational value. "We are going to get rid of 'militarism' not by abolishing the Army, but by expanding the Army to include everyone," he wrote. "It is only then that we shall consider the Army as we should consider it; the training place for citizens."[88]

Others defended military readiness and the CMCTs on more traditional grounds that echoed the proponents of the preparedness movement before the war: they were good for the manhood of the nation. Representative Anthony J. Griffin of New York could not sympathize with people who believed the camps promoted militarism. What these people really meant, according to Griffin, was that the military was not good enough for their sons. "If we do not stop this coddling and humoring of the youth of our country, we are going to raise up a race of weaklings," he bellowed. "We want men in this country, and we should not encourage sentiments that would take ambition and the fire of patriotism and loyalty out of boys who want to go into the Army or Navy."[89]

It was not long after all three services began advertising themselves as educational institutions that Captain E. S. West found it tiresome. He believed army recruiting claims that "a Certificate of honorable discharge from the army is the same as a certificate of graduation from a great school" to be false and misleading, which could lead to disillusionment and bad morale. "The United States has no army," the army officer heard people say, "it has been turned into a poor school." West submitted an editorial in support of his complaint. In it he lamented that no one wanted to be real soldiers or sailors anymore. A brief look at the recruiting literature of all three services revealed that "all who are of roving disposition are invited to join the world-roving marines." West continued, "If a man has red blood and wants to learn a trade," then the U.S. Army is waiting for him. And as for the U.S. Navy, "all it wants of men is to educate them and give them pleasure trips to foreign lands." All that the armed services require, it seemed to him, were for recruits to "have a good time and emerge from his period of service a better man physically, better educated, with personal knowledge of foreign countries even the best geography could not teach him." "Surely we are not militaristic in the United States," West concluded. "A lot of people have been worrying about it for nothing."[90] But the captain was not alone in his complaints within the army.

Several army colonels around the country complained that the educational and vocational reforms had caused problems in morale and training. Colonel W. C. Short of the Sixteenth Cavalry reported that "educational and vocational schools cause[d] a great deal of discontent" because schoolwork interfered with military training. Colonel Howard R. Hickock, the commanding officer of the Fourth Cavalry, complained that soldiers who elected not to attend schooling harbored resentment against those who did because they did not share the burdens of military discipline and training equally. Colonel Orrin R. Wolfe of the Eighteenth Infantry experienced increased numbers of soldiers going absent without leave in his regiment. He thought it was because of "the school situation, the large amount of fatigue, and small amount of real soldiering."[91] There is little doubt that some Marines complained about the educational reforms along similar lines. The full extent to which this is true, however, remains unknown.

The Quantico Football Team

The Marines Corps's plan to make the MCI at Quantico a military university had more than just the intellectual and moral development of men in mind. Marines had advertised their love of sports before the Great War. But it was during the war itself when they gained experience forming teams and playing against other services. The first successful Marine football team sprang up in 1917 at Marine Barracks, Mare Island, California, where many West Coast college and university students went for recruit training after they enlisted to fight in the Great War. Made up of experienced college football players such as Johnny Beckett from the University of Oregon, this team went 9–0 in 1917 against collegiate, club, and other military teams, including the army's Ninety-First Division team.[92]

When the armistice went into effect on November 11, 1918, most American troops did not return home from France immediately, and those who remained on occupation duty needed to maintain physical fitness and morale. The army, and by extension the Marines, therefore established football, baseball, and basketball teams and participated in boxing matches. Athletics among the allied armies became so popular immediately after the war that teams from all cobelligerent nations competed against each other in the 1919 Inter-Allied Games. By the time U.S. troops had returned from the Europe, the armed forces placed greater emphasis on athletics and team sports for officers and enlisted men.[93]

The Marines made athletics an important part of school planning from the very beginning. To them, sports were as necessary as education for developing manhood and attracting recruits. By the early 1920s, Marines were forming teams everywhere they were stationed. Interest in "manly sports" was common in the U.S. armed forces before, during, and after the Great War, and what Secretary Daniels said of the navy held equally true of all the services: "Much attention is devoted to athletics, which are necessary to keep men in prime physical condition, clean limbed, agile and mentally alert."[94] Baseball, football, basketball, and boxing gave Marines stationed around the globe chances to blow off steam, maintain morale, and keep physically fit.[95]

Athletic contests were also tests of manhood that put the Marines' reputation for manliness on full display. "We have always boasted that the Marine Corps is represented by the highest type of young America," Major Joseph Fegan wrote in the *Marine Corps Gazette*. "If we are to keep up this high standard, we must offer attractions which will appeal to this type of man."[96] In this way sports teams at Quantico would keep morale among the Marines high as well as enhance the collegiate atmosphere that Butler, Lejeune, and other officers wanted. But it would also help retain good Marines and appeal to high-quality recruits by presenting the Corps as a masculine (meaning male) institution with very high standards of manliness.

For this reason, Butler and his staff at Quantico wanted the Corps's athletic teams to be a part of the education initiative. "In addition to its military and educational work," one officer wrote of the MCI, "there will be a football, baseball, and track teams that will compete with the teams of other universities and colleges."[97] It would be Quantico's football team that would most attract Butler's attention because of the game's association with college athletics. After taking a tour of the base, which involved inspecting the educational facilities and watching the Marines play a football game, Secretary Daniels wrote to Butler: "I am happy that you are securing the true college spirit. . . . I had the pleasure of looking into the faces of these upstanding, ambitious, and sturdy young men."[98] With Daniel's blessing, Butler served as the driving force behind the Quantico football team. By November 1920, he had secured a game with Johns Hopkins University.[99]

Butler's inner sense of manliness and paternalism drove him to make sure the football team had opportunities to travel, compete, and draw crowds. Traveling was expensive, however, and he frequently complained about the cost of rail fares. After failing to secure tickets at a reduced rate to Baltimore to play Johns Hopkins, he ranted: "These Pennsylvania Railroad fellows are a lot of damned hogs. . . . [T]he railroads can go to hell." Incensed as he was at the rail line, however, he did not want to come across as whining. "We are men," he said, accepting the situation, "and are not going to cry because we can't get what we want."[100] In keeping with creating a collegiate atmosphere, Butler then took it upon himself to oversee the construction of an on-base football stadium with 33,000 seats. As with most things during this period, economy was key. "Not only have the men voted to build this with their own labor, but, also, to pay for it from their own funds, and it, therefore, behooves me, as the *father* of this family, to do it as cheaply as possible." Under Butler's management, Marines moved around 200,000 cubic yards of soil and built the grandstands themselves. The general procured cement from companies at a discounted price and wrote to railroad companies to acquire discarded steel in the form of fish plates and angle bars to finish constructing the grandstands.[101]

Butler planned on pitting the Quantico team against the best squads in the United States. This stadium (which would eventually be named Butler Field) would help by demonstrating the Marines' desire to be taken seriously. "We have gone to a tremendous amount of labor, although practically no expense, in the building of [a] huge stadium here in Quantico, and are naturally anxious to get into the best class of athletics, which means playing the very best teams," Butler wrote. "It is very hard for an organization such as ours to break into organized athletics and it is, therefore, necessary for us to appeal to anybody we know who has influence with first-class teams."[102] He reasoned that Americans, particularly at colleges and universities, did not care for military football teams during peacetime, which made "breaking into college athletics" difficult.[103] So, he invited teams to come play at Quantico, which would "open up our stadium and introduce us to the football world."[104]

The Quantico football team was a source of pride for Butler because it represented the quality of manhood that made up the Marine Corps. "We have 20,000 husky males to draw on, and we should be 'hot stuff,'" he wrote. Butler planned on pulling the best Marines from wherever he could to play on the team, whether they were stationed in the United States or overseas. Despite his insinuation that any Marine would naturally be good at the game, those with college football backgrounds manned the team for the most part. The general boasted that nearly all of the Marines on the team had been college stars, which was partially true, but most players did not come from university teams.[105] "We have collected the best football men in the Marine Corps and have a squad of seventy-five of the best players in this country, and our team will be as good as any in the United States," Butler claimed.[106]

Renowned athletes made up the Quantico team's roster. At six feet, three inches tall and weighing just shy of 200 pounds, no single player on the Marines' Quantico team had the prowess, skill, and physicality that Frank Bryan Goettge possessed. Goettge hailed from Ohio, where he played football for the University of Ohio. He joined the Marine Corps in 1918 and received a commission as a second lieutenant. He went on to fight with the Fifth Regiment of Marines in France at the Meuse-Argonne. He played football for the Corps while on occupation duty in Germany throughout 1919. While playing in the interservice games there, he developed a bit of reputation for being one of the Corps's best football players. Soon after returning to the States, Goettge assumed command of a company of Marines in Haiti. Butler yanked him out of Hispaniola to play for Quantico's new football team in 1921.[107]

In 1921, their first year of competition, the Marines went undefeated winning six games and beating teams from the Virginia Military Institute and George Washington University. That was the year that Goettge, playing quarterback, lead the team to a 20–0 win over the Third Army Corps, with Secretary of the Navy Denby, Major General Lejeune, and the secretary of war in attendance.[108] Goettge helped lead the Marines to a consecutive undefeated season in 1922, the year they defeated Georgetown University 9–6. This victory "established the right of the Marine team to consideration at the hands of strong college teams," claimed a writer for the *Leatherneck*.[109]

The game against Georgetown was everything Marines like Butler and Lejeune wanted: it attracted a crowd, it was a spectacle, it put Marine manhood up against a notable university team, and it was a victory. Calls for the matchup to become an annual event rang out from spectators and players alike, and newspaper around the country began to pay more attention to the Quantico Marines.[110] Butler served as the team's biggest cheerleader during these games. He was frequently on the sidelines wearing his lungs out with "wild" enthusiasm. According to one Marine witness, "everybody was highly amused by him."[111] Despite these wins, the Quantico football team mostly played what Butler called "second rate colleges."[112]

By 1923, Butler had secured games against more university teams, which accounts for their 6-2-1 record that season. Their biggest loss came from the University of Michigan on November 10, 1923, when the Wolverines walloped the Quantico Marines by a score of 26–6. Michigan was one of the dominant college football teams in the country that year, and at the time they played the Marines, not a single team had scored a touchdown on them that season. Goettge changed that early in the game when he ran a kickoff return back into their end zone, making it 6–0. It was all Michigan from there, however, as the Wolverines scored twenty-six unanswered points. Denby was again in attendance, which caused a bit of a stir. The University of Michigan was Denby's alma mater, but as the secretary of the navy and a former Marine himself, he officially supported the Marines to win the game.[113]

The Quantico Marines bounced back quickly after this defeat, finishing the 1923 season with another win over the Third Army Corps in December in front of an estimated 35,000 spectators in Washington, D.C. The Marines and soldiers battled all afternoon, and neither side scored any points until the last few minutes of the fourth quarter.

The Marines intercepted an army pass late in the game, which allowed Goettge to eventually score the game-winning (and only) touchdown after seven successive runs.[114] The Quantico Marines went on to defeat the Third Army Corps every year from 1924 to 1927, after which army teams fell off the Marines' schedule.[115]

Because of their victories between 1921 and 1923, the Quantico Marines began to be seen as prime examples of American manliness. H. C. Byrd, a prominent sportswriter at the time, drew inspiration from Goettge and the other players to write a rather hyperbolic story of Marine prowess on the gridiron that year. "Two thousand years ago," Byrd wrote, "Frank Goettge might have stood at Thermopylae. . . . [B]ut today Frank Goettge stands as supreme in the field of gridiron endeavor as he would have stood in only a little more heroic mold had he lived in those other times." Byrd attached to him manly qualities that served well in life, football, and battle. He was the epitome of manliness:

> Able to do everything in football and do it well—mentally the type of man who leads—Goettge physically is the mold which shows by example what leadership is. And as such a perfect example of the best that any type of physical combat offers, Goettge stood out yesterday in a contest in which were gathered athletes as able as any for whom vestal virgins raised their thumbs and won fame and glory for himself and the organization of which he is apart.[116]

Goettge's "physical power" provided the winning leverage over the Third Army Corps more than anything else. His performance led Byrd to draw conclusions about the makeup and traditions of the Marine Corps. "For nearly a century and a half the traditions of the Marine Corps have stood for what is good," he wrote, "that the Marine Corps makes the man." He asserted that "after watching for two hours Goettge and other men of his type, one comes to doubt that and to believe that [the] man makes the Marine Corps."[117]

Goettge may have received most of the public acclaim, but other prominent athletes manned the team as well. One was John W. Beckett, who had been the captain of the 1915 and 1916 University of Oregon football teams. Beckett joined the Marine Corps in 1917 and played for the Mare Island team during the Great War. He played defensive right tackle for the Quantico Marines in 1921 and went on to coach the team during the 1922, 1923, and 1924 seasons. Another star player for the Marines was Lieutenant Harry B. Liversedge. Described as a "giant,"

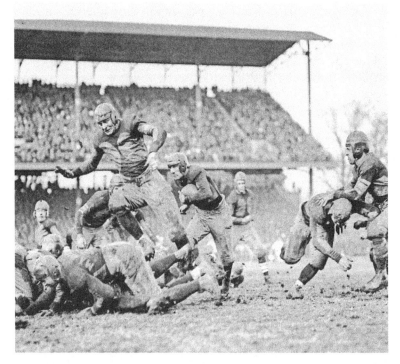

Fig. 52. Quantico Marines vs. Third Army Corps, December 1, 1923, Washington, D.C. History Division, Marine Corps Archives.

he weighed 194 pounds and played left tackle. Butler picked Liversedge because of his size, strength, and athletic résumé. He had played football for the University of California and had been a member of the U.S. track team in the 1920 Olympics in Antwerp, where he won the bronze medal in shot put.[118] Liversedge played with the Marines from 1921 to 1924 and was the captain of the 1924 team. He would serve in the Corps during World War II. He led the Twenty-Eighth Regiment on Iwo Jima; it was his Marines who raised both flags on Mount Suribachi in February 1945.

Frank Goettge, the star of the Quantico team and perhaps one of the best football players in the United States during the 1920s, would meet a violent end. A Japanese ambush killed him and nearly all the Marines of his patrol on Guadalcanal in 1942. Homer L. Overly served with Goettge in Haiti and remembered him fondly years later. "He was a man among men," Overly recalled, "a humane officer and [an] efficient leader." When learning of Goettge's death in action, he wrote,

Fig. 53. Quantico's football team captains: John W. Beckett, Harry B. Liversedge, and Frank Goettge. History Division, Marine Corps Archives.

"he is gone but will always remain the great big man Marine representative of the Marine Corps officers."[119]

Conclusion

The Quantico Marines football team afforded the Corps much needed positive publicity in 1920s postwar America. In the words of one historian, the games very much became a "metaphor for Marine prowess."[120] They showcased Marine manliness and athleticism before throngs of people, and Quantico's victories over army teams, Georgetown, and others earned them respect not just for the team but also for the branch of service—and as men. Football games made the Marines better acquainted with the public, and vice versa: "it educates those who are already members to be interested in what men of their ages are doing in civil life in the way of wholesome exercise."[121] Major Fegan asserted, "Publicity of this character cannot be purchased—it is not on the market."[122]

It was not all about publicity, however. Fegan went on to claim that athletics in general, and football in particular, encouraged esprit de corps, teamwork, and athleticism among the men. "Last, and most important," he argued, "it develops physically the young man; it makes him a better citizen; it makes him more able to combat hardship but does it all in a less irksome way than if it were done in a military fashion."[123] In a significant sense, therefore, the education initiatives and the Quantico football team reflected the centrality of manhood, its physical and mental development, within U.S. Marine culture.

The advertising of this culture rubbed off on the U.S. Army, which soon came to dominate national discourses on manhood and national military preparedness. The army followed the Marines' lead and began making overtly gendered appeals with their greater personnel needs and larger recruiting apparatus. While the Marines and navy claimed to "develop" men through education and vocational and physical training, the army promised to "build men" with the same means. Through the U.S. military's early 1920s advertising campaigns, therefore, the Marines' culture of manliness played an important role in linking military service with American citizenship and manhood.

Lejeune's promulgation of this culture during his first four years as Commandant paid dividends for the Marine Corps. "Due to the policy of its Commandant," read a navy press release, "the Marine Corps has been taught to consider itself not only a military force for the service of the Nation in war time but also a reservoir of educated, trained, technical men available at all times for the service of the Nation in peace."[124] Lejeune and Butler had turned Quantico into the intellectual hub of the Corps, replete with vocational courses and sports teams.

Academically, the Marine Corps Institute would never rise to the level of the Naval Academy at Annapolis or the Military Academy at West Point. Lack of funds and resources plagued the endeavor from the beginning. The Corps often had trouble acquiring textbooks for the courses it offered, for example. Soon the Marines had to outsource many of its basic courses to a correspondence school operating out of Scranton, Pennsylvania.[125] Marines taking correspondence classes fell short of the original plans to make Quantico more like a university than a military base.

The Corps's efforts at developing the manhood of Marines, making them more efficient men through education, reflects how manliness was a core ingredient of its early twentieth-century culture. Defining the relationship between his officers and men as "that of teacher and scholar," Lejeune made Marines' mental, physical, and moral development the responsibility of their superior officers. This idea remains a key tenet of Marine Corps University schools at Quantico to this day, a further indication of how lasting and pervasive this aspect of Marine culture has been. It also reflects a level of paternalism shared between Lejeune and Butler toward their Marines. They approached the moral and physical welfare of Marines in a fashion similar to how a father would raise a child. It is not clear whether Lejeune and Butler detected the irony of claiming Marines to be men while simultaneously considering them to be like their children.

Training and developing Marines remained Lejeune's mission for the rest of his tenure as Commandant. While he worked hard to prepare the Marine Corps for advance-base operations with the navy, he continued to promote the highest standards of manly character among Marines and to the public. His many speaking engagements sought to shape public opinion toward the Corps. Lejeune believed, "Our Corps is admired and beloved because of this constant fidelity to its trust, its unshakeable loyalty to the Government, its unselfish service to the nation, its dauntless courage in battle, and its unwavering esprit de corps."[126] He argued that fidelity, loyalty, unselfishness, and courage made Marines men of strong character, and such men were needed not only to defend the country but also to be productive citizens. These "military virtues constitute the very foundation of character building and are essential to right living whether our careers be within or without military service," the Commandant asserted.[127]

The Marine Corps would face more funding cuts during Lejeune's second four-year term, which he would have to accept. But his efforts to maintain good will with Congress and the American people through the development of manhood and public displays of manliness helped the Marines compete with the other services for recruits. Writing later in his memoirs, Lejeune explained why all the publicity and public relations were important to the postwar Corps. "The Marine Corps is dependent on the confidence and the affection of the American people for its maintenance and support," he asserted. When Lejeune wanted "officers and men to so conduct themselves as to gain and to keep the good opinion and the friendship of the Good Americans with whom they might come in contact," he meant, significantly, for Marines to be examples of trustworthy, efficient, and dependable manhood.[128] Lejeune retired in 1929, but not before building a strong case for the usefulness of the Marine Corps for the country's military readiness, education, and manhood.[129]

The Marine Corps "Trys to Make Men"

The men and women who appear in this book do so mostly as young people in the prime of their lives. Smedley Butler was thirty-seven when he frantically tried to get out of Haiti to see action on the western front. John Quick turned forty-eight at Belleau Wood, Dan Daly was forty-five, Clifton Cates was twenty-five, and Thomas Boyd, Francis Williams, and John Ausland, along with many of their fellow junior enlisted Marines, were in their early twenties or late teens. George Thorpe was forty-three when he fought his war in the Dominican Republic. Charles Merkel was twenty-nine years old when he committed suicide. For those who survived to old age, the Marine Corps and the Great War left their mark on them in ways that are impossible for the historian to capture completely.

To what extent were the Marines' claims to make men more manly and to benefit their lives true? How pervasive have these claims been throughout the rest of the twentieth century? The answers to these questions are complex. Historical evidence neither confirms nor denies the veracity of the Corps's promises to the men and women of the Great War era. While it is certainly true that Marines guaranteed manly reinvigoration, whether they benefited the lives of the men who joined their ranks is difficult to assess. What is clear is that the notion of manliness, and the Corps reputation for fostering and strengthening it, has carried on from one generation to the next. The notion that serving in the Marine Corps can serve as a rite of passage for young men is perhaps one of the most enduring legacies of the Great War era.

While Marines of that period did not always agree on what their experiences in the Great War–era Corps meant, their feelings were often based on their own interpretation of how war and the Corps affected their manhood and influenced their lives. While some veterans believed that it made men out of them, many others saw their experiences as detrimental to their health and well-being. Even though the wars of the twentieth century would exact terrible costs in American lives, the Marine Corps would continue to attract young men with promises of manhood.

World War I Veterans

Many Americans before and during World War I opposed claims that war and the military could strengthen the manhood of the country, much less benefit anyone at all. This group grew stronger after the armistice. Some Marines joined this camp after the war; others did not. But how true-to-life were the Corps's promises to the small group of Marines who served during the Great War era?

In the late 1970s and early 1980s, the U.S. Army Military History Institute conducted a World War I research project that contacted surviving veterans of the Great War and asked them to fill out a questionnaire about their service. This included members of the Fifth and Sixth Regiment of Marines, which were attached to Fourth Brigade, Second Army Division during the war. Fifty-one former Marines, by then all octogenarians or older, took the opportunity to fill out questionnaires. Twenty-one of them served with the Fifth Regiment, twenty-eight with the Sixth, and two with the Sixth Machine Gun Battalion. Now in the winter of their lives, the remaining old globe-and-anchor men left answers to many questions about their service.

Each questionnaire was about eleven pages long with myriad questions. One asked them where they trained as recruits (all replied Parris Island, South Carolina), followed by, "What do you recall about entering the military service (your initial reactions and experiences)?" Most tended to agree that boot-camp discipline was strict and training was tough. To the query, "If you were in the Regular Army or Marines, why did you choose to leave (or stay in) the service?" most indicated that they left the Marine Corps because the war was over, which further illuminates why they enlisted in the first place. Other questions on the form were "What do you think of the quality of leadership while you were in the service?" and "Was drinking a problem?" The level of detail each man provided varies a great deal. Some veterans only gave yes or no answers, while others wrote several sentences in reply.

The handwritten responses show which veterans remained lucid and which did not in the 1970s or early 1980s. Some wrote with a steady hand, others appeared to suffer from arthritis by their erratic strokes. Some of them could not write at all and had a relative do so for them. "I am completing this questionnaire for my father," wrote

Janet Hanson Weis, daughter of Marine private Arthur W. Hanson. "He will be 91 years old in April, living alone, mentally and physically alert—truly to be admired."[1] Richard O. Jordan, former corporal in the Sixth Marines, sent in his business card with his completed questionnaire, It reads, "Dick Jordan, Retired, No Phone, No Address, No Business, No Worries, No Job, No Money, No Prospects."

One of the first questions on the form was "Why did you enlist?" Many of them did so because they felt it was the patriotic thing to do. Private First Class (PFC) William A. Dodge of the Fifth Regiment responded, "Patriotism, save the world." PFC E. R. Adams answered: "I felt it my patriotic duty. The draft was slow in taking me, so I volunteered in the Marine Corps." Houston Donoho enlisted due to a "spirit of adventure mixed with some patriotism and perhaps some desire for the so called 'glory of war,'" while Jesse H. Garrett declared, "I thought my country needed me." Frank Lincoln Merrill became a Marine for more chivalric reasons: "To save the world for Democracy. To keep the Kaiser's crowd from ever over running the U.S. and abusing women and girls as reported from the low countries."[2]

Most of these old Marines still held fast to their love of country. One of the last questions on the form was, "Since the World War I era was a great national experience, did you learn anything about America or Americans?" Many indicated that their experiences strengthened their patriotism. Eighty-six-year-old Alpha C. Miller wrote, "I learned long before WWI that America was the greatest land on earth and that patriotism, which at this time [August 1982] seems waning, will be rekindled in the teenagers of today and that they will feel the thrill that I did when marching to the strains of the stars and stripes forever."[3] Other Marines like James E. Swiger learned about people from other parts of the country. "Knew a southern boy," he wrote, "all for Confederates."[4] Ned Rundell grew more critical of the manhood of younger generations, asserting, "We were the finest people in the world, now [September 1982] we have had too much prosperity and we are soft."[5]

Many of these veterans chose the Corps in part because of the efforts of recruiters. Private Anders L. Peterson wrote, "the Marine Recruiter told me the Marines would be the first to go [fight] so I enlisted in the Marines." "Desire for adventure," William Bihary claimed, "and the Recruiting Sergeant's talk was very effective." One of the reasons Malcom D. Aitken chose the Corps was because of the "appearance of [the] recruiting personage." Donoho may have enlisted for several reasons, but he chose the Marines because he "saw a bill board in the little country post office showing a Marine landing party going ashore with rifles etc., so I enlisted in the Marines." PFC George H. Donaldson must have been persuaded by the Marines' manly appeal: "I chose the Marines as I wanted men around me, who know how to fight if I was going to take part in a war."[6] Many of them also enlisted in the Corps because, if drafted, they could not choose their branch of service. Being able to choose their fate mattered.

The Marine Corps claimed to be good for the men who joined and promised specifically that it would strengthen their manhood. The questionnaires, however, give an indication of how true-to-life the Marines' masculine image was in the experience of these veterans. They also help uncover not just how former Marines felt about the Corps but also how Americans felt about U.S. involvement in the Great War itself.

The penultimate question on the questionnaire reads, "Was your service during World War I of any specific benefit (or detriment) when you returned to civilian life?" Those who believed that it hurt them in some way cited the war's effect on their health. Corporal Richard Lilliard of the Fifth Regiment wrote, "Detriment: chronic sickness." W. E. Almond of the Sixth responded likewise, referencing ulcers and a right leg that never properly healed.[7] Peterson seemed annoyed at the question when he jotted down, "As I said before I lost the use of my left arm so I would have to say it was a detriment."[8] Whether or not these men blamed the Marine Corps or the war itself for their disabilities is not clear on the surface and cannot be addressed without conjecture. It is possible that their war and Marine experiences were inseparably linked—being critical of one may mean being critical of the other.

Others mentioned that their time in the Marine Corps equaled lost time at their jobs and vocations back home. Wilbert H. Norton and Furman L. Nuss of the Fifth Regiment both cited "lost time" on their questionnaires but nothing more. Harold S. Ugland provided more detail. He wrote, "I had a hard time getting work and finally got a job as a helper with a fellow that learned a good trade during the war at home, and he made twice the money I did." Their time in the Corps hurt them in the sense that they lost out on opportunities to advance in their line of work, while those who stayed behind did not. World War I veterans received no special benefits when they returned home initially, unlike subsequent generations of returning servicemen and women have. Raymond F. Woerter responded: "Forget the war, No GI benefits no education no career opportunities . . . no pension so forget it." Oliver Freeman noted the lack of benefits, too, and concluded with, "I feel the world war one Veterans are the forgotten men."[9]

It is not known if any of these men participated in the 1932 Bonus Army march on Washington, D.C. Awarded in 1924 but not payable until 1945, World War I veterans suffering during the Great Depression wanted their bonus sooner rather than later. Soldiers and police forced them out of the capital instead. Rundell answered the question, "What were your expectations of G-I Benefits, educational, and career opportunities?" with, "None, this is WWI remember?"[10]

Other veterans, however, wrote that Marine discipline helped their careers after they returned home. Freeman may have lamented his lack of G.I. benefits, but he wrote, "The fact I was in the Marines gave me a boost in later life, I was a supervisor in a Rubber co." Samuel L. Crawford "went from laborer to Asst. Gen. Manager of a large company" and wrote that the Marine Corps was "of more benefit to me than a university education [because of] the discipline." Donoho, like all the men who filled out these questionnaires, was an infantryman. Although he did not find any of his combat training and experiences to be directly beneficial to his career, he did believe that "the strict training and discipline of the Marines . . . was beneficial to me later in civilian life." It is not entirely clear how exactly the discipline they were subjected to helped these men, but William H. Snead was more specific in his response. Being a Marine taught him "the art of disciplining ones [sic] self, I have never smoked, drank, gambled." Snead ultimately learned, "I must be bigger than the man that lives with me."[11]

The dichotomous nature of these Marines' answers reflects how many Americans felt about the Great War almost as soon as it ended. In 1917 the U.S. government and armed forces pitched the war to Americans as necessary to protect home and family. In that sense it was a defensive war, but it was also meant to be a crusade to save democracy from tyranny and oppression. It was a war to save civilization itself. To fight it, American men and women had to perform their particular roles in society: men needed to grab the musket off the mantelpiece to fend off the wolves, while women had the equally important responsibility of taking care of the family at home in her husband's absence. American manhood would be strengthened because of this experience, and the nation itself would be stronger as well. But recent scholarship has uncovered pervasive apathy and ambiguity after 1919 that coursed through the interwar period leading up to the Second World War.[12] Even the Marines who survived the war painted conflicting images of its meaning and its overall effect on the men who fought it.

After recovering from a chest wound sustained at Belleau Wood, Colonel Catlin published his 1919 combat memoir, *With the Help of God and a Few Marines*. Catlin clearly falls in with the crowd that believed the Corps and the war benefited those who survived. He who returned was undoubtedly "a cleaner and better man than when he went over."[13] Marines rushing to their deaths across an open wheat field without proper artillery support was no cause for scorn or resentment for Catlin. "Never did men advance more gallantly in the face of certain death; never did men deserve greater honour for valour," he wrote, with notable romantic flair.[14] Catlin even went so far as to describe the machine-gun infested woods as "some mythical monster belching smoke and fire from its lair." His Marines slew the beast "with heads up and the light of battle in their eyes."[15]

Nowhere in Catlin's account of Belleau Wood or his telling of the battles that came after (even though he did not witness them himself) is there a discouraging word about the effects of combat and fatigue on the men. Until the very end of his narrative, he maintains that the Germans were simply "no match for the flower of American manhood pitted against them."[16] Catlin believed that American involvement in the war was crucial to the allies' victory, and that the Marines' contribution was vital to the AEF's efforts.

Catlin's book was a part of an early wave of war narratives published in 1919. Eddie Rickenbacker's *Fighting the Flying Circus* and Kermit Roosevelt's *War in the Garden of Eden*, like *With the Help of God and a Few Marines*, all tend to focus on the glory, honor, and other romantic themes of war.[17] John W. Thomason, a Marine officer who was with the Fifth Marines at Belleau Wood and Soissons, tends to romanticize combat Marines in his *Fix Bayonets!* (published in 1925 and 1926 by Charles Scribner's Sons). Thomason portrays Marines as hardy, brave, and professional men sent to do the nasty but necessary business of war.

For many Americans, romantic and glory-filled interpretations of the Great War were hard to accept. Recently, Catlin has been described not as the voice of young men who fought, but as one of the generation of old men "who sent the youth of America into harm's way."[18] Soon after the war, conflicting visions surfaced in American literature, popular culture, and commemorative efforts as many became disillusioned with the war and its aftermath. Some veterans and popular authors saw the conflict as a tragic waste of men and resources, the cost of which was born by countless families across the country. Marine veterans of the Great War added significant voices to this critical reinterpretation of its legacy.

Thomas Boyd's novel *Through the Wheat* appeared in April 1923.

Boyd was a native Ohioan who joined the Marine Corps in May 1917 via a Chicago recruiting station. He fought at Belleau Wood, Soissons, and Mont Blanc with the First Battalion, Sixth Marines (the very same battalion I joined eighty-six years later). The novel follows William Hicks and his Marine comrades throughout these battles and is often referred to as a fictionalized account of Boyd's own experiences. None other than F. Scott Fitzgerald himself, who envied Boyd's combat experiences, helped get the book in print when no publishers seemed interested.[19]

Boyd's image of Marines in France was not in keeping with their manly ideal as promoted on the home front. Throughout the novel, the Marines descend from healthy and exuberant warriors to worn out, hateful, and hollow killers. In one scene he describes a young German soldier surrendering earnestly during the Battle of Soissons. "At the sight of him an uncouth, illiterate tatterdemalion from the south of Illinois snarled half animal-like" and killed the unarmed soldier with one shot. The unnamed Marine then spits on the corpse contemptuously. Marines were supposed to be morally upright and chivalrous, especially those who fought in France. But during this incident, Hicks and "the rest of the platoon looked on nonplussed, not knowing whether their comrade had done the ethical thing or not."[20] That ambivalence signifies how far these Marines had fallen. Far from becoming manlier, the battle, death, and fatigue of the western front had made these men physically, emotionally, and morally unhinged. The book sold around twelve thousand copies between its first printing and its second in 1924.

In 1924 Laurence Stallings joined Boyd in presenting a different image of Marines on the front lines. Stallings fought at Belleau Wood with the Third Battalion, Fifth Marines. After the war he became an author and a playwright. In his play *What Price Glory*, Marines are brave but are also human beings who can bend and even break under pressure. One of the most notable examples of this is Lieutenant Moore's breakdown, when he shouts:

What price glory now? Why in God's name can't we all go home? Who gives a damn for this lousy, stinking little French town but the poor French bastards who live here? God Damn it! You talk about courage, and all night long you hear a man who's bleeding to death on a tree calling you "Kamerad" and asking you to save him. God damn every son of a bitch in the world who isn't here! I won't stand for it. I won't stand for it! I won't have the platoon asking me every minute of the live long night when they are going to be relieved. . . . Flagg, I tell you, you can shoot me, but I won't stand for it. . . . I'll take 'em out tonight and kill you if you get in my way . . . [starts sobbing again].[21]

Moore has lost control of himself in this scene, crying more like a boy than a man. But that is what war does to grown men, even some Marines. Stallings's play, a serious treatment of American's wartime experience, was quite popular for a time, with strong ticket sales.

Even John W. Thomason's portrayal of Marines evolved as time went on. He continued to write stories of Marines that celebrated their own style of military manliness. The men in his collection of short stories entitled *Marines and Others* are tough and fierce. He had a clear preference for field Marines who endured the danger and death of war in France and in the tropics. There is the young private who assaults a sailor for making jokes about Marines after their expedition into Nicaragua.[22] Then there is Gunnery Sergeant William King, who has a thick neck and "beefy shoulders." At Belleau Wood he "kicked people to their feet, bullying and swearing and raging." Private Wilmer Douglas hates King because he constantly belittled him in training. But after Douglas's first battle, he thinks King "the finest fighting man I ever saw."[23]

Thomason's fictional characters often fall well below the Marines' manly ideal, however. Douglas eventually attempts to shoot King in a fit of rage but misses and instead wounds an innocent Marine on duty. The private faces a court-martial and goes to prison, although his parents eventually secure his release. Douglas carries a deep hatred of King with him for over ten years. He encounters him again when King, who has since retired, attempts to secure a loan through the bank that employs him. Douglas finds out that without the loan, King could lose the farm he has established since his retirement. Still filled with rage, he confides to his fiancée his plan to ruin his former tormentor's life: he will lie to his bosses and ruin King's credit. His fiancée threatens to leave him if he goes through with such an intolerable and decidedly unmanly act. Douglas eventually gives in to her pleas and allows King to get the loan not for her or for King, but for himself.[24] His redemption comes when he does the honorable, honest, and manly thing despite his hatred.

Then came William Edward Campbell's *Company K*, published in

1933. Campbell fought with the Fifth Marines at Belleau Wood, Soissons, Mont Blanc, and Saint-Mihiel and was awarded the Navy Cross and the Distinguished Service Cross for valor. Written under the penname "William March," *Company K* is a sharp rebuke of any romanticizing of war and the armed forces. As Philip Beidler has pointed out, the story of these Marines is a "litany of callousness, brutality, and degradation."[25] March's survivors return home shattered. Private Everatt Qualls, who participated in the execution of German prisoners, commits suicide believing the death of his boy was God punishing him.[26] Private Walter Webster's face, disfigured from battle, causes his new bride to shun him.[27] The German soldier who Manuel Burt killed by thrusting a bayonet through his skull keeps visiting him in his dreams.[28] Others have problems finding work, starting new lives, or simply staying sane. These Marines are not better equipped for the struggles of life.

Company K portrays the promises made by the Marine Corps and the rest of American propaganda to be unfulfilled at best and lies at worst. Regarding the Battle of Belleau Wood, March takes on the romanticism of Albertus Catlin and Floyd Gibbons. Private Sylvester Wendell is tasked with writing letters to the parents of Marines who have died there. Feeling all his letters are deceitful, he decides to write at least one honest letter, even though he decides at the last minute not to send it. "Your son Francis died needlessly in Belleau Wood," he states. The poor Marine suffered through several hours of agony before succumbing to his wounds. He died in misery after living like a "frightened animal, cold and hungry." March ensures this character dies cursing bitterly because he realizes that everything he has been told by his country and his own mother about "honor, courage and patriotism, were all lies."[29] March leaves no stone unturned when it comes to pointing out how bitterly ironic war could make things.

March targets Marines' supposed manliness, too. Corporal Clarence Foster believes every word of propaganda against the Germans. To him, they raped Belgian women and bashed out the brains of their children. He sees them as animals, which makes it easier for him to comply with his captain's orders to oversee the execution of twenty-two German prisoners. When other Marines in his squad express reservations, Foster snaps back: "What do you birds think this is? This is war! . . . Why didn't you bring along your dolls and dishes to play with!"[30] The Marines then carry out their captain's orders. The aim of *Company K* is to show the brutality of the war and how no man is immune to it. The profound cynicism of the novel, though, is reflective more of American attitudes about the Great War in the 1930s than anything else.

It was Smedley Butler, however, who perhaps shifted the furthest in his opinion on the Marines and the war. The apostacy of Butler probably began in 1929 when, in front of hundreds of guests at the Pittsburg Builder's Exchange, he publicly admitted how the Marines rigged elections and bullied residents in Haiti and the Dominican Republic. The secretary of the navy reprimanded him and ordered a retraction of the statement.[31] Rejected for the commandancy in 1930, he decided to retire in 1931, although not before stirring up another controversy. Butler addressed the Philadelphia Contemporary Club in January 1931, telling a story of how Italian prime minister Benito Mussolini allegedly ran over a child in the Italian countryside without stopping to help the boy. He told the audience that Mussolini said, "What is one life in the affairs of a State." Mussolini's government protested and denounced the speech, as did the Hoover administration, which ordered Smedley under house arrest pending a court-martial for conduct unbecoming an "officer and a gentleman."[32]

Fueling the controversy was the fact that Butler had little to no respect for President Herbert Hoover as a man. When Captain Pedro Del Valle visited the general at Quantico, the senior Marine recounted a story from the Boxer Rebellion. While manning the walls during the Battle of Tientsen, Butler and his Marines became aware of an American civilian "hiding with the women." Del Valle later recounted what Butler told him: "So they went and saw who it was, and it was this engineer chap. They hauled him up to the hideout and put him on the wall and treated him rough. He says, 'You know who that was? Herbert Hoover.'"[33] The State Department decided to drop charges against the general in exchange for a reprimand and a public apology. Butler retired in September 1931 but not before claiming that Naval Academy graduates had conspired to ruin his career.[34]

After retirement he joined the chorus of anti-imperialist and pro-isolationist sentiment then growing throughout the country. He became the most outspoken advocate for the Bonus Army during the veterans' attempts to get their bonuses early. In 1935 Butler published *War Is a Racket*, in which he argues that wars, particularly the U.S. interventions in Haiti and the Dominican Republic, were started by and benefited a cabal of wealthy capitalists at the expense of both the invaders and the invaded. Soldiers, Marines, and their families paid a high price and got nothing for it except "newly placed gravestones. Mangled bodies. Shattered minds. Broken hearts and homes. Economic instability. Depression and all its attendant miseries. Back-breaking taxation for generations and generations."[35] Old Gimlet Eye, as he was known in the Marines, became a staunch isolationist during the 1930s and was probably among the 70 percent of Americans who, according to a 1937 Gallup poll, believed that the United States had made a mistake fighting in the Great War.[36] Added to the milieu was the 1934–36 Nye Committee report that claimed banks and munitions companies had exercised undue influence in getting America into war with Germany in 1917. By 1940, with the international situation across both oceans looking bleak, Americans wanted no part of wars or military occupations.

The Marine Corps of the twenty-first century, however, has held fast to the notion that Belleau Wood was a glorious affair that demonstrated the Corps's usefulness to society. Marines' experiences in Hispaniola, however, receive much less attention. After 1918 society may have moved on quickly without ever forming a lasting and significant memory of the conflict within American culture. But this is simply not the case with the Marine Corps.

As an institution, the Corps remembers well the long summer of 1918, the battles, the gas, and those who fell in the woods and wheat fields of France. The Great War and Belleau Wood, in particular, stand out prominently among the Corps's collective memory in part because of the efforts of Marine historians (many of whom were Marines themselves) over the decades. Every general history of the Marine Corps published since 1918 has given special attention to the significance of Belleau Wood.[37] Paul Westermeyer's recent assertion captures well how Marines have attached meaning to a battle that many outside the Corps simply have not: at Belleau Wood "Marine tenacity and media savvy catapulted the Corps into even greater public consciousness, cementing the Marine Corps' self-proclaimed reputation as an elite force into reality."[38] The actual Marine veterans of Haiti, the Dominican Republic, and the Great War, however, were like most Americans of the time, unable to make up their collective minds on what the wars meant. In the end, they agreed to disagree and moved on with their lives.

How former Marines thought about the war and how they thought about the Corps were different things. Homer Overly never filled out a World War I questionnaire, but at the age of eighty-five, he did record his feelings about his time in the Corps during the Great War. Overly was one of the Marines who enlisted to fight the Germans but fought Haitian insurgents instead. He served only one enlistment. But posted up in his favorite rocking chair in his den decades later, he declared, "if I had stayed in the Marines, I would have been a better Marine, U.S. Citizen, father, husband and great grand father [*sic*]." Reminiscences like these brought up feelings of pride for Overly, manifested by lumps in his throat and tears in eyes. "I feel pretty much like the old adage which I have so many times found so true, that 'Once a Marine almost always a Marine,' and in my eighty-five years I'm proud to claim its worth."[39]

Merwin Silverthorne, whose letters from Belleau Wood were published in *Dear Folks at Home*, still felt strong loyalty to the Marine Corps fifty years after the Great War. He retired in 1954 after spending serving thirty-seven years in the Corps and reaching the rank of lieutenant general. "I still can generate some tears on Marine Corps birthdays and when I start singing the Marine Corps hymn," he told his interviewer. "I have no feelings of regret or bitterness whatsoever about any incidents in the Marine Corps."[40]

Marine Manliness and Masculinity in World War II

Manliness and masculinity pervaded Marines' culture, and their claims to benefit one's manhood continued following the Great War. In 1930 a writer for the *Leatherneck* asserted that the Corps made men into gentlemen. Marines had "evolved from the mere waterfront brawlers of a former day to gentlemen of the first order," and "it has not sapped their manhood or their ability to fight in the least."[41] During World War II, Captain Edward B. Irving claimed that the Corps had reached the "full stature of its military manhood" and still made "gentlemen who can fight like hell!"[42] The Marine Corps would expand to six combat divisions and nearly 475,000 troops on paper during this war. Nearly 20,000 Marines died in the conflict, with 68,000 wounded.[43] If the Corps matured into manhood, as Irving thought, then it cost many lives to do so.

Eugene Sledge, a Marine combat veteran of Peleliu and Okinawa and the author of the acclaimed memoir *With the Old Breed*, writes of the "hardening effect" of both Marine Corps training and combat. After boot camp, he recalls: "We were hard physically, had developed endurance. . . . Perhaps more importantly we were tough mentally." But combat brutalized him and his comrades to an exceptional degree. "The fierce struggle for survival in the abyss of Peleliu," he writes, "eroded the veneer of civilization and made savages of us all."[44] Sledge and his friends were no strangers to how, on one hand, the Corps strengthened their bodies and disciplined their minds but, on the other, how the war itself was a harmful experience.

Sledge referred to the older generation of Marines who trained him, and who he admired greatly, as the "Old Breed." He looked up to Gunnery Sergeant Haney, the ideal field Marine, who allegedly fought at Belleau Wood with the Third Battalion, Fifth Regiment. Haney's reputation for combat prowess, experience, and physique all commanded respect from Sledge's generation. Although just over fifty years old, Haney was tough as nails with muscles as hard as granite. "I felt like he was not a man born of woman," Sledge recalls, "but that God had issued him to the Marine Corps." Haney trained the new Marines when they arrived and set the standard for what was expected of them in garrison and in combat. He was Sledge's vital link between his own generation and that of the "Old Corps." "To us, he *was* the old breed," writes Sledge. "We admired him—and we loved him deeply."[45]

Beginning somewhere in the interwar period, the distinctions between "manhood" and "masculinity" began to blur. Recent scholars writing on the period have tended to use the terms either synonymously or let their moral and mental connotations of "manliness" and "manhood" apply equally to "masculinity."[46] Definitions of these terms are never fixed, but it appears that "masculinity" is the term of choice for scholars exploring gender from the 1930s forward. While it has tended to simply mean things associated with the male gender, the term appears to have taken on the physical, mental, and moral connotations formerly reserved for discussions of manliness and manhood. Despite this gradual shift in both preference and meaning, all three terms remained ways to describe male behavior and character. Historical context, therefore, requires using "masculinity" more loosely than in previous chapters as this analysis moves into the 1940s and beyond.

In his book *American Samurai*, Craig Cameron writes that the Marines like Sledge who fought in World War II "possessed a strongly self-conscious image of themselves as marines that was in part based on the interwar myths that had grown up around the corps."[47] The Marines of World War II, he argues, brought the masculine images of their World War I and interwar predecessors with them into battle in the Pacific. Gunnery Sergeant Haney very much fit that masculine image. The Marines formed their own style of military "masculinity"— Cameron uses this term instead of "manliness"—that helped them form a cohesive identity that differentiated themselves from outsiders, including soldiers in the army, sailors in the navy, or civilians back home, and influenced how they fought the Japanese. In an important sense the Marines of the Great War era became the standard of measurement for those of the 1940s. Cameron would perhaps have agreed that the images and stories surrounding the Great War–era Marines had a significant influence on the World War II–era Marines.

The Marine Corps did not open its ranks to African Americans until World War II, and resistance within the Corps was staunch. In one of the more despicable acts ever committed by a sitting Commandant, General Thomas Holcomb said to the navy's General Board in 1942: "There would be a definite loss of efficiency . . . if we have to take Negros. . . . [T]he negro race has every opportunity now to satisfy its aspirations for combat, in the Army, a very much larger organization than the Navy or Marine Corps—and their desire to enter the naval service is largely, I think, to break into a club that doesn't want them."[48] Holcomb's reference to loss of efficiency can be read two ways. On one hand, he may have been referring to concerns over diverting his already limited number of experienced noncommissioned officers and field officers to lead, train, and equip segregated Black units. On the other, it reflects his belief that Black men would dilute the Marines' ability to fight and, therefore, their own sense of prestige.

Holcomb's antipathy toward Black men in the Marine Corps was strong enough for him to consider precluding the service from expanding to perform its upcoming amphibious missions in the Pacific, missions his generation of Marines had spent years developing and training for. "If it were a question of having a Marine Corps of 5,000 whites or 250,000 Negroes," he said, "I would rather have the whites."[49] If history followed Holcomb's preference, then the Marine Corps probably would never have expanded to nearly 500,000 servicemen during World War II. Indeed, it is hard to imagine where the Corps would be today without the history of its drive across the central Pacific in the 1940s. But Holcomb was one of the globe-and-anchor men of the Great War era, a member of the "Old Breed" that Sledge writes about. He had fought at Belleau Wood and afterward had a distinguished career in the Marine Corps. He brought all the Great War–era racial animosity toward African Americans that he had into that hearing, the very same that considered the manhood of Black men to be lesser than that of white men.

How Black men and women have navigated through this predominately white male culture throughout the twentieth century was explored by Cameron McCoy, himself a Marine infantry officer. He points out that the first Black men and women to enter the Marines in World War II came into a "Jim Crow Marine Corps." It was an organization that segregated and relegated Black Marines to labor, not combat duty. Trained at Montford Point near Camp Lejeune, North Carolina, these Marines faced discrimination immediately. White Marines challenged their right to be one of them and thereby challenged their citizenship, equality, and dignity. It is not surprising that McCoy found that Montford Point Marines felt their manhood was also challenged.[50] Black men used their honorable service as Marines to assert their manhood and prove they deserved all the rights and privileges of white citizens.

The legislative and executive branches of the federal government forced the Marine Corps to enlist women as reservists in 1943. "Free a Marine to Fight" slogans helped enlist nearly 20,000 women during the war.[51] Women have joined the Marine Corps, although in paltry numbers, ever since. As of 2018 women only made up 8 percent of the officer corps and 9 percent of the enlisted ranks in the Marine Corps.[52] The army, navy, and air force have much higher populations of women. A 2018 research project conducted by the Center for Advanced Operational Culture Learning found that the Marine Corps can be quite hostile to women within its ranks. From the beginning, drill instructors instill negative perceptions about women into male recruits' heads during boot camp. Women then face prejudices when they reach the fleet operating forces and fear being seen as weak, perhaps to a greater extent than their male colleagues.[53]

Korea

The performance of Marines in Korea, much like their epic battles of World War II, seemed to further justify the Corps's claims of martial prowess. By 1952, Marines had added the Pusan Perimeter, the major amphibious assault at Inchon, and the Chosin Reservoir to their list of victories. Once again Marines garnered public praise despite the horrendous casualties they experienced and the fact that Chosin was a retreat and fight for survival against overwhelming Chinese forces. Marine veterans experienced terrible trauma from this war, having witnessed misery and brutality on a scale equivalent to what World War II veterans had witnessed. Over four thousand Marines died on the Korean Peninsula, while twenty-three thousand were wounded.[54] Korea was not a triumph for the other services, particularly the army, which despite having the main effort in the war, suffered from troop shortages, lackluster leadership, and much less positive public attention compared to the Marines.[55] The Korean War bolstered the Corps's place within the U.S. defense establishment and American culture in part because many Marines continued to espouse the benefits of war and military service over the costs.[56]

Despite the trauma of Korea, the Marines of the 1950s continued to espouse manliness and masculinity within their ranks and promised to make men out of the boys who joined them. In 1955 First Lieutenant Walter K. Wilson claimed that a man "should be sent to boot camp with the understanding that he is not only undergoing training and toughening up, but that he is encountering a test of manhood as well and is expected to face up to it." Once he becomes a Marine, "he should feel that he is accepted as a man and that he is capable of shouldering his responsibilities."[57] In 1957 Victor Krulak wrote a letter to Commandant Randolph McCall Pate explaining that the United States wants a Marine Corps in part because they believe that "our Corps is downright good for the manhood of our country."[58] The primary recruiting slogan at the time was quite similar to that of the army three decades earlier, "The Marine Corps Builds Men."

These explicit gendered appeals of the 1950s once again occurred during a time when historians have identified a version of a "crisis of masculinity." Early twentieth-century public officials argued that corporate capitalism, woman's suffrage, and poor military readiness had threatened American manhood. During the 1950s, American public intellectuals worried about the potential "softening" effects of male conformity and domesticity.[59] Fears of global communism and nuclear war, however, now raised the stakes. The fear of domestic communism, especially of communists within the federal government, fueled bitter and acrimonious public discourses in which the political right accused liberals of being unmanly and soft in the face of communism. Republican senator Joseph McCarthy, who served with a Marine air squadron in the Pacific theater during World War II, became notorious after claiming in a speech in Wheeling, West Virginia, to have a list of the names of communists working within the State Department. After this speech he "began a campaign to impugn the manhood and thus the political legitimacy of Democrats."[60] The senator's public notoriety grew until he eventually earned an official censure from the U.S. Senate for pushing his crusade too far, dying soon after in 1957. Before his death, however, McCarthy had stoked fears of a pervasive weaking of American masculinity by linking complacency, homosexuality, and timidity with communism expansion.

Within this cultural and political context, the reputation of the Marine Corps, in addition to its promise of manhood, continued to draw young men into the ranks. Zell Miller, who later would become a prominent Georgia politician, was one of these men. In 1953 he was a college student at Emory University and felt his life was going nowhere. After seeing a recruiting poster with the man-building slogan on it, he decided to become a Marine. After serving in the Corps between 1953 and 1956, he went on to have a successful career in politics. Miller later claimed to owe much of his accomplishments to the fact that he "sought to 'make a man of myself' by joining the Marine Corps as a troubled and insecure lad."[61]

The claim that Marines made men did not go unchallenged in the fifties, however. The most notable challenge to the Marine Corps's reputation came when Staff Sergeant Matthew C. McKeon, a drill instructor at Parris Island, marched his platoon of recruits at night through Ribbon Creek to punish them for lax discipline on the rifle range. Six recruits drowned, and McKeon faced a court-martial, one in which even Commandant Pate said the "entire Marine Corps is on trial." McKeon was reduced in rank to private and separated from the Corps a few years later. The media storm would blow over in time, as headlines moved on to other things and after the Corps had cracked down on overly zealous drill instructors. It is ironic, however, that despite the controversy surrounding Marine boot camp, recent scholarship shows how it remained the envy of army leadership, who admired Marine drill instructors for "creating a powerful connection between the service and many of its recruits."[62] It would not be until Vietnam that the public would again witness Marines failing to live up to their own standards.[63]

Vietnam

In the 1960s the conflict in Vietnam would draw millions of Americans into the armed forces. Many joined for patriotic reasons, while the draft forced over two million people into uniform. As U.S. involvement in South Vietnam intensified, a new generation of young men fell for the gendered appeals of the services. Fathered by World War II veterans and growing up in a culture that idealized John Wayne's masculine cowboy/soldier persona, many of these young men accepted, sometimes without question, the idea that the military turned boys into men.[64] They soon joined a world where, in addition to their duties, men and women were also responsible for upholding socially and militarily constructed gender roles prescribed to them. The 1960s U.S. military required men to be warriors. They required women, even those in uniform, to be "symbols of the home front support and comfort." While combat troops performed their masculine duty in violent clashes with Vietnamese communists, "the military mobilized women as conventionally feminine symbols" such as nurses and administrative clerks.[65] These men and women, therefore, entered military cultures very much shaped by wartime gender roles.

These gender roles found expression in men's pulp magazines and on the battlefield. Historian Gregory Daddis has argued these magazines "inundated American adolescents and men with idealized storylines of wartime heroism coupled with sexual conquest of women."[66] In many ways they were an extension of the prevailing cultural belief in American exceptionalism, which placed American men at the top of the world's racial and gender hierarchy. While these magazines celebrated an aggressive and highly sexualized form of masculinity (which in this context appears synonymous with early twentieth-century manliness), Americans from the White House down to the line platoons denigrated the masculinity of the North and South Vietnamese. President Lyndon B. Johnson called North Vietnam a "damn little pissant country" while U.S. troops in country referred to locals as "dinks," "gooks," and "slants."[67] Rank misogyny flourished in this environment, as male troops frequently referred to women, both Vietnamese and American servicewomen, either as dangerous or as prostitutes and subjects of sexual conquest.[68] These cultural beliefs and expressions surrounding gender made up significant aspects of the wartime environment in which this newest generation of Marines found themselves.

Philip Caputo remembered volunteering to be a Marine officer: "I needed to prove something—my courage, my toughness, my manhood."[69] Much like Miller, Caputo saw a "The Marine Corps Builds Men" poster and decided to become "one of its construction projects."[70] He went on to describe how Officer Candidate School hardened his body and mind before his being placed in the "masculine world of a Marine rifle battalion."[71] Major General Lew Walt was to Caputo what Gunnery Sergeant Haney was to Sledge: an archetypal Marine who exuded the Corps's manly ideal. "I was in awe of Walt," Caputo admitted. The young officer saw him as an "authentic hero," a man who led his troops from the front, "where generals had positioned themselves in the days when they were fighting-men like Lee, and not business managers like Westmoreland."[72]

Combat was the final test of Caputo's manhood, the event that cut forever any remaining ties he or his Marines had to boyhood. But much like the Marines whom came before him, Caputo experienced the brutal effects of combat on his mind. He grew to hate Vietnam, hate the Marines' mission there, and hate the Vietnamese communists. He admitted that his hatred and moral backsliding came from months of off-and-on combat in country and led to the deaths of innocent Vietnamese. He and a few of his Marines would face a court-martial for the murder of two Vietnamese in a night raid gone wrong. Although he was acquitted of murder charges, Caputo was a very much a "moral casualty of the war."

This case echoed Marine conduct on Hispaniola four and half decades earlier. Although relieved that his chain of command dropped the charges, Caputo ultimately felt that his innocent verdict meant that the Marine Corps in Vietnam was a faulty and misguided moral universe. He writes: "A verdict of innocent would solve the dilemma. It would prove no crime had been committed. It would prove what the others wanted to believe: that we were virtuous American youths, incapable of the act of which we had been accused. And if we were incapable of it, then they were too, which is what they wanted to believe of themselves."[73] The Marine Corps may have made a man of him, but the war in Vietnam had twisted him and turned him briefly into an unrestrained killer. Men of Caputo's generation and their children were dealing with the effects of that war long afterward. The entire conflict cast a pall over any claims the armed services (particularly the Marine Corps, with 13,091 killed and over 88,000 wounded) made regarding making men out of recruits.[74]

Wars in the Middle East and My Own Experience

Anthony Swofford, a Marine Desert Storm veteran and author of *Jarhead*, enlisted in the mid-1980s to become a man like his father, uncle, and grandfather, all of whom had served in the armed forces before him. Joining the Marine Corps infantry would "prove both my manhood and the masculinity of the [family] line," he reasoned.[75] Swofford became a scout sniper after having "grown up" in the Marine Corps on tales of men like the legendary Carlos Hathcock, who had nearly one hundred confirmed kills as a sniper in Vietnam. Swofford and his friends looked up to Caputo's Vietnam generation as living standards of manliness much the same way that Caputo had looked up to Walt and Sledge had looked up to the "Old Breed."[76] But Swofford believed that he never achieved the level of combat credibility that the preceding generations did. Although he saw the death and destruction of war and received the much-coveted Combat Action Ribbon during Desert Storm, he never got a chance to kill. "To be a marine, a true marine, you must kill," he writes, for if you do not, "you consider yourself less of a marine and even less of a man."[77] Swofford felt that he did not live up to his own perceptions of what it meant to be a man because of this. But his use of manhood and masculinity as primary lenses through which he interpreted his service is shared by the many generations of Marines that came before him and the ones that have come after.

I and others like me became quite taken with the masculine image of the Marine Corps. My recruiters used many of the same appeals that Marines of the Great War era used. I believed that the Corps would make a man out of me the way I believed it had made a man out of my father, who fought in Vietnam. I believed that the Corps would make me a more responsible and respectable citizen. Whether that is what happened I can no longer say. But as a former Marine infantryman, with combat tours in Afghanistan and Iraq, I feel confident in saying that the Corps I knew (in 2002–6) was indeed a "masculine haven" that, culturally speaking, was not all that different from the life Marines of the early twentieth century knew.

While together in training or on deployment, we were mostly free from feminine influences. We cussed, fought, read men's magazines, and drank too much. We also led strenuous lives that required a great deal of physical training for preparation. Our minds and bodies hardened in response to our experiences, and we believed ourselves to be men—young men, but men nonetheless. When we returned home to our loved ones, we were expected to open doors for women and the elderly, to be "gentlemen" and upstanding citizens. But my generation also fell short in maintaining that ideal in war, just like our predecessors. To name just one incident, Marines killed twenty-four unarmed civilians in Haditha, Iraq, in November 2005, and none of them faced any serious charges.[78]

That "masculine haven" was passed down to us from Dan Daly and Smedley Butler of the Great War era to Eugene Sledge and Lew Walt of the World War II era; from them on down to Korean veterans and then to Philip Caputo, Charles Krulak, and my own father who all fought in Vietnam; to Anthony Swofford and the Marines of the 1980s and the Persian Gulf War; down to my generation who fought in the Afghanistan and Iraq Wars. Marine notions of manhood and masculinity defined, motivated, and governed much of the behavior and traditions of us all. These latest wars, of course, came with a cost that families of the fallen and many surviving Marines will struggle with for the rest of their lives. Marines suffered over four hundred killed and over five thousand wounded in Afghanistan from 2001 to 2021. They lost over eight hundred killed and over ten times that many wounded in Iraq between 2003 and 2016.[79] Though lower casualty totals in comparison to the Vietnam War and World War II, for the Marines who died and for their families, the suffering and grief of the first two decades of the twenty-first century has not been any less.

Conclusion

Whether positive, negative, or somewhere in between, gender remains a key component of U.S. Marine culture. Notions of masculinity and manliness have helped shape Marines' experiences in recruiting, training, war, and counterinsurgencies. Several of the old globe-and-anchor men, despite the long passage of time, felt that the old Corps kept its promise to benefit their manhood. Dick Jordan recorded that by the time he had returned to civilian life, he "was much wiser and more of a *Man*." William Bihary filled out two veterans questionnaires, one in the early 1970s and another in August 1982. "I can recall most of my experiences in the Marine Corps," he wrote on the first one. "Left home a teenager, and returned as a man." In response to the same question about a decade later, he wrote: "I benefited greatly. Enlisted at 19, and I matured into manhood fast." Jordan and Bihary would have agreed with Kenneth L. Payne's answer to the same question. Payne noted that the Marine Corps and the Great War made him more mature: "The Marine Corps trys [*sic*] to make men."[80] How successful the Marine Corps was and continues to be will be judged by individual Marines themselves and, most importantly, by their families and the nation they serve. While Marines still proclaim that service benefits the citizen, war and all the potential physical and psychological harm that comes with it can make—or break—that promise.

Conclusion

A gendered analysis of the Marine Corps during the Great War era reveals that white manhood and manliness formed the basis of its identity and institutional culture. Manliness guided Marine behavior, established standards of decorum, and influenced recruiting, publicity, and image production. With this understood, it becomes possible to better appreciate the effect of the Great War era on the Marine Corps. Many Marines gained valuable combat experience in large combat formations in France as well as in counterguerrilla campaigns on Hispaniola. This generation of officers and men would eventually shift the Marine Corps's resources and training emphasis away from its more traditional pre–Great War duties toward advance-base operations with the navy. But the American people measured the Marines' usefulness not only in terms of military readiness and effectiveness but also according to standards of manliness set by popular culture and by the Marines themselves.

By the early twentieth century, the Corps had long possessed a culture influenced by notions of white manhood and manliness. Great War–era Marines frequently conformed to a white middle-class style of manliness that valued honor, bravery, self-restraint, and discipline. But they also promoted their own form of martial manliness that placed even greater emphasis on the above characteristics and added efficiency, combat prowess, and readiness into the mix. As the branch of service that had both military and naval attributes, Marines wanted men of good character who could be as competent at sea as on land. Those who did not measure up as men did not measure up as Marines. By 1914, the Corps had begun projecting that culture outward to society to recruit and gain favorable publicity. Marines offered to invigorate the manhood of young men and prepare them for the "battles of life."

The opportunity afforded by the Great War was a tremendous boon in terms of public image and reputation. War with Germany thrust military manliness to the forefront of U.S. culture. Suddenly, military service, values, and culture became exceedingly popular as millions of men joined the army and hundreds of thousands the navy. The Marines capitalized on their prewar publicity and expanded to unprecedented numbers while turning away thousands of applicants for not matching their standards and for lack of room. This pickiness enhanced the Corps's reputation as being an elite institution, one for the "best" of American manhood only. The imagery and advertisements it used during the war projected an elite warrior image to appeal to American wartime manhood.

The battles Marines fought against the Germans in France were not important solely because they were seen as triumphs. These victories meant so much more to the Marines themselves and to society. Their performance at Belleau Wood, Soissons, and other battles in France afforded Marines the opportunity to look like paragons of manliness in battle and, in doing so, made the manhood of the nation look every bit as virile and strong at a time when no one was sure how American men would measure up in a fight with militaristic Germans. The amount of goodwill this afforded the Corps in the realm of public opinion is incalculable. Marines had worked to persuade Americans that they were elite warriors. But deeper than that, through their service in the war, they convinced themselves and many others that they were real men. Even though the fighting clearly did not benefit the 2,461 Marines killed nor many of the 9,520 wounded, the Corps and the public interpreted these costs as necessary for victory and, therefore, as a credit to Marine manhood.

It was a different story entirely on Hispaniola. Even though Marine casualties were much lower there, some of the men's actions threatened to undermine the image and reputation the Corps had cultivated leading up to and during the Great War. Marines such as Charles Merkel, Dorcas Williams, Ernest Lavoie, and William F. Becker, accused as they all were of brutality, lack of self-control, and killing women and children, fell short of the Corps's moral standards. They besmirched their institution's reputation for upright manliness at a time when Marines in France won glory for themselves and their country. A gender analysis thus reveals that the Great War era's effect on the Corps is much more complex than traditional military histories have argued.

While Marines in France made American men look brave, strong, and willing to sacrifice for the greater good, those on Hispaniola made American manhood look corrupted, degenerate, and savage. Reports of Marine brutality against the people of Haiti and of the Dominican Republic far outnumbered reports of the same in France. As Smedley Butler's frantic efforts to transfer from Haiti to the western front demonstrates, as soon as the United States entered the Great War, many Marines desperately wanted off the island. Many of them saw fighting in France against Germans a much better way to prove their manhood than waging a counterinsurgency on Hispaniola against people they believed were racially inferior. Marines on the island became impatient and frustrated, and some of them committed crimes against the local populations. When news of these crimes leaked to the American reporters, it precipitated a firestorm of bad press for the Marines. High-profile journals and newspapers placed Marine actions on Hispaniola in the same genus of barbarity as the Germans in Belgium. Unfortunately for the peoples of Haiti and the Dominican Republic, the Marines who committed crimes against them did not treat them any differently than some white men treated Black Americans across the United States. White supremacy pervaded American and U.S. Marine culture during the Great War era.

The Marines would weather the public-relations storm via their postwar recruiting and publicity campaigns. Through peace, mobilization, and large and small wars, the Corps claimed to be good for the manhood of the nation. Boot camp supposedly turned young American boys into men. Life in the Corps, Marines claimed, injected the struggle and strife that old progressives believed American men had lost by the turn of the twentieth century. They promoted the idea that strong and properly developed manhood prepared them for life. During the preparedness movement in the United States, Marines had claimed they were already prepared. During the Great War, when the nation called upon American manhood to answer Germany's challenge, the Marines said they were ready. Haitian and Dominican insurgents appeared no match for the superior manliness of the Marines. After the armistice, the Corps's public relations and recruiting efforts fell back on gendered appeals to bolster its depleted ranks.

The end of the war saw a great demobilization of the armed forces along with the weakening hold of military manliness on American men's culture. The Marine Corps ditched the wartime imagery and conformed its public profile to the peacetime manliness that reemerged around 1920. Roving Marines, Civil War reenactments, guarding the U.S. Mail, and various publicity stunts projected an image of morally upright, dependable, and efficient Marines who maintained their readiness to serve at a moment's notice. The Marine Publicity Bureau used these activities to persuade the public that the Corps still made men.

Education reforms centered at Quantico, Virginia, served as the Corps's most ambitions and extensive effort to become more efficient and to enhance the lives of the men who joined its ranks. Inspired by civilian colleges and universities, Brigadier General Butler oversaw the establishment of the Quantico football team that soon played opponents around the country. This team came to represent Marine manhood as they tested their mettle against anyone who would agree to play them. That, in addition to the educational and vocational opportunities provided to officers and enlisted men, allowed the Publicity Bureau to advertise how the Marine Corps developed men physically, mentally, and morally. Recruiters and publicists claimed that men who transitioned from the Corps back to civilian life would do so having learned valuable life and vocational skills that would set them up for success.

There is perhaps no greater measure of the Marine Corps success and influence in this kind of endeavor than the U.S. Army taking advertising and publicity advice from the Marines. The army then began a massive publicity campaign of its own that made the very same claims that the Marines had been making for years previously. Army publicists now promoted their service as an educational institution in addition to a military one that, like the Marine Corps, "built men." Once the army began recruiting and advertising in this way, a threshold of nationwide military and naval recruiting and publicity had been crossed. The recruiting campaigns, civilian training camps, and the high visibility of army, navy, and Marine publicity sparked criticism of growing militarism in the United States. But the services' promotion and publicity of educational reforms shielded them partially from this criticism. Education, they argued, kept militarism at bay by making each service a path in life that readied men for citizenship. The Marine Corps, through its own publicity and its influence on the army's reforms, bears significant responsibility for the forging of that shield. It was a defense that Marines, and all the armed services, benefited from at a time of deep budget cuts and retrenchment.

Throughout the Great War era, Marine efforts to promote a culture of manliness directed attention away from the dangers of war and military life toward the potential benefits. As a military/naval institution that valued physical, mental, and moral strength, the Corps created an alluring image for young white men seeking a rite of passage into manhood. Within this context, the potential for danger and death only enhanced this appeal. Many who experienced the trauma of the Great

War, however, including Marine veterans-turned-authors Thomas Boyd, William March, and Laurence Stallings, pushed back against this idea that war and the armed forces benefited young men's lives. Even many of the surveys that the old veterans of the Fourth Brigade filled out in the 1970s and 1980s reveal that not all Marines walked away from their experiences feeling like "better men."

But the idea that the Marine Corps turned young boys into men remained firmly entrenched in its service culture and recruiting throughout the twentieth century. As Americans evolved their ideas on manliness and manhood during the Great Depression, World War II, and the Cold War, Marines continued to promote themselves as a bastion of martial manliness. As "masculinity" eventually became the term of choice over "manhood" in discourses about male behavior and culture, Marines held fast to claims of physical, mental, and moral development that had been linked with traditional manliness. Despite the casualties and destruction wrought by World War II, Korea, and Vietnam, many young Americans, including Philip Caputo, Anthony Swofford, and my own generation, fell for the allure of the Marines' masculine image. There are consequences to this pervasive and historically entrenched white-male culture that continues to affect the Marine Corps in the twenty-first century.

Gender, Race, and the Twenty-First-Century Marine Corps

The Marine Corps of the 2020s is still a mostly white and overwhelmingly masculine institution in terms of demographics and culture. Part of the legacy of the pervasive masculine culture addressed in this book is the ongoing problems with misogyny in the Corps. The "Marines United" scandal is the prime, most recent example. Marines United was a Facebook group of around 30,000 members. Authorities in 2017 discovered that members had been sharing nude and explicit photographs of female servicemembers. The scandal made national news and led to the identification of ninety-seven active-duty Marines who received some sort of reprimand, seven of them court-martialed. Investigations found these Marines guilty of posting inappropriate photos without the consent of the women in the photographs and of blackmailing women with threats of both rape and posting additional photos.[1] Instances of courts-martial in the Marine Corps have gone down since 2007, while instances of sexual assault and harassment have gone up.[2] It is perhaps because of this that the Corps today continues to have problems recruiting and retaining women in both the officer and enlisted ranks.[3]

One need look no further than the people who make it to the very top of the Marine Corps to see how pervasive white masculine identity continues to be. In 2013 the Corps had an unprecedented six four-star generals: John Kelly, James Mattis, Joseph Dunford, James Amos, John Allen, and John Paxton—all of them white males. Since 1943 only twenty-five Black officers have been promoted past colonel. Seven have made it lieutenant general, but none had been promoted to four-star rank. Seventy-two white men have become four-star generals since World War II.[4] It was not until 2018 that the Marine Corps promoted its very first Black woman past the rank of colonel. In June 2022 Secretary of Defense Lloyd Austin nominated Marine lieutenant general Michael Langley to lead U.S. Africa Command. When Langley was confirmed to this post in August 2022, he became the Corps's very first Black four-star general.[5] Prior to Langley's confirmation, the top leadership positions in the Marine Corps have all been held by white officers in part because Black officers tend to leave the service, thus taking themselves out of the pool of candidates, much more frequently than their white counterparts. The reasons for this may have to do with lingering racism within the Corps service culture, but this is not known and requires further study.

The top Corps leadership are all males, however, because only infantry officers (except for James Amos. who was a pilot) with combat leadership and command experience get promoted to these positions. Until very recently, all combat occupational specialties were closed to women. Therefore, the promotion system has been rigged against them for decades. There simply has not been a path for women to promote up as high as their male peers. They are just now beginning to incorporate into and even lead infantry platoons. Once again, the Marine Corps's civilian masters had to force the service to do this.

Opponents of gender integration of the Marine Corps infantry cite the negative effect women might have on unit cohesion, meaning infantry platoons will not work together as efficiently. A 2015 RAND Corporation study found that "gender integration is more likely to have negative consequences on unit cohesion when the social context of the unit creates a hostile work environment for women."[6] The hostile "social context" stems from the Corps's history of being a masculine institution. Historically speaking, one had to be a man first to be a Marine, much less a fighting one. What this gender history reveals is that in joining the infantry, not only are women up against a male-dominated culture and misogyny, but they are also fighting to alter a longstanding historical tradition. Historically and culturally speaking, nearly all the Marines' heroes, like Dan Daly, Chesty Puller, Carlos Hathcock, and Bradley Kasal, are men who distinguished themselves in combat. There are no female equivalents in the pantheon of Marine heroes yet. Women serving in the infantry have implications for the Corps's claim to benefit the youth of America. Given the knee-jerk hostility toward the notion of females in the infantry military occupational specialties, will women infantry officers and enlisted Marines say on the other end of their experience that they are better for it? Will the benefits of service justify the personal costs to them? Only time will tell.

The Marine Corps will continue to have problems with its own masculine culture because many of its leaders are ill equipped to understand gender in the first place. It is ironic that members of the most masculine institution of the armed services (demographically) pay so little attention to the gendered elements of their culture. Part of the problem is that there is not enough written about Marines and culture that address gender. James A. Warren's *American Spartans* (2005), based mostly on secondary sources, fails to include manliness as one of the "Elements of Marine Corps Culture" and thus paints an incomplete picture of the service since World War II.[7] Others are more blunt about the value of gender in Marine culture. Marion F. Sturkey commented in the preface to his work on Marine culture:

> Gender? There is only one kind of U.S. Marine, the lethal fighting kind. Gender? Who knows? Who cares? . . . Therefore, with respect to gender this book contains no deranged psycho-babble. Readers will find no *politically correct* "he or she" foolishness or "him or her" lunacy. The Male pronoun suffices for all. Any wacko liberal wimps who dislike this Warrior Culture ethos should find something else to read.[8]

These dismissals of gender as a form of cultural analysis regarding the Corps reflect a glaring gap in most Marine historians' understanding of their own subject matter.

Interest in the institutional culture of the armed forces is growing among academics and military professionals. With just a few exceptions, however, academic military historians omit gender when addressing culture.[9] Some of the most notable military history professors in the country do not teach it or assign readings on it, and their students steer clear of it. *The Culture of Military Organizations* (2019), edited by Peter Mansoor and Williamson Murray, is the latest and perhaps most glaring example of this trend. The entire body of the work reflects a complete rejection of gender as an analytical tool among academic military historians. Its contributors examine how military institutions develop certain biases for offensive action, technology, education, promotion, and even certain kinds of history. Allan Millett's chapter on Marine Corps culture is the only one of the eighteen chapters that addresses gender in any meaningful way by acknowledging that "masculine dominance values" exist within the Corps. But his exploration of Marine masculinity does not go much further than that.[10]

Learning how to use gender as an analytical tool is important for the Marine Corps (and the other services) because the armed forces need to better understand how gender works to recruit and retain the best personnel and cultivate the best leadership from American society. Contrary to who the Corps promotes to the highest enlisted and officer ranks, the best leaders are not necessarily white men. A serious examination of gender in the Marines forces readers to ask tough questions about culture, identity, history, and their core assumptions about what it means to be a Marine. Military institutions who do not align themselves to the cultural, political, social, and strategic situation surrounding them risk paying a high price, both on the home front and against enemies abroad. To ignore gender as an analytical tool to gain insight into one's own history and culture is to risk worsening the disconnect between the armed forces and U.S. society by courting disaster in the realm of public relations.

What has kept the Marine Corps in existence is fighting on the battlefield *and* developing and maintaining positive relationships with the society it serves through advertising and public relations. The Corps will need leadership that can do both, and its needs educators who can and are not afraid to use analytical tools like gender to teach them how. A large portion of the U.S. population today is sensitive to perceived exclusions based on gender, race, and sexual preference in both private and public institutions. Commandant General David Berger made efforts to promote this when he asserted that greater diversity of Marines in terms of gender, race, and cultural background adds to the Corps warfighting capabilities. "We're much more powerful when we have different people looking at the same issue from different perspectives," he argued.[11] Traditionally, Marine culture and recruit training aims to strip away individuality to create uniformity among troops to enhance discipline and effectiveness. By arguing that diversity will lead to victory, however, Berger flipped on its head a longstanding assumption about gender, racial, and cultural diversity in the armed services.

Gender continues to have a substantial part in contemporary discourses surrounding the Marine Corps and military readiness. In 2020 General Berger promulgated Force Design 2030, which calls for an overhaul of the Corps's force structure, capabilities, and readiness posture. Influenced heavily by the 2018 National Defense Strategy that placed China and Russia as central threats to U.S. security, Berger oversaw the Corps's divestment of all of its tank battalions and the shrinkage of its infantry and artillery units in favor of littoral regiments armed with sophisticated rocket systems whose mission will be to help the navy in sea-denial operations in the Pacific. The guiding assumption is that the Marine Corps is not ready to fight a peer adversary like China.[12]

Commandant Berger followed up Force Design 2030 with Talent Management 2030, which addresses recruiting, promotion, and retention. The Corps has long put most of its recruiting resources and efforts toward attracting qualified recruits for initial enlistment and decidedly less on retaining them. This has made the Marines the youngest force on average than the rest of the armed services, which some have argued works because of its continuous need for combat readiness. Marine infantry units are mostly populated by young men (in their late teens to early twenties) on their first and most likely only enlistment because of that demographic's ability to handle the mental and physical strain of training and combat better than older populations.[13]

This new management system also emphasizes diversity, equity, and inclusion to attract and retain Marines from different cultural and demographic backgrounds. Talent Management 2030 does not say it explicitly, but the clear implication is that the Marine Corps is trying to attract more nonwhite males. By doing this, the document claims, the Corps is gaining "a competitive warfighting advantage over our adversaries, particularly those who place a premium on uniformity of thought."[14] In a sense, greater diversity and inclusion equates to better performance in war. Considering how white males have historically dominated the Corps in terms of demographics, leadership, and culture, it will be interesting to see how these changes affect readiness.

Force Design and Talent Management 2030 triggered the strongest opposition against change that any sitting Commandant has endured. There are two main opposition groups: older retired Marine officers and enlisted Marine veterans. The retired general officers, including Charles Krulak, Anthony Zinni, and Paul Van Riper, and former Marine and ex–secretary of the navy James Webb argue that Berger's changes weaken the Corps's air-ground task forces and make the service vulnerable.[15] Medal of Honor winner and retired Major General James E. Livingston has gone so far as to bring back the old "crisis of masculinity" trope by arguing that because of General Berger's changes, "The Marine air-ground task force . . . is being *emasculated*."[16] For both sides of this debate, what is at stake is the very survival of the Marine Corps. The pro–Force Design 2030 camp thinks that the Marines must adapt to survive, while their opponents believe the recent changes will make the Corps irrelevant and will lead to its eventual demise.[17] This is an important debate that will have lasting implications for the U.S. defense establishment, not just the Marine Corps.

The Corps's history of race and gender influences this debate in three ways. The first is paternalism. Both sides use metaphors likening Marines to members of the same family. Robert Work has described the disagreement as a "custody fight between the grandparents and parents of a beloved child," while Van Riper, a retired lieutenant general, has called the argument "a fight for the life of a child."[18] Likening the Corps to a child and claiming to have its best interests in mind has historical precedent dating back to early twentieth-century Marine paternalism, which viewed Marines as young men embarking on a passage toward manhood. Marine leadership back then often saw the relationship between officers and enlisted as father figures leading and guiding young men on that path. A century later this paternalism allows the participants in this debate to cast the Marine Corps as a child and present themselves as caretakers fighting over its future.

Second, remarkably absent from this discussion are members of the minority communities within the Corps. Few, if any, women or Black Marines have come forward to add their voices to the force-design debate. The primary participants in this discussion derive their authority and credibility (even their paternalism) from their combat and leadership experience in the Marine Corps. Nearly all are either veterans of Vietnam, the Gulf War, Iraq, or Afghanistan. Since combat-leadership roles and military occupational specialties have been closed to women during their time in the service, and few Black Marines have stayed in the Corps as long and as frequently as their white counterparts, that means the discussion's participants are nearly all white males. The Corps's culture and future, therefore, are still very much dominated by this group. It is thus their perspective, more than any other, that is shaping this historic debate; where it will lead remains unknown.

Third, race and gender are a part of this discussion through the explicit rage on social media from a second main opposition group: Marine veterans. On June 1, 2022, Marine Corps official headquarters and recruiting Instagram accounts posted images supporting Lesbian, Gay, Bisexual, Trans, Queer (LGBTQ+) Pride month. The headquarters Instagram posted an image of a Kevlar helmet with multicolor-tipped rifle rounds under the helmet band. Underneath the image is the caption, "We remain committed to fostering an environment free from discrimination, and defend the values of treating all equally, with dignity and respect."[19] The official recruiting page posted text within a multicolored box with the caption, "The Marine Corps is committed to the values we defend, treating everyone equally—with dignity and respect."[20] These posts, which are in line with Talent Management 2030's emphasis on diversity, equity, and inclusion, attracted thousands of negative comments from people identifying as either Marines or Marine veterans.

The many complaints against these posts fall under one of three kinds. First is the backlash against the Corps recognizing or celebrating a particular group of people over any other. Second are those who believe that promoting diversity, equity, and inclusion detracts from combat readiness. This idea is founded on the assumption that the only thing that matters in the Marine Corps is "lethality" (meaning combat and killing). Proponents of this idea draw on the traditional notion that combat is a male domain and that making the Corps more diverse makes it less masculine, which they fear could weaken it. The third major grievance involves the Marine Corps becoming too "woke." In conservative and right-wing parlance, "woke" means, among other things, a soft, weak, insecure, and emotionally sensitive ideologue with insidious political agendas. A "woke" Marine Corps in this context means a "ruined" institution that has departed from its traditionally masculine reputation and public image toward one that is more open to women and the LGBTQ+ community. "Less masculine" to former Marines who want the Corps to be "hard" and focused on killing equates to the Corps becoming "soft" by focusing more on being "politically correct."

This uglier side of the debate is fueled by political and cultural forces outside of the Marine Corps. American gender norms are still changing and evolving in the 2020s. What has not changed, however, is how opposing sides use gender to cast aspersions on each other. The political right uses terms such as "soft," "woke," "beta male," and "snowflake" to describe men on the left. The political left, however, sees the right as the home of "toxic masculinity," a term frequently associated with and manifested by misogyny, bigotry, homophobia, and transphobia. With the disastrous withdrawal of U.S. forces and personnel from Afghanistan in August 2021, this gendered language has made its way into the discourses surrounding military readiness. Conservatives, long the traditional and unconditional supporters of the U.S. armed forces, now accuse them of being infested by "woke" and "soft" liberals who deserve the blame for the United States losing in Afghanistan. For them, the "liberal agenda," with its emphasis on diversity and celebration of "beta males," has literally cost American lives and global prestige.

The Marine Corps has evolved over the last century, however, in terms of how it uses gender in recruiting and publicity. In the public arena it no longer claims to make *men*, but it continues to promote the benefits of becoming a Marine. Those benefits are similar to what they were a century ago. Marines are given opportunities to travel, become physically fit, and even go to school. The training is supposed to harden bodies and sharpen minds so that Marines can not only survive in combat but also be successful in any walk of life. The Corps's goal is not to make misogynistic killers. According to the recruiting these days, the Marines train people who can win on the battlefield and one day return home to the country they served as honest and productive citizens. The public face of the Marine Corps still values honor, courage, selflessness, assertiveness, and discipline, but it now attributes these traits to men *and* women. Just like in the early twentieth century, institutional paranoia about survival continues to pervade the Corps. Military readiness, however, is not the only thing that matters in this context. What also matters is making Marines and the American public continue to believe that the Corps is good for the country and the lives of themselves and their children. Paying careful attention to how the Marines' history of gender and race have influenced their image, identity, and culture helps us understand why Americans see the benefits of the Corps as being worth its cost.

Notes

Abbreviations

Dear Folks at Home	Kemper F. Cowing, comp., *"Dear Folks at Home—": The Glorious Story of the United States Marines in France as Told by their Letters from the Battlefield*, ed. Courtney R. Cooper (New York: Houghton Mifflin, 1919)
LOC	Library of Congress, Washington, DC
NARA I	National Archives and Records Administration, Washington, DC
NARA II	National Archives and Records Administration, College Park, MD
NPRC	National Personnel Records Center, St. Louis, MO
OHC	Oral History Collection
PPC	Personal Papers Collections
RB	Reference Branch
RG 80	General Records of the Department of the Navy, 1798–1947
RG 127	Records of the U.S. Marine Corps
RG 165	Records of the War Department General and Special Staffs
USAHEC	U.S. Army Heritage and Education Center, U.S. Army War College, Carlisle, PA
USMCHD	U.S. Marine Corps History Division, Marine Corps Archives, Quantico, VA
WWIQF	World War I Questionnaire Files

Preface

Epigraph. Victor H. Krulak, *First to Fight: An Inside View of the U.S. Marine Corps* (Annapolis, MD: Naval Institute Press, 1984), xv.

1. Robert Coram, *Brute: The Life of Victor Krulak, U.S. Marine* (New York: Little, Brown, 2010), 3.

2. Charles Krulak, "The Crucible: Building Warriors for the 21st Century," *Marine Corps Gazette*, July 1997, 13. I remember my own November 2002 experience with the Crucible quite well.

3. Krulak, 13.

Introduction

1. Frederick J. Haskin, "U.S. Marines Have Earned Laurels on Many Fields after Hard Fight Hoisted the Stars," *New Orleans Times Picayune*, May 7, 1914. Haskin was a civilian journalist who had a long career in U.S. newspapers from the turn of the twentieth century to the 1940s. He wrote books such as *The American Government, The Immigrant: An Asset and a Liability, The Panama Canal, Uncle Sam at Work*, and *The American Government Today*. It is not clear where he gets his information about Marines based on the content of this article, with its focus on Marine identity, readiness, sharpshooting, etc., but likely from a Marine recruiting pamphlet.

2. "Marines Make Glory in Vera Cruz Fight," *Galveston (TX) Daily News*, May 10, 1914.

3. "Americans Laugh While under Fire from Concealed Enemy," *New Orleans Times Picayune*, Apr. 22, 1914.

4. Heather Venable, *How the Few Became the Proud: Crafting the Marine Corps Mystique, 1874–1918* (Annapolis, MD: Naval Institute Press, 2019), 12–13. For other recent discussions on this subject, see Leo Spaeder, "Sir Who Am I?: An Open Letter to the Incoming Commandant of the Marine Corps," *War on the Rocks*, Mar. 28, 2019, https://warontherocks.com/2019/03/sir-who-am-i-an-open-letter -to-the-incoming-commandant-of-the-marine-corps/; Gordon Emmanuel and Justin Gray, "The Marine Corps' Evolving Character and Enduring Purpose," *War on the Rocks*, May 6, 2019, https://warontherocks.com/2019/05/the-marine-co rps-evolving-character-and-enduring-purpose/; Mark Nostro, "Discarding the Ptolemaic Model of the Marine Corps," *War on the Rocks*, Apr. 10, 2019, https:// warontherocks.com/2019/04/discarding-the-ptolemaic-model-of-the-marine-co rps/; Brian Kerg, "Russell's Century-Old Plea for the Marine Corps, Updated for 2019," *War on the Rocks*, Apr. 5, 2019, https://warontherocks.com/2019/04/russe lls-century-old-plea-for-the-marine-corps-updated-for-2019/; and Mark Folse, "Marine Corps Identity from the Historical Perspective," *War on the Rocks*, May 13, 2019, https://warontherocks.com/2019/05/marine-corps-identity-from-the-his torical-perspective/.

5. Venable, *How the Few Became the Proud*, 6–10; James Warren, *American Spartans: The U.S. Marines: A Combat History from Iwo Jima to Iraq* (New York: Free Press, 2005), 16–17; Craig M. Cameron, *American Samurai: Myth, Imagination, and the Conduct of Battle in the First Marine Division, 1941–1951* (New York: Cambridge University Press, 1994), 24–28; Allan R. Millett, *Semper Fidelis: The History of the United States Marine Corps* (New York: Free Press, 1991), 267–286; Aaron O'Connell, *Underdogs: The Making of the Modern Marine Corps* (Cambridge, MA: Harvard University Press, 2012), 13–15; Keith Bickel, *Mars Learning: The Marine Corps Development of Small Wars Doctrine, 1915–1940* (Boulder, CO: Westview, 2001), 12, 248.

6. Michael Kimmel, *Manhood in America: A Cultural History*, 3rd ed., (New York: Oxford University Press, 2012), 88; Tom Pendergast, *Creating the Modern Man: American Magazines and Consumer Culture, 1900–1950* (Columbia, MO: University of Missouri Press, 2000), 2; Athena Delvin, *Between Profits and Primitivism: Shaping White Middle-Class Masculinity in the United States, 1880–1917* (New York: Routledge, 2005), 17; Martin Summers, *Manliness & Its Discontents: The Black Middle*

Class & the Transformation of Masculinity, 1900–1930 (Chapel Hill: University of North Carolina Press, 2004), 8; Joe L. Dubbert, "Progressivism and the Masculinity Crisis," in *The American Man*, ed. Elizabeth H. Pleck and Joseph H. Pleck (Englewood Cliffs, NJ: Prentice-Hall, 1980), 309–310; Peter N. Stearns, *Be a Man! Males in Modern Society*, 2nd ed. (New York: Holmes & Meier, 1990), 10–11.

7. Amy S. Greenberg, *Manifest Manhood and the Antebellum American Empire* (New York: Cambridge University Press, 2005), 11–12.

8. Gail Bederman, *Manliness and Civilization: A Cultural History of Gender and Race in the United States, 1880–1917* (Chicago: University of Chicago Press, 1995), 19.

9. Donald J. Mrozek, "The Habit of Victory; the American Military and the Cult of Manliness," in *Manliness and Morality: Middle-class Masculinity in Britain and America, 1800–1940*, ed. J. A. Mangan and James Walvin (Manchester: Manchester University Press, 1987), 222.

10. Pendergast, *Creating the Modern Man*, 27.

11. Luther H. Gulick, *The Dynamic of Manhood* (New York: Association, 1918), 9–14; Martyn Summerbell, *Manhood in Its American Type* (Boston: Richard G. Badger, 1916), 109; Kelly Miller, "Education for Manhood," *Kelly Miller's Monographic Magazine*, Apr. 1913, 12; George Walter Fiske, *Boy Life and Self-Government* (New York: Association, 1916), 28; R. Swinburn Clymer, *The Way to Godhood* (Allentown, PA: Philosophical Publishing, 1914), 89–90.

12. Mrozek, "Habit of Victory," 221–223; Peter G. Filene, *Him/Her/Self: Sex Roles in Modern America* (Baltimore: Johns Hopkins University Press, 1986), 93; Dubbert, "Progressivism and the Masculinity Crisis," 308; Michael Messner, "The Meaning of Success: The Athletic Experience and the Development of Male Identity," in *The Making of Masculinities: The New Men's Studies*, ed. Harry Brod (Boston: Allen & Unwin, 1987), 196; Michael Kimmel, "The Contemporary 'Crises' of Masculinity in Historical Perspective," in *The Making of Masculinities: The New Men's Studies*, edited by Harry Brod (Boston: Allen and Unwin, 1987), 143.

13. Gail Bederman's chapter on G. Stanley Hall goes into great depth about this. Bederman, *Manliness and Civilization*, 77–120.

14. Clymer, *Way to Godhood*, 77; U.S. Congress, *Congressional Record*, 65th Cong., 1st sess. (1917), 383.

15. Summerbell, *Manhood in Its American Type*, 40.

16. Theodore Roosevelt, *The Strenuous Life: Essays and Addresses* (New York: Century, 1903), 4; Bederman, *Manliness and Civilization*, 171–172.

17. The dichotomy between field and dress Marines is acknowledged but is not associated with masculinity in Allan R. Millett, "The U.S. Marine Corps, 1973–2017: Cultural Preservation in Every Place and Clime," in *The Culture of Military Organizations*, ed. Peter R. Mansoor and Williamson Murray (New York: Cambridge University Press, 2019), 399–400. See also Lorien Foote, *The Gentlemen and the Roughs: Violence, Honor, and Manhood in the Union Army* (New York: New York University Press, 2010), 1–5.

18. Hans Schmidt, *Maverick Marine: General Smedley D. Butler and the Contradictions of American Military History* (Lexington: University Press of Kentucky, 1987), 211–213.

19. Jiří Hutečka, *Men under Fire: Motivation, Morale, and Masculinity among Czech Soldiers in the Great War, 1914–1918* (New York: Berghahn Books, 2020), 8; Gregory

A. Daddis, *Pulp Vietnam: War and Gender in Cold War Men's Adventure Magazines* (New York: Cambridge University Press, 2021), 5.

20. Amy Greenberg, for example, defines martial and restrained manhood as forms of manliness *and* masculinity without clarifying any distinctions between the terms. *Manifest Manhood*, 11–12. Jiří Hutečka offers no distinction between the terms. *Men under Fire*, 6–13. Although gender is not the crux of Heather Venable's analysis, she also offers no significant distinction between "masculinity" and "manliness" but uses both terms. *How the Few Became the Proud*, 14–15, 134–135, 176–177. Gregory Daddis seems to favor "masculinity" over "manhood" or "manliness" because of the historical period he explores. But if there were any distinction between the terms by the 1950s and 1960s he leaves them undefined. Daddis, *Pulp Vietnam*, 5, 26.

21. Aaron Belkin, *Bring Me Men: Military Masculinity and the Benign Façade of American Empire, 1898–2001* (New York: Columbia University Press, 2012), 10–11; Hutečka, *Men under Fire*, 77, 208, 238.

22. *Armed Forces Decorations and Awards* (American Forces Information Service, Department of Defense, 1992), 2–3. https://history.army.mil/moh/Armed-Forces -Decorations-and-Awards.pdf (accessed Jan. 1, 2021).

23. *Armed Forces Decorations*, 4.

24. "Smedley Butler," Recipients, National Medal of Honor Museum, https:// mohmuseum.org/medal_of_honor/smedley-butler/ (accessed Jan. 1, 2021).

25. Medal of Honor Citation, "Captain Hiram I. Bearss, USMCR (Deceased)," Marine Corps University, https://www.usmcu.edu/Portals/218/HD/Histories /MHC/Bearss_H.I.pdf?ver=kR8bpuqjnHT5BLPwuFSvEg%3d%3d (accessed Jan. 1, 2021).

26. Jeff Hearn, "Forward: On Men, Women, Militarism, and the Military," in *Military Masculinities: Identity and the State*, ed. Paul R. Higate (Westport, CT: Praeger, 2003), xii.

27. Frederick M. Wise, *A Marine Tells It to You*, ed. by Meigs O. Frost (New York: J. H. Sears, 1929), 5.

28. For a comprehensive review of works dealing with gender in the Great War, see Andrew J. Huebner, "Gee! I Wish I Were a Man: Gender and the Great War," in *The Routledge History of Gender, War, and the U.S. Military*, ed. Kara Dixon Vuic (New York: Routledge, 2018), 68–82.

29. Belkin, *Bring Me Men*, 4; Kristin L. Hoganson, *Fighting for American Manhood*, 8.

30. R. W. Connell, *Masculinities*, 2nd ed. (Los Angeles: University of California Press, 2005), 71.

31. Scott, *Gender and the Politics of History*, 42.

32. Bederman, *Manliness and Civilization*, 18.

33. Ryan D. Wadle, *Selling Sea Power: Public Relations and the U.S. Navy, 1917–1941* (Norman: University of Oklahoma Press, 2019), 136; Venable, *How the Few Became the Proud*, 121; Connell, *Masculinities*, 73.

34. Kimmel, *Manhood in America*, 62–63.

35. Connell, *Masculinities*, 84; Mrozek, "Habit of Victory," 221–223; Peter G. Feline, *Him/Her/Self: Sex Roles in Modern America* (Baltimore: Johns Hopkins University Press, 1986), 93; Dubbert, "Progressivism and the Masculinity Crisis," 308;

Messner, "Meaning of Success," 196; Kimmel, "Contemporary 'Crises' of Masculinity," 143; James Gilbert, *Men in the Middle: Searching for Masculinity in the 1950s* (Chicago: University of Chicago Press, 2005), 15–33; K. A. Cuordileone, *Manhood and American Political Culture in the Cold War* (New York: Routledge, 2005), 9–14.

36. Kimmel, *Manhood in America*, 102; Delvin, *Between Profits and Primitivism*, 17; Rotundo, *American Manhood*, 242–246.

37. Fiske, *Boy Life and Self-Government*, 105.

38. Wanda Ellen Wakefield, *Sports and the American Military, 1898–1945* (New York: State University of New York Press, 1997), 35–78.

39. For more analysis on the importance of the male body to masculinity see Delvin, *Between Profits and Primitivism*, 4; Susan Bordo, *The Male Body: A New Look at Men in Public and Private* (New York: Farrar, Straus, & Giroux, 1999); Christina S. Jarvis, *The Male Body at War: American Masculinity during World War II* (Dekalb: Northern Illinois University Press, 2004), 4; John F. Kasson, *Houdini, Tarzan, and the Perfect Man: The White Male Body and the Challenge of Modernity in America* (New York: Hill & Wang, 2001), 19.

40. W. J. T. Mitchell, *Iconology: Image, Text, Ideology* (Chicago: University of Chicago Press, 1986), 44; Cameron, *American Samurai*, 8–9.

41. Mitchell, *Iconology*, 48.

42. Cameron, *American Samurai*, 49; O'Connell, *Underdogs*, 2–4; Venable, *How the Few Became the Proud*, 14; For more on Marine institutional culture sans gender analysis see Marion F. Sturkey, *Warrior Culture of the U.S. Marines*, 3rd ed. (Plum Branch, SC: Heritage Press International, 2010), xii; Paula Holmes-Eber, *Culture in Conflict: Warfare, Culture Policy, and the Marine Corps* (Stanford: Stanford University Press, 2014); Frank J. Tortorello, "An Ethnography of 'Courage' among U.S. Marines" (PhD diss., University of Illinois at Urbana-Champaign, 2010); Terry Terriff, "Warriors and Innovators: Military Change and Organizational Culture in the U.S. Marine Corps," *Defense Studies* 6, no. 2 (2006); and "'Innovate or Die': Organizational Culture and the Origins of Maneuver Warfare in the United States Marine Corps," *Journal of Strategic Studies* 29, no. 3 (2006).

43. For broad impact the Great War had on the United States see David M. Kennedy, *Over Here: The First World War and American Society* (New York: Oxford University Press, 1980); Robert H. Zieger, *America's Great War: World War I and the American Experience* (New York: Rowman & Littlefield, 2000); Jackson Lears, *Rebirth of a Nation: The Making of Modern America, 1877–1920* (New York: Harper Collins, 2009); Michael McGerr, *A Fierce Discontent: The Rise and Fall of the Progressive Movement in America, 1870–1920* (New York: Free Press, 2003); Jennifer D. Keene, *Doughboys, the Great War, and Remaking of America* (Baltimore, MD: Johns Hopkins University Press, 2001); Christopher Capozzola, *Uncle Sam Wants You: World War I and the Making of the Modern American Citizen* (New York: Oxford University Press, 2008); Robert H. Wiebe, *The Search for Order, 1877–1920* (New York: Hill & Wang, 1967).

44. Joseph Alexander, *Through the Wheat: The U.S. Marines in World War I* (Annapolis, MD: Naval Institute Press, 2008); Robert B. Asprey, *At Belleau Wood* (Denton: University of North Texas Press, 1996); Alan Axelrod, *Miracle at Belleau Wood: The Birth of the Modern Marine Corps* (Guilford, CT: Lyons, 2007); Henry Berry, *Make the Kaiser Dance* (New York: Doubleday, 1987); Ronald J. Brown, *A*

Few Good Men: The Story of the Fighting Fifth Marines (Novato, CA: Presidio, 2001); Dick Camp, *The Devil Dogs at Belleau Wood: U.S. Marines in World War I* (Minneapolis, MN: Zenith, 2008); George B. Clark, *Devil Dogs: Fighting Marines of World War I* (Novato, CA: Presidio, 1999); Edward M. Coffman, *The War to End All Wars: The American Military Experience in World War I* (New York: Oxford University Press, 1968); Mark Ethan Grotelueschen, *The AEF Way of War: The American Army and Combat in World War I* (New York: Cambridge University Press, 2007); Edward G. Lengel, *Thunder and Flames: Americans in the Crucible of Combat, 1917–1918* (Lawrence: University Press of Kansas, 2015); Robert J. Moskin, *The U.S. Marine Corps Story*, 3rd ed. (Boston: Little, Brown, 1992); Michael S. Neiberg, *The Second Battle of the Marne* (Bloomington: Indiana University Press, 2008); William D. Parker, *A Concise History of the United States Marine Corps 1775–1969* (Washington, DC: Historical Division Headquarters USMC, 1970); Millett, *Semper Fidelis*, 317–318.

45. For discussions of war making men more manly see Hoganson, *Fighting for American Manhood: How Gender Politics Provoked the Spanish-American and Philippine-American Wars* (New Haven, CT: Yale University Press, 1998); Mark Moss, *Manliness and Militarism: Educating Young Boys in Ontario for War* (New York: Oxford University Press, 2001); Michael C. C. Adams, *The Great Adventure: Male Desire and the Coming of World War I* (Bloomington: Indiana University Press, 1990), 49; and Peter G. Filene, "In Time of War," in *The American Man*, ed. Elizabeth H. Pleck and Joseph H. Pleck (Englewood Cliffs, NJ: Prentice-Hall, 1980), 323.

46. Stephen M. Fuller and Graham A. Cosmas, *Marines in the Dominican Republic* (Washington, DC: History and Museums Division Headquarters, U.S. Marine Corps, 1974), 68; Edwin H. Simmons, *The United States Marines: A History*, 3rd ed. (Annapolis, MD: Naval Institute Press, 1998), 110; Clyde H. Metcalf, *A History of the United States Marine Corps* (New York: G. P. Putnam's Sons, 1939), 370, 390–393; Moskin, *U.S. Marine Corps Story*, 187–188; Millett, *Simper Fidelis*, 186. A notable exception is Breanne Robertson, "Rebellion, Repression, and Reform: U.S. Marines in the Dominican Republic," *Marine Corps History* 2, no. 1 (Summer 2016): 31–54.

47. Alan McPherson, *The Invaded: How Latin Americans and Their Allies Fought and Ended U.S. Occupations* (New York: Oxford University Press, 2014), 2, 265; Bruce J. Calder, *The Impact of Intervention: The Dominican Republic during the U.S. Occupation of 1916–1924* (Princeton, NJ: Markus Wiener, 2006), xxviii; Frank Moya Pons, *The Dominican Republic: A National History* (Princeton, NJ: Markus Wiener, 1998); Ian Bell, *The Dominican Republic* (Boulder, CO: Westview, 1980); Steeve Coupeau, *The History of Haiti* (Westport, CT: Greenwood, 2008); Hans Schmidt, *The United States Occupation of Haiti, 1915–1934* (New Brunswick, NJ: Rutgers University Press, 1995).

48. Robert Lindsay, *This High Name: Public Relations and the U.S. Marine Corps* (Madison: University of Wisconsin Press, 1956), 36–39; Schmidt, *Maverick Marine*, 143.

49. David J. Ulbrich, *Preparing for Victory: Thomas Holcomb and the Making of the Modern Marine Corps, 1936–1943* (Annapolis, MD: Naval Institute Press, 2011), 1. See also David J. Bettez, *Kentucky Marine: Major General Logan Feland and the Making of the Modern USMC* (Lexington: University Press of Kentucky, 2014); Leo Joseph Daugherty, "To Fight Our Country's Battles: An Institutional History of the United States Marine Corps during the Interwar Era, 1919–1935" (PhD diss.,

Ohio State University, 2001), 55; Millett, *Semper Fidelis*, 318–323; Merril L. Bartlett, "John A. Lejeune," in *Commandants of the Marine Corps*, ed. Allan Millett and Jack Shulimson (Annapolis, MD: Naval Institute Press, 2004), 213; Lt. Col. Kenneth J. Clifford, *Progress and Purpose: A Developmental History of the United States Marine Corps, 1900–1970* (Washington, DC: USMC History and Museums Division, 1973), 31–36; John A. Lejeune, "The Mobile Defense of Advance Bases by the Marine Corps," *Marine Corps Gazette*, June 1916, 1; John H. Russell, "A Plea for a Mission and Doctrine," *Marine Corps Gazette*, June 1916, 109; Jeter A. Isely and Philip A. Crowl, *The U.S. Marines and Amphibious War: Its Theory and Its Practice in the Pacific* (Princeton, NJ: Princeton University Press, 1951), 3–45; Victor H. Krulak, *First to Fight: An Inside View of the U.S. Marine Corps* (Annapolis, MD: Naval Institute Press, 1984), 1–107; and Coram, *Brute*, 71–72.

1. Elements of the U.S. Marine Corps

Epigraph. "Our Marines," *Recruiters' Bulletin*, Mar. 1915, 8. The editors prefaced this poem by describing the author briefly. The writer was a young man who tried to enlist in the Marine Corps but was rejected because doctors determined he had a heart murmur. The applicant "felt very bad over his rejection, and remarked that if he could not be a Marine in the flesh he would be one in spirit." He gave this poem to the recruiters, who then forwarded it to the *Recruiters' Bulletin*, which published it.

1. "Essential elements" was originally inspired by Samuel P. Huntington, "National Policy and the Transoceanic Navy," *Naval Institute Proceedings*, May 1954, 483–493. His model, however, does not work well in explaining Marine Corps history or its place in the early twentieth-century U.S. defense establishment.

2. By no means was every American taken by the rhetoric of empire, nor did they believe its promises. David Mayers, *Dissenting Voices in America's Rise to Power* (New York: Cambridge University Press, 2007), 190–220; Jeffrey W. Meiser, *Power and Restraint: The Rise of the United States, 1898–1941* (Washington, DC: Georgetown University Press, 2015), 59–144.

3. Jackson Lears, *Rebirth of a Nation: The Making of Modern America, 1877–1920* (New York: Harper Collins, 2009), 279.

4. I use "Marine" with a capital "M" when talking about members of the U.S. Marine Corps and "marine" with a lower case "m" when discussing soldiers performing general maritime duties on ship who are not necessarily members of the U.S. Marine Corps or the Royal Marines.

5. Millett, *Semper Fidelis*, 6–7, 27–29.

6. Carroll Smith-Rosenberg, "The Republican Gentleman: The Race to Rhetorical Stability in the New United States," in *Masculinities in Politics and War: Gendering Modern History*, ed. Stefan Dudink, Karen Hagemann, and John Tosh (New York: Manchester University Press, 2004), 69.

7. Rotundo, *American Manhood*, 3.

8. Rotundo, 3.

9. Millett, *Semper Fidelis*, 34.

10. William Ward Burrows to Benjamin Strother, Mar. 31, 1800, Entry 4: Headquarters U.S. Marine Corps, Office of the Commandant, General Records Correspondence, Letters Sent, Aug. 1798–June 1801, vol. 2, RG 127, NARA I; Paul W. Westermeyer, "Marines, Masculinity, and Identity in the Frigate Navy" (paper presented at the McMullen Naval History Symposium, Annapolis, MD, Sept. 20, 2019).

11. William Ward Burrows to Benjamin Stoddert, July 31, 1800, Entry 4, vol. 2, RG 127, NARA I.

12. Burrows to Stoddert, July 31, 1800.

13. William Ward Burrows to Philip Edwards, May 30, 1800, Entry 4, vol. 2, RG 127, NARA I.

14. Rotundo, *American Manhood*, 20–21.

15. William Ward Burrows to Henry Caldwell, Sept. 22, 1800, Entry 4, vol. 2, RG 127, NARA I.

16. Burrows to Caldwell, Sept. 22, 1800.

17. Westermeyer, "Marines, Masculinity, and Identity in the Frigate Navy."

18. Merrill L. Bartlett, "Anthony Gale, 1819–1820," in *Commandants of the Marine Corps*, ed. Allan R. Millett and Jack Shulimson (Annapolis, MD: Naval Institute Press, 2004), 50.

19. Robert D. Heinl Jr., "The Cat with More Than Nine Lives," in *On the Corps: USMC Wisdom from the Pages of* Leatherneck, Marine Corps Gazette, *and* Proceedings, ed. Charles P. Neimeyer (Annapolis, MD: Naval Institute Press, 2008), 46–48. Heinl's essay was originally published in *US Naval Institute Proceedings*, June 1954.

20. Foote, *Gentlemen and the Roughs*, 6–7; Bertram Wyatt-Brown, *Southern Honor: Ethics and Behavior in the Old South* (New York: Oxford University Press, 1982), 5, 17, 34–36.

21. Greenberg, *Manifest Manhood*, 3–5.

22. Foote, *Gentlemen and the Roughs*, 6–7.

23. Wyatt-Brown, *Southern Honor*, 35.

24. Millett, *Semper Fidelis*, 97.

25. William H. Roberts, *Now for the Contest: Coastal & Oceanic Naval Operations in the Civil War* (Lincoln: University of Nebraska Press, 2004), 155–156; Millett, *Semper Fidelis*, 98–99.

26. Millett, *Semper Fidelis*, 99.

27. Craig L. Symonds, *The U.S. Navy: A Concise History* (New York: Oxford University Press, 2016), 55–64; Jack Shulimson, *The Marine Corps Search for a Mission, 1880–1898* (Lawrence: University Press of Kansas, 1993), 13; Millett, *Semper Fidelis*, 114.

28. Allan R. Millett, Petter Maslowski, and William B. Feis, *For the Common Defense: A Military History of the United States from 1607 to 2012*, 3rd ed. (New York: Free Press, 2012), 219–220.

29. Heinl, "Cat with More Than Nine Lives," 49; Millett, *Semper Fidelis*, 102.

30. Shulimson, *Marine Corps Search for a Mission*, 62.

31. Shulimson, 13–15.

32. Henry Clay Cochran quoted in Shulimson, 17.

33. Shulimson, xi.

34. "A Summary of Missions of the United States Naval Academy," 2, Naval Academy Reference Files, Special Collections and Archives, Chester A. Nimitz Library, U.S. Naval Academy, Annapolis, MD.

35. *Regulations of the United States Naval Academy* (Washington, DC: Government Printing Office, 1887), 63.

36. Thomas G. Ford, chap. 28, "General Reflections," 18, Box 3, Thomas G. Ford Manuscript, 1858–1908, Special Collections and Archives, Nimitz Library, U.S. Naval Academy.

37. William F. Fullam, "The System of Naval Training and Discipline Required to Promote Efficiency and Attract Americans," *Proceedings of the United States Naval Institute*, Oct. 1890, 475, available via subscription at https://www.usni.org/magazines/proceedings/1890/october/system-naval-training-and-discipline-required-promote-efficiency (accessed July 17, 2019).

38. Fullam, 495.

39. Paul Murphy, response to Fullam, "System of Naval Training," 518.

40. Shulimson, *Marine Corps Search for a Mission*, 111.

41. Fullam, "System of Naval Training," 494.

42. Richard White, *The Republic for Which It Stands: The United States during Reconstruction and the Gilded Age, 1865–1896* (New York: Oxford University Press, 2017), 657.

43. Alfred Thayer Mahan, *The Influence of Sea Power Upon History, 1660–1783* (Boston: Little, Brown, 1890), 29–58. See also Robert Seager II, "Alfred Thayer Mahan: Navalist and Historian," in *Quarterdeck and Bridge: Two Centuries of American Naval Leaders*, ed. James C. Bradford (Annapolis, MD: Naval Institute Press, 1997), 219–243; and Symonds, *U.S. Navy*, 60–61.

44. Jack Shulimson, "Charles Heywood, 1891–1903," in *Commandants of the Marine Corps*, ed. Allan R. Millett and Jack Shulimson (Annapolis, MD: Naval Institute Press, 2004), 117.

45. Heinl, "Cat with More Than Nine Lives," 51–52.

46. William F. Fullam, "The Organization, Training, and Discipline of the Navy Personnel as Viewed from the Ship," *Proceedings of the United States Naval Institute*, Jan. 1896, 105, available via subscription at https://www.usni.org/magazines/proceedings/1896/january/honorably-mentioned-organization-training-and-discipline-navy (accessed Feb. 20, 2020).

47. J. N. Hemphill, response to Fullam, "Organization, Training, and Discipline," 172; Heinl, "Cat with More Than Nine Lives," 52–53.

48. For a concise list and brief description of these landings, see Harry Alanson Ellsworth, *One Hundred Eighty Landings of the United States Marines, 1800–1934* (Washington, DC: Headquarters U.S. Marine Corps, Historical Section, 1934).

49. Fullam, "Organization, Training, and Discipline," 113–114.

50. Heinl, "Cat with More Than Nine Lives," 53.

51. Millett, *Semper Fidelis*, 135; Shulimson, *Marine Corps Search for a Mission*, 198.

52. Shulimson, *Marine Corps Search for a Mission*, 201; Millett, *Semper Fidelis*, 267–271.

53. Hoganson, *Fighting for American Manhood*, 158–159.

54. Hoganson, 164–165.

55. Millett, Maslowski, and Feis, *For the Common Defense*, 300–301.

56. Millett, *Semper Fidelis*, 139.

57. Heinl, "Cat with More Than Nine Lives," 57.

58. "Report of the Major General Commandant of the United States Marine Corps," in *Annual Report of the Navy Department for the Fiscal Year 1914* (Washington, DC: Government Printing Office, 1915), 462.

59. *Annual Report of the Navy Department . . . 1914*, 72; Frederick S. Harrod, *Manning the New Navy: The Development of a Modern Enlisted Force, 1899–1940* (Westport, CT: Greenwood, 1978), 174; *Report of the Adjutant General of the Army to the Secretary of War for the Fiscal Year 1914* (Washington, DC: Government Printing Office, 1915), 8.

60. *Report of the Adjutant General of the Army . . . 1914*, 7–8.

61. Gordon L. Rottman, *U.S. Marine Corps World War II Order of Battle: Ground and Air Units in the Pacific War, 1939–1945* (Westport, CT: Greenwood, 2002), 15.

62. 1st Marines, Lineage and Honors, Ground Units, Marine Corps University, https://www.usmcu.edu/Research/Marine-Corps-History-Division/Information-for-Units/Lineage-and-Honors-by-Unit/ (accessed July 23, 2019).

63. *Annual Report of the Navy Department . . . 1914*, 470.

64. Among researchers, too.

65. 1st, 2nd, 3rd, and 4th Marines, Lineage and Honors, Ground Units, Marine Corps University, https://www.usmcu.edu/Research/Marine-Corps-History-Division/Information-for-Units/Lineage-and-Honors-by-Unit/ (accessed July 23, 2019).

66. M. Almy Aldrich, *History of the United States Marine Corps* (Boston: Henry L. Shepard, 1875), 7. Collum compiled for Aldrich various official reports and other documents.

67. Editorial, "Reckless Recruiting," *United States Army and Navy Journal*, Aug. 20, 1887, 67. See also Shulimson, *Marine Corps Search for a Mission*, 67–68.

68. Charles G. McCawley, "Recruiting for Marine Corps," *United States Army and Navy Journal*, Aug. 27, 1887, 80. See also Shulimson, *Marine Corps Search for a Mission*, 67–68.

69. "Report of the Colonel Commandant of the United States Marine Corps," in *Annual Report of the Navy Department for the Fiscal Year 1914*, 525; Shulimson, *Marine Corps Search for a Mission*, 68.

70. Shulimson, *Marine Corps Search for a Mission*, 70.

71. Quoted in Shulimson, 120.

72. Editorial, "Reckless Recruiting," 67.

73. Shulimson, *Marine Corps Search for a Mission*, 118.

74. Simmons, *United States Marines*, 42–47, 59.

75. Millett, *Semper Fidelis*, 113.

76. "Heroism of Americans: Many Instances Shown to Prove the Bravery of the Yankee Nation," *Kansas City Journal*, June 17, 1917, 9.

77. Millett, *Semper Fidelis*, 129.

78. Millett, 186–187.

79. Millett, 134; Colin Colburn, "Esprit de Marine Corps: Making of the Modern Marine Corps through Public Relations, 1898–1945" (PhD diss., University of Southern Mississippi, 2018), 33–34.

80. Editorial, "Record of the Marines: Praises of the Corps Sounded by Officers of the Ships at Santiago," *New York Times*, Oct. 23, 1898, 13.

81. Hoganson, *Fighting for American Manhood*, 68–69.

82. Venable, *How the Few Became the Proud*, 62.

83. Brain McAllister Linn, "'We Will Go Heavily Armed': The Marines' Small War on Samar, 1901–1902," in *U.S. Marines and Irregular Warfare, 1898–2007: Anthology and Selected Bibliography*, ed. Stephen S. Evans (Quantico, VA: Marine Corps University, 2008), 47; Millett, *Semper Fidelis*, 154–155.

84. Edward H. Crosby, "The Military Idea of Manliness," *Independent*, Apr. 1901, 873. See also Rotundo, *American Manhood*, 236–237.

85. Editorial, "The Week," *Nation*, May 1, 1902, 337; "A Court-Martial for Major Waller: Hero of Samar Accused of Executing Natives without Trial," *New York Times*, Mar. 7, 1902, 3; "Praise for the Work of Marines," *San Francisco Chronicle*, Oct. 29, 1902, 2; "Waller Boasts Samar Work," *St. Louis Post*, June 13, 1902, 3.

86. Sgt. Thomas G. Sterrett, "Working the Newspapers," *Recruiters' Bulletin*, Nov. 1914, 10; Cpl. Lester E. Smith, "Old-Time Publicity Bureaus," *Marines Magazine*, June 1916, 8. See also Lindsay, *This High Name*, 9–11.

87. Colburn, "Esprit de Marine Corps," 43–44.

88. Lindsay, *This High Name*, 10–11.

89. Millett, *Semper Fidelis*, 113.

90. Colburn, "Esprit de Marine Corps," 24; Lindsay, *This High Name*, 11.

91. Editorial, "Relative Efficiency of Divisions and Districts for Calendar Year, up to March 1, 1915," *Recruiters' Bulletin*, Mar. 1915, 11.

92. *Annual Report of the Navy Department for the Fiscal Year 1915* (Washington, DC: Government Printing Office, 1916), 773.

93. *Report of the Adjutant General of the Army . . . 1914*, 32–38.

94. Venable, *How the Few Became the Proud*, 6.

95. *The Marine's Catechism—Who Am I?* (New York: U.S. Marine Corps Publicity Bureau, 1917), cover page.

96. *Marine's Catechism*, 7 (emphasis added).

97. Edward A. Callan, "Editorial," *Marines Magazine*, Dec. 1915, 1.

98. "The Marine Corps Association: Its Formation and Objects," *Marine Corps Gazette*, June 1916, 73.

99. Pendergast, *Creating the Modern Man*, 30.

100. Edward A. Callan, "Editorial," *Marines Magazine*, Dec. 1915, 1.

101. John A. Lejeune, "The Mobile Defense of Advance Bases by the Marine Corps," *Marine Corps Gazette*, June 1916, 1. The footnote on the first page of this article reads: "Lecture delivered to officers of Advance Base School, Philadelphia, in May, 1915. This paper is based very largely on Captain Earl Ellis' lectures on Advance Bases."

102. Lejeune, 2–3.

103. Lejeune, 1–2.

104. Lejeune, 2.

105. Lejeune, 2.

106. John H. Russell, "A Plea for a Mission and Doctrine," *Marine Corps Gazette*, June 1916, 109.

107. Lejeune, "Mobile Defense," 1–2.

108. Russell, "Plea for a Mission and Doctrine," 122.

109. Lejeune, "Mobile Defense," 9.

110. Russell, "Plea for a Mission and Doctrine," 112–113.

111. Kimmel, *Manhood in America*, 101–102; Rotundo, *American Manhood*, 232–244.

112. Editorial, "One Definition of a Marine," *Recruiters' Bulletin*, Dec. 1915, 16.

2. With Hard Two-Fisted Hands

Epigraph. Berton Braley, "The Leathernecks," *Marines Magazine*, June 1917, 14.

1. William J. Candee, "Sergeant McNab's Strategy," *Marines Magazine*, May 1917, 7.

2. Candee, 8.

3. Candee, 8.

4. Kimmel, *Manhood in America*, 88; Summers, *Manliness & Its Discontents*, 16; Delvin, *Between Profits and Primitivism*, 9; Dubbert, "Progressivism and the Masculinity Crisis," 309–310.

5. *Annual Report of the Navy Department for the Fiscal Year 1914* (Washington, DC: Government Printing Office, 1915), 462.

6. Millett, *Semper Fidelis*, 216.

7. Paul S. Reinsch, *An American Diplomat in China* (Garden City, NY: Doubleday, Page, 1922), 17.

8. Henry C. Hines, "A Day in the Field," *Marines Magazine*, Dec. 1915, 52.

9. Charles A. Ketcham, "Marine Corps Efficiency," *Marines Magazine*, Mar. 1917, 12.

10. Cpl. F. E. Turin, "Active Man," *Marines Magazine*, Jan. 1916, 14.

11. C.L.S., "Say!," *Marines Magazine*, Mar. 1917, 13.

12. Charley Dunbeck, "Marine—Efficiency—Synonym," *Marines Magazine*, Mar. 1917, 11.

13. Charles A. Ketcham, "Recruiting by Wire," *Marines Magazine*, Mar. 1917, 8.

14. Rotundo, *American Manhood*, 224–225; Bederman, *Manliness and Civilization*, 172; Kimmel, *Manhood in America*, 88.

15. Kimmel, *Manhood in America*, 134; Filene, *Him/Her/Self*, 70; Filene, "In Time of War," 321–324.

16. Alfred Percival, "Our Readiness for War," *Syracuse (NY) Herald*, Dec. 10, 1914.

17. Millett, Maslowski, and Feis, *For the Common Defense*, 303–304.

18. John Patrick Finnegan, *Against the Specter of a Dragon: The Campaign for American Military Preparedness, 1914–1917* (Westport CT: Greenwood, 1974), 3.

19. Finnegan, 13.

20. Leonard Wood, introduction to *The Military Unpreparedness of the United States: A History of American Land Forces from Colonial Times until June 1, 1915*, by Frederick L. Huidekoper (New York: Macmillan, 1915), xiv.

21. Sgt. Claud Johnson, "Soldier of the Sea," *Recruiters' Bulletin*, Apr. 1916, 13.

22. Capt. L. M. Harding "Mr. American Citizen," *Recruiters' Bulletin*, July 1916, 18. See also Pvt. T. E. Dwyer, "Preparedness," *Recruiters' Bulletin*, June 1916, 12.

23. Greenberg, *Manifest Manhood*, 11; Foote, *The Gentlemen and the Roughs*, 3–5.

24. Homer Lea, *The Valor of Ignorance* (New York: Harper & Brothers, 1909), 20–21. Homer Lea was a diminutively small Coloradoan born in 1876 who had a penchant for military history and a desire to command troops in battle from a young age. His physical disabilities (i.e. bad eyes, chronic headaches, and he most likely had scoliosis) kept him out of military service in the United States. He went to China where he allegedly commanded Chinese troops in battle. Lea came back to the United States after his adventures and felt deeply disturbed by the indifference to national defense that he saw there; Clare Boothe, introduction to Homer Lea's 1942 edition of *Valor of Ignorance*, xxii–xxiii.

25. Lea, *Valor of Ignorance*, 9.

26. Lea, 16.

27. R. Swinburne Clymer, *The Way to Godhood* (Allentown, PA: Philosophical Publishing, 1914), 77.

28. Clymer, *The Way to Godhood*, 89–90.

29. U.S. War Department, *Outline of Plan for Military Training in Public Schools of the United States* (Washington, DC: Army War College, 1915), 8.

30. Wood, introduction to Huidekoper, *Military Unpreparedness of the United States*, xiii.

31. Huidekoper, *Military Unpreparedness of the United States*, 271–272.

32. Unsigned review of *The Military Unpreparedness of the United States*, by Frederick Louis Huidekoper, *Marine Corps Gazette*, June 1916, 184.

33. G. Stanley Hall, *Adolescence: Its Psychology and Its Relations to Physiology, Anthropology, Sociology, Sex, Crime, Religion, and Education*, vol. 2 (New York: D. Appleton, 1905), 620.

34. Michael Kimmel, "The Contemporary 'Crisis' of Masculinity in Historical Perspective," in *The Making of Masculinities: The New Men's Studies*, ed. Harry Brod (Boston: Allen & Unwin, 1987), 143–153, and *Manhood in America*, 62; E. Anthony Rotundo, "Body and Soul: Changing Ideals of American Middle-Class Manhood, 1770–1920," *Journal of Social History* 16 (Summer 1983): 23–38; Zieger, *America's Great War*, 136; Bederman, *Manliness and Civilization*, 10–13; Hoganson, *Fighting for American Manhood*, 9.

35. Filene, *Him/Her/Self*, 70; Filene, "In Time of War," 321–324; Kimmel, *Manhood in America*, 132–135; Bederman, *Manliness and Civilization*, 12; Rotundo, "Body and Soul," 23–38.

36. Dr. William Howard Lee, *Boston Sunday Post*, Aug. 29, 1915. For more on tenderness being a feminine trait, see Luther H. Gulick, *The Dynamic of Manhood* (New York: Association Press, 1918), 14.

37. Editorial, "Kind Words for the Marine Corps," *Recruiters' Bulletin*, Dec. 1915, 16.

38. Peter Buitenhuis, *The Great War of Words: British, American, and Canadian Propaganda and Fiction, 1914–1933* (Vancouver: University of British Columbia, 1987), 54.

39. Zieger, *America's Great War*, 33; Kennedy, *Over Here*, 49; Finnegan, *Against the Specter of a Dragon*, 122.

40. Norman Angell, *The Great Illusion: A Study of the Relation of Military Power to National Advantage* (New York: Putnam & Sons, 1910), x.

41. Ernest R. May, *The World War and American Isolation, 1914–1917* (Cambridge, MA: Harvard University Press, 1959), 37.

42. "Let Us Lead a World at War to a World at Peace Former Secretary of State Urged against Military Preparedness by U.S.," *Columbus (GA) Ledger*, Nov. 25, 1915.

43. Robert E. Speer, *The Stuff of Manhood: Some Needed Notes in American Character* (New York: Fleming H. Revell, 1917), 11; Bederman, *Manliness and Civilization*, 102.

44. Arthur P. Schultz, "A Saturday Sermon," *Iola (KS) Register*, Nov. 14, 1914.

45. Sgt. W. W. Seibert, "I Didn't Raise My Boy to Be a Soldier," *Recruiters' Bulletin*, May 1916, 9.

46. Jack O'Donovan, "Remember the U.S. Marine," *Marines Magazine*, Jan. 1917, 44.

47. O'Donovan, "Remember the U.S. Marine," 44.

48. O'Donovan, 14.

49. William J. Candee, "The Marine," *Marines Magazine*, Apr. 1917, 20.

50. Edwin H. Simmons quoted by John W. Ripley in the Forward of Henry I. Shaw Jr. and Ralph W. Donnelly, *Blacks in the Marine Corps* (Washington, DC: History and Museums Division, Headquarters, U.S. Marine Corps, 2002), iii.

51. Shaw and Donnelly, *Blacks in the Marine Corps*, x.

52. "Negro Wears Blouse of U.S. Marine, Starts Chase," *Recruiters' Bulletin*, June 1915, 17.

53. "Negro Wears Blouse of U.S. Marine," 17.

54. Barney Nolan to G. Whata Lyer, "Identified," *Marines Magazine*, Apr. 1917, 59.

55. "Bunks," *Marines Magazine*, Nov. 1917, 15.

56. "Spun Yarns," *Marines Magazine*, Aug. 1917, 60.

57. Anna Stubblefield, "'Beyond the Pale': Tainted Whiteness, Cognitive Disability, and Eugenic Sterilization," *Hypatia* 22, no. 2 (2007): 163.

58. Junius Aryan, *The Aryans and the Mongrelized America: The Remedy* (Philadelphia: Eagle Printing House, 1912), iv.

59. Charles Morris, *The Aryan Race: Its Origin and its Achievements* (Chicago: S. C. Griggs, 1888), 6; Oscar Grow, *The Antagonism of Races* (St. Louis: Nixon-Jones Printing, 1912), 62.

60. Luther H. La Barre, "Preparedness," *Marines Magazine*, Sept. 1917, 61. One Marine officer who could be construed as an exception was Pedro del Valle, who entered the Marine Corps via the U.S. Naval Academy in 1915. Del Valle was born in Puerto Rico of Spanish descent. His complexion was as Caucasian as the rest of his peers. Pedro A Del Valle, interviewed by Benis M. Frank, Nov. 15, 17, 29, Dec. 1, 1966, OHC, USMCHD.

61. Ray I. Hoppman, "Ask Them," *Recruiters' Bulletin*, June 1917, 14.

62. Hoppman, 14.

63. Hoppman, 14.

64. Braley, "Leathernecks," 14.

65. Braley, 14.

66. A. A. Kuhlen, "Kipling," *Marines Magazine*, Apr. 1917, 63.

67. Kevin P. Murphy, *Political Manhood: Red Bloods, Mollycoddles, & the Politics of Progressive Era Reform* (New York: Columbia University Press, 2008), 2–3.

68. Rudyard Kipling, "Soldier and Sailor, Too" (1892), in *The Cambridge Edition of the Poems of Rudyard Kipling*, vol. 1, ed. Thomas Pinney (Cambridge: Cambridge University Press, 2013), 427–429.

69. Kuhlen, "Kipling," 63; Kuhlen asserted that "Kipling has gone far towards acquainting the uninitiated with the life of the serviceman, English or American. We belong to the same fraternity," 65.

70. Kipling, "Soldier and Sailor, Too," 427.

71. Thomas F. Carney, "Kipling Cult," *Marines Magazine*, Feb. 1917, 8.

72. Carney, 8.

73. Carney, 8.

74. Carney, 9. The "mark" he refers to was an image used by recruiters and seen on recruiting pamphlets before and during World War I.

75. Paul F. Howard, "Iona Island," *Marines Magazine*, Apr. 1917, 25.

76. Carney, "Kipling Cult," 8; Kipling, "Soldier an' Sailor Too," 427.

77. Kuhlen, "Kipling," 64.

78. Kuhlen, 63–64.

79. Pvt. William A. Honing, "Training the Marine Recruit," *Recruiters' Bulletin*, July 1917, 9.

80. C. Hundertmark, "The Three Sons," *Marines Magazine*, Jan. 1917, 14.

81. Hundertmark, 14.

82. Percy Webb, "Paris Island Camp: Around the World in Eighty Days," *Recruiters' Bulletin*, Oct. 1917, 1–3.

83. Levi Hemrick, *Once a Marine* (Staunton, VA: Clarion, 2013), 13.

84. Hemrick, 13.

85. Hemrick, 13.

86. Hemrick, 19.

87. See Michael Kimmel, *Manhood in America*, 98–201; and Gaddis, *Pulp Vietnam*, 38–40.

88. Unidentified author, in *Dear Folks at Home*, 3.

89. Letter from Rubin Jaffe, n.d., in *Dear Folks at Home*, 4.

90. E. John Solano describes Swedish Exercises as "a judicious combination of scientific corrective and preventative exercises and active recreative games and athletic sports." Solano, *Physical Training (Junior Course): Swedish Exercises, Games, Swimming, Diving, Life-Saving* (Indianapolis: Bobbs-Merrill, 1914), 3rd page of preface. See also Raymond B. Fosdick and Edward Frank Allen, *Keeping Our Fighters Fit: For War and After* (New York: Century, 1918).

91. Letter from Rubin Jaffe, n.d., in *Dear Folks at Home*, 5.

92. Letter from Rubin Jaffe, 8.

93. Letter from Rubin Jaffe, 7.

94. Letter from Rubin Jaffe, 9.

95. Conrad Hundertmark, "Sergeant Canavan's Own," *The United States Marines: Twenty-Five Poems about Live in the Marine Corps* (Paris Island, SC: T. N. Miller, 1915), 2, Library of Congress, https://www.loc.gov/resource/gdclccn.1600 5979/?sp=1&st=text (accessed Mar. 1, 2022).

96. *Annual Report of the Navy Department for the Fiscal Year 1915* (Washington, DC: Government Printing Office, 1916), 149–152; *Annual Report of the Navy Department for the Fiscal Year 1916* (Washington, DC: Government Printing Office, 1917), 147, 183–186.

97. *Annual Report of the Navy Department . . . 1915*, 149–152; *Annual Report of the Navy Department . . . 1916*, 183–186.

98. *Report of the Adjutant General of the Army to the Secretary of War for the Fiscal Year 1916* (Washington, DC: Government Printing Office, 1916), 30; *Annual Report of the Navy Department . . . 1916*, 164.

99. Millett, *Semper Fidelis*, 290–292.

100. C.L.S., "War!" *Marines Magazine*, May 1917, 10.

101. Charles Ketcham, "Shrapnel," *Marines Magazine*, Sept. 1917, 10.

102. Candee, "Sergeant McNab's Strategy," 9.

103. Candee, 8.

3. A "Sure-'Nough" Man

Epigraph. Pvt. C. Hundertmark, "The United States Marine," *Recruiters' Bulletin*, Apr. 1915, 7.

1. Frederick J. McIntosh, "U.S. Marines Most Diversified Soldier in the World," *Ogden (UT) Standard*, May 18, 1918, 28; *U.S. Marines—Soldiers of the Sea: Duties, Experiences, Opportunities, Pay*, 8th ed. (New York: U.S. Marine Corps Publicity Bureau, 1918), 31.

2. "Report of the Major General Commandant of the United States Marine Corps," in *Annual Report of the Navy Department for the Fiscal Year 1915* (Washington, DC: Government Printing Office, 1916), 755.

3. "Report of the Major General Commandant," 756.

4. "Train for Warfare," *New Orleans Times Picayune*, Oct. 17, 1915.

5. "Big Men of Country Learn Use of Rifle in Instruction Combat [at] Plattsburg N.Y.," *Wilmington (DE) Evening Journal*, Aug. 14, 1915 (also in *Mount Vernon (OH) Democratic Banner*, Aug. 17, 1915).

6. George Barnett, "Biddle Preparedness Camp," *Recruiters' Bulletin*, Dec. 1915, 7.

7. Millett, Maslowski, and Feis, *For the Common Defense*, 308.

8. David F. Trask, "The U.S. Navy in a World at War, 1914–1919," in *In Peace and War: Interpretations of American Naval History*, 30th anniv. ed., ed. Kenneth J. Hagan (Westport, CT: Praeger Security International, 2008), 172.

9. Sgt. L. W. Ahl, "An Idea for Producing Better Recruiting Results," *Recruiters' Bulletin*, Jan. 1915, 10.

10. Harrod, *Manning the New Navy*, 11; Wadle, *Selling Sea Power*, 136.

11. First Lt. R. H. Kelly, "Recruiting," *Infantry Journal*, July–Aug. 1914, 60.

12. Ahl, "Idea for Producing Better Recruiting Results," 10.

13. Capt. William Brackett, "The Public's Misconception of the Enlisted Man," *Recruiters' Bulletin*, Jan. 1915, 11.

14. Brackett, 11.

15. *U.S. Marines—Soldiers of the Sea: Duties, Experiences, Opportunities, Pay*, 7th ed. (New York: U.S. Marine Corps Publicity Bureau, 1917), 18.

16. Sgt. Birger F. Westergard, "A Recruiter's Varied Experiences," *Recruiters' Bulletin*, Dec. 1914, 16.

17. Cpl. Michael DeBoo, "Too Many Foreigners in Pittsburg," *Recruiters' Bulletin*, Dec. 1914, 4.

18. Capt. William E. Parker, "Marine Corps Recruiting," *Infantry Journal*, Sept.–Oct. 1914, 230–231.

19. *National Service Magazine*, Feb. 1917, 128.

20. Editorial, "Recruits and Recruiting," *Infantry Journal*, Jan. 1917, 429.

21. Sgt. Frank R. Busch, "The Recruiting Sergeant's Trouble," *Recruiters' Bulletin*, Jan. 1915, 16.

22. Theodore Roosevelt, "The College Man: An Address Delivered at the Harvard Union," in *Theodore Roosevelt as an Undergraduate*, by Donald Wilelm (Boston: John W. Luce, 1910), 84. See also Kevin P. Murphy, *Political Manhood: Red Bloods, Mollycoddles, & the Politics of Progressive Era Reform* (New York: Columbia University Press, 2008), 1–2.

23. Rev. Jasper S. Hogan, *Manhood as an Objective in College Training: An Address Delivered before Alumni of Rutgers College, Wednesday, June 19, 1912*, Rutgers College Publications 16 (Association of the Alumni of Rutgers College, 1913), 6–8.

24. Pvt. C. Hundertmark, "College vs. Marine Corps," *Recruiters' Bulletin*, Feb. 1915, 1. It is not clear if Hundertmark went to college himself.

25. "Report of the Colonel Commandant of the United States Marine Corps," in *Annual Report of the Secretary of the Navy for the Year 1888* (Washington, DC: Government Printing Office, 1888), 525; Shulimson, *Search for a Mission*, 68.

26. "Report of the Major General Commandant of the United States Marine Corps," in *Annual Report of the Navy Department for the Fiscal Year 1914* (Washington, DC: Government Printing Office, 1914), 462.

27. "Report of the Major General Commandant of the United States Marine Corps," in *Annual Report of the Navy Department for . . . 1915*, 772.

28. "Report of the Major General Commandant of the United States Marine Corps," in *Annual Report of the Navy Department for the Fiscal Year 1916* (Washington, DC: Government Printing Office, 1916), 772.

29. "Report of the Major General Commandant of the United States Marine Corps," in *Annual Report of the Navy Department for the Fiscal Year 1917* (Washington, DC: Government Printing Office, 1918), 842.

30. Clifford Bleyer, "'Stimulating Recruiting': Suggested by an Advertising Expert," *Recruiters' Bulletin*, Jan. 1917, 14.

31. Bleyer, 13.

32. Bleyer, 14.

33. Bleyer, 13–14.

34. C. S. McReynolds, "Odds and Ends from Lusty Files," *Recruiters' Bulletin*, Jan. 1917, 5.

35. Mollie Shelton to C. S. McReynolds, Dec. 18, 1916, in *Recruiters' Bulletin*, Jan. 1917, 15.

36. C. S. McReynolds to Mollie Shelton, Jan. 3, 1917, in *Recruiters' Bulletin*, Jan. 1917, 15.

37. Bleyer, "Stimulating Recruiting," 14.

38. Bleyer, 14–15.

39. Bleyer, 15 (emphasis added).

40. H. G. Youard, *Showing Ourselves Men: Addresses for Men's Services* (New York: E. S. Gorham, 1911), 8.

41. Ernest Howard Crosby, "The Military Idea of Manliness," *Independent*, Apr. 19, 1901, 873–875; Rotundo, *American Manhood*, 236–237; Hoganson, *Fighting for American Manhood*, 180; McGerr, *Fierce Discontent*, 296–298.

42. Nancy K. Bristow, *Making Men Moral: Social Engineering during the Great War* (New York: New York University Press, 1996), 1–3; Raymond B. Fosdick and Edward Frank Allen, *Keeping Our Fighters Fit for War and After* (New York: Century, 1918), 191; Kennedy, *Over Here*, 145–146; Zieger, *America's Great War*, 89.

43. Winfield S. Hall, *Developing into Manhood* (New York: Association Press, 1911), 29.

44. Fiske, *Boy Life and Self-Government*, 105.

45. Ross E. Rowell, "Ex-Marines Who Have Made Good," *Recruiters' Bulletin*, Feb. 1917, 16.

46. "Ex-Marine Who Has Made Good," *Recruiters' Bulletin*, Apr. 1917, 8.

47. "Marine Training Leads to Success," *Recruiters' Bulletin*, Mar. 1918, 15.

48. *U.S. Marines—Soldiers of the Sea*, 7th ed., 32.

49. "Entering Naval Academy by Enlistment in Marine Corps," *Recruiters' Bulletin*, Jan. 1917, 13.

50. "Report of the Major General Commandant of the United States Marine Corps," in *Annual Report of the Navy Department for . . . 1917*, 836.

51. Maj. H. Lay, Memorandum for "Regimental Commanders, 5th and 6th, Commanding Officer, M.G. Battalion," Jan. 25, 1918, Adolph Bradlee Miller Papers, Box 4, MCA.

52. "Report of the Major General Commandant of the United States Marine Corps," in *Annual Report of the Navy Department for the Fiscal Year 1918* (Washington, DC: Government Printing Office, 1919), 2632–2633. See also Daugherty, "To Fight Our Country's Battles," 101–102.

53. Venable, *How the Few Became the Proud*, 13.

54. George Kneller, "M.C. Employment Bureau," *Recruiters' Bulletin*, Dec. 1916, 5.

55. *U.S. Marines—Soldiers of the Sea*, 7th ed., 5.

56. *U.S. Marines—Soldiers of the Sea*, 13 (emphasis added).

57. *U.S. Marines—Soldiers of the Sea*, 16.

58. *U.S. Marines—Soldiers of the Sea*, 16; Gulick, *Dynamic of Manhood*, 90.

59. Hall, *Developing into Manhood*, 19. See also Murphy, *Political Manhood*, 12.

60. Hogan, *Manhood as an Objective in College Training*, 6.

61. Sgt. Charles D. Baylis, "Athletics an Argument," *Recruiters' Bulletin*, Nov. 1916, 14.

62. Kneller, "M.C. Employment Bureau," 6.

63. *U.S. Marines—Soldiers of the Sea*, 7th ed., 16.

64. *U.S. Marines—Soldiers of the Sea*, 16.

65. Harrod, *Manning the New Navy*, 6.

66. Harrod, 49. Determining which men had "higher character" often meant that those of a certain class were sought after within the U.S. Navy and Marine Corps. Officer candidates for the Naval Academy were often from the middle to upper classes. For more on this, see Peter Karsten, *The Naval Aristocracy: The*

Golden Age of Annapolis and the Emergence of Modern American Navalism (New York: Free Press, 1972), 8–13; and Christopher McKee, *A Gentlemanly and Honorable Profession: The Creation of the U.S. Naval Officer Corps, 1794–1815* (Annapolis, MD: Naval Institute Press, 1991), 28.

67. *Annual Report of the Navy Department for . . . 1916*, 52.

68. "The Making of a Man-o'-Wars-Man," *Detroit Times*, Nov. 19, 1917, 4.

69. *Annual Report of the Navy Department . . . 1916*, 52–53.

70. Andrew Birtle, *U.S. Army Counterinsurgency and Contingency Operations Doctrine, 1860–1941* (Washington, DC: U.S. Army Center of Military History, 1998), 86–92, 122.

71. "Recruiting Office," *Bennington (VT) Evening Banner*, Nov. 2, 1917 (emphasis added).

72. Colbourn, "Esprit de Marine Corps, "87–88.

73. *"Four Thousand Enlistments by Saturday Night": Plan of Action U.S. Marine Corps National Recruiting Week June 10 to 16, 1917* (Washington, DC: Headquarters U.S. Marine Corps, 1917), 7. Each one of these booklets went through several editions leading up to U.S. entry into the Great War. This package most likely contained the seventh edition of *U.S. Marines—Soldiers of the Sea* and the third edition of *U.S. Marines in Rhyme, Prose, and Cartoon*, both of which came out in 1917. The *Marines Magazine* gave an indication of how many pieces of recruiting literature Marines distributed: "During the fiscal year ended June 30, 1917, the Marine Corps Recruiting Service distributed 4,785,389 pieces of recruiting literature, comprising 1,547,690 handbooks, booklets, pamphlets, etc., 2,717,348 handbills of various kinds, 467,453 posters and 52,907 hangers." *Marines Magazine*, Aug. 1917, 16.

74. *"Four Thousand Enlistments by Saturday Night,"* 3.

75. James J. Montague, "The Marines: Who Are Now doing Police Duty at Santiago," in *U.S. Marines in Rhyme, Prose, and Cartoon*, 3rd ed. (New York: U.S. Marine Corps Publicity Bureau, 1917), 27.

76. Theodore Roosevelt's life and doctrine of the "Strenuous Life" directly associated these attributes with strong manhood leading up to American entry into World War I. Kimmel, *Manhood in America*, 133–135; Bederman, *Manliness and Civilization*, 193; Hoganson, *Fighting for American Manhood*, 139.

77. Sgt. Bert Van Moss, "Mobilize the Athletes," *Recruiters' Bulletin*, May 1917, 4.

78. *"Four Thousand Enlistments by Saturday Night,"* 9.

79. *"Four Thousand Enlistments by Saturday Night,"* 9.

80. *"Four Thousand Enlistments by Saturday Night,"* 12.

81. *"Four Thousand Enlistments by Saturday Night,"* 12.

82. Kimmel, *Manhood in America*, 115.

83. Kennedy, *Over Here*, 51.

84. *"Four Thousand Enlistments by Saturday Night,"* 12.

85. Zieger, *America's Great War*, 79.

86. George Creel, *How We Advertised America: The First Telling of the Amazing Story of the Committee on Public Information That Carried the Gospel of Americanism to Every Corner of the Globe* (1920; repr., New York: Arno, 1972), 4; McGerr, *Fierce Discontent*, 290–292; Kennedy, *Over Here*, 59–61.

87. *Newspaper Advertising Campaign for Recruits—U.S. Marine Corps* (Philadel-

phia: Donovan and Armstrong Advertising, ca. 1917), Box 7, Entry 18: General Correspondence, Office of the Commandant, 1913–1938, RG 127, NARA I. Copy also in Lee S. Rose Papers, PPC, MCA.

88. *"Four Thousand Enlistments by Saturday Night,"* 5.

89. Pendergast, *Creating the Modern Man*, 51. See also Jan Cohn, *Creating America: George Horace Lorimer and the* Saturday Evening Post (Pittsburg: University of Pittsburgh Press, 1989).

90. Pendergast, *Creating the Modern Man*, 55.

91. *"Four Thousand Enlistments by Saturday Night,"* 5.

92. Edward G. Lowry, "The Marines Have Landed and Have the Situation Well in Hand," *Saturday Evening Post*, June 9, 1917, 28.

93. Lowry, 30.

94. Mary Roberts Rinehart, "The Gray Mailed Fist," *Saturday Evening Post*, June 23, 1917, 45.

95. The bureau claimed that this image was "reproduced from the May 5 issue of the Saturday Evening Post" and that "it is the first of a special series of heavy-caliber advertisements, advancing on and including Marine Corps Week." "Publicity Foundation for Marine Corps Week Laid by Advertising in The Saturday Evening Post," in *"Four Thousand Enlistments by Saturday Night,"* 5. This advertisement never made it to that particular issue, however, as the magazine went with smaller ads instead.

96. U.S. Marine Corps Publicity Bureau, "U.S. Marines," *Saturday Evening Post*, May 19, 1917, 37.

97. "U.S. Marines," 37.

98. "U.S. Marines," *Saturday Evening Post*, June 30, 1917, 69.

99. "U.S. Marines," *Saturday Evening Post*, June 2, 1917, 37.

100. Charles A. Ketcham, "Marine Corps Week," *Marines Magazine*, July 1917, 5.

101. Albert S. McLemore, "Well Done Recruiters," *Recruiters' Bulletin*, Aug. 1917, 19.

102. George Barnett, "Marine Corps Recruited to Full Strength," *Recruiters' Bulletin*, Aug. 1917, 32.

103. For U.S. Army figures, see *Annual Report of the Secretary of War, 1917* (Washington, DC: Government Printing Office, 1917), 7. For U.S. Navy and Marine figures, see *Annual Report of the Navy Department for . . . 1917*, 164, 845.

104. "Crack Yale Athletes Join Marines," *Recruiters' Bulletin*, May 1917, 27.

105. "College Students Doing Their Bit," *Recruiters' Bulletin*, Aug. 1917, 21; "Harvard's Football Captain a Marine," *Recruiters' Bulletin*, July 1917, 28. George B. Ryan, the editor of the *Boston Herald*, claimed: "Marines appealed only to the best. Only the best could take the tests and pass. The publicity served to bring to the office the finest young men in Boston. Records of the men enlisted at the Marine Corps office show that young men prominent in college, civic, business and social life chose that branch of the service." *Recruiters' Bulletin*, Dec. 1917, 17.

106. "Former Congressman a Marine," *Recruiters' Bulletin*, May 1917, 32.

107. George T. Hughes, "Newspaper Men Write about Marines," *Recruiters' Bulletin*, Dec. 1917, 16.

108. F. M. Knowles, "Newspaper Men Write about Marines," *Recruiters' Bulletin*, Dec. 1917, 16.

109. Eli J. Fouts, "Newspaper Men Write about Marines," *Recruiters' Bulletin*, Dec. 1917, 34.

110. William H. Richardson, "Marines Work Together like Clockwork," *Recruiters' Bulletin*, Mar. 1918, 13.

111. Thomas Boyd to Aunt Mattie, July 24, 1917, Thomas Boyd Papers, Manuscripts/Audiovisual Collections, Ohio Historical Society, Columbus.

112. John W. Thomas Jr., "The Marine Brigade," *Proceedings of the United States Naval Institute*, Nov. 1928, 964, available via subscription at https://www.usni.org /magazines/proceedings/1928/november/marine-brigade (accessed Jan. 21, 2020).

113. *Annual Report of the Navy Department for the Fiscal Year 1918* (Washington, DC: Government Printing Office, 1920), 1609.

114. Newton D. Baker to Woodrow Wilson, May 8, 1917, in Wilson, *The Papers of Woodrow Wilson*, ed. Arthur S. Link, vol. 42 (Princeton, NJ: Princeton University Press, 1983), 250.

115. Joseph Arthur Simon, *Greatest of All Leathernecks: John Archer Lejeune and the Making of the Modern Marine Corps* (Baton Rouge: Louisiana State University Press, 2019), 105; John A. Lejeune, *The Reminiscences of a Marine* (Philadelphia: Dorrance, 1930), 238; Millett, *Semper Fidelis*, 289–290.

116. John A. Lejune, "The United States Marine Corps: Talk Given by Major General John A. Lejeune, Commandant, U.S. Marine Corps 14 December, 1923, to the class of 1924, U.S. Naval War College," 17, Box 19, RG 4, Publications, nos. 820A–869, Archival Records, U.S. Naval War College, Newport, RI.

117. Edwin N. McClellan, *The United States Marine Corps in the World War*, 3rd ed. (Quantico, VA: U.S. Marine Corps History Division, 2014), 13–14.

4. The Cleanest and Strongest of Our Young Manhood

Epigraph. Isabel Likens Gates, "The United States Marines," *Washington Post*, Aug. 12, 1919, 6.

1. Lewis A. Holmes to Mother, May 12, 1918, in *Dear Folks at Home*, 9; Pvt. Reuben E. Goldblatt, "The Game in Progression," *Marines Magazine*, Dec. 17, 1917, 64.

2. Albertus W. Catlin, *With the Help of God and a Few Marines*, with Walter A. Dyer (New York: Doubleday, Page, 1919), 268.

3. Millett, *Semper Fidelis*, 318. See also Daugherty, "To Fight Our Country's Battles," 55.

4. Axelrod, *Miracle at Belleau Wood*, 229.

5. Venable, *How the Few Became the Proud*, 176–179.

6. Adams, *Great Adventure*, 8; Filene, "In Time of War," 323; Mrozek, "Habit of Victory," 222; Kimmel, *Manhood in America*, 139; Bristow, *Making Men Moral*, 19–21; Kennedy, *Over Here*, 145–146; Zieger, *America's Great War*, 89; McGerr, *Fierce Discontent*, 296–298; Lears, *Rebirth of a Nation*, 341.

7. Kennedy, *Over Here*, 163–166.

8. Woodrow Wilson quoted in Coffman, *War to End All Wars*, 76.

9. U.S. Congress, *Congressional Record Containing the Proceedings and Debates of the First Session of the Sixty-Fifth Congress* (Washington, DC: Government Printing Office, 1917), 137.

10. Edwin Denby quoted in Catlin, *With the Help of God and a Few Marines*, 292.

11. Youard, *Showing Ourselves Men*, 9. For more on cleanliness and manhood, see Summerbell, *Manhood in Its American Type*, 99; John S. P. Tatlock, *Why America Fights Germany* (Washington, DC: Committee on Public Information, 1918), 11.

12. U.S. War Department, *Outline of Plan for Military Public Schools of the United States* (Washington, DC: Army War College, 1915), 8.

13. C.L.S., "The Red Badge of Courage," *Marines Magazine*, July 1917, 14.

14. C.L.S., 14.

15. Bishop Junior, "Jim Bitter—Coward," *Marines Magazine*, June 1918, 4–6.

16. Youard, *Showing Ourselves Men*, 9.

17. *Manitoba Free Press*, Aug. 3, 1918, 19.

18. C.L.S., "Red Badge of Courage," 14.

19. Josephus Daniels, "The Test of an American," in *The Navy and the Nation: The War-Time Addresses by Josephus Daniels Secretary of the Navy* (New York: George H. Doran, 1919), 116.

20. Daniels, 117.

21. Capozzola, *Uncle Sam Wants You*, 21–33; David Mayers, *Dissenting Voices in America's Rise to Power* (New York: Cambridge University Press, 2007), 237–242; Ernest R. May, *The World War and American Isolation, 1914–1917* (Cambridge, MA: Harvard University Press, 1959), 37.

22. Woodrow Wilson, "Our Whole Nation an Army," in *Liberty, Peace, and Justice* (Chicago: Houghton Mifflin, 1918), 84.

23. Gerald E. Shenk, *"Work or Fight!": Race, Gender, and the Draft in World War One* (New York: Palgrave Macmillan, 2005), 5.

24. Wilson, "Our Whole Nation an Army," 84.

25. Adams, *Great Adventure*, 51.

26. Edwin Denby, "One Day in Detroit Proved the World Will Be Safe for Democracy," *Recruiters' Bulletin*, Oct. 2017, 6.

27. Denby, 6.

28. Lears, *Rebirth of a Nation*, 340; Kennedy, *Over Here*, 165.

29. Lears, *Rebirth of a Nation*, 340; Zeiger, *America's Great War*, 61–63.

30. "Woman Flayed as Traitor," *Washington Herald*, July 24, 1917, 1.

31. Mayers, *Dissenting Voices*, 239.

32. Andrew G. Huebner, *Love and Death in the Great War* (New York: Oxford University Press, 2018), 135–136.

33. Woodrow Wilson, "Flag Day Address," in *Liberty, Peace, and Justice*, 86. This speech was delivered in Washington, D.C., on June 14, 1917.

34. U.S. Congress, *Congressional Record . . . of the First Session of the Sixty-Fifth Congress*, 383–384 (emphasis added).

35. Adams, *Great Adventure*, 25.

36. Fiske, *Boy Life and Self-Government*, 17.

37. Summerbell, *Manhood in Its American Type*, 112–113.

38. Wilson, "Flag Day Address," 87.

39. Tatlock, *Why America Fights*, 5.

40. Tatlock, 5.

41. Ralph Tyler Flewelling, *Philosophy and the War* (New York: Abingdon, 1918), 35.

42. Josephus Daniels, "As They Go Forth to Battle," in *Navy and the Nation*, 171.

43. McClellan, *Marine Corps in the World War*, 33–76. This information also can be found in most histories concerning the Marines in World War I.

44. Lengel, *Thunder and Flames*, 63.

45. Elton E. Mackin, *Suddenly We Didn't Want to Die: Memoirs of a World War I Marine*, ed. George B. Clark (Novato, CA: Presidio, 1996), 27.

46. Mackin, 29.

47. Catlin, *With the Help of God and a Few Marines*, 118.

48. Thomas Boyd, *Points of Honor: Short Stories of the Great War by a U.S. Combat Marine*, ed. Steven Trout (Tuscaloosa: University of Alabama Press, 2018), 164.

49. Clifton B. Cates to Mother, June 14, 1918, Clifton B. Cates Papers, PPC, MCA.

50. Grotelueschen, *AEF Way of War*, 209–226; Lengel, *Thunder and Flames*, 203; Clark, *Devil Dogs*, 101.

51. Diary of the 4th Marine Brigade, June 1918, Adolph Bradlee Miller Papers, PPC, MCA.

52. Diary of Pvt. William A. Francis, William A. Francis File, 5th Marine Regiment, WWI QF, USAHEC.

53. Fourth Brigade to C.G., 2nd Division, "resume for 11 June," in Diary of the 4th Marine Brigade, June 1918, Miller Papers, MCA.

54. See the discussion in Heather P. Marshall, "'It Means Something These Days to be a Marine': Image, Identity, and Mission in the Marine Corps, 1861–1918" (PhD diss., Duke University, 2010), 342–343.

55. Quoted in Millett, *Semper Fidelis*, 304.

56. Quoted in Millett, 304.

57. Boyd, *Points of Honor*, 164–165. John Quick was awarded a Distinguished Service Cross for his actions at Bouresches. Oliver Lyman Spaulding and John Womack Wright, *The Second Division American Expeditionary Force in France, 1917–1919* (New York: Hillman, 1937), 372.

58. Arthur R. M. Ganoe, "The Battle of Soissons as I Saw It," *Marines' Bulletin*, Dec. 1918, 18.

59. Ganoe, 47.

60. Simmons, *United States Marines*, 102; McClellan, *Marine Corps in the World War*, 115; Millett, *Semper Fidelis*, 305–306.

61. Lengel, *Thunder and Flames*, 283.

62. John E. Ausland, "The Last Kilometer," John E. Ausland File, 5th Marine Regiment, WWI QF, USAHEC.

63. Diary of Pvt. William A. Francis, Francis File, 5th Marine Regiment, WWI QF, USAHEC.

64. Spaulding and Wright, *Second Division American Expeditionary Force*, 295–296.

65. McClellan, *Marine Corps in the World War*, 115.

66. The literature on this subject is broad. See Russell F. Weigley, *The American Way of War: A History of United States Military Strategy and Policy* (New York: Macmillan, 1973), 192–200; Grotelueschen, *AEF Way of War*, 10–58; Michael Howard, "Men against Fire: The Doctrine of the Offensive in 1914," in *Makers of Modern Strategy: From Machiavelli to the Nuclear Age*, ed. Peter Paret (Princeton, NJ: Princeton University Press, 1986), 510–511; and Peyton C. March, "Lessons of World

War I," in *American Military Thought*, ed. Walter Millis (New York: Bobbs-Merrill, 1966), 354.

67. John H. Russell, "Plea for a Mission and Doctrine," *Marine Corps Gazette*, June 1916, 122.

68. McClellan, *Marine Corps in the World War*, 115. See also "Marine Casualties at Belleau Wood," *Wall Street Journal*, Dec. 20, 1918, 9.

69. Paul Fussell, *The Great War and Modern Memory* (New York: Oxford University Press, 1975), 7–18. Also see Mary Loeffelholz, ed., "World War I and Its Aftermath," in *The Norton Anthology of American Literature, 1914–1945*, vol. D, 7th ed. (New York: Norton, 2007), 1371–1372; and Jon Stallworthy and Jahan Ramazani, eds., "Voices from World War I," in *The Norton Anthology of English Literature: The Twentieth Century and After*, vol. F, 8th ed. (New York: Norton, 2006), 1954–1955.

70. Walter Scott Hiller to family, June 16, 1918, in *Dear Folks at Home*, 118.

71. Merwin Silverthorne to parents, July 1, 1918, in *Dear Folks at Home*, 118.

72. Silverthorne to parents, July 1, 1918, 119.

73. John F. Pinson to family, n.d., in *Dear Folks at Home*, 160.

74. Pinson to family n.d., 160.

75. E. A. Wahl to Ann, June 27, 1918, in *Dear Folks at Home*, 143–144.

76. George W. Hamilton to family, June 25, 1918, in *Dear Folks at Home*, 127.

77. Henry N. Manney to Mother, June 10, 1918, in *Dear Folks at Home*, 135–136.

78. Silverthorne to parents, July 1, 1918, 117–118.

79. *Dear Folks at Home*, 169.

80. Silverthorne to parents, July 1, 1918, 118.

81. Williard P. Nelligan to mother, June 27, 1918, in *Dear Folks at Home*, 211.

82. Floyd Gibbons, *"And They Thought We Wouldn't Fight"* (New York: George H. Doran, 1918), 298. Another version of Gibbons's report can be found in Willis J. Abbot, *Soldiers of the Sea: The Story of the United States Marine Corps* (New York: Dodd, Mead, 1918), 298–300.

83. *Activities of the Committee on Public Information*, Jan. 27, 1918, Box 24, NM-84, General Correspondence ("Subject") File, Entry 376: War College Division and War Plans Division, Subordinate Offices, Morale Branch, 1918–1921, RG 165, NARA II.

84. Millett, *Semper Fidelis*, 303; Lengel, *Thunder and Flames*, 111–112; Simmons, *United States Marines*, 99; Moskin, *Marine Corps Story*, 99–100.

85. "U.S. Marines Smash Huns: Gain Glory in Brisk Fight on the Marne," *Chicago Daily Tribune*, June 6, 1918, 1; "Associated Press Dispatches Citing Marines in France," *Marine Corps Gazette*, June 1918, 158–159.

86. Gibbons, *"And They Thought We Wouldn't Fight,"* 312–322.

87. "Valor of Marines Stirs All America," *New York Times*, June 9, 1918, 2.

88. Don Martin, "Heroic Marines Whip Back Huns and Hold Gains," *New Orleans Times Picayune*, June 9, 1918.

89. Don Martin, "U.S. Marines Scored One of Biggest Allied Success in Marne Fighting," *Washington Post*, June 8, 1918. "When the Marines at Château Thierry surprised their foes by the determination of their advance they evidenced the kind of enthusiasm that is characteristic of all Americans and more intensely characteristic of the Marine than any other branch of the American military establishment."

"Marines Carve Lasting Niche in Fame's Hall: Recruits Flock to Ranks of Corps Whose Slogan Is 'First to Fight,'" *New Orleans Times Picayune*, June 24, 1918, 7.

90. "Marines Break Through!," *New York Tribune Review*, June 16, 1918, 1. It was an "onrushing horde of Germans at Chateau-Thierry. The Germans were stopped. Paris was saved. The turning-point in the war was reached. The Marines made themselves immortal." Lt. Newton Jenkins (U.S. Army), "Fighting in France with the Marines," *Scribner's Magazine Illustrated*, Jan. 1919, 99.

91. Millett, *Semper Fidelis*, 317; Moskin, *Marine Corps Story*, 144.

92. For how gender can be understood as a performance, see Judith Butler, *Gender Trouble: Feminism and the Subversion of Identity* (New York: Routledge, Chapman, & Hall, 1990).

93. Reginal Wright Kauffman, "The American Marines," *Living Age*, July 1918, 45.

94. Kemper F. Cowing, "Floyd Gibbons, Devil Dog by Nature," *Marines Magazine*, Oct. 1918, 15.

95. Gibbons, *"And They Thought We Wouldn't Fight,"* 304.

96. Simmons, *United States Marines*, 99.

97. "Three Times, but Not Out Yet," *Marines Magazine*, Oct. 1918, 11–12; "Heroes of Belleau Wood Come Back Smiling," *Recruiters' Bulletin*, Sept. 1918, 49; Abbot, *Soldiers of the Sea*, 309–310.

98. "Bois Brigade de Marines, Name Given Belleau Wood, in Honor of U.S. Forces," *Washington Post*, Aug. 11, 1918. See also "Belleau Wood Given New Name in Honor of U.S. Marine Brigade," *Washington Post*, July 12, 1918. McClellan, *Marine Corps in the World War*, 62–63; and Millett, *Semper Fidelis*, 303–304.

99. "U.S. Marines, Fighting like Tigers, Hurl Foe Back nearly a Mile," *Washington Post*, June 7, 1918.

100. "French Artist Depicts U.S. Marines' Victory," *Louisville (KY) Courier-Journal*, Oct. 10, 1918, 2.

101. Editorial, "The Labor Problem," *New Republic*, Oct. 20, 1917, 316.

102. Susan R. Grayzel, *Women and the First World War* (New York: Pearson, 2002), 33–34; Lettie Gavin, *American Women in World War I: They Also Served* (Niwot: University Press of Colorado, 1997), x; Zieger, *America's Great War*, 144; Kennedy, *Over Here*, 285.

103. Gavin, *American Women in World War I*, 2; Millett, *Semper Fidelis*, 308.

104. Memo, Barnett to Daniels, "Enrollment of Women in the Marine Corps Reserve for Clerical Duty," Aug. 2, 1918, Box 126, Entry 18: General Correspondence, Office of the Commandant, 1913–1938, RG 127, NARA I.

105. Linda L. Hewitt, *Women Marines in World War I* (Washington, DC: History and Museums Division, U.S. Marine Corps, 1974), 2.

106. *Dear Folks at Home*, 15.

107. Gavin, *American Women in World War I*, 26.

108. John A. Lejeune to Isabel Smith, Oct. 14, 1920, Box 126, Entry 18, RG 127, NARA I.

109. Venable, *How the Few Became the Proud*, 175.

110. Gavin, *American Women in World War I*, ix; Grayzel, *Women in the First World War*, 77–78; Huebner, "Gee! I Wish I Were a Man," 68–70.

111. "Uniform Women Marines Will Wear," *Recruiters' Bulletin*, Sept. 1918, 23.

112. Kimberly Jensen, *Mobilizing Minerva: American Women in the First World War* (Chicago: University of Illinois Press, 2008), ix; Venable, *How the Few Became the Proud*, 195.

113. "Those Girl Marines!," *Recruiters' Bulletin*, Dec. 1918, 61.

114. Martha L. Wilchinski, "Breaking the News to Bill," *Recruiters' Bulletin*, Sept. 1918, 26.

115. Martha L. Wilchinski, "It's 'Us Corporals' Now, Martha Tells Bill," *Marines' Bulletin*, Nov. 1918, 31.

116. Martha L. Wilchinski, "War Is Terrible but It Hasn't Anything on Peace So Corporal Martha Discovers," *Marines' Bulletin*, Dec. 1918, 52.

117. Martha L. Wilchinski, "Hurdling Hatches," *Marines' Bulletin*, Jan. 1919, 7.

118. Wilchinski, 7.

119. Martha L. Wilchinski, in *Dear Folks at Home*, 24.

120. Pearl Oagley, "Memory Bits of a Girl Marine of World War I," n.d., Pearl Oagley Papers, PPC, MCA.

121. "Devil Dog Division Captures Fifth Ave," *New York Times*, Aug. 9, 1919, 9.

122. "March of Marines Thrills the Capital," *New York Times*, Aug. 13, 1919; "Governor Hugs Hero Marines at Glory Fete," *Chicago Daily Tribune*, Aug. 24, 1919, 3; "More 'Leathernecks,' World War Heroes, Back in America," *Chicago Daily Tribune*, Aug. 7, 1919.

123. Edwin L. James, "Stories of the War That Didn't Happen: Even the Marines Themselves Admit They Have Received an Oversupply of Credit," *New York Times*, May 25, 1919.

124. Isabel Likens Gates, "The United States Marines," *Washington Post*, Aug. 12, 1919, 6.

125. Bessie B. Croffut, "U.S. Marines," *Washington Post*, Aug. 19, 1919, 8.

126. "And Now the Tributes!," *Marines' Bulletin*, Dec. 1918, 27.

127. William Almon Wolff, "Leading Advertising Experts Commend Success of Marines' Publicity Campaign," *Marines Bulletin*, Dec. 1918, 6. See also Colbourn, "Esprit de Marine Corps," 111–112.

128. Wolff, "Leading Advertising Experts," 5.

129. W. W. Yerkes, "Leading Advertising Experts," *Marines Bulletin*, Dec. 1918, 68.

130. William C. Freeman quoted by Wolff, "Leading Advertising Experts," 6.

131. Horace Lorimer, "The Blank Division," *Marines' Bulletin*, Dec. 1918, 48.

132. Melville E. Stone, interviewed by QM Sgt. Raymond Soat, *Marines' Bulletin*, Dec. 1918, 53.

133. Werner S. Allixon, "Leading Advertising Experts," *Marines Bulletin*, Dec. 1918, 70.

134. John A. Sleicher, "They Could Not Pass the Marines," *Marines' Bulletin*, Dec. 1918, 49.

135. Frederick D. Gardner, "Governors Endorse the Marine Corps," *Recruiters' Bulletin*, Dec. 1919, 6.

136. Ganoe, "Battle of Soissons," 47.

137. Fosdick and Allen, *Keeping Our Fighters Fit for War and After*, 17; Bristow, *Making Men Moral*, 11.

138. Hugh M. Dorsey, "Governors Endorse the Marine Corps," *Recruiters' Bulletin*, Dec. 1919, 6.

139. Oliver H. Shoup, "Governors Endorse the Marine Corps," *Recruiters' Bulletin*, Dec. 1919, 29.

140. Simon Bamberger, "Governors Endorse the Marine Corps," *Recruiters' Bulletin*, Dec. 1919, 6.

141. Emerson C. Harrington, "Governors Endorse the Marine Corps," *Recruiters' Bulletin*, Dec. 1919, 30.

142. *Honest Pride, Recruiters' Bulletin*, Dec. 1919, 21.

143. *Annual Report of the Navy Department for the Fiscal Year 1918* (Washington, DC: Government Printing Office, 1919), 405.

144. *Annual Report of the Navy Department*, 420.

145. *Annual Report of the Navy Department*, 422.

146. *Annual Report of the Navy Department*, 405.

147. "Marine Officer on Trial to Prove His War Air Exploits," *New York Tribune*, Mar. 25, 1919, 11.

148. "Chamberlain and Courts-Martial," *Le Meschacébé* (Lucy, LA), Sept. 27, 1919, 1; "Would Free All Yank Prisoners," *Washington Times*, July 21, 1919, 1; "May Cancel Court-Martial," *Seattle Star*, July 21, 1919, 1.

149. "Race Rioting Is Resumed in Washington City, Many Civilians and Soldiers Attack Negro Quarters," *Albuquerque Morning Journal*, July 22, 1919, 1; "Washington Race Riots Worse Monday Night," *Hickory (NC) Daily Record*, July 22, 1919, 1.

150. Thomas Boyd, *Through the Wheat: A Novel of the World War I Marines* (Lincoln: University of Nebraska Press, 2000), 179; William March, *Company K* (Tuscaloosa: University of Alabama Press, 1918), 123–130.

151. Graves Blanchard Erskin, interviewed by Benis M. Frank, History and Museums Division, Headquarters, U.S. Marine Corps, Washington, DC, Dec. 4, 1979, Oral History Collection, MCA, 37 (transcript).

152. J. G. Harbord, Memorandum, June 8, 1918, Headquarters, 4th Brigade, Confidential Diary of 4th Brigade Marines, May 30–June 30, 1918, Miller Papers, MCA.

153. Catlin, *With the Help of God*, 306.

154. Catlin, 306.

155. F. M. Johnson Jr., "Those Gone West," *Our Navy*, Aug. 1924, 5.

156. McClellan, *United States Marine Corps in the World War*, 10.

157. *Annual Report of the Navy Department for . . . 1918*, 1595; McClellan, *United States Marine Corps in the World War*, 9.

5. Tropicalitis

Epigraphs. James Bardin, "Hi, There, You Leatherneck!," *Leatherneck*, May 6, 1922, 5; John H. Craige, *Black Bagdad: The Arabian Nights Adventures of a Marine Captain in Haiti* (London: Stanley Paul, 1933), 99.

1. Smithson Taylor to Maj. Gen. George Barnett, June 11, 1917, Thad Taylor Personnel Files, NPRC, St. Louis.

2. "Memoir on the Political, Economic, and Financial Conditions Existing in the Republic of Haiti Under the American Occupation by the Delegates to the Unites States of the Union Pariotique d'Haiti," in U.S. Senate, *Inquiry into the Occupation and Administration of Haiti and Santo Domingo: Hearings before a Select Committee of Haiti and Santo Domingo*, 2 vols., 67th Cong., 1st and 2nd sess., 1922, 1:5–6 (hereafter referred to as Senate, *Hearings*). See also Millett, *Simper Fidelis*, 184–185; Renda, *Taking Haiti*, 29–30; Coupeau, *History of Haiti*, 68; Lester Langley, *The Banana Wars: United States Intervention in the Caribbean, 1898–1934* (Wilmington, DE: Scholarly Resources, 2002), 127–128.

3. Langley, *Banana Wars*, 122.

4. The declaration of martial law gave Marines a great deal of power while in country: "The commanding officer of the United States Expeditionary force, Colonel Littleton W. T. Waller, United States Marine Corps, is empowered to issue the necessary regulations and appoint the necessary officers to make this martial law effective." RAdm. William B. Caperton, "Proclamation to the People of Port Au Prince, Haiti," Sept. 3, 1915, John H. Russell Papers, PPC, USMCHD. The Marines vowed not to hinder the freedom of the press, yet by proclaiming "the publishing of false or incendiary propaganda of Haiti, or publishing any false, indecent or obscure propaganda, letters signed or unsigned, or matter which tends to disturb the public peace will be dealt with by the military courts," they essentially stated that they would, in fact, hinder the press at their discretion. Capt. Alexander S. Williams, "Office of the Provost Martial," Port au Prince, Haiti, Sept. 3, 1915, ibid. See also Millett, *Semper Fidelis*, 186.

5. "Synopsis-Santo Domingo," May 15, 1916, Dominican Republic Geographic Files, History Division, USMCHD; Langley, *Banana Wars*, 133–134; McPherson, *Invaded*, 34–36; Bickel, *Mars Learning*, 107–108; Calder, *Impact of Intervention*, 8–9; Simmons, *United States Marines*, 92–93; Millett, *Semper Fidelis*, 191–192; Moskin, *Marine Corps Story*, 191–193.

6. A Marine private commanding a platoon of gendarmes, for example, would have a special and temporary rank of lieutenant in the Gendarmerie but would still retain his normal rank within the Marine Corps itself. A Marine sergeant would have the rank of captain in the Gendarmerie and so forth. Marines in the Dominican Republic used the same system.

7. "America's Handy Man," *U.S. Marines in Rhyme, Prose, and Cartoon*, 3rd ed. (New York: U.S. Marine Corps Publicity Bureau, 1917), 29.

8. "The Busy Marine," *U.S. Marines in Rhyme, Prose, and Cartoon*, 29.

9. Bederman, *Manliness and Civilization*, 20.

10. Renda, *Taking Haiti*, 18; McPherson, *Invaded*, 128–129.

11. Paul Woyshner, *The Missionary*, Marines Magazine, Apr. 1917, 2. Woyshner won an award "for the most original acceptable cartoon" in January 1917 for this drawing. Paul Woyshner Papers, PPC, USMCHD.

12. [Artist's name illegible], *A Bad Child*, Marines Magazine, Jan. 1917, 37.

13. Kimmel, *Manhood in America*, 88.

14. Hoganson, *Fighting for American Manhood*, 136.

15. The word "spick" is a racial pejorative in contemporary parlance. Marines claimed to have invented the word: "The Marines refer to the natives of Latin-American countries as 'hombres' or 'spicks.' The former is a Spanish word for

man, picked up by Marines in the Philippines. The latter is a corruption of the word 'spiggoty' and owes its incorporation into the leatherneck lingo to the natives who have long tried to tell the Marines that they 'no spiggoty English.'" Unknown author, ca. 1921, Entry 37: General Correspondence, Recruitment 1921–1939, RG 127, NARA I.

16. Scott Nearing, *The Super Race: An American Problem* (New York: B. W. Huebsch, 1912), 77; Thomas Pearce Bailey, *Race Orthodoxy in the South and Other Aspects of the Negro Question* (New York: Neale, 1914), 17.

17. Henry F. Suksdorf, *Our Race Problems* (New York: Shakespeare, 1911), 98, 315; J. L. Kesler, "The Negro in Relation to Our Public Agencies and Institutions," in *Selected Articles on the Negro Problem*, ed. Julia E. Johnsen (New York: H. W. Wilson, 1921), 62–66; Fiske, *Boy Life and Self-Government*, 45; G. Stanley Hall, *Adolescence: Its Psychology and Its Relations to Physiology, Anthropology, Sociology, Sex, Crime, Religion, and Education*, vol. 2 (New York: D. Appleton, 1905), 649.

18. Roy Thomas Smith, *The Sacred Honor and Duty Black American Citizens Owe the Ethiopian Race* (Kansas City, KS: R. T. Smith, 1918), 17.

19. Francis J. Grimke, "The Race Problem—Two Suggestions as to Its Solution," Aug. 1919, Emory University digitized document via Hathi Trust, https://catalog.hathitrust.org/Record/100657881 (accessed Feb.7, 2017).

20. Chad L. Williams, *Torchbearers of Democracy: African American Soldiers in the World War I Era* (Chapel Hill: University of North Carolina Press, 2010), 7, 126–127; Adriane Lentz-Smith, *Freedom Struggles: African Americans and World War I* (Cambridge, MA: Harvard University Press, 2009), 20; Capozzola, *Uncle Sam Wants You*, 34–35.

21. See Walter W. Delsarte, *The Negro, Democracy, and the War* (Detroit: Wolverine Printing, 1919), 134; Wiebe, *Search for Order*, 156–157; McGerr, *Fierce Discontent*, 184–186; and Lulu Daniel Hardy, "Some Aspects of the Negro Question," *Biloxi (MS) Daily Herald*, June 25, 1919, 4. See also "The Same Everywhere," *Hattiesburg (MS) Daily American*, Oct. 1, 1919, 4; Frederick J. Haskin, "The Race Conflict," *Fitchburg (MA) Daily Sentinel*, Oct. 7, 1919, 4; "State Press Comment," *Hattiesburg (MS) Daily American*, Oct. 22, 1919, 4; A. M. Carpenter, "Negroes Demand Citizenship," *Topeka (KS) Plaindealer*, Apr. 18, 1919, 1; and Savoyard, "The Race Question," *Quanah Tribune-Chief* (Bryan, TX), Nov. 25, 1921, 3.

22. Unnamed brigade commander's report quoted in Brig. Gen. George Barnett to Secretary of Navy, "Report on Affair in the Republic of Haiti, June 1915 to June 30, 1920," Haitian Geographic Files, RB, USMCHD.

23. Millett, *Semper Fidelis*, 196.

24. L. Nogart to Joseph Pendleton, Apr. 16, 1918, Joseph Pendleton Papers, PPC, USMCHD.

25. "Marines with the Poilus," *Marines Magazine*, Oct. 1917, 48.

26. Col. L. W. T. Waller to Col. S. D. Butler, July 13, 1916, Smedley Butler Papers, PPC, USMCHD; Millett, *Semper Fidelis*, 187.

27. A. B. Miller, Personal Log, 15th Company Dope Book, USMC, Aug. 5–6, 1915, Adolf Bradlee Miller Papers, PPC, USMCHD.

28. Miller, Personal Log, Jan. 9, 1916; H. Hesketh Prichard, *Where Black Rules White: A Journey across and about Hayti* (New York: Thomas Nelson & Sons, 1910), 361.

29. Miller, Personal Log, Feb. 23, 1916.

30. Alexander A. Vandegrift, *Once a Marine: The Memoirs of General A. A. Vandegrift United States Marine Corps*, as told to Robert B. Asprey (New York: W. W. Norton, 1964), 53.

31. Vandegrift, *Once a Marine*, 53.

32. Schmidt, *Maverick Marine*, 1.

33. Smedley D. Butler to parents, Oct. 6, 1917, Butler Papers, PPC, USMCHD.

34. Butler to parents, Oct. 6, 1917.

35. Butler to parents, Oct. 6, 1917.

36. Butler to parents, Oct. 6, 1917.

37. H. C. Haines to John H. Russell, June 27, 1917, Russell Papers, PPC, USMCHD. Writing ten years after the fact, one journalist described Russell's feelings about missing the war in France: "Not to have served with his men in the biggest show of his lifetime was a crushing blow to the general. He felt that the career he valued most had been blighted. When he and his extraordinarily able and attractive wife were newly married, they had resolved to work hard and faithfully, and hope as a reward to head the corps. To them the chance seemed gone forever." Arthur Krock, "Russell of the Marines Justifies Cleveland's Faith," *New York Times*, Feb. 24, 1934.

38. George Barnett to Joseph Pendleton, Aug. 23, 1918, Pendleton Papers, PPC, USMCHD.

39. H. W. Houck, "Tropicalitis," *Marines Magazine*, Sept. 1917, 24 (emphasis added).

40. Renda, *Taking Haiti*, 132.

41. Craige, *Black Bagdad*, 193. See also Renda, *Taking Haiti*, 132.

42. John H. Russell, "Statement of Colonel John H. Russell, U.S. Marine Corps, Commanding 1st Brigade, U.S. Marines, Port-au-Prince, Haiti," n.d., Russell Papers, PPC, USMCHD.

43. Miller, Personal Log, May 31, 1916.

44. W. J. Simpson, *The Maintenance of Health in the Tropics* (London: John Bale, Sons, & Danielsson, 1916), 5.

45. Russell, "Statement."

46. Frederic May Wise, *A Marine Tells It to You* (New York: J. H. Sears, 1929), 334.

47. Craige, *Black Bagdad*, 89.

48. Craige, 91–92.

49. Warwick Anderson, "The Trespass Speaks: White Masculinity and Colonial Breakdown," *American Historical Review* 102, no. 5 (1997): 1343–1370; Catherine Cocks, "The Pleasures of Degeneration: Climate, Race, and the Origins of the Global Tourist South in the Americas," *Discourse* 29, nos. 2–3 (2007): 215–235.

50. Ellsworth Huntington, "The Adaptability of the White Man to Tropical America," *Journal of Race Development* 5, no. 2 (Oct. 1914): 193.

51. Huntington, 195.

52. Smedley Butler to F. M. Wise, Nov. 13, 1919, Butler Papers, PPC, USMCHD.

53. See Capt. John H. Craig, "Development of the Republic of Haiti," 1919, H-134 Haiti, Box 14, Entry 38: General Correspondence, Operations and Training Division, Intelligence Section, 1915–1934, RG 127, NARA I.

54. Memorandum, "General Courts-Martial, Haiti, July 28, 1915, to July, 1920, Inclusive," Haitian Geographic Files, RB, USMCHD.

55. "General Courts-Martial, Haiti."

56. Eli K. Cole, Feb. 27, 1917, in "Reports Relating to U.S. Navy and Marine Corps Operations in Haiti and Santo Domingo," 1915–1921, Box 2, Entry 38, RG 127, NARA I. For more information on how the Germans had established themselves in the social and economic milieus of Haiti and the Dominican Republic, see Calder, *Impact of Intervention*, 22; Schmidt, *Occupation of Haiti*, 34–35, 68–69, 95; and Renda, *Taking Haiti*, 51.

57. Eli K. Cole, Apr. 19, 1917, in "Reports Relating to U.S. Navy and Marine Corps Operations in Haiti and Santo Domingo."

58. John Russell to George Barnett, Oct. 17, 1919, Russell Papers, PPC, USMCHD.

59. J. L. Perkins to John H. Russell, "Account of Patrol Made in Company with Mr. Herbert J. Seligman," July 26, 1920, Russell Papers, PPC, USMCHD.

60. Col. George C. Thorpe to Joseph Pendleton, Aug. 18, 1918, Pendleton Papers, PPC, USMCHD.

61. L. Nogart to Joseph Pendleton, Apr. 16, 1918, Pendleton Papers, PPC, USMCHD; Thorpe to Pendleton, Aug. 18, 1918.

62. Brig. Gen. Joseph Pendleton to the Secretary of the Navy, July 24, 1919, Pendleton Papers, PPC, USMCHD. Historian Hans Schmidt argues that in Haiti, "all the investigations of rumors, surveillance of German firms, censoring of letters, and other counterespionage work failed to turn up much concrete evidence of German intrigue." Schmidt, *Occupation of Haiti*, 92.

63. Bruce Calder, "Caudillos and Gavilleros versus the United States Marines: Guerilla Insurgency during the Dominican Intervention, 1916–1924," *Hispanic American Historical Review* 58, no. 4 (Nov. 1978): 656. See also Millett, *Semper Fidelis*, 196.

64. "Germans Plot Negro Uprising in the South," *New York Tribune*, Apr. 4, 1917, 1. See also Janet G. Hudson, "The Great War and Expanded Equality: Black Carolinians Test Boundaries," in *The American South and the Great War, 1914–1924*, ed. Matthew L. Downs and M. Ryan Floyd (Baton Rouge: Louisiana State University Press, 2018), 142–144.

65. Herman Bernstein, "Inner Workings of Teuton Spy System Revealed to World," *Albuquerque Morning Journal*, July 30, 1918, 6.

66. Ellis Parker Butler, "U.S. Not Waiting to Be Destroyed," *Knoxville (TN) Independent*, June 8, 1918, 3.

67. Robert J. Bender, "War Plot Confirmed—Check Delivery of Note to Mexico," *Day Book* (Chicago), Mar. 1, 1917, available online at https://chroniclingameri ca.loc.gov/lccn/sn83045487/1917-03-01/ed-2/seq-1/ (accessed Feb. 22, 2020).

68. Millett, *Semper Fidelis*, 200.

69. Lt. Col. George C. Thorpe, "Confidential Report upon Conditions in Seibo and Macoris Provinces," May 30 1918, Pendleton Papers, PPC, USMCHD.

70. Thorpe, "Confidential Report."

71. Thorpe, "Confidential Report." Thorpe also believed that Taylor's actions corrupted the methods of many officers around him. "Captain Taylor," he observed, "had a very bad effect upon other officers, who acquired the idea that law-

lessness and utter disregard of civilians' rights was proper and admirable conduct for military forces." Ibid.

72. Major General Commandant to Judge Advocate General of the Navy, Nov. 9, 1925, General Correspondence, RG 80, NARA I. Agapito was also known as Azepto Jose. He was a Syrian and a storeowner in the Dominican Republic. His real name was Habib Koziah.

73. Senate, *Hearings*, 2:1136.

74. Headquarters Battalion, 3rd Provisional Regiment, USMC, Campaign Orders No. 1, San Pedro de Macoris, DR, Aug. 20, 1918, Pendleton Papers, PPC, USMCHD.

75. Millett, *Semper Fidelis*, 154–155; Birtle, *U.S. Army Counterinsurgency*, 130–131.

76. Senate, *Hearings*, 2:1119; Langley, *Banana Wars*, 146; Calder, *Impact of Intervention*, 149.

77. Arrest of Capt. Charles F. Merkel, M.C., Oct. 18, 1918, Dominican Republic Geographic Files, 1917–1919, RB, USMCHD; Mark Folse, "The Tiger of Seibo: Charles Merkel, George C. Thorpe, and the Dark Side of Marine Corps History," *Marine Corps History* 1, no. 2 (Winter 2016): 4–18.

78. Charles F. Merkel to Russell W. Duck, Oct. 2, 1918, Charles F. Merkel Personnel Files, NPRC.

79. George C. Thorpe to Joseph Pendleton, Aug. 21, 1918, Pendleton Papers, PPC, USMCHD (emphasis added).

80. Special Agent Carlos J. Rohde to Director of Naval Intelligence, "Conditions in Dominican Republic," Nov. 26, 1918, George C. Thorpe Personnel Files, NPRC, 8.

81. Rohde to Director of Naval Intelligence, 3–7.

82. Rohde to Director of Naval Intelligence, 3.

83. George C. Thorpe to Brigade Commander, "Report Special Agt. Carlos J. Rodhe [*sic*], re Dom. Rep." Dec. 23, 1918, Thorpe Personnel Files, 3.

84. Rohde to Director of Naval Intelligence, "Conditions in Dominican Republic," 7.

85. Testimony of Alexander S. Williams, in Senate, *Hearings*, 2:1822.

86. Testimony of Alexander S. Williams, 1820. See also Millett, *Semper Fidelis*, 196.

87. Wise, *Marine Tells It to You*, 307.

88. Russell, "Statement"; Tasker L. Oddie, "Report," in *Inquiry into Occupation and Administration of Haiti and the Dominican Republic*, June 26, 1922, https://www.history.navy.mil/research/library/online-reading-room/title-list-alphabetically/i/inquiry-occupation-administration-haiti-dominicanrepublic.html#amer.

89. Proclamation posted in Port-au-Prince, Mar. 14, 1919, in Russell, "Statement."

90. R. S. Hooker, "Proclamation to the Haitian People in the Districts Where There Are Bandits," 1919, Russell Papers, PPC, USMCHD.

91. Maj. John L. Doxey, "Notes on Situation in Hinche District," Feb. 28, 1919, Haiti Investigations, Entry 38, RG 127, NARA I.

92. Maj. Thomas C. Turner, "Report of Investigation of Certain Irregularities Alleged to Have Been Committed by Officers and Enlisted Man in the Republic of Haiti," Nov. 3, 1919, Haitian Geographic Files, RB, USMCHD. See also Senate, *Hearings*, 2:1809.

93. Brig. Gen. George Barnett to the Secretary of the Navy, "Report on the Affairs in the Republic of Haiti, June 1915 to June 30, 1920," Oct. 11, 1920, 70–72, Box 1E, PC-31, Office of the Secretary of the Navy, 1804–1947, Entry 113: Office of Public Relations, Press Releases, Jan. 1917–Dec. 1936, RG 80, NARA I; Renda, *Taking Haiti*, 174; Schmidt, *Occupation of Haiti*, 102–103; Millett, *Semper Fidelis*, 198.

94. Medal of Honor Citation, "Brigadier General Herman Henry Hanneken, USMC (Deceased)," Marine Corps University, https://www.usmcu.edu/Research /Marine-Corps-History-Division/Information-for-Units/Medal-of-Honor-Reci pients-By-Unit/Sgt-Herman-Henry-Hanneken/.

95. Crosby, "Military Idea of Manliness," 873.

96. Russell, "Statement."

97. George Barnett to John H. Russell, Oct. 2, 1919, George Barnett Papers, PPC, USMCHD.

98. Senate, *Hearings*, 1:425.

99. Wise, *Marine Tells It to You*, 304.

100. Barnett to Russell, Oct. 2, 1919, Barnett Papers, PPC, USMCHD.

101. "What Other Papers Say," *Washington Post*, Oct. 16, 1920.

102. "What Other Papers Say."

103. Millett, *Semper Fidelis*, 202.

104. Lt. Col. Douglas. C. McDougal to Brig. Gen. Smedley Butler, Sept. 17, 1921, Butler Papers, PPC, USMCHD.

105. Harry A. Franck, "Lays Haiti Killings to Southern Men," *New York Times*, Oct. 15, 1920.

106. Franck even calls into question Marine marksmanship:

I read in one account that it was a testimonial to the marksmanship of the ma-rines that only twelve of them had been killed, whereas they had killed more than 3,000 blacks. This is partly so, but the poor arms of the natives is another cause. Almost the only firearms they possess are eighteenth century weapons, relics of French days. You frequently see natives swaggering about with a re-volver or two, neither of which has been capable of firing a shot for years. Some were armed with scythes. In some instances, a single American with a rifle or machine gun has routed forty or fifty natives with arms of the sort I described. I know Americans who have killed or wounded six or eight natives in a single brief encounter.

Franck, "Lays Haiti Killings to Southern Men."

107. Gulian Lansing Morrill, *Sea Sodoms: A Sinical Survey of Haiti, Santo Do-mingo, Porto Rico, Curacao, Venezuela, Guadeloupe, Martinique, Cuba* (Minneapolis: Pioneer Printers, 1921), 48.

108. Herbert J. Seligmann, "The Conquest of Haiti," *Nation*, July 10, 1920, 35.

109. Logand Feland to John A. Lejeune, June 22, 1920, Reel 12, Container 14, Papers of John A. Lejeune, LOC.

110. Earl Ellis to John A. Lejeune, June 24, 1920, Reel 12, Container 14, Papers of John A. Lejeune, LOC.

111. John A. Lejeune, "To the Editor," *Nation*, July 24, 1920, 101.

112. "Marine Officer on Haiti," *New York Times*, Oct. 31, 1920.

113. CFB to the Editor, "Marines in Haiti and San Domingo," *Montgomery (AL) Advertiser*, Oct. 22, 1920, 4.

114. H. H. McNeill, "Racial Antipathy: The Sentiment Has Existed since Man's Beginning," *Montgomery (AL) Advertiser*, Aug. 16, 1919, 4; George W. Murray, *Race Ideals: Effects, Cause, and Remedy for the Afro-American Race Troubles* (Pittsburgh: Art Engraving & Printing, 1914), 22; Suksdorf, *Our Race Problems*, 314; Junius Aryan, *The Aryans and Mongrelized America: The Remedy* (Philadelphia: Eagle Printing House, 1912), vi; Bailey, *Race Orthodoxy in the South*, 17. See also Bailey, "Race Orthodoxy in the South," *Neale's Monthly*, Nov. 1913, 585; and Bederman, *Manliness and Civilization*, 110–113.

115. Richard Henry Edwards, *The Negro Problem* (Madison, WI, 1908), 12.

116. Edwards, 217.

117. McNeill, "Racial Antipathy," 4.

118. Josephus Daniels, Press Conference, Oct. 15, 1920, Box 1E, PC-31, Office of the Secretary of the Navy, 1804–1947, Entry 113, RG 80, NARA I.

119. Daniels, Press Conference, Oct. 15, 1920.

120. Daniels, Press Conference, Dec. 17, 1920.

121. Major General Commandant to the Secretary of the Navy, "Report of the Military Situation in Haiti during the Period of July 1, 1920, to Date, and a Report of My Inspection of the First Brigade, U.S. Marines, Stationed in the Republic of Haiti," Oct. 4, 1920, Box 2, Sept. 1–Nov. 30, 1929, PC-31, Office of the Secretary of the Navy, 1804–1947, Entry 113, RG 80, NARA I.

122. "Finding of Facts and Conclusion of Board of Investigation on Conditions in Haiti Ordered by the Secretary of the Navy" Oct. 19, 1920, Papers of John A. Lejeune, LOC.

123. "Marines Quieted Haiti, General Lejeune Says," *Sun*, Oct. 6, 1920.

124. "The Haitian-Dominican Scandal," *Washington Post*, Oct. 17, 1920. This paper went on to level charges of mismanagement and willful ignorance against Secretary of the Navy Daniels but not at the Marine Corps.

125. Bishop stated the following as the purpose of his book: "It is the author's desire in this volume to explain just who the marines are, what they do, where they go, so as to make every red-blooded American boy familiar with the services rendered by the United States Marine Corps to the nation in peace and war." Giles Bishop Jr., *The Marines Have Landed* (Philadelphia: Penn Publishing, 1920), 5.

126. Bishop, *Marines Have Landed*, 84.

127. Bishop, 203.

128. Editorial, "Fit for Boys," *Nation*, Jan. 19, 1921, 75.

129. E. H. Ellis, "Bush Brigades," *Marine Corps Gazette*, Mar. 1921, 1.

130. Ellis, 15.

131. "Memoir on the Political, Economic, and Financial Conditions Existing in the Republic of Haiti under the American Occupation by the Delegates to the United States of the Union Patriotique d'Haiti," *Nation*, May 25, 1921, 767–768. The "Haitian Memoir" can also be found in complete form in Senate, *Hearings*, 1:5–46 (hereafter "Haitian Memoir"). The Union Patriotique d'Haiti described itself as "a nonpartisan organization founded at Port-au-Prince, November 17, 1920, to crystallize the national aspirations of the Haitians for the return of their independence, maintained until the American invasion for one hundred and eleven

years. Every one of the twenty-seven districts which constitute the Republic of Haiti is represented and the Union has virtually the unanimous support of the entire Haitian people." *Nation*, May 25, 1921, 775.

132. "Haitian Memoir," 32.

133. It leveled this condemnation of the naval court of inquiry:

> Not a single rule was ever established for the inquiry and no form of procedure was indicated. The court never made known where it would hold its sessions, on what days they would take place, whether they would be public, whether the court itself would call in witnesses, whether the people who were acquainted with the whole thing or who were victims of acts at the hands of the forces of occupation could go and testify freely before the court, or what guarantees of safety it offered to Haitian citizens who wished to prove charges of criminal acts against officers who still had military authority, knowing well the cruelty of martial law in the country for the past five years.

"Haitian Memoir," 32.

134. "Haitian Memoir," 28.

135. "Protest Raised by the Anti-Election League of the Santo Domingo Province against the Order of Convocation Promulgated on July 14, 1921, by the United States of America in the Subjugated Territory of the Dominican Republic," in Senate, *Hearings*, 2:1121.

136. Editorial, *Nation*, May 25, 1921, 727; "Haiti Speaks!: Southern American Democrats Despoil Little Black Republic," *Cleveland Gazette*, June 4, 1921, 1; Hoganson, *Fighting for American Manhood*, 186–187.

137. Editorial, *Nation*, May 25, 1921, 727.

138. Editorial, 727.

139. "A Terrific Indictment: Haiti Speaks!," *Cleveland Gazette*, June 4, 1921, 1; Hoganson, *Fighting for American Manhood*, 187.

140. "Terrific Indictment," 1.

141. *Cleveland Gazette*, June 25, 1921.

142. *Cleveland Gazette*, June 25, 1921.

143. "Haitians Request Troops Withdrawal: Southern Democratic U.S. Marines Responsible," *Cleveland Gazette*, May 14, 1921, 1; "Haitian Delegates Ask Withdrawal of Marines: Many Atrocities Charged to the Devil Dogs," *Washington Bee*, June 4, 1921, 1.

144. Philip Douglas, "Americanizing Santo Domingo," *Cleveland Gazette*, June 18, 1921, 1.

145. "NAACP Secretary Testifies on Haiti," *Washington Bee*, Dec. 3, 1921. See also Henry Lewis Suggs, "The Response of the African American Press to the United States Occupation of Haiti, 1915–1934," *Journal of Negro History* 73 (Winter–Autumn, 1988), 33–45.

146. Senate, *Hearings*, 2:1132; Folse, "Tiger of Seibo," 12–13.

147. McDougal to Butler, Sept. 17, 1921, Butler Papers, PPC, USMCHD.

148. Senate, *Hearings*, 2:909.

149. Senate, *Hearings*, 917.

150. Senate, *Hearings*, 1547.

151. Summerbell, *Manhood in Its American Type*, 131.

152. Morrill, *Sea Sodoms*, 29.

153. Hoganson, *Fighting for American Manhood*, 186–187; Bederman, *Manliness and Civilization*, 84–45; Hall, *Adolescence*, 373.

154. Senate, *Hearings*, 1:28, 146–147, 231, 238, 257, 264, 290, 459, 2:1252, 1301, 1591–1592, 1778.

155. Daniel. P. Rhodes, *Our Immortality* (New York: Macmillan, 1919), 157.

156. U.S. War Department, *Outline of Plan for Military Training in Public Schools of the United States* (Washington, DC: Army War College, 1915), 8; RAdm. Casper F. Goodrich, "Training," *National Service Magazine*, Nov. 1917, 369–370; Bishop, *Marines Have Landed*, 84; Summerbell, *Manhood in Its American Type*, 99; Youard, *Showing Ourselves Men*, 8; Tatlock, *Why America Fights Germany*, 11.

157. Aryan, *Aryans and Mongrelized America*, v. Aryan wanted Congress to pass a law banning marriage and cohabitation between white people and darker races. The mixing with "any other race or person belonging to, or a mongrel of any branch of, the Negro, Mongolian or Semitic race" threatened the "racial manhood" of whites, he declared. Ibid., 351.

158. Lothrop Stoddard, *The Rising Tide of Color against White World-Supremacy* (New York: Charles Scribner's Sons, 1920), 303. See also Savoyard, "The Race Question," *Quanah Tribune-Chief* (Bryan, TX), Nov. 25, 1921, 3.

159. Joseph Pendleton, untitled speech, ca. 1919–20, Pendleton Papers, PPC, USMCHD.

160. "Record of Weekly Conference Held in Office of the Major General Commandant, Friday, November 18, 1921," Entry 37, RG 127, NARA I.

161. Oddie, "Report," in *Inquiry into Occupation and Administration of Haiti and the Dominican Republic*, June 26, 1922.

162. Samuel Guy Inman, *Through Santo Domingo and Haiti: A Cruise with the Marines* (New York: Committee on Cooperation in Latin America, 1919), 14.

163. James P. Hornaday, "Aid for Service Men Everywhere," *Poseyville (IN) News*, Sept. 24, 1920, 2.

164. Craige, *Black Bagdad*, 97.

165. Seligmann, "Conquest of Haiti," 36. A Marine captain whose patrol in the Haitian hills was accompanied by Seligmann, wrote, "he was surely an unscrupulous, irresponsible writer, inspired perhaps by the politicians who were looking for flaws, and that he had come to Haiti burdened with delusions and in search of such news as he might need in preparing an article of Bolshevik nature." Capt. J. L. Perkins to Brigade Commander, "Account of Patrol Made in Company with Mr. Herbert J. Seligman, Apr. 3–7, 1920," July 26, 1920, Russell Papers, PPC, USMCHD.

166. Inman, *Through Santo Domingo and Haiti*, 70.

167. "The Rape of Haiti! The Most Shocking Assertion Ever Made by a Responsible Government Official," *Cleveland Gazette*, Sept. 25, 1920, 1.

168. "The Haitian Scandal," *Washington Post*, Dec. 20, 1920, 6; "A Horrible Record in Hayti," *New York Tribune*, Oct. 23, 1920, 10.

169. Perkins to Russell, "Account of Patrol," July 26, 1920; Henry C. Davis to Regimental Commander, "Report of Field Operations," June 1, 1917, 1, USMCHD; Edward A. Craig, interviewed by L. S. Tatem, 1968, OHC, USMCHD, transcript, 23.

170. Board of Investigation on Conditions in Haiti, "Finding of Facts and Conclusions," Oct. 19, 1920, Russell Papers, PPC, USMCHD.

171. Oddie, "Report," in *Inquiry into Occupation and Administration of Haiti and the Dominican Republic*, June 26, 1922.

172. George Barnett, "Report of the Major General Commandant of the United States Marine Corps," in *Annual Report of the Navy Department for the Fiscal Year 1919* (Washington, DC: Government Printing Office, 1920), 2638.

173. Board of Investigation on Conditions in Haiti, "Finding of Facts and Conclusions," Oct. 19, 1920, Russell Papers, PPC, USMCHD.

174. Oddie, "Report," in *Inquiry into Occupation and Administration of Haiti and the Dominican Republic*, June 26, 1922.

175. Stephen Kantrowitz, "White Supremacist Justice and the Rule of Law: Lynching, Honor, and the State in Ben Tillman's South Carolina," in *Men and Violence: Gender, Honor, and Rituals in Modern Europe and America*, ed. Pieter Spierenburg (Columbus: Ohio State University Press, 1998), 218. See also Williams, *Torchbearers of Democracy*, 228; and Lears, *Rebirth of a Nation*, 105–107.

176. "Negro Taken from Train in Miss. Town and Severely Beaten," *Thomasville (GA) Times-Enterprise*, Sept. 30, 1919, 1; "Mob Attempts to Lynch Mayor of Omaha," *Thomasville (GA) Times-Enterprise*, Sept. 30, 1919, 1.

177. "Negro Advocate Beaten by Texans," *Atlanta Constitution*, Aug. 25, 1919, 1, 6. See also *Anniston (AL) Star*, Aug. 22, 1919, 6.

178. James E. Gregg, "Lynching: A National Menace," in Johnsen, *Selected Articles on the Negro Problem*, 152.

179. Quoted in Terence Finnegan, "'The Equal of Some White Men and the Superior of Others': Masculinity and the 1916 Lynching of Anthony Crawford in Abbeville County, South Carolina," in *Men and Violence: Gender, Honor, and Rituals in Modern Europe and America*, ed., Pieter Spierenburg (Columbus: Ohio State University Press, 1998), 240.

180. "For Action on Race Riot Peril," *New York Times*, Oct. 5, 1919, 10.

181. Millett, *Semper Fidelis*, 186.

182. Percy Webb, "Our Side of It," in "Rhymes of a Marine," n.d., Percy Webb Papers, PPC, USMCHD (emphasis added).

6. An Invitation to Brave Men

Epigraph. "The Trail of the Roving Marines," *Recruiters' Bulletin*, Feb. 1920, 4.

1. "The Roving Marines," *Recruiters' Bulletin*, Feb. 1920, 3; "The Weather," *Washington Herald*, Jan. 31, 1920, 4.

2. John A. Lejeune, "Report of the Major General Commandant of the United States Marine Corps," in *Annual Report of the Navy Department for the Fiscal Year 1920* (Washington, DC: Government Printing Office, 1920), 1056.

3. "Trail of the Roving Marines," 4.

4. Kimmel, *Manhood in America*, 88; Pendergast, *Creating the Modern Man*, 13; Delvin, *Between Profits and Primitivism*, 17; Summers, *Manliness & Its Discontents*, 8; Dubbert, "Progressivism and the Masculinity Crisis," 309–310; Stearns, *Be a Man!*, 10–11.

5. Lejeune, "Report of the Major General Commandant" (1920), 1055.

6. Lejeune, 1056.

7. "Dan Daly Joins Reserve," *Recruiters' Bulletin*, Aug. 1920, 2.

8. "Honored by Department," *Recruiters' Bulletin*, Apr. 1916, 3.

9. "Medals Don't Count with Dan Daly," *Recruiters' Bulletin*, May 1919, 22.

10. "Devil Dog Dan Daly Retires," *Brooklyn Eagle*, Feb. 10, 1929.

11. "Medals Don't Count with Dan Daly," 22.

12. "Roving Marines to Stage Big Jazz Show," *Boston Post*, Apr. 19, 1920, 13.

13. "Roving Marines Make a Big Hit," *Recruiters' Bulletin*, Feb. 1920, 3. See also "Roving Marines Coming to Boston," *Boston Evening Globe*, Apr. 6, 1920, 6; and "Marines Please Large Crowds of Syracusans," *Syracuse (NY) Herald*, Apr. 11, 1920, 10.

14. "Roving Marines Make a Big Hit," 4.

15. "'Roving Marines,' to Be Seen at Armory Friday Evening, Free," *Waterloo (IA) Evening Courier*, Mar. 3, 1920, 12.

16. "Roving Marines Make a Big Hit," 3; "'Roving Marines,' to Be Seen at Armory Friday Evening, Free," 12; "The Roving Marines Please Big Audience," *Montgomery (AL) Advertiser*, June 15, 1920, 2; "Roving Marines to Stage Big Jazz Show," 13; "Marines Stage Show in Butte," *Anaconda (MT) Standard*, May 2, 1920, 5.

17. Ralph D. Borst to Col. D. P. Hall quoted in "Roving Marines Make a Big Hit," 21.

18. "Roving Marines Coming to Boston," 6.

19. Newspaper quoted in "Roving Marines Make a Big Hit," 4.

20. "Roving Marines Make a Big Hit," 4.

21. "Roving Marines Leave Thursday for Georgia City," *Montgomery (AL) Advertiser*, June 17, 1920, 2.

22. "Roving Marines Leave Thursday for Georgia City," 2.

23. Officer in Charge to Officer in Charge, Eastern Recruiting Division, "Report of Roving Marines," Mar. 22, 1920, Entry 18: General Correspondence, Office of the Commandant, 1913–1938, RG 127, NARA I.

24. R. F. Avery, "Memorandum for the Officer in Charge, Eastern Recruiting Division, Philadelphia, PA.," Mar. 27, 1920, Entry 18, RG 127, NARA I.

25. Simon, *Greatest of All Leathernecks*, 152–153.

26. Simon, 153.

27. Glenn M. Harned, *Marine Corps Generals, 1899–1936*, 2nd ed. (North Charleston, SC: CreateSpace Independent Publishing Platform, 2017), 87–90.

28. Simon, *Greatest of All Leathernecks*, 79.

29. Sen. Thomas Butler to Lejeune, July 6, 1920, Container 14, Reel 12, Papers of John A. Lejeune, LOC; Mark R. Folse, "The (R)-Evolutionary Tenure of Commandant Lejeune," *Naval History* 35, no. 4 (Aug. 2020): 22–27.

30. Schmidt, *Maverick Marine*, 110–111.

31. Navy News Bureau, "Immediate Release," June 19, 1920, Box 1E, PC-31, Office of the Secretary of the Navy, 1804–1947, Office of the Secretary of the Navy, 1804–1947, Entry 113: Office of Public Relations, Press Releases, Jan. 1917–Dec. 1936, RG 80, NARA I.

32. Clifton B. Cates, interviewed by Benis M. Frank, 1973, OHC, USMCHD, transcript, 65–66, https://www.usmcu.edu/Portals/218/Gen%20Clifton%20B_%

20Cates.pdf (accessed Apr. 13, 2020). See also Merrill L. Bartlett, "George Barnett, 1914–1920," in *Commandants of the Marine Corps*, ed. Allan R. Millett and Jack Shulimson (Annapolis, MD: Naval Institute Press, 2004), 191–192. For other versions of this encounter, see Schmidt, *Maverick Marine*, 114–117.

33. Bartlett, "George Barnett," 191–193.

34. John A. Lejeune to Earl H. Ellis, July 7, 1920, Reel 12, Container 14, Papers of John A. Lejeune, LOC. See also Officer in Charge of Recruiting to the Major General Commandant, Sept. 12, 1921, Entry 37: General Correspondence, Recruitment, 1921–1939, RG 127, NARA I.

35. Maj. Gen. John A. Lejeune to Maj. Adolf B. Miller, July 19, 1920, Adolf B. Miller Papers, PPC, USMCHD.

36. Maj. Gen. John A. Lejeune statement, Mar. 8, 1922, in U.S. House of Representatives, Committee on Naval Affairs, *Statements of Maj. Gen. John A. Lejeune, Commandant, U.S. Marine Corps, Hearings before the United States House Committee on Naval Affairs, Sixty-Seventh Congress, Second Session, on Mar. 8, 9, 1922*, committee serial 68 (Washington, DC: Government Printing Office, 1923), 641.

37. Colbourn, "Esprit de Marine Corps," 115–116.

38. Lejeune, "Report of the Major General Commandant" (1920), 1056.

39. Lejeune, 1056. See also "Report of Roving Marines from O.I.C. District of Pittsburg," Mar. 24, 1920, Entry 18, RG 127, NARA I.

40. Officer in Charge of Recruiting to Major General Commandant, "Data for Annual Report," Sept. 12, 1921, Entry 37, RG 127, NARA I.

41. Officer in Charge of Recruiting to Major General Commandant, "Data for Annual Report," Sept. 12, 1921.

42. Bederman, *Manliness and Civilization*, 19.

43. Kimmel, *Manhood in America*, 140.

44. John A. Lejeune, "Preparation," *Marine Corps Gazette*, Mar. 1922, 54. This article is a copy of an address Lejeune delivered on January 12, 1922, at Marine Corps Schools, Quantico, VA.

45. Lejeune, 54.

46. Lejeune, 54–55.

47. E. B. Manwaring, "Recruit Training at Parris Island," Jan. 21, 1921, Entry 18, RG 127, NARA I.

48. Letter by F.H.W. of New York, Jan. 25, 1921, quoted in "Addendum: Recruit Training at Parris Island,".

49. Letter by J.L.O. of New York, Jan. 25, 1921, quoted in "Addendum: Recruit Training at Parris Island."

50. Letter by E.A.M. of Indiana, Jan. 25, 1921, quoted in "Addendum: Recruit Training at Parris Island."

51. Letter by J.A.S. of New York, Jan. 25, 1921, quoted in "Addendum: Recruit Training at Parris Island."

52. Letter by F.E. of New Jersey, Jan. 25, 1921, quoted in Manwaring, "Recruit Training."

53. Letter by F.X. MacD. of Massachusetts, Jan. 25, 1921, quoted in Manwaring, "Recruit Training."

54. Letter by J.H.V.S. of Pennsylvania, Jan. 25, 1921, quoted in "Addendum: Recruit Training at Parris Island."

55. Letter by H.O.A. of Kentucky, Jan. 25, 1921, quoted in "Addendum: Recruit Training at Parris Island."

56. Letter by A.A.S. of Pennsylvania, Jan. 25, 1921, quoted in "Addendum: Recruit Training at Parris Island."

57. Manwaring, "Recruit Training," 1.

58. Commanding Officer to Major General Commandant, "Letters for Publicity Purposes," Feb. 1, 1921, Entry 18, RG 127, NARA I.

59. Commanding Officer to Major General Commandant, "Letters for Publicity Purposes."

60. Commanding Officer to Major General Commandant, "Letters for Publicity Purposes" (emphasis added).

61. John A. Lejeune quoted in Krulak, *First to Fight*, 168.

62. Lejeune quoted in Krulak, 169.

63. RAdm. William L. Rodgers, "Address to the Graduating Class of Marine Officers at Quantico on June 9," *Marine Corps Gazette*, June 1923, 91.

64. Rodgers, 88.

65. Venable, *How the Few Became the Proud*, 136–137.

66. Lejeune, "Report of the Major General Commandant" (1920), 1056.

67. Lejeune, 1074.

68. Norris A. Brisco, *Economics of Efficiency* (New York: Macmillan, 1921), vii; Vanderveer Custis, *The Foundations of National Industrial Efficiency* (New York: Macmillan, 1923), 3.

69. Brisco, *Economics of Efficiency*, 83, 123; Custis, *Foundations of National Industrial Efficiency*, 150, 247.

70. Daugherty, "To Fight Our Country's Battles," 103–116; Millett, *Semper Fidelis*, 323; Robert Debs Heinl Jr., *Soldiers of the Sea: The United States Marine Corps, 1775–1962* (Annapolis, MD: Naval Institute Press, 1962), 228–229; Simon, *Greatest of all Leathernecks*, 159.

71. Heinl, *Soldiers of the Sea*, 228; Daugherty, "To Fight Our Country's Battles," 104.

72. Daugherty, "To Fight Our Country's Battles," 105; Heinl, *Soldiers of the Sea*, 229; Simon, *Greatest of All Leathernecks*, 159.

73. John A. Lejeune, "Report of the Major General Commandant of the United States Marine Corps," in *Annual Report of the Navy Department for the Fiscal Year 1921* (Washington, DC: Government Printing Office, 1921), 49.

74. Lejeune quoted in "Promotion Bill before Congress," *Marine Corps Gazette*, Dec. 1922, 323.

75. "Promotion by Selection—Discussion," *Marine Corps Gazette*, June 1922, 185–200; Daugherty, "To Fight Our Country's Battles," 115–116.

76. Edwin Denby, Press Release, n.d., Box 3, PC-31, Office of the Secretary of the Navy, 1804–1947, Entry 113, RG 80, NARA I.

77. Bettez, *Kentucky Marine*, 154–156.

78. "Marines to Stop Mail Robberies," *Bedford (IN) Daily Mail*, Nov. 10, 1921, 2; "Armed Guards Common Sight in Washington," *Charleston (WV) Daily Mail*, Nov. 18, 1921, 17.

79. "Mail or Dead Marine Says Denby Message," *New York Times*, Nov. 13, 1921, 14.

80. "Mail or Dead Marine," 14.

81. John J. Blaine quoted in "Mail Marine Guards Scorned by Governor Blaine

of Wisconsin, Renewing Demand for Hanson's Trial, Assails Hays Policy," *New York Times*, Dec. 9, 1921, 15.

82. "Want Marine Guard for Mail Shooting," *New York Times*, Nov. 26, 1921, 15.

83. "Mail Guard Is Exonerated: Marine Did His Duty in Firing at Man, Says Naval Board," *New York Times*, Jan. 6, 1922, 15.

84. Denby, Press Release, n.d.

85. "Backs Marine for Shooting: Post Office Department Endorses Action in Firing on Youths on Train," *New York Times*, Dec. 24, 1921, 5.

86. "Shot by Mail Guard: Marine in Indiana Thought Man Was Breaking into a Car," *New York Times*, Dec. 2, 1921, 18.

87. "Marine Mail Guard Shoots Farmer Dead: Witnesses Say Victim Was Ordered to Move While Standing near Train," *New York Times*, Dec. 5, 1921, 18; "Say Marine Was Menaced: Shooting of Man in Texas Said to Be Due to His Attitude," *New York Times*, Dec. 6, 1921, 17.

88. "Mail Car Marine Shoots 2: Fired Sawed-off Gun at Three Stealing Parcels near Savannah," *New York Times*, Dec. 9, 1921, 18.

89. Victor France Bleasdale, interviewed by Benis M. Frank, Dec. 4, 1979, OHC, USMCHD, transcript, 173.

90. Bleasdale, 174.

91. Lejeune statement, Mar. 8, 1922, in U.S. House, Committee on Naval Affairs, *Statements of Maj. Gen. John A. Lejeune*, 645. See also Hubert Work to the Major General Commandant, Mar. 14, 1922, Logan Feland Papers, PPC, USMCHD; and "No Robberies of Mail during Marines' Tour of Postal Duty," *Leatherneck*, Apr. 1, 1922, 1.

92. Lejeune statement, Mar. 8, 1922, in U.S. House, Committee on Naval Affairs, *Statements of Maj. Gen. John a. Lejeune*, 645.

93. "On the Threshold of 1922," *Leatherneck*, Jan. 7, 1922, 1.

94. Lejeune statement, Mar. 8, 1922, in U.S. House, Committee on Naval Affairs, *Statements of Maj. Gen. John a. Lejeune*, 644.

95. "Naval Activities from March 4, 1921 to March 4, 1922, Released Sunday, March 5th, 1922," Box 4, PC-31, Office of the Secretary of the Navy, 1804–1947, Entry 113, RG 80, NARA I.

96. "Record of Weekly Conference Held in Office of the Major General Commandant, Friday, November 18, 1921," Entry 37, RG 127, NARA I.

97. "On the Threshold of 1922," 1. Begun in late 1917, *Leatherneck* was originally the *Quantico Leatherneck*, run by Marines stationed in Virginia who had worked in the newspaper business as civilians. Angus A. Aull, "Who Started the *Leatherneck?*," *Editor and Publisher* (New York), Feb. 19, 1921, 38.

98. First Sgt. Percy Webb, "MAIL-O!" *Leatherneck*, Dec. 3, 1921, 5.

99. Smedley Butler to Thomas Butler, Sept. 2, 1921, Smedley Butler Papers, PPC, USMCHD.

100. Schmidt, *Maverick Marine*, 134–136; Millett, *Semper Fidelis*, 324. Moskin, *Marine Corps Story*, 207; Simmons, *United States Marines*, 111.

101. Millett, Maslowski, and Feis, *For the Common Defense*, 348–349; Weigley, *American Way of War*, 228; David MacIsaac, "Voices from the Central Blue: The Air Power Theorists," in *Makers of Modern Strategy: From Machiavelli to the Nuclear Age*, ed. Peter Paret (Princeton NJ: Princeton University Press, 1986), 630–631.

102. Butler to Butler, Sept. 2, 1921.

103. John A. Lejeune, "The Mobile Defense of Advance Bases by the Marine Corps," *Marine Corps Gazette*, June 1916, 1; John H. Russell, "A Plea for a Mission and Doctrine," *Marine Corps Gazette*, June 1916, 109; Earl H. Ellis, "Advanced Base Operations in Micronesia," in *21st Century Ellis: Operational Art and Strategic Prophecy for the Modern Era*, ed. B. A. Friedman (Annapolis, MD: Naval Institute Press 2015), 86–139; Isely and Crowl, *U.S. Marines and Amphibious War*, 3–45; Krulak, *First to Fight*, 1–107; Millett, *Semper Fidelis*, 319–343; Coram, *Brute*, 71–72.

104. "Record of Conference Held in the Office of the Major General Commandant," Oct. 7, 1921, Entry 37, RG 127, NARA I.

105. *Fall Exercises, 1924: Marine Corps Expeditionary Force* (Publicity Bureau: Force Headquarters MCEF, 1924), 3, copy in Civil War Reenactments, Subject Files, RB, USMCHD.

106. "President in Marine Camp during Night," *Sedalia (MO) Democrat*, Oct. 7, 1921, 6; "Harding at Field Maneuvers," *Lincoln Nebraska State Journal*, Oct. 2, 1921, 11; "Harding Reviews Force of Marines," *Oneonta (NY) Daily Star*, Oct. 3, 1921, 1; "Marines Go Over Top at Wilderness as in Days of '61," *Hattiesburg (MS) American*, Sept. 30, 1921, 5.

107. "Harding Lauds Corps: Praises Marines after 24 Hours in Camp in the Wilderness," *Washington Post*, Oct. 3, 1921, 1; "Harding Reviews Force of Marines," 1.

108. "Marine Show Energy in Wilderness Battle: Expeditionary Force Digs in Behind Smoke Screen amid Scenes of Civil War Conflicts," *New York Times*, Sept. 30, 1921, 2.

109. "Record of Conference Held in the Office of the Major General Commandant," Oct. 7, 1921.

110. H.A.M. to Smedley Butler, Nov. 1, 1921, Butler Papers, PPC, USMCHD.

111. "Marines to 'Hike' to Gettysburg and Return," *Leatherneck*, June 17, 1922, 1.

112. "Marine Aviators Commended for Work during Maneuvers," *Leatherneck*, July 15, 1922. See also Richard D. L. Fulton and James Rada Jr., "The Last to Fall: The 1922 March, Battles, and Deaths of the U.S. Marines at Gettysburg," *Marine Corps History* 3, no. 1 (Summer 2017): 15.

113. "Marines to 'Hike' to Gettysburg and Return," 1.

114. Clifford, *Progress and Purpose*, 32; Millett, *Semper Fidelis*, 327; Isely and Crowl, *U.S. Marines and Amphibious War*, 30–31; Krulak, *First to Fight*, 89. Simmons, *United States Marines*, 112.

115. "Impressive Ceremony," *Sioux City (IA) Sunday Journal*, Mar. 23, 1924, 25.

116. "For Release Sunday, February 3, 1924," Box 6, PC-31, Office of the Secretary of the Navy, 1804–1947, Entry 113, RG 80, NARA I.

117. Marine Recruiting Bureau, "Yearly Statement of Recruiting by Divisions, Districts and Stations" (Washington DC, Headquarters Marine Corps, Fiscal Years 1920, 1922, and 1923), Recruiting, Subject Files, RB, USMCHD.

7. To Build Up a Class of Men

Epigraph. H.K., "Bits o' Mud from Quantico," *Leatherneck*, Dec. 3, 1921, 5. This poem was accompanied by a preface: "The long-looked-for additional verse to the

Marine Hymn has been written and all Quantico is singing it. It was written for the football game in Baltimore with the Third Army Corps Area champs and just about predicts what is going to happen."

1. "Marines Victors over Third Army Corps, 20–0, Goettge Outstanding Star of Annual Service Battle," *Washington Herald*, Dec. 4, 1921, 13; "Leathernecks Down Third Area Machine," *Washington Post*, Dec. 4, 1921, 29; "Army and Marines on Edge for Game," *Washington Post*, Dec. 1, 1921, 18; "Prominent Government Officials See Marines Down 3rd Army Corps-20–0," *New York Times*, Dec. 4, 1921, 114.

2. Kimmel, *Manhood in America*, 274; Bederman, *Manliness and Civilization*, 15.

3. Millett, Maslowski, and Feis, *For the Common Defense*, 339.

4. Edward M. Coffman, *The Regulars: The American Army, 1898–1941* (Cambridge, MA: Harvard University Press, 2004), 231–232, 234; Richard W. Stewart, ed., *American Military History*, vol. 2, *The United States Army in a Global Era, 1917–2008*, 2nd ed. (Washington, DC: Center of Military History, 2010), 57–58; Millett, Maslowski, and Feis, *For the Common Defense*, 343–345.

5. Craig C. Felker, "Finding Certainty in Uncertain Times: The Navy in the Interwar Years," in *America, Sea Power, and the World*, ed. James Bradford (Malden, MA: John Wiley & Sons, 2016), 179–182; Millett, Maslowski, and Feis, *For the Common Defense*, 342–343; Wadle, *Selling Sea Power*, 165.

6. Charles E. Sawyer, "Physical Manhood of America Is Weak," *Bar Harbor (ME) Times*, Feb. 8, 1922, 3. Also in *Quanah Tribune Chief* (Bryan, TX), Feb. 3, 1922, 3.

7. Henry Herbert Goddard, *Human Efficiency and Levels of Intelligence* (Princeton, NJ: Princeton University Press, 1920), vii; Edward Earle Purinton, *Personal Efficiency and Business* (New York: Robert M. McBride, 1920), 16; Henry Louis Smith, *Your Biggest Job School or Business: Some Words of Counsel for Red-Blooded Young Americans Who Are Getting Tired of School* (New York: D. Appleton, 1921), viii, 56–59, 64; Indiana State Board of Health, *Keeping Fit (For Boys)* (Indianapolis: Bureau of Venereal Diseases, 1921), 3, 7, 10; Young Men's Christian Associations of North America, *Physical Education* (New York: Association Press, 1920), 59.

8. Indiana State Board of Health, *Keeping Fit*, 3, 7, 10.

9. Young Men's Christian Associations, *Physical Education*, 59.

10. Albert Sidney Gregg quoted in introduction to James Samuel Knox, *Personal Efficiency* (Cleveland: Knox Business, 1920), unpaginated.

11. Lt. Col. Charles A. Fleming et al., *Quantico: Crossroads of the Marine Corps* (Washington, DC: History and Museums Division, USMC, 1978), 24.

12. Folse, "(R)-Evolutionary Tenure of Commandant Lejeune"; Fleming et al., *Quantico*, 39.

13. John A. Lejeune, "Statement of Maj. Gen. John A. Lejeune, U.S. Marine Corps, before House Committee on Naval Affairs," Feb. 26, 1920, in *Annual Report of the Navy Department for the Fiscal Year 1920* (Washington, DC: Government Printing Office, 1921), 382.

14. *Annual Report*, 105.

15. *Annual Report*, 105–109.

16. Josephus Daniels, n.d., Box 1E, PC-31, Office of the Secretary of the Navy, 1804–1947, Entry 113: Office of Public Relations, Press Releases, Jan. 1917–Dec. 1936, RG 80, NARA I. Also in *Annual Report of the Navy Department . . . 1920*, 112.

17. Press Conference, Sept. 20, 1920, Box 1E, PC-31, Office of the Secretary of the Navy, 1804–1947, Entry 113, RG 80, NARA I.

18. Josephus Daniels, "Training Men for the Navy and the Nation," *Saturday Evening Post*, Apr. 9, 1921, 24.

19. Daniels, 80.

20. Josephus Daniels to Smedley Butler, Jan. 10, 1920, Smedley Butler Papers, PPC, USMCHD.

21. Smedley Butler to Maj. L. S. Schmitt, Feb. 27, 1920, Butler Papers.

22. Smedley Butler to Josephus Daniels, Jan. 13, 1920, Butler Papers. See also Fleming et al., *Quantico*, 39.

23. Butler to Daniels, Jan. 13, 1920.

24. Butler to Daniels, Jan. 13, 1920; Fleming et al., *Quantico*, 39.

25. Butler to Daniels, Jan. 13, 1920; Fleming et al., *Quantico*, 39.

26. Butler to Daniels, Jan. 13, 1920.

27. Butler to Daniels, Jan. 13, 1920.

28. *Annual Report of the Navy Department for the Fiscal Year 1919* (Washington, DC: Government Printing Office, 1920), 325.

29. Butler to Daniels, Jan. 13, 1920.

30. Edward Garstin Smith, *Americanism* (Chicago: Edward Garstin Smith, 1920), 7.

31. Thames Ross Williamson, *Problems in American Democracy* (New York: D. C. Health, 1922), 255–256.

32. Basil A. Yeaxlee, *An Educated Nation* (New York: Oxford, 1921), 25.

33. Smith, *Your Biggest Job School or Business*, 64.

34. Smith, 69.

35. "Behold the Triumph of the Prussian School Master," *Hartford (KY) Herald*, May 25, 1921; *Rockingham (NC) Post-Dispatch*, May 26, 1921, 3.

36. Smith, *Americanism*, 15.

37. Smith, *Your Biggest Job School or Business*, 76.

38. Julius A. Schaad, *Christianity: A Man's Religion* (Chicago: Witness, 1922), 35.

39. Capt. Earl H. Jenkins, "Character—Building the Basis for High Morale," *Marine Corps Gazette*, Mar. 1920, 46–47.

40. Jenkins, 51.

41. First Lt. J. H. Craige, "Vocational Training in the Marine Corps," *Marine Corps Gazette*, Mar. 1920, 36.

42. Craige, 36.

43. Craige, 42.

44. "Men Have Chance to Join 5th Regiment of Marines," *Boston Evening Globe*, Mar. 30, 1920, 16.

45. "Uncle Sam Gives Free Scholarships," *Boston Globe*, Apr. 28, 1920, 8.

46. Frederick J. Haskin, "A New School for Marines," *Chester (PA) Times*, Apr. 7, 1920, 6; "Plan New School for U.S. Marines," *Dubuque (IA) Telegraph Herald*, Apr. 15, 1920, 16; "New School for Marines," *Janesville (WI) Daily Gazette*, Apr. 7, 1920, 6; "Haskin Letter on Live Topics," *Canton (OH) Daily News*, Apr. 6, 1920, 6.

47. Haskin, "New School for Marines," 6.

48. "Marine Corps Institute Attains Magnitude of a University," *Ogden (UT) Standard Examiner*, July 4, 1920, 10.

49. "U.S. Marines Are Being Educated," *Thomasville (GA) Dailey Times Enterprise*, Feb. 9, 1920, 3.

50. Daniels, "Training Men for the Navy and the Nation," 83.

51. Logan Feland to Smedley Butler, Aug. 25, 1920, Butler Papers, PPC, USMCHD.

52. O. C. Lightner to Maj. Gen. Wendel C. Neville, Mar. 24, 1923, Entry 18: General Correspondence, Office of the Commandant, 1913–1938, RG 127, NARA I.

53. Sen. Kenneth McKellar, Apr. 12, 1920, 66th Cong., 2nd sess., *Congressional Record* 59, no. 105:5951–5952, ("Subject") File 1918–1921, Box 12, NM-84, Entry 376: War College Division and War Plans Division, Subordinate Officers, Morale Branch, 1918–1921, RG 165, NARA II.

54. J. E. Cutler, Memorandum for Chief, Morale Branch, "Recruiting Volunteer Army of 500,000 in Peace Times," Dec. 5, 1918, Morale Branch General Correspondence File 1918–1921, Box 24, NM-84, Entry 376, RG 165, NARA II.

55. Lt. R. F. Fuller, Memorandum for the Chief, Morale Branch, "Voluntary Enlistment," Dec. 5, 1918, Morale Branch General Correspondence File 1918–1921, Box 24, NM-84, Entry 376, RG 165, NARA II.

56. Col. H. I. Rees, Memorandum for Officer in Charge, Recruiting Service, Office of the Adjutant General of the Army, Dec. 23, 1919, Morale Branch General Correspondence File 1918–1921, Box 24, NM-84, Entry 376, RG 165, NARA II.

57. C. R. Dickinson, "Report on Recruiting Methods, Relation of Recruiting to Morale, and Suggestions," Jan. 18, 1919, Morale Branch General Correspondence File 1918–1921, Box 24, NM-84, Entry 376, RG 165, NARA II.

58. Dickinson, 7.

59. Dickinson, 7.

60. Dickinson, 9.

61. The General Recruiting Service operated out of ten corps areas around the country: Boston, New York City; Pittsburg; New Orleans; Evansville, Indiana; Chicago; Omaha, Nebraska; El Paso, Texas; Los Angeles; and Washington, DC. Each infantry division, seven total, had their own recruiting responsibilities as well.

62. Maj. Edmund F. Hackett to Chief, Morale Branch, General Staff, "Report of Work for A.G.O.," July 30, 1919, Morale Branch General Correspondence File 1918–1921, Box 24, NM-84, Entry 376, RG 165, NARA II.

63. Hackett, "Report of Work for A.G.O."

64. Maj. William T. Morgan, Memorandum for the Chief, Morale Branch, "Recruiting for the Regular Army," Feb. 7, 1919, Morale Branch General Correspondence File 1918–1921, Box 24, NM-84, Entry 376, RG 165, NARA II.

65. *United States Army in the World War 1917–1919: Bulletins, GHQ, AEF*, CMH publication 23-23, vol. 17 (1948; repr., Washington, DC: Center of Military History, U.S. Army, 1992), https://history.army.mil/html/books/023/23-23/CMH_Pub_23-23.pdf. See also *Extracts from General Orders and Bulletins*, War Department (Washington DC: Government Printing Office, Jan. 1919), 10, via Hathi Trust, https://babel.hathitrust.org/cgi/pt?id=hvd.hl29dl&seq=112.

66. Hackett, "Report of Work for A.G.O."

67. Maj. R. J. Burt, Memorandum for the Adjutant General of the Army, "Reasons for Enlisting," Nov. 18, 1919, General Correspondence ("Subject") File 1918–1921, Box 24, NM-84, Entry 376, RG 165, NARA II.

68. For navy figures, see Harrod, *Manning the New Navy*, 174–175. For the Marines, see John A. Lejeune, "Report of the Major General Commandant of the United States Marine Corps," in *Annual Report of the Navy Department for . . . 1920*, 1055. For army figures, see Stewart, *American Military History*, 2:56.

69. Coffman, *Regulars*, 233.

70. Newton D. Baker, "Letter from the Secretary of War to Presidents of all Universities and Colleges," Mar. 13, 1920, Box 13, General Correspondence ("Subject") File 1918–1921, Entry 376, RG 165 NARA II.

71. Chaplain George C. Stull, "The American Soldier," in *U.S. Army Schools: Vocational, Educational, Recreational* (Camp Gordon, GA: Printing Class, Educational and Vocational Schools, 1920), General Correspondence ("Subject") File 1918–1921, Box 12, NM-84, Entry 376, RG 165, NARA II.

72. Sen. Kenneth McKellar, Apr. 12, 1920, 66th Cong., 2nd sess., *Congressional Record* 59, no. 105:5951–5952, ("Subject") File 1918–1921, Box 12, NM-84, Entry 376, RG 165, NARA II.

73. Maj. A. G. Rudd, "Slogans Valuable in Publicity," *U.S. Army Recruiting News*, July 1, 1924, 12.

74. "Notice to Recruiters," *U.S. Army Recruiting News*, June 15, 1924, 15.

75. "To the Mothers of America," *U.S. Army Recruiting News*, May 1, 1924, 2.

76. "Army Personnel and Material: Extracts from the Final Report of General John J. Pershing as Chief of Staff," *U.S. Army Recruiting News*, Dec. 15, 1924, 4; John Garry Clifford, *The Citizen Soldiers: The Plattsburg Training Camp Movement, 1913–1920* (Lexington, KY: University Press of Kentucky, 2015); Donald M. Kington, *Forgotten Summers: The Story of the Citizens' Military Training Camps, 1921–1940* (San Francisco, CA: Two Decades, 1995), 10.

77. "Navy and USMC Aid CMTC," *U.S. Army Recruiting News*, May 21, 1921, 15.

78. R. E. Greenwood, *At a Citizen's Military Training Camp, U.S. Army Recruiting News*, May 1, 1921, 14.

79. "Economic Value of CMTC Training: Testimony of Major Archibald G. Thacher, Member of the Easter Department Governing Committee, Military Training Camps Association, before the House Appropriations Committee, January 19, 1921," *U.S. Army Recruiting News*, May 1, 1921, 14.

80. "Navy and USMC Aid CMTC," 15.

81. Adele Daniel, "A Young Man I Know Should Attend the ACMTC," *U.S. Army Recruiting News*, June 15, 1924, 5.

82. "The Radio Corporation and C.M.T.C." *U.S. Army Recruiting News*, Dec. 15, 1924, 7.

83. Kington, *Forgotten Summers*, 165–168.

84. W. E. B. DuBois, untitled article, *Crisis*, Feb. 1924, 151; Kington, *Forgotten Summers*, 166.

85. Michael S. Sherry, *In the Shadow of War: The United States since the 1930s* (New Haven, CT: Yale University Press, 1995), 10–11.

86. Hiram Johnson quoted in Coffman, *Regulars*, 228.

87. Sen. Kenneth McKellar, Apr. 12, 1920, 66th Cong., 2nd sess., *Congressional Record* 59, no. 105:5951–5952, ("Subject") File 1918–1921, Box 12, NM-84, Entry 376, RG 165, NARA II.

88. Frank Crane, "The Army as Educator," *U.S. Army Recruiting News*, May 15, 1924, 8.

89. Rep. Anthony J. Griffin, "Army and Navy Training for Boys," speech in the House, Mar. 26, 1924, in *U.S. Army Recruiting News*, May 15, 1924, 12.

90. Capt. E. S. West, Morale Officer to Chief, Morale Branch, "Erroneous Statement and Comment in Public Press," Mar. 16, 1920, General Correspondence ("Subject") File 1918–1921, Box 24, NM-84, Entry 376, RG 165, NARA II.

91. Memorandum for the Director, War Plans Division, "Certain Views from Officers of the Army in Educational and Recreation Work," Jan. 10, 1921, General Correspondence ("Subject") File 1918–1921, Box 24, NM-84, Entry 376, RG 165, NARA II.

92. R. A. McMullen, "A Study of the History of Marine Corps Football on the West Coast 1917–1940," 1972, 1–4, Football, Subject Files, RB, USMCHD.

93. Wanda Ellen Wakefield, *Playing to Win: Sports and the American Military, 1898–1945* (Albany: State University of New York Press, 1997), 35–37; Daniels, "Training Men for the Navy and the Nation," 24; Craige, "Vocational Training in the Marine Corps," 41–42.

94. Daniels, "Training Men for the Navy and the Nation," 24.

95. *U.S. Marines: Duties, Experiences, Pay*, 10th ed. (New York: U.S. Marine Corps Publicity Bureau, 1919), 15–14.

96. Maj. Joseph C. Fegan, "Athletics as Publicity," *Marine Corps Gazette*, Mar. 1923, 16.

97. Craige, "Vocational Training in the Marine Corps," 41–42.

98. Josephus Daniels to Smedley Butler, Dec. 6, 1920, Butler Papers, PPC, USMCHD.

99. Smedley Butler to Thomas Butler, Nov. 19, 1920, Butler Papers, PPC, USMCHD.

100. Butler to Butler, Nov. 19, 1920.

101. Smedley Butler to Eppa Hunton Jr., President, R.R.&P. Railroad, Sept. 21, 1922, Butler Papers, PPC, USMCHD; Smedley Butler to T. L. Eyre, Sept. 22, 1922, Butler Papers, PPC, USMCHD; "Marines Build Stadium with Waste Material," *Syracuse (NY) Herald*, Nov. 1, 1922, 15; "Marines' Stadium Built of Waste," *Boston Globe*, Nov. 1, 1922, 10. See also John A. Lejeune, "Report of the Major General Commandant of the United States Marine Corps," in *Annual Report of the Navy Department for the Fiscal Year 1923* (Washington, DC: Government Printing Office, 1923), 970.

102. Smedley Butler to Richard Peters Jr., Apr. 26, 1922, Butler Papers, PPC, USMCHD.

103. Butler to Eyre, Sept. 22, 1922.

104. Butler to Peters, Apr. 26, 1922.

105. Butler to Peters, Apr. 26, 1922; Schmidt, *Maverick Marine*, 139.

106. Butler to Eyre, Sept. 22, 1922; Schmidt, *Maverick Marine*, 129–143. The 1923 Quantico football team had approximately fifty players. They ranged in age from nineteen to thirty-four, but most of the Marines were in their middle to late twenties. They ranged in weight from 140 to 198 pounds, with most of them being between 160 and 185 pounds. Harry Keck, "Third Corps again Humbled by Marines," *Marines Review*, Jan. 1924, 10, clipping, Football 1920s, Subject Files, RB, USMCHD.

107. Edna Loftus Smith, "Stop Goettge!," Mar. 15, 1956, Football, Subject Files, RB, USMCHD; Frank Goettge, 1921 Players, Football 1920s, Subject Files, RB, USMCHD.

108. "Prominent Government Officials See Marines Down 3rd Army Corps, 20–0," *New York Times*, Dec. 4, 1921, 114.

109. "Marines Defeat Georgetown," *Leatherneck*, Nov. 4, 1922, 1–2.

110. "Marines Defeat Georgetown," 1–2; "Baseball Is Losing Out," *New Castle (PA) News*, Sept. 22, 1920, 11; Arthur L. Knapp, "Famous Goettge among Stars Not to Play in 1925," *Washington Post*, Dec. 19, 1924, 23; "Tom Henry Stars for Marine Football Team," *Alton (IL) Evening Telegraph*, Nov. 28, 1923, 2.

111. Ford Ovid Rogers, interview by Benis M. Frank, Oral History Unit, Historical Branch, G-3 Division, Apr. 1966, OHC, USMCHD, transcript, 107; Schmidt, *Maverick Marine*, 139.

112. Butler to Peters, Apr. 26, 1922.

113. "Michigan Defeats Marines by 26–6," *New York Times*, Nov. 11, 1923, 4.

114. "Marines Vanquish Third Army Corps," *New York Times*, Dec. 2, 1923, 1.

115. "Schedules of Marine Corps Football Teams," Football, Subject Files, RB, USMCHD.

116. H. C. Byrd, "Goettge Is Outstanding Star of Tense Struggle," newspaper clipping, ca. Dec. 1923, Football Famous Players, Subject Files, RB, USMCHD.

117. Byrd, "Goettge Is Outstanding Star."

118. John W. Beckett and Harry B. Liversedge, Football Famous Players, Subject Files, RB, USMCHD; Keck, "Third Corps again Humbled by Marines," Football 1920s, Subject Files, RB, USMCHD.

119. Homer L. Overly, "A Marine Patrol," 37, Homer L. Overly Papers, PPC, USMCHD.

120. Cameron, *American Samurai*, 27.

121. Fegan, "Athletics as Publicity," 16.

122. Fegan, 16.

123. Fegan, 17.

124. "Naval Activities from March 4, 1921 to March 4, 1922," Box 4, PC-31, Office of the Secretary of the Navy, 1804–1947, Entry 113, RG 80, NARA I.

125. Schmidt, *Maverick Marine*, 132.

126. John A. Lejeune, "Address Delivered by Major General John A. Lejeune, Commandant, U.S. Marine Corps, at Philadelphia, PA., on the 151st Birthday of the Corps, 10 November 1926," Speeches 1926–29, Speeches and Writings File, Reel 10, Container 11, Papers of John A. Lejeune, LOC.

127. John A. Lejeune, "Address Delivered by Major General John A. Lejeune, Major General Commandant, U.S. Marine Corps, at the Commencement Exercises of Norwich University, Northfield, Vermont, June 16, 1927," 5, Speeches 1926–29, Speeches and Writings File, Reel 10, Container 11, Papers of John A. Lejeune, LOC.

128. John Lejeune, *The Reminiscences of a Marine* (Philadelphia: Dorrance, 1930), 465.

129. Parts of this conclusion appear in Folse, "(R)-Evolutionary Tenure of Commandant Lejeune," 22–27.

8. The Marine Corps "Trys to Make Men"

1. Arthur W. Hanson File, 6th Marine Regiment, WWIQF, USAHEC.

2. William A. Dodge and Frank Lincoln Merrill Files, 6th Marine Regiment, WWIQF, USAHEC; Edward R. Adams, Houston D. Donoho, and Jesse H. Garrett Files, 5th Marine Regiment, ibid.

3. Alpha C. Miller File, 6th Marine Regiment, WWIQF, USAHEC.

4. James E. Swiger File, 6th Marine Regiment, WWIQF, USAHEC.

5. Ned B. Rundell File, 6th Marine Regiment, WWIQF, USAHEC.

6. Anders L. Peterson, William A. Bihary, Donoho, and George H. Donaldson Files, 6th Marine Regiment, WWIQF, USAHEC; Malcom D. Aitken File, 5th Marine Regiment, WWIQF, USAHEC.

7. Richard Lilliard File, 5th Marine Regiment, WWIQF, USAHEC; William E. Almond File, 6th Marine Regiment, WWIQF, USAHEC.

8. Peterson File, 6th Marine Regiment, WWIQF, USAHEC.

9. Wilbert H. Norton, Furman L. Nuss, and Raymond F. Woerter, 5th Marine Regiment, WWIQF, USAHEC; Oliver Freeman and Rundell Files, 6th Marine Regiment, WWIQF, USAHEC; Huebner, *Love and Death in the Great War*, 278.

10. Rundell File, 6th Marine Regiment, WWIQF, USAHEC; Huebner, *Love and Death in the Great War*, 278.

11. Freeman, William H. Snead, and Donoho Files, 5th Marine Regiment, WWIQF, USAHEC; Samuel Lindsay Crawford, 6th Marine Regiment, WWIQF, USAHEC.

12. Lisa M. Budreau, *Bodies of War: World War I and the Politics of Commemoration in America, 1919–1933* (New York: New York University Press, 2010), 3; Kimberly J. Lamay-Licursi, *Remembering World War I in America* (Lincoln: University of Nebraska Press, 2018), xv; Huebner, *Love and Death in the Great War*, 281; Steven Trout, *On the Battlefield of Memory: The First World War and American Remembrance, 1919–1941* (Tuscaloosa: University of Alabama Press, 2010), 12.

13. Catlin, *With the Help of God and a Few Marines*, 27.

14. Catlin, 114.

15. Catlin, 116.

16. Catlin, 296.

17. Lamay-Licursi, *Remembering World War I in America*, 58–59.

18. Lamay-Licursi, 60.

19. Lamay-Licursi, 122; Huebner, *Love and Death in the Great War*, 281; Trout, *Battlefield of Memory*, 7.

20. Boyd, *Through the Wheat*, 179–180.

21. Anderson Maxwell and Laurence Stallings, *What Price Glory: A Play in Three Acts* (New York: Harcourt Brace, 1926).

22. John W. Thomason, *Marines and Others* (New York: Charles Scribner's Sons, 1929), 194.

23. Thomason, 146.

24. Thomason, 152–156.

25. Philip D. Beidler quoted in introduction to William March, *Company K* (Tuscaloosa: University of Alabama Press, 1989), xvii.

26. March, 222–223.

27. March, 227.

28. March, 251–253.

29. March, 101–102.

30. March, 127.

31. Schmidt, *Maverick Marine*, 204–205.

32. Schmidt, 209–210.

33. Schmidt, 210; Pedro Augusto Del Valle, interviewed by Benis M. Frank, Nov. 15, 1966, OHC, USMCHD, transcript, 45.

34. Schmidt, *Maverick Marine*, 212.

35. Smedley D. Butler, *War Is a Racket*, ed. Adam Parfrey (Los Angeles: Feral House, 2003), 24.

36. John Milton Cooper Jr., "The World War and American Memory," in *Beyond 1917: The United States and the Global Legacies of the Great War*, ed. Thomas W. Zeiler, David K. Ekbladh, and Benjamin C. Montoya (New York: Oxford University Press, 2017), 59.

37. Abbot, *Soldiers of the Sea*, 297–306; Metcalf, *History of the United States Marine Corps*, 482–490; John H. Craige, *What You Should Know about the Marines* (New York: Norton, 1941), 22; Philip N. Pierce and Frank O. Hough, *The Compact History of the United States Marine Corps*, 2nd ed. (New York: Hawthorn Books, 1964), 182–183; Simmons, *United States Marines*, 97–100. Moskin, *U.S. Marine Corps Story*, 112–124.

38. Paul Westermeyer, "The Rise of the Early Modern Marine Corps and World War I," in *The Legacy of Belleau Wood: 100 Years of Making Marines and Winning Battles*, ed. Paul Westermeyer and Breanne Robertson (Quantico, VA: History Division, USMC, 1918), 2.

39. Homer L. Overly, "A Marine Patrol," 39–40, Hover L. Overly Papers, PPC, USMCHD.

40. Merwin W. Silverthorne, interviewed by Benis M. Frank, Feb. 28, 1969, OHC, USMCHD, transcript.

41. "Yesterday and Today," *Leatherneck*, Aug. 1930, 26.

42. Edward B. Irving, "How Does the Marine Corps of 1918 Compare with the Marine Corps of 1942?," *Leatherneck*, Nov. 1942, 272.

43. "Marine Corps Fiscal Year End Strengths, 1798–2015," History Division, Marine Corps University, https://www.usmcu.edu/Research/Marine-Corps-History-Division/Research-Tools-Facts-and-Figures/End-Strengths/ (accessed Feb. 16, 2022); "Marine Corps Casualties: 1775–2016," History Division, Marine Corps University, https://www.usmcu.edu/Research/Marine-Corps-History-Division/Research-Tools-Facts-and-Figures/Marine-Corps-Casualties-1775-2016/ (accessed Feb. 16, 2022).

44. Eugene Sledge, *With the Old Breed: At Peleliu and Okinawa* (New York: Oxford University Press, 1990), 13, 121.

45. Sledge, 38.

46. Historian James Gilbert makes no distinction. Gilbert, *Men in the Middle: Searching for Masculinity in the 1950s* (Chicago: University of Chicago Press, 2005), 15–17. Although Kyle A. Cuordileone addresses the differences between the terms, he does not apply those differences to his analysis. Cuordileone, *Manhood and*

American Political Culture in the Cold War (New York: Routledge, 2005), 12. Gregory A. Daddis favors "masculinity." See Daddis, *Pulp Vietnam*.

47. Cameron, *American Samurai*, 48.

48. Ulbrich, *Preparing for Victory*, 119; John W. Gordon, "Thomas Holcomb," in *Commandants of the Marine Corps*, ed. Allan R. Millett and Jack Shulimson (Annapolis, MD: Naval Institute Press, 2004), 274.

49. Holcomb quoted in Gordon, "Thomas Holcomb," 274.

50. Cameron McCoy, "Mr. President, What of the Marines?: The Politics of Contested Integration and the Domestic Legacy of the Modern Black Leatherneck in Cold War America" (PhD diss., University of Texas at Austin, 2017), 14.

51. Zayna N. Bizri, "From Making Men to Making Marines: Marine Corps Recruiting during World War II," *Marine Corps History* 1, no. 1 (2015): 33.

52. Council on Foreign Relations, "Demographics of the U.S. Military," last updated July 13, 2020, https://www.cfr.org/backgrounder/demographics-us-military (accessed Dec. 17, 2020).

53. Rebecca Lane et al., "Marine Corps Organizational Culture Research Project Report to Personnel Studies and Oversight Office: Marines' Perspectives on Various Aspects of Marine Corps Organizational Culture," Mar. 30, 2018, 49–50, https://www.usmcu.edu/Portals/218/CAOCL/files/MCOCR%20Report%20to%20PSO%2030Mar18_wDem_FINAL.pdf?ver=2019-09-05-135301-060 (accessed Dec. 17, 2020).

54. "Marine Corps Casualties: 1775–2016" (accessed Feb. 16, 2022).

55. William M. Donnelly, "'The Best Army That Can Be Put in the Field in the Circumstances': The U.S. Army, July 1951–July 1953," *Journal of Military History* 71, no. 3 (July 2007): 839–841. See also Donnelly, "A Damn Hard Job: James A. Van Fleet and the Combat Effectiveness of U.S. Army Infantry, July 1951–February 1953," *Journal of Military History* 82, no. 1 (Jan. 2018).

56. For an in-depth discussion of the Korean War's influence on Marine culture, see in O'Connell, *Underdogs*, 148–150, 187–191. See also Andrew J. Huebner, *The Warrior Image: Soldiers in American Culture from the Second World War to the Vietnam Era* (Chapel Hill: University of North Carolina Press, 2008), 98–99.

57. Walter K. Wilson III, "Reality: The Basic Premise of Democracy Is Philosophically Incompatible with the Efficiency of a Military Organization," *Marine Corps Gazette*, Feb. 1955, 37.

58. Krulak, *First to Fight*, xv. See also Krulak, "Who Needs a Marine Corps?," *Leatherneck*, July 1975, 11.

59. Gilbert, *Men in the Middle*, 4.

60. Cuordileone, *Manhood and American Political Culture*, 46–47.

61. Zell Miller, *Corps Values* (Atlanta: Longstreet, 1997), 8.

62. William M. Donnelly, "From Sergeant Snorkels to Drill Sergeants: Basic Training of Male Soldiers in the U.S. Army, 1953–1964," *Journal of Military History* 86, no. 2 (Apr. 2022).

63. O'Connell, *Underdogs*, 188–189; Millett, *Semper Fidelis*, 528–531.

64. Heather M. Stur, *Beyond Combat: Women and Gender in the Vietnam War Era* (New York: Cambridge University Press, 2011), 4; Huebner, *Warrior Image*, 250; Daddis, *Pulp Vietnam*, 7; Bobby A. Wintermute and David J. Ulbrich, *Race and Gender in Modern Western Warfare* (Boston: De Gruyter, 2018), 314.

65. Kara Dixon Vuic, *The Girls Next Door: Bringing the Home Front to the Front Lines* (Cambridge, MA: Harvard University Press, 2019), 3.

66. Daddis, *Pulp Vietnam*, 5.

67. Wintermute and Ulbrich, *Race and Gender in Modern Western Warfare*, 315–316.

68. Stur, *Beyond Combat*, 1–2, 38–40; Vuic, *Girls Next Door*, 196–198.

69. Philip Caputo, *A Rumor of War* (1977; repr., New York: Henry Holt, 1996), 6.

70. Caputo, 7. See also Daddis, *Pulp Vietnam*, 5, 17, 185.

71. Caputo, *Rumor of War*, 35.

72. Caputo, 188.

73. Caputo, 331.

74. "Marine Corps Casualties: 1775–2015" (accessed May 26, 2022).

75. Anthony Swofford, *Jarhead: A Marine's Chronicle of the Gulf War and Other Battles* (New York: Scribner, 2003), 203.

76. Swofford, 56, 110.

77. Swofford, 247.

78. P. J. Neal, "Forgetting Victor Krulak," U.S. Naval Institute *Proceedings* 146 (Oct. 2020), https://www.usni.org/magazines/proceedings/2020/october/forgetting-victor-krulak (accessed Dec. 17, 2020).

79. "Marine Corps Casualties: 1775–2015" (accessed May 26, 2022).

80. Richard O. Jordan, William A. Bihary, and Kenneth L. Payne Files, 6th Marine Regiment, WWIQF, USAHEC.

Conclusion

1. Shawn Snow, "Seven Marines Court-Martialed in Wake of Marines United Scandal," *Marine Corps Times*, Mar. 1, 2018, https://www.marinecorpstimes.com/news/your-marine-corps/2018/03/01/seven-marines-court-martialed-in-wake-of-marines-united-scandal/ (accessed Dec. 17, 2020).

2. Geoff Ziezulewicz, "UCMJ Crackdown: Why Mattis Thinks Commanders Have Gone Soft on Misconduct," *Military Times*, Sept. 10, 2018, https://www.militarytimes.com/news/your-military/2018/09/10/ucmj-crackdown-why-mattis-thinks-commanders-have-gone-soft-on-misconduct/ (accessed Dec. 18, 2020); Meghann Myers, "A Culture That Fosters Sexual Assaults and Sexual Harassment Persists despite Prevention Efforts, a New Pentagon Study Shows," *Military Times*, Apr. 30, 2020, https://www.militarytimes.com/news/your-military/2020/04/30/a-culture-that-fosters-sexual-assaults-and-sexual-harassment-persists-despite-prevention-efforts-a-new-pentagon-study-shows/ (accessed Dec. 18, 2020).

3. Heather Venable, "How the Few Become the Valued: Improving Recruitment and Retention of Female Marines," *U.S. Naval Institute Proceedings* 146 (Oct. 2020), https://www.usni.org/magazines/proceedings/2020/october/how-few-become-valued-improving-recruitment-and-retention-female (accessed Dec. 18, 2018).

4. James Joyner, "Fear of a Black General?," Ideas, Defense One, Sept. 1, 2020, https://www.defenseone.com/ideas/2020/09/race-and-marine-corps-generals/168162/ (accessed Dec. 17, 2020).

5. Mallory Shelborne, "White House Nominates First Black Marine for Fourth

Star," *USNI News*, June 9, 2022, https://news.usni.org/2022/06/09/white-house-no minates-first-black-marine-for-fourth-star (accessed June 10, 2022).

6. Agnes Gereben Scheafer et al., *Implications of Integrating Women into the Marine Corps Infantry* (RAND Corporation, 2015), xiv.

7. Warren, *American Spartans*, 11–33.

8. Sturkey, *Warrior Culture of the U.S. Marines*, xii.

9. Cameron, *American Samurai*; O'Connell, *Underdogs*; Venable, *How the Few Became the Proud.*

10. Allan R. Millett, "The U.S. Marine Corps, 1973–2017: Cultural Preservation in Every Place and Clime," in *The Culture of Military Organizations*, ed. Peter Mansoor and Williamson Murray (New York: Cambridge University Press, 2019), 383; Mark R. Folse, "Tell This to the Marines: Gender and the Marine Corps," *War on the Rocks*, Mar. 5, 2020, https://warontherocks.com/2020/03/tell-this-to-the-marin es-gender-and-the-marine-corps/ (accessed Dec. 18, 2020).

11. David Berger quoted in Philip Athey, "The Corps Can't Complete Its Missions without Women, Minorities, Top Marine Says," *Marine Times*, Sept. 11, 2020, https://www.marinecorpstimes.com/news/your-marine-corps/2020/09/11/the -corps-cant-complete-its-missions-without-women-minorities-top-marine-says/ (accessed Dec. 18, 2020).

12. U.S. Marine Corps Headquarters, "Force Design 2030," Mar. 2020, 1–3, https://www.hqmc.marines.mil/Portals/142/Docs/CMC38%20Force%20Design %202030%20Report%20Phase%20I%20and%20II.pdf?ver=2020-03-26-121328 -460 (accessed June 13, 2022).

13. U.S. Marine Corps Headquarters, "Talent Management 2030," Nov. 2021, 6, https://www.hqmc.marines.mil/Portals/142/Users/183/35/4535/Talent%20Man agement%202030_November%202021.pdf (accessed June 13, 2022).

14. "Talent Management 2030," 6.

15. Charles Krulak, Jack Sheehan, and Anthony Zinni, "War Is a Dirty Business. Will the Marine Corps Be Ready for the Next One?," *Washington Post*, Apr. 22, 2022, https://www.washingtonpost.com/opinions/2022/04/22/marines-restruc turing-plan-scrutiny-generals/ (accessed June 10, 2022); Paul K. Van Riper, "Jeopardizing National Security: What Is Happening to Our Marine Corps?," *Marine Corps Times*, Mar. 21, 2022, https://www.marinecorpstimes.com/opinion/comment ary/2022/03/21/jeopardizing-national-security-what-is-happening-to-our-marine -corps/ (accessed June 10, 2022); Stephen W. Larose, "A View from the Trenches on the Debate Wracking the Marine Corps," *War on the Rocks*, May 6, 2022, https:// warontherocks.com/2022/05/a-view-from-the-trenches-on-the-debate-wracking -the-marine-corps/ (accessed June 10, 2022).

16. James Livingston and Jay Vargas, "How the Nation's Corps of Marines Has Lost Its Way," *Marine Times*, Apr. 10, 2023, https://www.marinecorpstimes.com /opinion/commentary/2023/04/10/how-the-nations-corps-of-marines-has-lost -its-way/ (accessed Apr. 13, 2023).

17. Todd South, "Lethal and Survivable or Irrelevant and Vulnerable?: Marine Redesign Debate Rages," *Marine Corps Times*, May 16, 2022, https://www.marine corpstimes.com/news/your-marine-corps/2022/05/16/lethal-and-survivable-or-ir relevant-and-vulnerable-marine-corps-redesign-debate-rages/ (accessed June 10, 2022); Worth Parker, "How the Marine Corps Went to War with Itself over the

Next War," *Task & Purpose*, June 10, 2022, https://taskandpurpose.com/news/ma
rine-corps-warfighting-force-design/ (accessed June 11, 2022).

18. Robert Work, "Force Design 2030: A Threat or Big Opportunity?," *1945*,
May 15, 2022, https://www.19fortyfive.com/2022/05/usmc-force-design-2030-thre
at-or-opportunity/ (accessed June 11, 2022); Van Riper quoted in Smith, "Lethal
and Survivable" (accessed June 10, 2022).

19. U.S. Marine Corps (@marines), "Kevlar helmet in recognition of Pride
Month," Instagram photo, June 1, 2022, https://www.instagram.com/p/CeQ8K6
1O_iv/?igshid=YmMyMTA2M2Y= (accessed June 15, 2022).

20. U.S. Marine Corps Recruiting (@usmarinecorps), "The Marine Corps Is
Committed to the Values We Defend, Treating Everyone Equally—with Dignity
and Respect," Instagram photo, June 1, 2022, https://www.instagram.com/p/CeRB
zSZs9bI/?igshid=YmMyMTA2M2Y= (accessed June 15, 2022).

Bibliography

Archival Sources

Chester A. Nimitz Library, Special Collections and Archives, U.S. Naval Academy, Annapolis. MD
RG 405.2.1 Office of the Superintendent, Correspondence
Entry 3: Press Copies of Letters Sent by the Superintendent, 1865–1911
Entry 21: Letters and Memorandums Sent by the Superintendent to Academy Officers, Instructors, and Cadets, 1881–1885
Entry 22: Press Copies of Letters and Memorandums Sent by the Superintendent to Academy Officers, Instructors, and Cadets, 1884–1908

Library of Congress, Washington, DC
Chronicling America: Historic American Newspapers. https://chroniclingameri ca.loc.gov/
Papers of John A. Lejeune
World War I Posters. https://www.loc.gov/pictures/collection/wwipos/

National Archives and Records Administration, College Park, MD
RG 127 Records of the U.S. Marine Corps
    Division of Public Relations, Radio Scripts, 1933–45
RG 165 Records of the War Department General and Special Staffs
    Entry 376: War College Division and War Plans Division, Subordinate Offices, Morale Branch, 1918–21
RG 287 Publications of the Federal Government
    Navy Department, 1828–1947

National Archives and Records Administration, Washington, DC
RG 80 General Records of the Department of the Navy, 1798–1947
    Office of the Secretary of the Navy, 1804–1947
        Entry 113: Office of Public Relations, Press Releases, January 1917–December 1936
RG 127 Records of the U.S. Marine Corps
    Entry 18: General Correspondence, Office of the Commandant, 1913–38
    Entry 37: General Correspondence, Recruitment, 1921–39
    Entry 38: General Correspondence, Operations and Training Division, Intelligence Section, 1915–34
    Expeditionary Forces and Detachments, 1835–1949

National Personnel Record Center, St. Louis, MO
Charles F. Merkel Personnel Files
George C. Thorpe Personnel Files
Thad Taylor Personnel Files

Ohio Historical Society, Columbus
Manuscripts/Audiovisual Collections
    Thomas Boyd Papers

U.S. Army Heritage and Education Center, U.S. Army War College, Carlisle, PA
World War I Questionnaire Files
    5th Marine Regiment
        Edward R. Adams File
        Malcom D. Aitken File
        John E. Ausland File
        William N. Betts File
        Lester D. Birdsong File
        Edward L. Brown File
        Houston D. Donoho File
        William A. Francis File
        Jesse H. Garrett File
        William J. Larson File
        Richard Lilliard File
        Hilding O. Magney File
        Richard B. Millin File
        Wilbert H. Norton File
        Furman L. Nuss File
        Albert E. Powis File
        Carl L. Snare File
        William H. Snead File
        Harold S. Ugland File
        George W. Weingart File
        Raymond F. Woerter File
    6th Machine Gun Battalion
        John C. Ashworth File
        Melvin N. Johnson File
    6th Marine Regiment
        William E. Almond File
        Robert J. Benedict File
        William A. Bihary File
        Lessiter Brownwell File
        Peter P. Bymers File
        Samuel Lindsay Crawford File
        Alvis E. Curl File
        Carlton B. Davis File
        William A. Dodge File
        George H. Donaldson File

Oliver W. Freeman File
Arthur W. Hanson File
James S. Harrington File
John S. Johnson File
Richard O. Jordan File
Norman I. Lott File
Frank Lincoln Merrill File
Alpha C. Miller File
George D. Monroe File
Kenneth L. Payne File
Anders L. Peterson File
Howard Pfeifer File
Ned B. Rundell File
Benjamin F. Shuller File
Raymond H. Stenback File
James F. Swiger File
Rollie K. Waggoner File
Frank Winchester Jr. File

U.S. Marine Corps History Division, Marine Corps Archives, Quantico, VA
Oral History Collection
Victor France Bleasdale
Clifton B. Cates
Edward Arthur Craig
Karl Schmolsmire Day
Pedro Augusto Del Valle
Robert Livingston Denig
Graves Blanchard Erskine
Lewis J. Fields
Walter Scott Gaspar
Leo David Hermle
Louis Reeder Jones
Robert C. Kilmartin Jr.
Melvin Levin Krulewitch
Ivan W. Miller
Francis Patrick Mulcahy
David Rowan Nimmer
Alfred Houston Noble
Pearl Oagley
DeWitt Peck
Omar Titus Pfeiffer
Edwin Allen Pollock
Lewis Burwell Puller
Bennet Puryear Jr.
Ray Albert Robinson
Ford Ovid Rogers
William Walter Rogers

Christian Frank Schilt
Lemuel Cornick Shepherd Jr.
Merwin Silverthorne
Julian Constable Smith
Gerald Carthrae Thomas
William Jennings Wallace
William Arthur Worton
Personal Papers Collections
George Barnett Papers
Hiram Bearss Papers
Smedley Butler Papers
Clifton B. Cates Papers
Albert W. Catlin Papers
Edward A. Craig Papers
Earl Ellis Papers
Logan Feland Papers
Ben Fuller Papers
Robert Huntington Papers
Adolph Bradlee Miller Papers
Homer L. Overly Papers
Joseph Pendleton Papers
Herman Priebe Papers
Lee S. Rose Papers
John H. Russell Papers
George C. Thorpe Papers
Alexander Vandegrift Papers
Littleton Waller Jr. Papers
Percy A. Webb Papers
Paul Woyshner Papers
Reference Branch, Biographical and Subject Files
Dominican Republic Geographic Files
Famous Football Players
Football
Football 1920s
1921 Players
Haitian Geographic Files

Newspapers and Magazines

Ada (OK) Evening News
Anniston (AL) Star
Atlantic Monthly
Bar Harbor (ME) Times
Biloxi (MS) Daily Herald
Boston Daily Globe
Boston Evening Globe

Bryan (TX) Daily Eagle
Cleveland Gazette
Chicago Daily Tribune
Des Moines Daily News
Hattiesburg (MS) American
Helena (MT) Independent Record
Journal of Race Development
Literary Digest
Madison Wisconsin State Journal
Manitoba Free Press
Metropolitan Magazine
Montgomery (AL) Advertiser
Nation
National Service Magazine
New Republic
New York Times
New York Tribune
Pan American Magazine
Poseyville (IN) News
Quanah Tribune-Chief (Bryan, TX)
Rural Manhood
Saturday Evening Post
Scribner's Magazine Illustrated
Thomasville (GA) Times-Enterprise
Washington Bee
Washington Post

Armed Forces Newspapers, Magazines, and Journals

Marine Corps Gazette
Marines' Bulletin
Marines' Magazine
National Service Magazine
Our Navy
Recruiters' Bulletin
United States Army and Navy Journal
U.S. Army Recruiting News
U.S. Naval Institute *Proceedings*

Books, Articles, and Dissertations

Abbot, Willis J. *Soldiers of the Sea: The Story of the United States Marine Corps.* New York: Dodd, Mead, 1918.
Adams, Michael C. C. *The Great Adventure: Male Desire and the Coming of World War I.* Bloomington: Indiana University Press, 1990.

Alexander, Joseph. *Through the Wheat: The U.S. Marines in World War I*. Annapolis, MD: Naval Institute Press, 1996.

Annual Reports of the Navy Department for the Fiscal Year [1913–1932]. Washington, DC: Government Printing Office, [1914–33].

Asprey, Robert B. *At Belleau Wood*. Denton: University of North Texas Press, 1996.

Axelrod, Alan. *Miracle at Belleau Wood: The Birth of the Modern U.S. Marine Corps*. Guilford, CT: Lyons, 2007.

Babb, Valerie. *Whiteness Visible: The Meaning of Whiteness in American Literature and Culture*. New York: New York University Press, 1998.

Baldwin, Hanson W. *What the Citizen Should Know about the Navy*. New York: W. W. Norton, 1941.

Ballendorf, Dirk A., and Merrill Lewis Bartlett. *Pete Ellis: An Amphibious Warfare Prophet, 1880–1923*. Annapolis, MD: Naval Institute Press, 1997.

Bederman, Gail. *Manliness and Civilization: A Cultural History of Gender and Race in the United States, 1880–1917*. Chicago: University of Chicago Press, 1996.

Belkin, Aaron. *Bring Me Men: Military Masculinity and the Benign Façade of American Empire, 1898–2001*. New York: Columbia University Press, 2012.

Bell, Ian. *The Dominican Republic*. Boulder, CO: Westview, 1980.

Berry, Henry. *Make the Kaiser Dance*. New York: Doubleday, 1978.

Bettez, David J. *Kentucky Marine: Major General Logan Feland and the Making of the Modern USMC*. Lexington: University Press of Kentucky, 2014.

Bickel, Keith B. *Mars Learning: The Marine Corps Development of Small Wars Doctrine, 1915–1940*. Boulder CO: Westview, 2001.

Birtle, Andrew J. *U.S. Army Counterinsurgency and Contingency Operations Doctrine, 1860–1941*. Washington, DC: U.S. Army Center of Military History, 2009.

Bishop, Giles. *Lieutenant Comstock, U.S. Marine*. Philadelphia: Penn Publishing, 1922.

———. *The Marines Have Landed*. Philadelphia: Penn Publishing, 1920.

Bizri, Zayna N. "Recruiting Women into the World War II Military: The Office of War Information, Advertising, and Gender." PhD diss., George Mason University, 2017. https://www.proquest.com/openview/158f6b29e6d1ec865f1bofe408fd3065/1.pdf?pq-origsite=gscholar&cbl=18750&diss=y.

Boeckmann, Cathy. *A Question of Character: Scientific Racism and the Genres of American Fiction, 1892–1912*. Tuscaloosa: University of Alabama Press, 2000.

Boot, Max. *The Savage Wars of Peace: Small Wars and the Rise of American Power*. New York: Basic Books, 2002.

Bordo, Susan. *The Male Body: A New Look at Men in Public and Private*. New York: Farrar, Straus, & Giroux, 1999.

Boyd, Thomas. *Through the Wheat: A Novel of the World War I Marines*. Lincoln: University of Nebraska Press, 2000.

———. *Points of Honor: Short Stories of the Great War by a U.S. Combat Marine*. Edited by Steven Trout. Tuscaloosa: University of Alabama Press, 2018.

Brinck-Johnsen, Kim. "Playing the Man: Masculinity, Performance, and United States Foreign Policy, 1901–20." PhD diss., University of New Hampshire, 2004.

Brisco, Norris A. *Economics of Efficiency*. New York: Macmillan, 1921.

Bristow, Nancy K. *Making Men Moral: Social Engineering during the Great War*. New York: New York University Press, 1996.

Brown, Ronald J. *A Few Good Men: The Story of the Fighting Fifth Marines*. Novato, CA: Presidio Press, 2001.

Browne-Marshall, Gloria J. *Race, Law, and American Society, 1607 to Present*. New York: Routledge, 2007.

Budreau, Lisa M. *Bodies of War: World War I and the Politics of Commemoration in America, 1919–1933*. New York: New York University Press, 2010.

Butler, Smedley Darlington. *General Smedley Darlington Butler: The Letters of a Leatherneck, 1898–1931*. Edited by Anne Cipriano Venzon. New York: Praeger, 1992.

Calder, Bruce J. *The Impact of Intervention: The Dominican Republic during the U.S. Occupation of 1916–1924*. Austin: University of Texas Press, 1984.

Cameron, Craig M. *American Samurai: Myth, Imagination, and the Conduct of Battle in the First Marine Division, 1941–1951*. Cambridge: Cambridge University Press, 1994.

Capozzola, Christopher. *Uncle Same Wants You: World War I and the Making of the Modern American Citizen*. New York: Oxford University Press, 2008.

Carnes, Mark C. "Middle Class Men and the Solace of Fraternal Ritual." In *Meanings for Manhood*, edited by Mark C. Carnes and Clyde Griffen, 37–66. Chicago: University of Chicago Press, 1990.

———. *Secret Ritual and Manhood in Victorian America*. New Haven, CT: Yale University Press, 1989.

Catlin, Albertus W. *With the Help of God and a Few Marines*. With Walter A. Dyer. New York: Doubleday, Page, 1919.

Clark, George B. *Devil Dogs: Fighting Marines of World War I*. Novato, CA: Presidio, 1999.

———. *The Second Infantry Division in World War I: A History of the American Expeditionary Force Regulars, 1917–1919*. Jefferson, NC: McFarland, 2007.

Clifford, Kenneth J. *Progress and Purpose: A Developmental History of the United States Marine Corps 1900–1970*. Washington, DC: History and Museums Division, Headquarters, U.S. Marine Corps, 1973.

Clymer, R. Swinburne. *The Way to Godhood*. Allentown, PA: Philosophical Publishing, 1914.

Coffman, Edward M. *The Old Army: A Portrait of the American Army in Peacetime, 1784–1898*. New York: Oxford University Press, 1986.

———. *The Regulars: The American Army, 1898–1941*. Cambridge, MA: Harvard University Press, 2004.

———. *The War to End All Wars: The American Military Experience in World War I*. Lexington: University Press of Kentucky, 1998.

Colbourn, Colin. "Esprit de Marine Corps: The Making of the Modern Marine Corps through Public Relations, 1898–1945." PhD diss., University of Southern Mississippi, 2018. https://aquila.usm.edu/dissertations/1593/.

Cole, Bernard D. *Gunboats and Marines: The Unites States Navy in China, 1925–1928*. Newark, NJ: University of Delaware Press,1983.

Coletta, Paolo E., and Jack K. Bauer, eds. *United States Navy and Marine Corps Bases, Overseas*. Westport CT: Greenwood, 1985.

Connable, Ben. "Warrior-Maverick Culture: The Evolution of Adaptability in the U.S. Marine Corps." PhD diss., Kings College London, 2016. https://kclpure

.kcl.ac.uk/portal/en/theses/warriormaverick-culture(b9316ae2-345f-4bde-8e
e9-790260261fd4).html.

Connell, R. W. *Masculinities*. 2nd ed. Los Angeles: University of California Press, 2005.

Cooper, John Milton, Jr. "The World War and American Memory." In *Beyond 1917: The United States and the Global Legacies of the Great War*, edited by Thomas W. Zeiler, David K. Ekbladh, and Benjamin C. Montoya, 54–68. New York: Oxford University Press, 2017.

Coram, Robert. *Brute: The Life of Victor Krulak, U.S. Marine*. New York: Little, Brown, 2010.

Coupeau, Steeve. *The History of Haiti*. Westport, CT: Greenwood, 2008.

Cowing, Kemper F., comp. *"Dear Folks at Home—": The Glorious Story of the United States Marines in France as Told by Their Letters from the Battlefield*. Edited by Courtney R. Cooper. New York: Houghton Mifflin, 1919.

Craige, John H. *Black Bagdad: The Arabian Nights Adventures of a Marine Captain in Haiti*. London: Stanley Paul, 1933.

Crowell, Benedict, and Robert F. Wilson. *Demobilization: Our Industrial and Military Demobilization after the Armistice, 1918–1920*. New Haven, CT: Yale University Press, 1921.

Curtis, Susan. "The Son of Man and God the Father: The Social Gospel and Victorian Masculinity." In *Meanings for Manhood*, edited by Mark C. Carnes and Clyde Griffen, 67–78. Chicago: University of Chicago Press, 1990.

Custis, Vanderveer. *The Foundations of National Industrial Efficiency*. New York: Macmillan, 1923.

Daddis, Gregory A. *Pulp Vietnam: War and Gender in Cold War Men's Adventure Magazines*. New York: Cambridge University Press, 2021.

Dalleo, Raphael. *American Imperialism's Undead: The Occupation of Haiti and the Rise of Caribbean Anticolonialism*. Charlottesville: University of Virginia Press, 2016.

Daugherty, Leo J. "To Fight Our Country's Battles': An Institutional History of the United States Marine Corps during the Interwar Era, 1919–1935." PhD diss., Ohio State University, 2001.

———. *The Marine Corps and the State Department: Enduring Partners in United States Foreign Policy, 1798–2007*. Jefferson, NC: McFarland, 2009.

Delvin, Athena. *Between Profits and Primitivism: Shaping White Middle-Class Masculinity in the United States, 1880–1917*. New York: Routledge, 2005.

Donnelly, William M. "'The Best Army That Can Be Put in the Field in the Circumstances': The U.S. Army, July 1951–July 1953." *Journal of Military History* 71, no. 3 (July 2007): 809–847.

———. "A Damn Hard Job: James A. Van Fleet and the Combat Effectiveness of the U.S. Army Infantry, July 1951–February 1953." *Journal of Military History* 82, no. 1 (January 2018): 147–179.

———. "From Sergeant Snorkels to Drill Sergeants: Basic Training of Male Soldiers in the U.S. Army, 1953–1964." *Journal of Military History* 86, no. 2 (April 2022): 399–426.

Douglas, Roy. *The Great War, 1914–1918: The Cartoonists' Vision*. New York: Routledge, 1995.

Dubbert, Joe L. "Progressivism and the Masculinity Crisis." In *The American Man*, edited by Elizabeth H. Pleck and Joseph H. Pleck, 303–320. Englewood Cliffs, NJ: Prentice-Hall, 1980.

Dubois, Laurent. *Haiti: The Aftershocks of History*. New York: Metropolitan Books, 2012.

Ebbert, Jean, and Marie-Beth Hall. *The First the Few the Forgotten: Navy and Marine Corps Women in World War I*. Annapolis, MD: Naval Institute Press, 2002.

Fatton, Robert J. *The Roots of Haitian Despotism*. Boulder, CO: Lynne Rienner, 2007.

Faulkner, Richard S. *Pershing's Crusaders: The American Soldier in World War I*. Lawrence: University Press of Kansas, 2017.

Filene, Peter G. *Him/Her/Self: Sex Roles in Modern America*. Baltimore, MD: Johns Hopkins University Press, 1986.

———. "In Time of War." In *The American Man*, edited by Elizabeth H. Pleck and Joseph H. Pleck, 321–338. Englewood, NJ: Prentice-Hall, 1980.

Finnegan, John Patrick. *Against the Specter of a Dragon: The Campaign for American Military Preparedness, 1914–1917*. Westport, CT: Greenwood, 1974.

Fiske, George Walter. *Boy Life and Self-Government*. New York: Association, 1916.

Flewelling, Ralph Tyler. *Philosophy and the War*. New York: Abingdon, 1918.

Foote, Lorien. *The Gentlemen and the Roughs: Violence, Honor, and Manhood in the Union Army*. New York: New York University Press, 2010.

Fosdick, Harry Emerson. *The Manhood of the Master*. New York: Association, 1916.

Fosdick, Raymond B., and Edward Frank Allen. *Keeping Our Fighters Fit for War and After*. New York: Century, 1918.

Friedman, B. A., ed. *21st Century Ellis: Operational Art and Strategic Prophecy for the Modern Era*. Annapolis, MD: Naval Institute Press, 2015.

Fuller, Stephen M., and Graham A. Cosmas. *Marines in the Dominican Republic*. Washington, DC: History and Museums Division, Headquarters, U.S. Marine Corps, 1974.

Gaddis, Gregory A. *Pulp Vietnam: War and Gender in Cold War Men's Adventure Magazines*. New York: Cambridge University Press, 2021.

Gavin, Lettie. *American Women in World War I: They Also Served*. Niwot: University Press of Colorado, 1997.

Gibbons, Floyd. *"And They Thought We Wouldn't Fight."* New York: George H. Doran, 1918.

Gilbert, James. *Men in the Middle: Searching for Masculinity in the 1950s*. Chicago: University of Chicago Press, 2005.

Gilmore, David D. *Manhood in the Making: Cultural Concepts of Masculinity*. New Haven, CT: Yale University Press, 1990.

Goddard, Henry Herbert. *Human Efficiency and Levels of Intelligence*. Princeton, NJ: Princeton University Press, 1920.

Goldstein, Joshua S. *War and Gender: How Gender Shapes the War System and Vice Versa*. New York: Cambridge University Press, 2001.

Gossett, Thomas F. *Race: The History of an Idea in America*. New York: Oxford University Press, 1997.

Grayzel, Susan R. *Women and the First World War*. New York: Pearson Longman, 2002.

Greenberg, Amy S. *Manifest Manhood and the Antebellum American Empire*. New York: Cambridge University Press, 2005.

Grotelueschen, Mark Ethan. *The AEF War of War: The American Army and Combat in World War I*. New York: Cambridge University Press, 2007.

Gulick, Luther H. *The Dynamic of Manhood*. New York: Association, 1918.

Gutiérrez, Edward A. *Doughboys on The Great War: How American Soldiers Viewed Their Military Service*. Lawrence: University Press of Kansas, 2014.

Hall, G. Stanley. *Adolescence: Its Psychology and Its Relations to Physiology, Anthropology, Sociology, Sex, Crime, Religion, and Education*. Vol. 2. New York: D. Appleton, 1905.

Hall, Winfield S. *Developing into Manhood*. New York: Association, 1911.

Haney-López, Ian F. *White by Law: The Legal Construction of Race*. New York: New York University Press, 1996.

Harrod, Frederick S. *Manning the New Navy: The Development of a Modern Enlisted Force, 1899–1940*. Westport CT: Greenwood, 1978.

Hemrick, Levi E. *Once a Marine*s. Staunton, VA: Clarion, 2013.

Heinl, Robert Debs. *Soldiers of the Sea: The United States Marine Corps, 1775–1962*. Annapolis, MD: Naval Institute Press, 1962.

Hoffman, Jon T. *Chesty: The Story of Lieutenant General Lewis B. Puller, USMC*. New York: Random House, 2001.

Hoganson, Kristin L. *Fighting for American Manhood: How Gender Politics Provoked the Spanish-American and Philippine American Wars*. New Haven, CT: Yale University Press, 1998.

Holmes-Eber, Paula. *Culture in Conflict: Warfare, Culture Policy, and the Marine Corps*. Stanford, CA: Stanford University Press, 2014.

Hudson, Janet G. "The Great War and Expanded Equality: Black Carolinians Test Boundaries." In *The American South and the Great War, 1914–1924*, edited by Matthew L. Downs and M. Ryan Floyd, 140–161. Baton Rouge: Louisiana State University Press, 2018.

Huebner, Andrew J. "Gee I Wish I Were a Man: Gender and the Great War." In *The Routledge History of Gender, War, and the U.S. Military*, edited by Kara Dixon Vuic, 68–86. New York: Routledge, 2018.

———. *Love and Death in the Great War*. New York: Oxford University Press, 2018.

———. *The Warrior Image: Soldiers in American Culture from the Second World War to the Vietnam Era*. Chapel Hill: University of North Carolina Press, 2008.

Hundertmark, Conrad. *The United States Marines: Twenty-Five Poems about Life in the Marine Corps*. Parris Island, SC, 1915.

Hunter, W. J. *Manhood Wrecked and Rescued: How Strength, or Vigor, Is Lost, and How It Can Be Restored by Self-Treatment*. New York: Physical Culture, 1900.

Hutečka, Jiří. *Men under Fire: Motivation, Morale, and Masculinity among Czech Soldiers in the Great War, 1914–1918*. New York: Berghahn Books, 2020.

Irwin, Julia F. *Making the World Safe: The American Red Cross and a Nation's Humanitarian Awakening*. Oxford: Oxford University Press, 2013.

Isely, Jeter A., and Philip A. Crowl. *The U.S. Marines and Amphibious War: Its Theory and Its Practice in the Pacific*. Princeton, NJ: Princeton University Press, 1951.

Jackson, Warren R. *His Time in Hell: A Texas Marine in France: The World War I*

Memoir of Warren R. Jackson. Edited by George B. Clark. Novato, CA: Presidio, 2001.

Jarvis, Christina S. *The Male Body at War: American Masculinity during World War II*. Dekalb: Northern Illinois University Press, 2004.

Jensen, Kimberly. *Mobilizing Minerva: American Women in the First World War*. Chicago: University Press of Illinois Press, 2008.

Johnsen, Julia. *Selected Articles on the Negro Problem*. New York: H. W. Wilson, 1921.

Karsten, Peter. *The Naval Aristocracy: The Golden Age of Annapolis and the Emergence of Modern Navalism*. New York: Free Press, 1972.

Kasson, John F. *Houdini, Tarzan, and the Perfect Man: The White Male Body and the Challenge of Modernity in American*. New York: Will and Wang, 2001.

Kauffman, Reginald W. "The American Marines." *Living Age*, July 6, 1918.

Keene, Jennifer D. *Doughboys, the Great War, and the Remaking of America*. Baltimore: Johns Hopkins University Press, 2001.

Kennedy, David M. *Over Here: The First World War and American Society*. Oxford: Oxford University Press, 1980.

Kimmel, Michael. "The Contemporary 'Crisis' of Masculinity in Historical Perspective." In *The Making of Masculinities: The New Men's Studies*, edited by Harry Brod, 121–154. Boston: Allen and Unwin, 1987.

———. *Manhood in America: A Cultural History*. 3rd ed. New York: Oxford University Press, 2012.

Kington, Donald M. *Forgotten Summers: The Story of the Citizens' Military Training Camps, 1921–1940*. San Francisco, CA: Two Decades, 1995.

Krulak, Victor H. *First to Fight: An Inside View of the U.S. Marine Corps*. Annapolis, MD: Naval Institute Press, 1984.

Lamay-Licursi, Kimberly J. *Remembering World War I in America*. Lincoln: University of Nebraska Press, 2018.

Langley, Lester D. *The Banana Wars: United States Intervention in the Caribbean, 1898–1934*. Wilmington, DE: Scholarly Resources, 2002.

Laskin, David. *Long Way Home: An American Journey from Ellis Island to the Great War*. New York: Harper Perennial, 2010.

Lears, Jackson. *Rebirth of a Nation: The Making of Modern America, 1877–1920*. New York: Harper Collins, 2009.

Leed, Eric J. *No Man's Land: Combat & Identity in World War I*. New York: Cambridge University Press, 1979.

Lejeune, John A. *The Reminiscences of a Marine*. Philadelphia: Dorrance, 1930.

Lengel, Edward G. *Thunder and Flames: Americans in the Crucible of Combat, 1917–1918*. Lawrence: University Press of Kansas, 2015.

———, ed. *A Companion to the Meuse-Argonne Campaign*. Malden, MA: Wiley Blackwell, 2014.

Lindsay, Robert. *This High Name: Public Relations and the U.S. Marine Corps*. Madison: University of Wisconsin Press, 1956.

Logan, Rayford W. *Haiti and the Dominican Republic*. New York: Oxford University Press, 1968.

Mackin, Elton E. *Suddenly We Didn't Want to Die: Memoirs of a World War I Marine*. Novato, CA: Presidio, 1993.

Mahan, Alfred Thayer. *Naval Strategy*. Washington, DC: Headquarters, U.S. Marine Corps, 1991.

Marshall, Heather P. "'It Means Something These Days to Be a Marine': Image, Identity, and Mission in the Marine Corps, 1861–1918." PhD diss., Duke University, 2010. https://dukespace.lib.duke.edu/dspace/bitstream/handle/10161/3040/D_Marshall_Heather_a_201008.pdf?.

McClellan, Edwin N. *The United States Marine Corps in the World War*. 3rd ed. Quantico, VA: U.S. Marine Corps History Division, 2014.

McCoy, Cameron D. "Mr. President, What of the Marines?: The Politics of Contested Integration and the Domestic Legacy of the Modern Black Leatherneck in Cold War America." PhD diss., University of Texas at Austin, 2017. https://repositories.lib.utexas.edu/handle/2152/47367.

McCrocklin, James H. *Garde d'Haiti: Twenty Years of Organization and training by the United States Marine Corps*. Annapolis, MD: Naval Institute Press, 1956.

McGerr, Michael. *A Fierce Discontent: The Rise and Fall of the Progressive Movement in America*. New York: Oxford University Press, 2003.

McKee, Christopher. *A Gentlemanly and Honorable Profession: The Creation of the U.S. Naval Officer Corps, 1794–1815*. Annapolis, MD: Naval Institute Press, 1991.

McKee, Patricia. *Producing American Races: Henry James, William Faulkner, Toni Morrison*. Durham, NC: Duke University Press, 1999.

McPherson, Alan. *The Invaded: How Latin Americans and Their Allies Fought and Ended U.S. Occupations*. New York: Oxford University Press, 2014.

Meade, Gary. *The Doughboys: America and the First World War*. New York: Penguin Putnam, 2001.

Meiser, Jeffrey W. *Power and Restraint: The Rise of the United States, 1898–1941*. Washington, DC: Georgetown University Press, 2015.

Messner, Michael. "The Meaning of Success: The Athletic Experience and the Development of Male Identity." In *The Making of Masculinities: The New Men's Studies*, edited by Harry Brod, 193–210. Boston: Allen and Unwin, 1987.

Metcalf, Clyde H. *A History of the United States Marine Corps*. New York: G. P. Putnam's Sons, 1939.

Millett, Allan R. "Assault from the Sea: The Development of Amphibious Warfare between the Wars—the American, British, and Japanese Experiences." In *Military Innovation in the Interwar Period*, edited by Williamson Murray and Allan R. Millett, 50–95. Cambridge: Cambridge University Press, 1996.

———. *Semper Fidelis: The History of the United States Marine Corps*. 2nd ed. New York: Free Press, 1991.

———. "The U.S. Marine Corps, 1973–2017: Cultural Preservation in Every Place and Clime." In *The Culture of Military Organizations*, edited by Peter Mansoor and Williamson Murray, 378–402. New York: Cambridge University Press, 1996.

Millett, Allan R., Petter Maslowski, and William B. Feis. *For the Common Defense: A Military History of the United States, 1607–2012*. 3rd ed. New York: Free Press, 2012.

Mitchell, W. J. T. *Iconology: Image, Text, Ideology*. Chicago: University of Chicago Press, 1986.

Morrill, Gulian Lansing. *Sea Sodoms: A Sinical Survey of Haiti, Santo Domingo, Porto Rico, Curacao, Venezuela, Guadeloupe, Martinique, Cuba*. Minneapolis: Pioneer Printers, 1921.

Moskin, Robert J. *The U.S. Marine Corps Story*. 3rd ed. Boston: Little, Brown, 1992.

Moss, Mark. *Manliness and Militarism: Educating Young Boys in Ontario for War*. New York: Oxford University Press, 2001.

Mrozek, Donald J. "The Habit of Victory: The American Military and the Cult of Manliness." In *Manliness and Morality: Middle-Class Masculinity in Britain and America, 1800–1940*, edited by J. A. Mangan and James Walvin, 220–241. Manchester: Manchester University Press, 1987.

Murphy, Gretchen. *Shadowing the White Man's Burden: U.S. Imperialism and the Problem of the Color Line*. New York: New York University Press, 2010.

Murphy, Kevin P. *Political Manhood: Red Bloods, Mollycoddles, & the Politics of Progressive Era Reform*. New York: Columbia University Press, 2008.

Neiberg, Michael S. *The Second Battle of the Marne*. Bloomington: Indiana University Press, 2008.

Neumann, Brian F. "Pershing's Right Hand: General James G. Harbord and the American Expeditionary Forces in the First World War." PhD diss., Texas A&M University, 2006. https://oaktrust.library.tamu.edu/handle/1969 .1/4424.

O'Connell, Aaron B. "Underdogs: A Cultural History of the United States Marine Corps, 1941–1965." PhD diss., Yale University, 2009.

———. *Underdogs: The Making of the Modern Marine Corps*. Cambridge, MA: Harvard University Press, 2012.

Ortiz, Stephen R. *Beyond the Bonus March and GI Bill: How Veteran Politics Shaped the New Deal Era*. New York: New York University Press, 2010.

Paine, Ralph D. *Roads of Adventure*. New York: Houghton Mifflin, 1922.

Painter, Nell Irvin. *The History of White People*. New York: W. W. Norton, 2010.

Paradis, Don V. *The World War 1 Memoirs of Don V. Paradis: Gunnery Sergeant, USMC*. Edited by Peter F. Owen. Peter F. Owen, 2010.

Paret, Peter. "The Function of History in Clausewitz's Understanding of War." *Journal of Military History* 82 (October 2018): 1049–1066.

Parker, William D. *A Concise History of The United States Marine Corps 1775–1969*. Washington, DC: Historical Division, Headquarters, U.S. Marine Corps, 1970.

Patterson, Sarah E. "The Few, the Proud: Gender and the Marine Corps Body." PhD diss., Florida State University, 2019.

Peguero, Valentina. *The Militarization of Culture in the Dominican Republic, from the Captains General to General Trujillo*. Lincoln: University of Nebraska Press, 2004.

Pendergast, Tom. *Creating the Modern Man: American Magazines and Consumer Culture, 1900–1950*. Columbia: University of Missouri Press, 2000.

Pierce, Philip N., and Frank O. Hough. *The Compact History of the United States Marine Corps*. 2nd ed. New York: Hawthorn Books, 1964.

Pons, Frank Moya. *The Dominican Republic: A National History*. Princeton, NJ: Markus Wiener, 1998.

Prichard, H. Hesketh. *Where Black Rules White: A Journey across and about Hayti*. New York: Thomas Nelson & Sons, 1910.

Purintan, Edward Earle. *Personal Efficiency and Business*. New York: Robert M. McBride, 1920.

Reinsch, Paul S. *An American Diplomat in China*. Garden City, NY: Doubleday, Page, 1922.

Renda, Mary A. *Taking Haiti: Military Occupation and the Culture of U.S. Imperialism, 1915–1940*. Chapel Hill: University of North Carolina Press, 2001.

Report of the Adjutant General of the Army to the Secretary of War for the Fiscal Year [1914–1921]. Washington, DC: Government Printing Office, [1914–22].

Richardson, Norman E. *The Religion of Modern Manhood or Masculine Topics for Men's Bible Classes*. New York: Eaton and Mains, 1911.

Roediger, David R. *The Wages of Whiteness: Race and the Making of the American Working Class*. New York: Verso, 1991.

Rogoziński, Jan. *A Brief History of the Caribbean: From the Arawak and the Carib to the Present*. New York: Facts on File, 1992.

Rolt-Wheeler, Francis. *The Boy with the U.S. Marines*. Boston: Lothrop, Lee, & Shepard, 1926.

Rosenberg, Emily S. "War and the Health of the State: The U.S. Government and the Communications Revolution during World War I." In *Selling War in a Media Age: The Presidency and Public Opinion in the American Century*, edited by Kenneth Osgood and Andrew K. Frank, 48–66. Gainesville: University Press of Florida, 2010.

Ross, Stewart Halsey. *Propaganda for War: How the United States Was Conditioned to Fight the Great War of 1914–1918*. Jefferson NC: McFarland, 1996.

Rotundo, Anthony E. *American Manhood: Transformations in Masculinity from the Revolution to the Modern Era*. New York: Basic Books, 1993.

Rutenberg, Amy S. *Manifest Manhood and the Antebellum American Empire*. New York: Cambridge University Press, 2005.

Schmidt, Hans. *Maverick Marine: General Smedley D. Butler and the Contradictions of American Military History*. Lexington: University Press of Kentucky, 1987.

———. *The United States Occupation of Haiti, 1915–1934*. New Brunswick, NJ: Rutgers University Press, 1995.

Scott, Joan Wallach. *Gender and the Politics of History*. New York: Columbia University Press, 1988.

Shenk, Gerald R. *"Work or Fight!": Race, Gender, and the Draft in World War One*. New York: Palgrave Macmillan, 2005.

Sheriff, Mary D. "How Images Got Their Gender: Masculinity and Femininity in the Visual Arts." In *A Companion to Gender History*, edited by Teresa A. Meade and Merry E. Wiesner-Hanks, 146–169. Malden, MA: Blackwell, 2004.

Shulimson, Jack. *The Marine Corps' Search for a Mission, 1880–1898*. Lawrence: University Press of Kansas, 1993.

Simmons, Edwin H. *Through the Wheat: The U.S. Marines in World War I*. With Joseph Alexander. Annapolis, MD: Naval Institute Press, 2008.

———. *The United States Marines: A History*. 3rd ed. Annapolis, MD: Naval Institute Press, 1998.

Simon, Joseph Arthur. *The Greatest of All Leathernecks: John Archer Lejeune and the Making of the Modern Marine Corps*. Baton Rouge: Louisiana State University Press, 2019.

Smith, Henry Louis. *Your Biggest Job School or Business: Some Words of Counsel for Red-Blooded Young Americans Who Are Getting Tired of School*. New York: Appleton, 1921.

Smith, Holland M., and Percy Finch. *Coral and Brass*. New York: Charles Scribner's Sons, 1949.

———. *The Development of Amphibious Tactics in the U.S. Navy*. Washington, DC: History and Museums Division, Headquarters, U.S. Marine Corps, 1992.

Spaulding, Oliver Lyman, and John Womack Wright, eds. *The Second Division American Expeditionary Force in France, 1917–1919*. New York: Hillman, 1937.

Speer, Robert E. *The Stuff of Manhood: Some Needed Notes in American Character*. New York: Fleming H. Revell, 1917.

Stearns, Peter N. *Be a Man!: Males in Modern Society*. 2nd ed. New York: Holmes & Meier, 1990.

Stewart, David Melville. *Jesus and Modern Manhood*. London: James Clarke, 1911.

Sturkey, Marion F. *Warrior Culture of the U.S. Marines*. 3rd ed. Plum Branch, SC: Heritage Press International, 2010.

Suksdorf, Henry F. *Our Race Problems*. New York: Shakespeare, 1911.

Summerbell, Martyn. *Manhood in Its American Type*. Boston: Richard G. Badger, 1916.

Summers, Martin. *Manliness & Its Discontents: The Black Middle Class & the Transformation of Masculinity, 1900–1930*. Chapel Hill: University of North Carolina Press, 2004.

Suskind, Richard. *The Battle of Belleau Wood: The Marines Stand Fast*. Toronto, ON: Macmillan, 1969.

Tatlock, John S. P. *Why America Fights Germany*. Washington, DC: Committee on Public Information, 1918.

Thomason, John W. *Fix Bayonets!: With the U.S. Marine Corps in France, 1917–1918*. New York: Charles Scribner's Sons, 1925.

Tosh, John. "Hegemonic Masculinity and the History of Gender." In *Masculinities in Politics and War: Gendering Modern History*, edited by Stefan Dundink, Karen Hagemann, and John Tosh, 41–60. New York: Manchester University Press, 2004.

Trask, David F. "The U.S. Navy in a World at War, 1914–1919." In *In Peace and War: Interpretations of American Naval History*, 30th anniv. ed., edited by Kenneth Hagan and Michael T. McMaster, 169–181. Westport, CT: Praeger Security International, 2008.

Traxel, David. *Crusader Nation: The United States in Peace and the Great War, 1898–1920*. New York: Alfred A. Knopf, 2006.

Trout, Steven. *On the Battlefield of Memory: The First World War and American Remembrance, 1919–1941*. Tuscaloosa: University of Alabama Press, 2010.

Ulbrich, David J. *Preparing for Victory: Thomas Holcomb and the Making of the Modern Marine Corps, 1936–1943*. Annapolis, MD: Naval Institute Press, 2011.

U.S. House of Representatives. Committee on Naval Affairs. *Statements of Maj. Gen. John A. Lejeune, Commandant, U.S. Marine Corps, Hearings before the United States House Committee on Naval Affairs, Sixty-Seventh Congress, Second Session, on Mar. 8, 9, 1922*. Committee Serial 68. Washington, DC: Government Printing Office, 1922.

U.S. Senate. Select Committee on Haiti and Santo Domingo. *Inquiry into the Occupation and Administration of Haiti and Santo Domingo: Hearings before a Select Committee of Haiti and Santo Domingo*. 2 vols. Washington, DC: Government Printing Office, 1922.

Vandegrift, Alexander A. *Once a Marine: The Memoirs of General A. A. Vandegrift*. As told to Robert B. Asprey. New York: W. W. Norton, 1964.

Venable, Heather. *How the Few Became the Proud: Crafting the Marine Corps Mystique, 1874–1918*. Annapolis, MD: Naval Institute Press, 2019.

Venzon, Anne Cipriano. *From Whaleboats to Amphibious Warfare: Lt. Gen. "Howlin Mad" Smith and the U.S. Marine Corps*. Westport CT: Praeger, 2003.

Wadle, Ryan D. "The Fourth Dimension of Naval Tactics: The U.S. Navy and Public Relations, 1919–1939." PhD diss., Texas A&M University, 2011. https://hdl.handle.net/1969.1/ETD-TAMU-2011-05-9166.

———. *Selling Sea Power: Public Relations and the U.S. Navy, 1917–1941*. Norman: University of Oklahoma Press, 2019.

Warren, James A. *American Spartans: The U.S. Marines: A Combat History from Iwo Jima to Iraq*. New York: Free Press, 2005.

Watson, Elwood, and Marc E. Shaw, eds. *Performing American Masculinities: The 21st Century Man in Popular Culture*. Indianapolis: Indiana University Press, 2011.

Weigley, Russell F. *The American Way of War: A History of United States Military Strategy and Policy*. New York: Macmillan, 1973.

———. *History of the United States Army*. New York: Macmillan, 1967.

Wiebe, Robert H. *The Search for Order, 1877–1920*. New York: Hill and Wang, 1967.

Williams, Chad L. *Torchbearers of Democracy: African American Soldiers in the World War I Era*. Chapel Hill: University of North Carolina Press, 2010.

Williams, Robert Hugh. *The Old Corps: A Portrait of the U.S. Marine Corps between the Wars*. Annapolis, MD: Naval Institute Press, 1982.

Wilson, Woodrow. *The Papers of Woodrow Wilson*. Edited by Arthur S. Link. Vol. 42. Princeton, NJ: Princeton University Press, 1983.

Wintermute, Bobby A., and David J. Ulbrich. *Race and Gender in Modern Western Warfare*. Boston: De Gruyter, 2018.

Wise, Frederic May. *A Marine Tells It to You*. Edited by Meigs O. Frost. New York: J. H. Sears, 1929.

Wonham, Henry B. *Playing the Races: Ethnic Caricature and American Literary Realism*. New York: Oxford University Press, 2004.

Woodward, David R. *The American Army and the First World War*. Cambridge: Cambridge University Press, 2014.

Wyatt-Brown, Bertram. *Southern Honor: Ethics and Behavior in the Old South*. New York: Oxford University Press, 1982.

Youard, H. G. *Showing Ourselves Men: Addresses for Men's Services*. New York: E. S. Gorham, 1911.

Zeeland, Steven. *The Masculine Marine: Homoeroticism in the U.S. Marine Corps*. Binghamton, NY: Haworth, 1996.

Zieger, Robert H. *America's Great War: World War I and the American Experience*. New York: Rowman & Littlefield, 2000.

Index

Please note that italicized page numbers in this index indicate illustrations.